"This volume tackles an incredibly important issue that has been so far understudied: the way far-right movements appropriate the language of liberalism. The authors offer us a series of vivid examples of how the semantics of freedom and rights can be instrumentalized by forces promoting exclusionary policies. They also invite us to question the loss of meaning associated with illiberal Newspeak. A must-read for everyone interested in understanding the challenges of liberalism today."

Marlene Laruelle, *Director, Illiberalism Studies Program, The George Washington University, USA; Editor,* Illiberalism.org

"It is easy to assume that the language of freedom, equality, individual and collective rights, and pluralism belongs inextricably to liberal and leftist egalitarians. This assumption has been very much put in question by the strategic rhetoric deployed by a range of right-wing (including radical-right) theoreticians and political actors in many different societies today. The aim of this instructive and important book by A. James McAdams and Samuel Piccolo, and their collaborators, is to warn us of the serious perils we face when concepts intended to promote progress, enlightenment, and justice are hijacked in order to serve opposing ideological purposes."

Ronald Beiner, *author of* Dangerous Minds: Nietzsche, Heidegger, and the Return of the Far Right

"One of the biggest questions of our time is how democracies globally will be challenged by the rise of conservative nationalists who are savvy with communications and messaging. After covering the January 6, 2021, attack on the US Capitol, I am highly aware of the power of words to influence voters. This book provides a vivid roadmap for understanding these forces, taking readers far beyond the headlines and delving into analysis and research that offers important perspectives."

Robert Costa, *CBS News chief election & campaign correspondent; co-author of the # 1 New York Times bestseller* Peril

"This fascinating volume traces how far-right politicians, intellectuals, and opinion-makers use the language of democracy to hollow out basic liberal principles and institutions—and how this form of Newspeak can divide societies in the name of protecting them. The chapters are provocative, controversial, and always engaging. Importantly, the authors analyze the concept of the 'far-right' itself, and assess its boundaries and analytical utility. An invaluable guide for all scholars and supporters of liberal democracy."

Anna Grzymala-Busse, *Michelle and Kevin Douglas Professor of International Studies, Stanford University, USA*

FAR-RIGHT NEWSPEAK AND THE FUTURE OF LIBERAL DEMOCRACY

This book is the first systematic, multicountry exploration of far-right Newspeak.

The contributors analyze the ways in which contemporary far-right politicians, intellectuals, and pundits use and abuse traditional liberal concepts and ideas to justify positions that threaten democratic institutions and liberal principles. They explore cases of both far-right and right-wing thought in eastern and western Europe, the United States, and Canada. Subjects include well-known figures, such as Marine Le Pen, Tucker Carlson, Peter Thiel, Nick Griffin, Thierry Baudet, Jordan Peterson, Russell Brand, and Viktor Orbán, and lesser-known names, such as the Czech politician Tomio Okamura and the Internet personality "Raw Egg Nationalist." The contributors examine these figures' claims about hot-button issues, including immigration, Islam, race, Covid-19 policies, feminism, monetary policy, and free speech. The book demonstrates that mainstream politicians and intellectuals are at risk of losing control over the definitions of the very concepts, including equal rights, racial and ethnic diversity, and political tolerance, that undergird their vision of liberal democracy.

It will be of interest to scholars, journalists, policymakers, political scientists, historians, political theorists, sociologists, and general audiences concerned about the sophisticated efforts of far-right and right-wing politicians and pundits to undermine the foundations of liberal democracy.

A. James McAdams is the William M. Scholl Professor of International Affairs in the Department of Political Science at the University of Notre Dame, USA.

Samuel Piccolo is Assistant Professor of Political Science at Gustavus Adolphus College, Saint Peter, Minnesota, USA.

Routledge Studies in Fascism and the Far Right

Series editors: Nigel Copsey, *Teesside University, UK* and Graham Macklin, *Center for Research on Extremism (C-REX), University of Oslo, Norway*

This book series focuses upon national, transnational and global manifestations of fascist, far right and right-wing politics primarily within a historical context but also drawing on insights and approaches from other disciplinary perspectives. Its scope also includes anti-fascism, radical-right populism, extreme-right violence and terrorism, cultural manifestations of the far right, and points of convergence and exchange with the mainstream and traditional right.

Organisation of Ukrainian Nationalists on Emigration
Its Formation and Transnational Connections in 1929–1934
Magdalena Gibiec

Fascist Italy in the Age of Corporatism
Searching for a Third Way
Alessio Gagliardi

Christian Nationalism and Anticommunism in Twentieth-Century South Africa
Ruhan Fourie

Far-Right Newspeak and the Future of Liberal Democracy
Edited by A. James McAdams and Samuel Piccolo

Neo-Nazi Terrorism and Countercultural Fascism
The Origins and Afterlife of James Mason's Siege
Spencer Sunshine

For more information about this series, please visit: www.routledge.com/Routledge-Studies-in-Fascism-and-the-Far-Right/book-series/FFR

FAR-RIGHT NEWSPEAK AND THE FUTURE OF LIBERAL DEMOCRACY

Edited by A. James McAdams and Samuel Piccolo

LONDON AND NEW YORK

Designed cover image: © Getty Images

First published 2024
by Routledge
4 Park Square, Milton Park, Abingdon, Oxon OX14 4RN

and by Routledge

605 Third Avenue, New York, NY 10158

Routledge is an imprint of the Taylor & Francis Group, an informa business

© 2024 selection and editorial matter, A. James McAdams and Samuel Piccolo; individual chapters, the contributors

The right of A. James McAdams and Samuel Piccolo to be identified as the authors of the editorial material, and of the authors for their individual chapters, has been asserted in accordance with sections 77 and 78 of the Copyright, Designs and Patents Act 1988.

All rights reserved. No part of this book may be reprinted or reproduced or utilised in any form or by any electronic, mechanical, or other means, now known or hereafter invented, including photocopying and recording, or in any information storage or retrieval system, without permission in writing from the publishers.

Trademark notice: Product or corporate names may be trademarks or registered trademarks, and are used only for identification and explanation without intent to infringe.

British Library Cataloguing-in-Publication Data
A catalogue record for this book is available from the British Library

Library of Congress Cataloging-in-Publication Data
Names: McAdams, A. James, editor. | Piccolo, Samuel, editor.
Title: Far-right newspeak and the future of liberal democracy / edited by A. James McAdams and Samuel Piccolo.
Description: Abingdon, Oxon ; New York, NY : Routledge, 2024. | Series: Routledge studies in fascism and the far right | Includes bibliographical references and index.
Identifiers: LCCN 2023055585 (print) | LCCN 2023055586 (ebook) | ISBN 9781032566771 (hardback) | ISBN 9781032566269 (paperback) | ISBN 9781003436737 (ebook)
Subjects: LCSH: Right-wing extremists—Language. | Right and left (Political science) | Rhetoric—Political aspects | Political oratory.
Classification: LCC HN49.R33 F37 2024 (print) | LCC HN49.R33 (ebook) | DDC 320.5—dc23/eng/20240108
LC record available at https://lccn.loc.gov/2023055585
LC ebook record available at https://lccn.loc.gov/2023055586

ISBN: 978-1-032-56677-1 (hbk)
ISBN: 978-1-032-56626-9 (pbk)
ISBN: 978-1-003-43673-7 (ebk)

DOI: 10.4324/9781003436737

Typeset in Sabon
by Apex CoVantage, LLC

A. James McAdams
To my friends

Samuel Piccolo
To my teachers

CONTENTS

Preface   *xii*
Note to the Reader   *xiv*
List of Contributors   *xvi*

PART I
Introduction   **1**

1 Far-Right Newspeak and the Fragility of Liberal Democracy   3
  A. James McAdams

PART II
The Language of Liberalism   **25**

2 Masters of Contemporary Newspeak: Tucker Carlson, Marine Le Pen, and Jordan Peterson   27
  A. James McAdams

3 "We Are Looking for a New Feminism": Marine Le Pen's Reappropriation of the Liberal Language of Women's Rights and Gender Equality   48
  Sarah Shurts

4 Far-Right Politics in the Czech Republic: Tomio Okamura's Liberal Language and Populist Playbook   65
  Petra Mlejnková

PART III
Far-Right Newspeak in Practice   85

5 The Transition From Liberal to Illiberal Constitutionalism in Poland and Hungary: The Language of Rights and Equality   87
Tímea Drinóczi and Agnieszka Bień-Kacała

6 When Legal Language Meets Apocalypse Anxiety: Democracy, Constitutional Scholars, and the Rise of the German Far Right After 2015   106
Frank Wolff

7 From Practical Critics to Hateful Malcontents: The Rise and Fall of the Online "Manosphere"   126
George Hawley

PART IV
The Ambiguities of a Concept   143

8 Forced to Be Free? America's "Postliberals" on Freedom and Liberty   145
Laura K. Field

9 Shine a Light or Burn It Down? Conspiracism and Liberal Ideas   166
Steven Pittz

PART V
Beyond Far-Right Newspeak   187

10 Against the Global Prison-Society: The Far Right's Language of the Opposition to the Great Reset   189
José Pedro Zúquete

11 Hard Men, Hard Money, Hardening Right: Bitcoin, Peter Thiel, and Schmittian States of Exception   205
Josh Vandiver

PART VI
Conclusion 231

12 Liberalism's Vulnerabilities and Two Paths for the Future 233
   Samuel Piccolo

Bibliography 260
Index 285

PREFACE

Far-Right Newspeak and the Future of Liberal Democracy began with a précis that one of us (McAdams) circulated among the eventual contributors in fall 2021. The purpose of this document—"'Speaking the Language of Liberalism': Far-Right Intellectuals, Pundits, and Politicians and the New Threat to Liberal Democracy"—was to initiate a conversation among European and American scholars about the contemporary far right's use and abuse of key words in the liberal-democratic vocabulary, such as freedom, liberty, equality, rights, tolerance, and democracy. We discussed three questions: What makes the appropriation of this language new and different from the efforts of earlier generations of far-right actors to propagate their views? How have these contemporary figures used this language to gain the attention and support of previously inaccessible middle-of-the-road audiences? Finally, what does the success of these actors portend for the future of liberal democracy?

From the beginning, we conceived of this project as a collaborative undertaking that would result in the publication of a truly cohesive volume. To this end, the contributors met on four separate occasions to share ideas and seek to identify common approaches to our subject. In a virtual meeting on May 31, 2022, the participants shared ideas about how the subjects of their research related to the précis's topics. In a second virtual meeting on September 12, 2022, we discussed brief summaries of prospective papers. We then met in person on December 9–10, 2022, at the University of Notre Dame (United States) to discuss draft chapters of an eventual volume. Because we had already circulated these drafts beforehand, there was no need for formal presentations. We were free to engage in informal discussions about each chapter and how it corresponded to the arguments in the other chapters.

Finally, we met again virtually on April 4, 2023, to discuss the integration of our chapters into a coherent and unified statement about the topic of Far-Right Newspeak. In the process of producing final chapters, it makes sense that the contributors have come to different conclusions about important issues, such as who should or should not be counted as "far right" and whether our actors' challenges to liberal democracy are universally negative or positive. Meaningful comparison must always include the identification of notable differences. Nonetheless, we hope the reader will recognize that our collaborative approach has enabled us to produce a volume in which all of the chapters speak to each other and shed a collective light on a major challenge to liberal democracy.

We are greatly indebted to Notre Dame's Nanovic Institute for European Studies and its director Clemens Sedmak and the Kellogg Institute for International Studies and its directors Paolo Carozza and Aníbal Pérez-Liñán for sponsoring our project over so many years. A third sponsor, the Dr. William M. Scholl Foundation, has generously supported McAdams' research for nearly a quarter of a century and made it possible for him to explore an array of pressing issues, including Far-Right Newspeak. Naturally, a long-running research project would not be imaginable without the concerted assistance of specific individuals. From the beginning, Beka Prince of the Nanovic Institute took responsibility for every aspect of the organization of our meetings. We are deeply grateful for her help in arranging everything from Zoom sessions in eight different time zones to her careful attention to our contributors' travel schedules and accommodations at Notre Dame. Beka was joined by Therese Hanlon of the Kellogg Institute whose vast knowledge about the challenges of organizing events was instrumental to the conference's success. In addition, we benefited from the insights and expertise of Alice Blum, Lars Erik Berntzen, and Alejandro Castrillon, who were involved at different stages of our collaboration. We also extend our thanks to Alexandra Conley for her excellent research on key far-right figures. In the final stages of our project, Cathy Bruckbauer played a huge role in bringing the disparate pieces of our volume together, editing every chapter, and lending endless words of wisdom and advice. Finally, we thank our editors at Routledge. Craig Fowlie offered his support, encouragement, and expertise from the moment we began circulating our précis. We are also grateful to Elizabeth Hart for her assistance throughout the production of this volume.

A. J. M.
S. P.

NOTE TO THE READER

We would like to offer the reader a few words about the title of this book: *Far-Right Newspeak and the Future of Liberal Democracy*. Anyone who has studied the politicians, pundits, and intellectuals whom we examine knows there is a challenge in what to call them. There are undeniable differences in both their arguments and their varied agendas and audiences. Understandably, scholars have chosen a variety of names to describe their particular subjects, such as New Right, Alt-right, paleoconservative, libertarian, Catholic integralist, identitarian, national conservative, and postliberal. The problem with this approach is that it makes meaningful comparison nearly impossible. In contrast, we use a single term, "far right," to characterize these individuals' positions. No term is perfect. Nevertheless, "far right" is a useful umbrella concept because it allows for the systematic examination of the similarities and differences among a wide variety of cases. The challenge of identifying the defining features of a single concept also provides an inducement for wrestling with the question of inclusion. Who should—or should not—be categorized as "far right"? As the reader will see, the contributors to this volume carefully distinguish between those aspects of their subjects' positions that should be classified under this rubric and those that should not. In several cases, they conclude that their subjects are not far right at all.

The second concept in our title is "liberal democracy." Library book stacks and scholarly journals are filled with debates about the meaning of this term, as well the specific words "liberal" and "democracy." Due to the vicissitudes of history, liberal democracy itself is a moving target. Scholars are unlikely to build a solid consensus on the meaning of the concept. In any case, we have no intention of joining these debates. Instead, we treat the term as an ideal type. By "democracy," we mean a variety of fully functioning institutions such as courts, parliaments, constitutions, and constitutional principles that allow citizens to play an active role in public affairs. In ensuring access to the public realm, leaders of democratic states must deal with a panoply of questions about the form these institutions take. These include the most desirable forms of political representation, the proper distribution of power among different branches of government, the appropriate balance between majority rule and minority protections, the instantiation of the rule of law, and the guarantee of free and fair elections. Naturally, democratic regimes respond to these questions in different ways. By "liberal," we refer to the principles that democratic leaders are obliged to follow in their interactions with citizens. These principles include the rights to free speech, assembly, religious practice, and privacy as well as the guarantee of full equality. These values are also based upon universal norms, such as political tolerance and respect for the dignity of every person. The interpretation and application of these principles vary from country to country. But there is one liberal constant that is directly relevant to the cases in this volume. For the "liberal" part of liberal democracy to mean anything, we maintain that these ideals are not simply whatever the ruling majority says they are at any given time or in any given place.

CONTRIBUTORS

Agnieszka Bień-Kacała is a university (associate) professor of constitutional law at the University of Szczecin, Poland; she is the Leader of the research group Gender and Constitution in Poland, affiliated at the Faculty of Law and Administration of the University of Szczecin, Poland; she serves as Principal Investigator within the Polish National Science Centre project titled *Illiberal Constitutionalism in Poland and Hungary*; she is the author of over a hundred publications; and she recently co-authored (with Tímea Drinóczi) *Illiberal Constitutionalism in Poland and Hungary: The Deterioration of Democracy, Misuse of Human Rights and Abuse of the Rule of Law*, which was published by Routledge in 2022.

Tímea Drinóczi is a Hungarian professor of law, currently a visiting professor at the Faculty of Law at the Federal University of Minas Gerais. She was a full professor at the University of Pécs (Hungary) and Kenyatta University (Kenya). She is an independent expert of OSCE ODIHR on constitutional and legislative matters. Her newest co-authored book is *Illiberal Constitutionalism in Poland and Hungary: The Deterioration of Democracy, Misuse of Human Rights and Abuse of the Rule of Law* (Routledge 2022, with Agnieszka Bień-Kacała). Besides illiberal constitutionalism, her research interest covers constitutional identity, constitutional change, and the quality of legislation.

Laura K. Field is a writer and political theorist who has worked extensively on the intellectuals who rose to prominence under the Trump administration and is currently working on a book on the subject.

George Hawley is Associate Professor of political science at the University of Alabama. He is the author of seven books, including *Right-Wing Critics of American Conservatism*, *Demography, Culture, and the Decline of America's Christian Denominations*, and *In a Divided America: The Right and Identity Politics*.

A. James McAdams is the William M. Scholl Professor of International Affairs at the University of Notre Dame. His primary fields of research and teaching are in comparative and international politics, and political history. Between 2002 and 2018, he was Director of the Nanovic Institute for European Studies at Notre Dame. His publications include *Judging the Past in Unified Germany* and *Vanguard of the Revolution: The Global Idea of the Communist Party*, which was named one of the best books of 2018 by *Foreign Affairs*. McAdams' most recent book (co-edited with Alejandro Castrillon), *Contemporary Far-Right Thinkers and the Future of Liberal Democracy*, appeared in Routledge's book series *Fascism and the Far Right*. McAdams is the recipient of honorary degrees from the Catholic University of Ukraine and the John Paul II Catholic University of Lublin, Poland.

Petra Mlejnková is Assistant Professor at the Department of Political Science, Faculty of Social Studies, Masaryk University (Czech Republic). She focuses on research of extremism and radicalism in Europe, propaganda, and information warfare. She has published or co-edited several publications on these topics, including *Challenging Online Propaganda and Disinformation in the 21st Century*.

Samuel Piccolo is Assistant Professor of political science at Gustavus Adolphus College, Saint Peter, Minnesota. His articles have appeared in venues including *American Journal of Political Science*, *Journal of Politics*, *European Journal of Political Theory*, *Politics and Poetics*, *Arendt Studies*, and *Security Studies*. He is at work on a book about Native American political thought and Western political theory.

Steven Pittz is Associate Professor of Political Science and Associate Director of the Center for the Study of Government and the Individual at the University of Colorado in Colorado Springs. He is the author of several articles, chapters, and books, including *Recovering the Liberal Spirit: Nietzsche, Individuality, and Spiritual Freedom* and *American Citizenship and Constitutionalism in Principle and Practice*, edited with Joseph Postell.

Sarah Shurts is Professor of History at Bergen Community College in New Jersey. She is the author of *Resentment and the Right: French Intellectual*

Identity Reimagined, 1898–2000, and has published articles on twentieth-century French intellectuals and the extreme right in *Historical Reflections/ Réflexions Historiques, European History Quarterly, French Politics, Culture & Society*, the *Journal of Modern European History*, and the *Journal of the History of Ideas*.

Josh Vandiver is Assistant Professor of Political Science at the University of Colorado, Colorado Springs. His research interests include radical thought, organizations, and strategic cultures in Europe and the USA, with focus upon men and masculinities. He has published in the journals *Polis, Political Theory, Politics, Religion, and Ideology*, and the *Journal for the Study of Radicalism*, as well as several edited volumes, including *Global Identitarianism* (Routledge) and *Contemporary Far-Right Thinkers and the Future of Liberal Democracy* (Routledge).

Frank Wolff, PhD habil., is senior researcher and Privatdozent for Modern and Contemporary History at Osnabrück University and a member of its Institute for Migration Research and Intercultural Studies (IMIS). He received his PhD from Bielefeld University (2011), habilitated at Osnabrück University, and has held various international fellowships and guest professorships, for example at Johns Hopkins University, the University of Notre Dame, and Bard College Berlin. In 2023/24 he is leading the international research group "Internalizing Borders: The Social and Normative Consequences of the European Border Regime" at the Center for Interdisciplinary Studies at Bielefeld University. His main research interests include modern global migration, transnational Jewish history, and the formation of modern border law. His books include *Die Mauergesellschaft: Kalter Krieg, Menschenrechte und die deutsch-deutsche Migration 1961–1989* and the bestseller *Hinter Mauern: Geschlossene Grenzen als Gefahr für die offene Gesellschaft* (with Volker M. Heins).

José Pedro Zúquete is Research Fellow at the Institute of Social Sciences at the University of Lisbon, Portugal. He is a political scientist whose research focuses mainly on comparative politics, social movements, and extremism. His previous books include *The Identitarians: The Movement Against Globalism and Islam*. He is also the editor of the *Routledge International Handbook of Charisma* and the *Palgrave Handbook of Left-Wing Extremism*.

PART I
Introduction

1
FAR-RIGHT NEWSPEAK AND THE FRAGILITY OF LIBERAL DEMOCRACY

A. James McAdams

If you control the meaning of words, you can dictate how people think. George Orwell vividly conveyed this insight into the power of language in his dystopian novel *1984*. Writing with the bitter lessons of Nazism and Stalinism in mind, Orwell alerted his readers to the fragility of liberal democracy. He warned that democracy's future enemies would not rule by force alone. They would bring their countries' populations fully under their sway by creating new vocabularies of domination. One of their first steps would be to abolish the Oldspeak idiom of classical liberalism, including such words as "freedom," "equality," "rights," "tolerance," and "democracy," and replace it with the dictatorial Newspeak of "goodthink" and "thoughtcrime."[1]

In this light, if Orwell were to come back to life today, he might not be surprised to find that liberal democracy's contemporary foes are no less intent upon manipulating ordinary language to serve their purposes. Yet, contrary to his predictions after World War II, he would discover that these figures have adopted a much different vocabulary than the fictional Newspeak of *1984*. On the far right in particular, politicians, public intellectuals, and activists consciously present themselves as adherents to the same liberal principles that Orwell was determined to protect. Indeed, many invoke both his name and *1984* to justify their claims. When Twitter and Facebook banned Donald Trump from their platforms because of his use of incendiary language during the violent assault on the US Capitol on January 6, 2021, the ex-president's son, Donald Trump, Jr., denounced the corporations for ostensibly violating his father's constitutional rights. "We are living in Orwell's 1984," Trump Jr., proclaimed. "Free speech no longer exists in America."[2] Shortly thereafter, when the publishing house Simon & Schuster canceled the publication of a book by US Senator Josh Hawley for spreading disinformation about

DOI: 10.4324/9781003436737-2

the 2020 presidential election, Hawley retorted, "This could not be more Orwellian. . . . [This is] a direct assault on the First Amendment. . . . I will fight this 'cancel culture' with everything I have."[3] Three months later, in April 2021, when the Covid-19 pandemic was spreading across Europe, the British anti-vax media group, the Centre for Research on Globalization, described public-safety measures to combat the virus as "Orwellian lockstep and a loaded syringe."[4] Likewise, in 2021, the British far-right news celebrity, Steve Hilton, characterized proposed vaccine passports as a "nightmare, Orwellian infrastructure" and "an unprecedented, anti-democratic power grab."[5] In each instance, a reborn Orwell would likely be mortified by the appropriation of both his name and his words to attack plainly justifiable—if politically controversial—steps to safeguard liberal democracy and human welfare.

This volume is dedicated to examining the invocation of this rhetoric: Far-Right Newspeak. Strictly speaking, the manipulation of the language of liberalism and democracy has been around for some time, but almost exclusively on the political margins. From the American Independent Party to the British National Party, extreme-right and neofascist politicians in the post–World War II era have sought—and failed—to win over skeptical electorates by professing to respect democratic institutions. However, I will argue in this chapter that the Far-Right Newspeak of the 2000s is far more sophisticated and appealing than the clumsy formulations of the parties and movements of the past. In advanced democracies throughout the world, far-right actors have opened the so-called Overton window of acceptable political discourse to normalize white supremacist ideas, anti-Islamic prejudice, hate crimes against immigrants, and overt discrimination against minority groups.[6] Two decades ago, mainstream politicians and political pundits worried about alienating their supporters if they espoused views that were clearly contrary to their countries' fundamental values. However, in these actors' confident use of the vocabulary of Far-Right Newspeak today, there are fewer signs of restraint. If one were to take them at their word, as their followers do, one would think they are simply well-meaning citizens, dedicated to defending liberal principles and democracy against the purportedly anti-democratic designs of their political adversaries on the left.

Just as important, the purveyors of Far-Right Newspeak have been strikingly successful. From France to Hungary, Germany, the United States, and many other democracies, voters have elected far-right politicians into office at every level of government. In 2022, the French politician Marine Le Pen came close to winning her country's presidency by cultivating disaffected conservative and working-class voters; in Italy, a former leader of the country's neofascist student movement, Giorgia Meloni, was named prime minister; and in Sweden, a party with neo-Nazi roots, the Sweden Democrats, was the second largest vote-getter in the country's parliamentary elections. In 2023, the far-right German party, Alternative for Germany (AfD), defied predictions of its inevitable demise at the height of the pandemic and won major local elections. It was even outpacing the mainstream Social Democratic Party in popular opinion surveys.[7] In Spain, the anti-immigrant populist party, Vox, mounted a serious challenge to the country's conservative People's Party in provincial elections before falling short in the general election. In the Netherlands, the nationalist Farmer-Citizen Movement won significant victories in provincial elections by campaigning against the government's efforts to combat climate change.

Concurrently, like-minded cable news commentators, electronic publishers, and bloggers, such as Walter Asperl, the Austrian director of the online site, unzensuriert.at; Daniel Friberg, the owner of the influential European publishing house Arktos Media; Katie Hopkins, the British columnist; and Tucker Carlson, the former Fox News host, have capitalized on new communications technologies and popular social media platforms to spread their views among mainstream audiences. Casting themselves as defenders of their countries' founding values, they have roiled discontent among their followers by adeptly pushing disinformation and divisive conspiracy theories about Covid vaccines, Muslim immigration, election results, and global corporations.

Nonetheless, one cannot attribute the growing salience of Far-Right Newspeak to words alone. Whatever one might think about the Le Pens, Melonis, and Asperls of the day, these individuals could not have made their views known, let alone built sizable followings, without the turbulent political, social, and economic conditions of the early 2000s. They have found receptive audiences among disgruntled citizens who feel unjustly deprived of their share of their countries' economic prosperity, worry about being displaced by immigrant populations, and fear that their children are being corrupted by postmodern ideas and Woke capitalism. In these circumstances, it has been substantially easier than in past decades for far-right actors to present themselves as modern-day Joan of Arcs (Le Pen), poised to save their compatriots from the power-hungry politicians, arrogant intellectuals, and global financiers who, in their depiction, bear sole responsibility for these misfortunes.[8]

In this introductory chapter, I will set the stage for this volume's assessment of Far-Right Newspeak by addressing three questions. First, how do we recognize this particular type of political language when we encounter it? Its expositors do not have a monopoly on far-right views. One can easily find political activists and intellectuals who still explicitly use the incendiary rhetoric of the National Socialist and fascist movements of the first half of the twentieth century. Nonetheless, as I shall argue—and as the contributors to this volume confirm—their numbers are dwarfed by the great majority of today's far-right actors who have consciously adopted both liberal and democratic vocabularies to communicate their views.[9] To illustrate this shift from the old to the new, I will provide brief sketches of two contemporary personalities who, in the fashion of the old right, unabashedly use antidemocratic and neofascist rhetoric: Aleksandr Dugin and Richard Spencer.[10] I will then compare their claims to the contrasting, democracy-friendly idiom of several of their contemporaries, including two early exponents of Far-Right Newspeak, Alain de Benoist and Pat Buchanan, and three of their current acolytes, Götz Kubitschek, Carlson, and Jarosław Kaczyński.

Second, when the expositors of Far-Right Newspeak speak, why do people listen and, in many cases, go on to align themselves with their views? Although the political and social polarization of the 2000s has provided them with a favorable climate to propagate their arguments, these conditions are not sufficient to account for their success. One must still *explain* why populations that have known no other form of government than liberal democracy, such as those in the United States, the United Kingdom, the Netherlands, and Canada, should suddenly be receptive to perspectives about race, ethnicity, and religious faith that are contrary to the attitudes of preceding generations. This question is equally valid for portions of the populations of the post-dictatorial democracies of east-central Europe and Latin America. In all of these cases, one might expect that people who were born long after their countries' transition to democracy would naturally appreciate what they have inherited. Instead, many have proven to be surprisingly susceptible to illiberal and anti-liberal appeals.

I shall argue that the appeal of Far-Right Newspeak is that it draws upon a contradiction, or "perpetual antinomy," in the words of the Polish philosopher Leszek Kolakowski, that is inherent to all liberal-democratic regimes. This is the abiding tension between these regimes' obligation to safeguard a panoply of rights and freedoms—to speech, assembly, religion, and much more—and their corresponding responsibility to attend to the welfare of all citizens.[11] To show how the tension between these obligations has been available for exploitation by the far right, I will single out three concepts that we typically associate with liberal democracy: individual freedom, equal rights, and democratic representation. I shall contend that these figures' selective approach to these concepts is precisely what makes them far-right, and not just right.

Finally, why should we be concerned about the appeal of Far-Right Newspeak? Answering this question is more challenging than the casual observer might expect. For one thing, while many far-right positions are inimical to liberal democracy, one should not assume that this is true of all of them. Figures like Carlson and Le Pen are not alone when they attack preferential hiring policies for racial minorities and the provision of welfare services to immigrants. The representatives of conservative catch-all parties and public intellectuals have a long history of deriding left-leaning governments for such measures. Nor are far-right actors the only critics of liberal claims to neutrality, neoliberal economic policies, and the self-seeking behavior of politicians and global corporations. In fact, in some cases, their arguments dovetail with equally vociferous critiques on the left and far-left sides of the political spectrum.[12]

Furthermore, even in cases where far-right positions are clearly contrary to liberal-democratic principles, we are well advised to avoid the assumption that democracy's future is predetermined. To guard against this temptation, I shall outline three contrasting scenarios. The first scenario is that liberal democracy survives despite its trials into the foreseeable future. One possibility, for which there is considerable evidence, is that democratic institutions are strong enough to withstand the challenges of their far-right adversaries. Another equally plausible possibility is that precisely because of democracy's resilience, the system's opponents adopt more moderate views as they acquire vested interests in the status quo.

A second scenario is that the leaders of liberal-democratic states gradually steer their countries in the direction of illiberal democracy. With the exception of Hungary's prime minister, Viktor Orbán, most European and American far-right politicians have avoided using the word "illiberal," preferring instead to identify themselves with less provocative terms, like "national conservative" and "postliberal."[13] Still, many openly express their sympathy for a conception of democracy that would not be governed by some of the most important liberal precepts, including the tolerance of cultural diversity and the freedoms of assembly and speech.

A third scenario is the death of democracy. In this scenario, citizens lose the will to defend democratic institutions against would-be dictators because the reasons for putting them into place, that is, certain conceptions of human worth and convictions about how people should live together, have lost their appeal. Each of these scenarios is possible, but none is inevitable. Thus, we can only reflect on a day-to-day basis about which scenario has the greatest chance of coming to fruition.

The Far Right Speaks: What Do They Say?

One of the surest ways to understand something is to ask what it is not. This maxim holds true for the study of Far-Right Newspeak. Only a few decades ago, the task of interpreting the views of the most visible far-right politicians and intellectuals was relatively straightforward. Until the 1970s and 1980s, the Oldspeak of the extreme right had more in common with the idiom of the fascist movements of the 1920s and 1930s than with the language of contemporary democracy. For its exponents, the victory of liberal democracy over totalitarian dictatorship in 1945 came at an enormous cost. From their standpoint, the triumph of liberal values, including the idea of universal human rights and the concomitant devaluation of traditional norms, had corrupted Western society and left citizens struggling to find meaning in their lives. Accordingly, the foes of democracy maintained that the only hope for the survival of Western civilization lay in restoring the values and shared racial, ethnic, religious, and national identities of earlier generations. Moreover, in contrast to moderate conservatives whom they routinely condemned, they conceived of this mission in zero-sum terms. Whether their opponents were on the right or left, they regarded them as mortal enemies with whom no compromise was possible. Of course, the path to fulfilling these ambitions was open to debate. Although their views remained unchanged, some far-right actors sought to influence their governments by pursuing political office. Others were barely distinguishable from the proponents of fascism in the first half of the twentieth century and openly called for the overthrow of the democratic system.[14]

One can still identify outspoken exponents of these positions in the 2020s, even if their ability to advance extremist agendas is slight. For example, the Russian philosopher Aleksandr Dugin has unabashedly advocated replacing democracy with an authentically "fascist fascism."[15] In Dugin's characterization, the nearly universal acceptance of the principles of the European Enlightenment in Western democracies—individual freedom, human rights, secularism, and rationalism—has torn human beings from their natural moorings. Without an immediate intervention from the right, Dugin would have us believe that humanity is doomed. Because he bases his claims on a hodgepodge of occultist, neopagan, and mystical sources, Dugin has never made it easy for his readers to understand how he proposes to reverse this trend. Nevertheless, he has committed himself to two points that justify his inclusion among the most extreme forms of old-right thought. First, Dugin frankly states that only the adoption of a new form of totalitarian rule will suffice to return society to its premodern foundations. In particular, he argues that the states that lie within what he calls the "Eurasian sphere"—roughly, the territory of the old Soviet Union—should be governed entirely by the inherited cultural and religious values of Russian civilization. Second, Dugin leaves no doubt that this will require a revolution. To save humanity, one must destroy the enemy's ideas. Hence, the new regime should begin its rule with an act of purgation, a "Nuremberg of liberalism."[16]

The American white supremacist Richard Spencer is specific where Dugin is obscure. Like many of his extreme right allies, Spencer reduces his diagnosis of the ills of American democracy to a single issue: race. The values of white America, he warns, are on the verge of being swept away by the onslaught of alien peoples: African-Americans, Hispanic Americans, and non-white immigrants. If white identity is not defended, everything that has made the US great will be lost. "Our bones are in the ground," Spencer declared in 2016. "We own it. At the end of the day America can't exist without us."[17]

Like Dugin, Spencer looks to the past for explanations of what went wrong. He finds them in the Founding Fathers' decision to commit their new nation to the principle of universal equality. Once this step was taken, Spencer contends, white Americans were fated to lose everything that made them naturally superior to other groups. Over time, they became "race-less, family-less, class-less, history-less individuals."[18] To restore this lost identity, Spencer proposes to found the US all over again. He would replace the Declaration of Independence with a "declaration of difference and distance— We hold these truths to be self-evident; that all men are created unequal."[19] Then, he would establish an all-white "ethnostate" which, in turn, would be allied with equally racially homogenous European ethnostates. As a rule, Spencer has been cagey about pinning himself down on how these entities are to come into being. For example, in 2013, he painted a peaceful picture of the transition. The path to these states, he said, would be no more conflictual than the creation of ethnically based nations at the Versailles Conference of 1919.[20] Not long thereafter, however, Spencer let down his guard, conceding that a redrawing of ethnic boundaries would likely be violent. "Look," he admitted, "maybe it will be horribly bloody and terrible."[21]

In stark contrast, the purveyors of Far-Right Newspeak invoke a far different language than these contemporary extremists. Words like "Nuremberg," "horribly bloody," and "terrible" are nowhere to be found in their speeches, television interviews, and communications on social media. Moreover, they would never associate themselves with fascism. If we take far-right politicians and would-be opinion-makers at their word, as I do for illustrative purposes in this section, they have no intention of dismantling the institutions of post–World War II democracy. Quite the contrary. They are quick to affirm their support for institutional constraints on the use of political power, the rigorous application of the rule of law, and free and fair elections. Similarly, they formulate their critiques of liberalism in nuanced and selective ways. On the one hand, they decry the left's assaults on traditional values and purported attempts to eliminate racial, ethnic, gender, and class differences through social engineering. On the other, they consciously lay claim to specific elements of the liberal vocabulary, which they then reframe to serve less than liberal purposes. Whereas neofascist thinkers like Dugin regard the idea of individual freedom as a threat to Western civilization, the proponents of Far-Right Newspeak describe it as a fundamental right and an essential defense against leftist extremism. In addition, while Dugin, Spencer, and other extremists treat the idea of equal rights as incompatible with the preservation of distinctive racial, ethnic, and cultural identities, the expositors of Far-Right Newspeak resolve the issue by advancing a specific conception of equality that accentuates these identities.

The Far-Right Newspeak of the twenty-first century did not spring from thin air. One can trace its roots to the 1970s when a rising generation of French far-right intellectuals and political organizers voiced their frustration over the old-right's failure to offer a compelling vision to their country's citizens. In the view of thinkers like Alain de Benoist, the leading light of France's *Nouvelle droite* ("New Right"), French citizens were essentially being presented with a false choice between two equally unsatisfactory positions. Either they could align themselves with the antediluvian attitudes and anti-democratic disposition of the extreme right or they could sell their souls and embrace the values of France's conservative establishment which, the critics argued, were barely distinguishable from the agenda of classical liberalism. Although few of these figures were ever welcomed into the intellectual mainstream—de Benoist was unusual for gaining a couple years of respectability—their efforts to craft a "third way" between these options showed how the language of liberalism could be utilized to advance illiberal and anti-liberal claims.

De Benoist laid the conceptual foundations for transforming the classical idea of equal rights into a rationale for devaluing the rights of minority populations. In a polemical collection of essays, *Vu de Droite* (1977), he argued that the overwhelming majority of French citizens were the actual victims of discrimination in his country. Because of the political elites' "pseudo-anti-racist" policies and deluded attempts to create a totally homogenous society, ordinary Frenchmen and Frenchwomen were denied the right to act on those aspects of their personality, such as their race, religious faith, and cultural heritage, that made each of them unique. On the basis of this logic, de Benoist concluded that one could only speak of equality in a meaningful sense by restoring each citizen's "right to difference." Luckily for France, in his view, these citizens were naturally equipped to preserve the culture and traditions of their nation.[22]

One of De Benoist's contemporaries, the American far-right journalist and three-time presidential candidate, Pat Buchanan, used a different and less nuanced rationale to justify an exclusionary version of majoritarianism. Beginning in the 1970s, he tapped into the distinctively American glorification of heroic individualism and distrust of political authority to castigate establishment politicians, including those in his own Republican Party, for sacrificing basic freedoms at the altar of big government and the welfare state. In part, Buchanan's message was consistent with mainstream conservatism. He echoed the long-standing conservative lament about the "fading away of the free society, when men advanced [on the basis of] ability, merit, and performance."[23] What set Buchanan apart from the mainstream was his use of apocalyptic language to make his case. In his depiction, left-wing Democrats were the real enemies of democracy. While they claimed to be defending equal rights and combating racism and poverty, their real goal was to destroy the "soul of America." The only way to bring the United States back to good health, Buchanan argued, in an unmistakable nod to his country's white majority population, was for the American people to wrench power from the hands of the ruling class. At this point, they could put their faith in those good people who were prepared to fight for the country's founding ideals: traditional social values, the sanctity of the family, faith in God, and unflinching patriotism.[24]

Admittedly, it is difficult to judge the extent to which either de Benoist's or Buchanan's thinking continues to influence the contemporary far right. Although European identitarian activists and intellectuals often cite de Benoist's name to embellish their arguments, there is little to indicate that they have taken the time to struggle through his continuing output of abstruse tomes. Similarly, while Buchanan won millions of votes in his three presidential campaigns, one does not need to go back to his speeches or follow his current op-ed columns to understand the populist appeals of far-right politicians and intellectuals like Donald Trump and Steve Bannon.

Nonetheless, the ideas with which the two figures were associated are thriving thanks to the efforts of a younger, successor generation of purveyors of Far-Right Newspeak. For example, Götz Kubitschek, the director of the rightwing German Institute for National Policy and the online journal *Sezession im Netz*, has made a name for himself by applying a quasi-intellectual gloss to his attacks on his government's immigration policies and its failure to safeguard supposedly authentic German values. Like his French counterpart, Kubitschek presents himself as an advocate of the right of every citizen to defend his or her personal identity ("*Verteidigung des Eigenen*").[25] In a bitter exchange with a former colleague, Karlheinz Weißmann, in November 2021 over anti-Covid lockdowns and vaccination mandates, Kubitschek condemned Germany's leaders for supposedly violating the constitution by depriving citizens of their freedom, as individuals, to make personal decisions about their well-being. In assuming this role, it seems, they had paralyzed the population with the fear that things could only get worse. These measures, he warned, were harbingers of darker days to come for German democracy. It was even possible that they were a test run by the government to use its arbitrary conception of the common good to subjugate the people (*das Volk*) to its total command.[26]

In much the same manner, Tucker Carlson has used the idea of equal rights to buttress the case that white Americans are the real victims of discrimination. In a beguiling manner, Carlson tells his viewers that the advocates of preferential policies to address racial and gender disparities are not sincerely interested in equality. If they were, he explains, they would insist upon judging people on the basis of their skills and natural talents. Since they do the opposite, they are the real "racists" in American society. Taking this argument one step further, Carlson has played into his viewers' anxieties about the rapidly changing racial and ethnic composition of the US population. He has openly endorsed the racist "replacement theory," contending that liberal and left-wing politicians are bent upon replacing white Americans with peoples of color from other countries. In the name of prompting freedom of speech, Carlson has also given precious airtime to avowed white nationalists, such as Curtis Yarvin, a defender of slavery and terrorism. He has even warned of a coming race war if American politicians fail to heed his warnings.[27]

In this light, both Kubitshek and Carlson could find much to admire in the example of Jarosław Kaczyński, who for eight years practically defined Poland's political priorities thanks to his leadership of the country's Law and Justice Party (PiS). From his position at the pinnacle of political power between PiS's victory in the presidential and parliamentary elections in 2015 and the party's unexpected defeat in 2023, Kaczyński rallied supporters around the idea that Poland had only completed half of its transition to democracy. In his characterization, the country's first postcommunist leaders had played a heroic role in setting up legitimate democratic institutions. Nonetheless, this happy transition had been abruptly cut short by the machinations of left-wing "totalitarian" ideologues and meddling European Union officials who stood in the way of infusing these bodies with the values of the Polish nation. As a result, Kaczyński advised his followers, the moral authority of traditional institutions, like the family and the Catholic Church, had been eroded and the reputation of the nation was tarnished.[28]

Beyond making these claims, Kaczyński was in the position to effect political changes about which Carlson and Kubitschek could only dream. During PiS's years as the majority party in Parliament, he used his arguments as a justification for hollowing out many of his country's democratic achievements. Taking advantage of both his party's political position and the opportunity to make strategic appointments to the constitutional court, he successfully expanded executive power over the judiciary, compromised the integrity of state television and other media, and imposed new constraints on the freedom of assembly.[29] In the process of forcing through these changes, Kaczyński labeled anyone who disagreed with these measures an enemy of democracy and threatened to "destroy" them if they stood in his way.[30]

The Contemporary Far Right Speaks: Why Do People Listen and Then Follow?

It is one thing to argue that far-right actors like Kubitschek, Carlson, and Kaczyński invoke the language of Far-Right Newspeak because it allows them to reach the middle-of-the-road audiences that were inaccessible to their old-right predecessors. However, it is a much greater challenge to explain why they have succeeded in using this language to motivate people to follow them. In my view, the key to understanding the attraction of Far-Right Newspeak is that these figures do not ask potential supporters to make the choice against democracy. If they took this approach, many of their listeners would likely look elsewhere for more palatable sources of inspiration. Instead, they take advantage of the tension between freedom and the common good that Kolakowski has described as liberalism's "perpetual antinomy" to argue that mainstream politicians have betrayed their own principles. According to this logic, they, the purveyors of Newspeak, are the supposed defenders of these ideals.

Briefly, Kolakowski's argument is that all liberal-democratic regimes are engaged in a balancing act.[31] On the one hand, their leaders approach policymaking with the goal of maximizing the rights and freedoms of those whom they serve. Each human being, this principle holds, is entitled to seek personal fulfillment. Hence, leaders must approach every decision with an awareness of their limitations in making responsible decisions about the good of others. Furthermore, as the people's elected representatives, they would unjustly impinge upon the rights of their fellow citizens if they used their positions to impose their personal preferences. Accordingly, they must foster conditions in which every person has an equal opportunity to prosper. Just as no individual should be deprived of his or her freedom, it would be unjust to allow one person to prosper at the expense of another.

On the other hand, Kolakowski emphasizes that democratic leaders should be equally committed to advancing the common good. If the needs of all citizens are not adequately addressed, the rights of the individual will never be secure. Accordingly, Kolakowski argues that there can be no absolute right to freedom. A society based upon this principle would descend into anarchy. Moreover, because power is always distributed unequally, the failure to address entrenched disparities would reinforce conditions in which only the powerful have the chance to realize their potential. Thus, Kolakowski emphasizes that when democratic leaders intervene to "protect the weak from the strong," they are not violating the rights of the powerful. To the contrary, they are fostering conditions in which meaningful equality is extended to every citizen.[32]

For Kolakowski, a democracy is robust when its leaders affirm both parts of this antinomy. The fact that the tension between freedom and the common good is perpetual serves everyone's interests. In a complex world, people with different political and cultural perspectives are obliged to work together to identify solutions to difficult problems. To ensure that their views have equal weight, political compromise about the degree to which they should use the state's power to resolve these issues is unavoidable. Ideally, when all sides abide by this principle, each has a chance to realize at least some of its objectives.

In contrast, the propagators of Far-Right Newspeak, including many, though not all, of those who are covered in this volume, take the opposite position. In effect, they advise their audiences that the antinomy is resolvable—not through compromise or accommodation, but essentially by choosing one side over the other. One can still be a defender of freedom and equal rights, they insist, but this does not mean that one should be forced to consider the common good of all. In this respect, the exponents of this perspective part ways with a basic precondition for the flourishing of any liberal democracy. They absolutize one side of the antinomy—generally, the interests of the majority—while dismissing the side that would otherwise force leaders to seek solutions to complex problems on the basis of compromise. This step, as I have suggested earlier, is what makes their arguments far-right, and not simply right.

Consider Kubitschek's selective characterization of the concept of freedom. In his depiction, even measures to safeguard the health of the German population in a pandemic are unjustifiable because they threaten the individual's right to decide for himself or herself what is consonant with their personal needs. In this one-sided depiction of a basic liberal value, one need not worry about a contradiction between freedom and the welfare of all citizens. Because this narrow definition of freedom excludes other rights, one can justify any type of behavior as an exercise in individual judgment, even if it is antithetical to the well-being of others.

For his part, Carlson absolves his viewers of any guilt for opposing efforts to combat vestiges of racial and ethnic discrimination and the continuing burdens of poverty by summoning an equally selective and deracinated conception of equal rights. In his portrayal, state intervention in these matters is antithetical to the American dream. When leftist politicians break this rule to appease the demands of minorities, they are actually intent upon creating new inequalities. As a result, the majority of Americans find themselves struggling to survive in circumstances where the cards of opportunity are stacked against them.

Taken together, these truncated conceptions of freedom and equality help to explain why far-right politicians, like Kaczyński, have been able to persuade voters that a true democracy is defined by the will of the majority. This populist and essentially problematic application of the majoritarian principle is appealing because it implies that there is no need to engage in the protracted process of reconciling the contending needs and desires of the diverse segments of society, especially those of minorities. By defining political priorities in terms of the ostensible wishes of the majority, far-right leaders are free to treat the thorny issue of democratic representation as resolved. By this logic, the majority population can rest content in the assumption that its leaders are acting in its best interest.

Ironically, there is a trace of utopian thinking in all of these arguments. Whereas moderate politicians welcome disagreement and conflict as essential features of democratic politics, far-right actors regard these tensions as an impediment to the realization of their conception of a just society. In this one respect, their arguments are akin to those of far-left utopians, like Karl Marx and V. I. Lenin, who sought to eliminate the challenge of political complexity by prioritizing the interests of one segment of society over others.[33] While these contemporary personalities also claim to maximize individual freedom and realize true equality, the perverse consequence of this approach to politics is that the precondition for its realization for some people, as Orwell once observed, is its denial to others.[34]

The Far-Right Speaks: Should We Be Worried?

Will Orwell's dystopian vision of liberal democracy's future prove to be accurate? Even the most sanguine observer will find it impossible to avoid this question. The undeniable success of far-right populist politicians and extremist movements in the 2010s and 2020s has already spurred a cottage industry of academic and journalistic publications on the health of liberal democracy and the prospects for its survival. The key words in the titles of countless books and articles reflect the seriousness of this concern: "Twilight of Democracy," "Democracy Against Liberalism," "How Democracy Ends," "The Politics of Fear," and "The Extreme Gone Mainstream."[35] Moreover, public opinion surveys in advanced democracies and sophisticated analyses of democratic performance confirm that there is growing skepticism among citizens about the system's virtues and, paradoxically, widespread public apathy about the need to address its shortcomings.[36] These surveys also indicate that sympathy for illiberal and anti-liberal alternatives is on the rise.[37]

Nonetheless, one should not be fatalistic about the prospects for liberal democracy.[38] True, like all forms of political organization, liberal democracy is destined to be superseded at some point by new forms of human governance. Understandably, many of the possibilities are beyond our imagination. However, although all things must pass, they need not pass today. Just as far-right actors have ridden the waves to power and influence over the past couple decades by taking advantage of propitious conditions—successive economic crises, the movement of desperate people from one part of the world to another, and a global pandemic—the fate of liberal democracy will depend upon highly contingent circumstances. This is why it makes sense to weigh the probability of a range of outcomes as time moves along and reflect upon the conditions that will favor one of them over the others.

One scenario is that the democratic institutions and principles that undergird the current political order survive for the foreseeable future. As I have noted at the beginning of this chapter, the far right does not have a monopoly on denouncing the positions of politicians and parties on the left. Mainstream conservatives in North America and Europe routinely vilify their moderate-left opponents for their stands on immigration, government spending, and supposed hostility to traditional and Judeo-Christian values. Moreover, the fact that the political right and the left engage in heated debates over these issues is not an indication that democracy is on the verge of collapse.

Kolakowski's observations about the "perpetual antinomy" in democratic life teach us that the opposite may be true. To the extent that political rivals are ultimately willing to engage in compromise on contested issues, democracy is alive and well. In the 2020s, democratic institutions and liberal values in many countries have proven to be remarkably resilient in the face of significant challenges to their authority. In both Slovenia and the Netherlands, popular support for the far-right Slovenian National Party and the Forum for Democracy, respectively, surged for a brief period but then plummeted. In Norway and the Czech Republic, far-right parties have notable followings, but their numbers are, as yet, insufficient to mount a serious threat to middle-of-the-road parties and their governing coalitions. Even in Germany, where the AfD has registered significant gains in the public eye, the party's ability to challenge established institutional practices will be constrained by the population's continuing faith in the democratic system.[39]

A second scenario is that liberal democracy gradually slips into "illiberal" democracy, or simply "illiberalism." The meaning of both terms is notoriously difficult to pin down. In some studies, the concept of illiberal democracy is simply a convenient shorthand to fill in the space between healthy pluralistic politics and authoritarianism. Still, there is a rough scholarly consensus about a set of objectives that is shared by all illiberal actors. Typically, these figures promote policies that elevate the authority of traditional institutions, such as the family, the church, and other sources of group identity, over the supposed hegemony of secular values and excessive individualism. They attempt to turn their followers' sense of victimization by liberal elites into a source of political power. And, they use this power to transform formal political institutions, such as the electoral system and the courts, in ways that cement their gains.[40]

These aims not only play a significant role in the thinking of the five expositors of Far-Right Newspeak whom I have described in this chapter. One can also find them in the goals of most of the far-right actors, as well as other variations in right-wing thinking, in this volume. The consistent refrain in these figures' arguments is that there is no contradiction between the rejection of some, or even all, liberal values and one's sincere commitment to democracy. As I have noted, they contend that they are the real supporters of the system, even though many of the policies they advocate contradict these claims. Among the functioning democracies of Europe and America, Viktor Orbán has done more than any other leader, including Kaczyński, to manipulate the levers of power to transform the democratic system to his liking. While claiming to abide by democratic norms, he has steered government funding to political allies and putatively patriotic organizations, extended voting rights to ethnic Hungarians who live abroad, and overseen the promulgation of a constitution that gives him broad authority over judicial appointments and a wide variety of public institutions.[41]

To be sure, with the arguable exception of Poland's PiS government, it would be difficult to demonstrate that any other European or American democracy would qualify as truly illiberal. Still, one can find Orbán and Kaczyński *Doppelgänger* everywhere. In every country in these regions, far-right politicians routinely take advantage of opportunities to promote illiberal and anti-liberal platforms and push legislation to advance their preferred policies. In the United States in particular, state legislatures have used formally democratic means to pass discriminatory voting laws, ban controversial books, restrict freedom of speech, and prohibit programs that foster diversity awareness. Just as in Poland and Hungary, sympathetic courts have produced legal opinions that justify these illiberal measures. Making these developments even more significant, politicians once known for their middle-of-the-road positions have supported these steps simply to increase their appeal among far-right voters.

The third scenario is the passing of democracy. While the proponents of illiberalism insist that they remain unequivocally committed to democratic institutions, one must wonder whether democracy can survive if the authority of the liberal values that undergird it is discounted or dismissed. In the words of one expert on democracy, "Can't have one without the other."[42] Formal constitutions, courts, and competitive elections make liberalism possible by guaranteeing citizens equal access to the public sphere, safeguarding fundamental rights, and enforcing the rule of law. However, the liberal idea is the source of the political sensibilities and commitment to the good of all persons that determines how politicians behave within these institutional boundaries. Indeed, the preservation of liberal values is even more important given the fact that democratic institutions were created to serve them. Whether future leaders be classified as far-right or fall under related categories, such as libertarian, identitarian, Alt-right, or postliberal, their success in compromising and distorting traditional liberal conceptions of freedom, equality, and democratic representation will put them in the position to hollow out these institutions from within. They can impose new constraints on vital rights by rewriting their countries' constitutions, chip away at the autonomy and independence of the judiciary, persuade compliant parliaments to end limits on their terms in office, and manipulate election rules to ensure that they and their allies gain even greater power.

Aside from the extreme cases of Russia and Belarus, whose leaders have turned their political institutions into rubber stamps to justify autocratic rule, democracy's day of reckoning has not yet come to Europe and the Americas. Still, the supplanting of established democracies with autocracy does not happen overnight.[43] It may already be approaching on "extremist cat feet." Should the opportunity to subvert liberal democracy arise, the expositors of Far-Right Newspeak can provide powerful arguments to beguile trusting populations into believing that conventional approaches to securing the common good of all are no longer worth defending.

'Tis a fragile thing, this idea of liberal democracy.

Four Substantive Themes

This volume is divided into four thematic sections. We have designed each of these sections to address specific issues that arise in the study of Far-Right Newspeak. In the first section, "The Language of Liberalism," the contributors consider the ways in which exponents of Far-Right Newspeak from four different countries use and abuse liberal vocabularies to appeal to mainstream audiences. I begin the section by exploring the similarities and differences in the language and arguments of three well-known personalities: the American social media pundit Tucker Carlson; the French politician Marine Le Pen; and, somewhat controversially, the Canadian psychologist Jordan Peterson. Despite the significant differences in how each figure frames liberal principles, such as freedom and equality, to make the case against the political establishment, I contend that all three converge around a set of ideas that would justify making their societies less free, less equal, and ultimately less democratic. Sarah Shurts follows with an analysis of Le Pen's arguments about women's rights and gender equality. To understand the popular appeal of Le Pen's approach among women voters, Shurts argues that we should be skeptical when scholars argue that her use of liberal terms is nothing more than a ruse or a façade. Rather, it is important to recognize that Le Pen has successfully shifted French political culture rightward by appropriating and reinterpreting the liberal and republican values that have long defined French identity. Finally, Petra Mlejnková examines the Far-Right Newspeak vocabulary of the Czech far-right politician Tomio Okamura. In many ways, Okamura's liberal vocabulary is more simplistic and transparently opportunistic than Le Pen's. However, as Mlejnková demonstrates, Okamura is an illuminating example of how a far-right politician in a postcommunist state can exploit his country's trials to convince voters that only an illiberal conception of democracy can protect them from a return to dictatorship.

In the second section, "Far-Right Newspeak in Practice," the contributors examine several concrete cases in which the use and abuse of liberal concepts is reflected in the behavior of far-right politicians, influential legal scholars, and ordinary citizens. Tímea Drinóczi and Agnieszka Bień-Kacała open the section with a discussion of the role of Far-Right Newspeak in postcommunist Poland and Hungary. The countries' most prominent politicians, Kaczyński and Orbán, respectively, have adeptly manipulated the language of individual rights and equality to hollow out constitutional protections of these rights and foreclose the possibility of adapting the law to evolving social values. Despite Kaczyński's and Orbán's undeniable impact, however,

Drinóczi and Bień-Kacała remind us that Far-Right Newspeak is only as powerful as political and social conditions will allow. Thus, in Poland, far-right politicians and judges were able to join forces to impose significant limits on the right to an abortion, whereas in Hungary, the law remains comparatively permissive. In contrast, Hungarian advocates of constitutional provisions for traditional conceptions of the family and gender roles have been more successful than their Polish counterparts.

In the following chapter, Frank Wolff examines the mutually beneficial relationship that arose between a small but influential group of legal scholars and politicians in the wake of the German government's controversial decision in 2015 to allow large numbers of migrants to stay in the country. In their subsequent denunciations of the decision and the implementation of related human rights protections, the scholars have used liberal constitutional rhetoric to contend that German democracy is on the verge of collapse. Then, far-right politicians and even leading figures in mainstream parties appropriated these claims and skillfully used them to condemn the government for violating the law and the letter of the constitution. In the final chapter of this section, George Hawley explores a more down-to-earth manifestation of right-wing and far-right thinking, the online anti-feminist movement called the "manosphere." In its early years, Hawley argues, this movement was not at all illiberal. Far from advancing a form of Newspeak, its adherents limited themselves to making modest claims about cultural stereotypes of men and critiquing the preferential legal treatment of women. In the 2000s, however, the manosphere degenerated into a platform for misogyny and misanthropy. In recent years, this extremist forum for male grievance has practically disappeared. However, Hawley points out that the issues that precipitated the movement have not gone away. They are currently being exploited and normalized by such diverse personalities as Jordan Peterson, Tucker Carlson, and "Raw Egg Nationalist."[44]

In the third thematic section, "The Ambiguities of a Concept," the contributors wrestle with the challenge of distinguishing between actors who unmistakably embody far-right positions and others who either straddle the fine line between right-wing and far-right ideas or take positions that cannot be usefully described as Far-Right Newspeak. This task is essential to making sense of the far right. If one were to put all of the subjects in this volume into a Procrustean bed of far-right identity, it would be impossible to make meaningful comparisons among them. In her chapter, Laura K. Field focuses on so-called postliberals and singles out two sophisticated Catholic intellectuals, Patrick Deneen and Adrian Vermeule. Both thinkers argue that democracies should not be governed by the traditional liberal ideal of freedom from state interference in citizens' private lives. Instead, Deneen and Vermeule advocate a qualitatively different definition of freedom that is understood as the capacity of individuals to self-regulate and orient their lives in accordance with an objective good. Field warns that enemies of democracy could use these arguments to justify authoritarianism. In her view, this would make the word "postliberal" as Orwellian as Far-Right Newspeak. In the following chapter, Steven Pittz argues that it is a mistake to treat all forms of conspiratorial thinking as manifestations of far-right positions. Drawing a distinction between "pragmatic" and "systemic" conspiracy theories, he maintains that "pragmatic conspiracism" is potentially consistent with classical liberal attitudes about active citizen engagement in democratic politics and the necessity of questioning political authority. The purveyors of "systemic conspiracism," in contrast, abuse and pervert liberal language to serve anti-liberal ends.

In the fourth thematic section, "Beyond Far-Right Newspeak," José Pedro Zúquete and Josh Vandiver speculate about where the ideas underlying Far-Right Newspeak might be headed. Zúquete centers on the far-right opponents of "The Great Reset," purportedly an organized effort by the World Economic Forum to subvert individual freedoms in order to further the interests of corporate and political elites. These resisters of the Great Reset are especially concerned with "biopolitics," the management of human activity and health through technology. In particular, Zúquete highlights their use of the liberal idea of freedom to depict vaccine passport mandates during the Covid-19 pandemic as tyrannical. In the following chapter, Vandiver speculates about the emergence of action groups on the "technological right" that advocate preparations for supposedly impending crises on the democratic horizon. Vandiver shows how Peter Thiel—the most prominent and influential of these tech-right figures—has sought to cultivate "hard men" who are committed to defending individual freedom by employing non-democratic and extra-constitutional means. Vandiver identifies similar themes in the arguments of cryptocurrency enthusiasts. These "Bitcoin bros" and "cryptopartisans" contend that liberal-democratic governments have manipulated the money supply to the exclusive benefit of capital and financial markets, not workers. For this reason, in their view, only non-state-backed currencies like Bitcoin can be trusted to put power back into the hands of ordinary people.

Finally, in the concluding chapter, Samuel Piccolo reflects on the implications of the arguments in this volume for the future of liberal democracy. First, he contends that liberal democrats must acknowledge contemporary liberal democracy's vulnerabilities, rather than focusing solely on the views of their political opponents. This approach will also help them recognize liberal democracy's ability to self-correct. Second, he connects Far-Right Newspeak to a deeper and, as yet, insufficiently explored problem in defining liberal concepts: Can we say definitively that something is liberal and democratic?

Notes

I would like to thank Agnieszka Bień-Kacała, Laura K. Field, and Samuel Piccolo for their detailed and quite helpful comments on this chapter.
1 George Orwell, *1984* (New York: Signet Classic, 1961).
2 https://twitter.com/DonaldJTrumpJr/status/1347697226466828288.
3 www.theguardian.com/us-news/2021/jan/18/josh-hawley-book-publisher-simon-schuster.
4 www.globalresearch.ca/orwellian-lockstep-loaded-syringe/5710144.
5 Fox News, March 21, 2021, www.foxnews.com/video/6245003952001.
6 The concept of the "Overton window" refers to the range of possibilities through which ideas that are considered socially unacceptable (outside the window) can be transformed into acceptable ideas (inside the window) and then enacted as policy. Interestingly, the politicization and propagation of the concept originated in a right-libertarian think tank, the Mackinac Center for Public Policy. However, I would not characterize the Center as far right. For the Center's interpretation of its mission, see www.mackinac.org/about.
7 Sabine Kinkartz, "Far-Right AfD Emerges as Germany's Second Strongest Party," *Deutsche Welle*, July 7, 2023, www.dw.com/en/far-right-afd-emerges-as-germanys-second-strongest-party/a-66154675.
8 Le Pen likes to portray herself as a modern-day Joan of Arc saving "French freedoms" (a motto for her 2022 presidential campaign) in the same way that France's patron saint sought to save Christianity. See Daniel Rueda, "A Certain Idea of France's Past: Marine Le Pen's History Wars," *European Politics and Society* (2022): 1–15, www.tandfonline.com/doi/full/10.1080/23745118.2022.2058751.
9 Also, see the important study by Lars Erik Berntzen, one of the original participants in the meetings that led to this volume, *Liberal Roots of Far Right Activism: The Anti-Islamic Movement in the 21st Century* (London: Routledge, 2020).
10 On the manipulation of political rhetoric to support extremist and proto-fascist ideas, see Ruth Wodak and John E. Richardson, eds., *Analyzing Fascist Discourse: European Fascism in Talk and Text* (London: Routledge, 2013); and Paul Jackson, Matthew Feldman, Anton Shekhovtsov, Roger Griffin, Janet Wilson, Ruth Wodak, and Graham Macklin, eds., *Doublespeak: The Rhetoric of the Far Right Since 1945* (Stuttgart: Ibidem, 2014).
11 Kołakowski, "The Self-Poisoning of the Open Society," in *Modernity on Endless Trial* (Chicago and London: The University of Chicago Press, 1990), 162–74. Kołakowski also argues that liberal democracies have "self-poisoning" tendencies. For an insightful application of this idea to contemporary Europe, see Ivan Krastev, "Europe's Democracy Paradox," www.the-american-interest.com/2012/02/01/europes-democracy-paradox/.
12 While there is no lack of outspoken critics of liberalism on the left, the major difference between them and the far right is that they are supportive of democracy. See Aurelian Mondon and Aaron Winter, *Reactionary Democracy: How Racism and the Populist Far Right Became Mainstream* (London: Verso, 2020); and Ishay Landa, *The Apprentice's Sorcerer: Liberal Tradition and Fascism* (Chicago: Haymarket Books, 2012).
13 See Laura Field's argument about the relationship between far-right thinkers and postliberal thinkers in Chapter 8.

14 For diverse approaches to this topic, see Richard Saull, Alexander Anievas, Neil Davidson, and Adam Fabry, eds., *The Long Durée of the Far Right* (London: Routledge, 2015); and Mark Sedgwick, ed., *Key Thinkers of the Radical Right* (Oxford: Oxford University Press, 2019).
15 Cited in Ronald Beiner, *Dangerous Minds: Nietzsche, Heidegger, and the Return of the Far Right* (Philadelphia: University of Pennsylvania, 2019), 69.
16 Marlene Laruelle, "Aleksandr Dugin and Eurasianism," in *Key Thinkers of the Radical Right: Behind the New Threat to Liberal Democracy*, edited by Mark Sedgwick (Oxford: Oxford University Press, 2019), 155–69. Also see Laruelle, ed., *Eurasianism and the European Far Right: Reshaping the Europe-Russia Relationship* (Lanham, MA: Lexington Books, 2015).
17 www.splcenter.org/fighting-hate/extremist-files/individual/richard-bertrand-spencer-0.
18 This article, "The God of White Dispossession" (January 20, 2014) was originally published on the website radixjournal.com, which apparently no longer exists. However, it can be found in the archive of the internet site Wayback Machine, https://web.archive.org/web/20140125004533/http://www.radixjournal.com/journal/2014/1/20/the-god-of-white-dispossession/.
19 This article, "The Metapolitics of America," from July 4, 2014, is available on the Wayback Machine site, https://web.archive.org/web/20170719203514/http:/www.radixjournal.com/journal/2014/7/4/the-metapolitics-of-america, and see www.splcenter.org/fighting-hate/extremist-files/individual/richard-bertrand-spencer-0.
20 Lauren Fox, "The Hate Monger Next Door," *Salon*, September 13, 2013, www.salon.com/2013/09/29/the_hatemonger_next_door/. Spencer is apparently unaware that the Versailles Conference was hardly a successful exercise in peacemaking. Spencer is also credited with coining the term "Alt-right." On Spencer and other white supremacist currents, see George Hawley, *Making Sense of the Alt-Right* (New York: Columbia University Press, 2019).
21 Bulent Kenes, "Richard B. Spencer: The Founder of Alt-Right Presents Racism in a Chic New Outfit," *European Center for Populism Studies*, June 28, 2021, www.populismstudies.org/richard-b-spencer-the-founder-of-alt-right-presents-racism-in-a-chic-new-outfit/.
22 Alain de Benoist, *Vu de Droite. Anthologie critique des idées contemporaines* (Paris: Éditions du Labyrinthe, 1977), 30–31.
23 "The Voice in the Desert," June 11, 1990, https://buchanan.org/blog/pjb-the-voice-in-the-desert-146.
24 See "1992 Republican Convention Speech," August 17, 1992, https://buchanan.org/blog/1992-republican-national-convention-speech-148, and "The Cultural War for the Soul of America," September 14, 1992, https://buchanan.org/blog/the-cultural-war-for-the-soul-of-america-149.
25 Cited in Thomas Wagner, *Die Angstmacher: 1968 und die neuen Rechten* (Berlin: Aufbau, 2017), 81.
26 "Drohen Finstere Tage?" November 25, 2021, https://sezession.de/65101/drohen-finstere-tage. Weißmann supported the measures. See "Gemeinwohl hat Vorrang," *Junge Freiheit*, November 28, 2021, https://jungefreiheit.de/debatte/kommentar/2021/fuer-impfpflicht/.
27 For example, "Equity Is Racism," *Fox News*, May 20, 2021, and Tucker Carlson, "The Key Difference Between 'Equality' and 'Equity,'" *Fox News*, March 3, 2021.

28 See "We Are Dealing With a Rebellion," *TVN Poland*, June 4, 2016. https://tvn24.pl/polska/zjazd-okregowy-pis-w-warszawie-przemowienie-jaroslawa-kaczynskiego-ra649572-3186955 (English translation), and "Speech at the Polona Institute," May 2, 2016, https://poloniainstitute.net/poland-current-issues/jaroslaw-kaczynski-speech-of-may-2-2016/ (English translation).

29 See Tímea Drinóczi and Agnieszka Bień-Kacała, *Rule of Law, Common Values, and Illiberal Constitutionalism: Poland and Hungary Within the European Union* (London: Routledge, 2022). Also, see their analysis in Chapter 5 of this volume.

30 Daniel Tiles, "'We Will Destroy These People,' Says Polish Leader Kaczyński in Response to Protests," *Notes from Poland*, December 8, 2022, https://notesfrompoland.com/2022/12/08/we-will-destroy-these-people-says-polish-leader-kaczynski-in-response-to-protests/.

31 Kołakowski, "The Self-Poisoning of the Open Society," 173–74.

32 Ibid., 168.

33 See A. James McAdams, *Vanguard of the Revolution: The Global Idea of the Communist Party* (Princeton: Princeton University Press, 2017), Chapters 2 and 3.

34 Orwell captured this paradox in his classic fable, *Animal Farm* (New York: Signet, 2004). Interestingly, in his *Communist Manifesto*, Marx made a similar point in his case against capitalism, although he failed to recognize the tragic implications of his revolutionary prescriptions. In this sentence, I am deliberately borrowing his formulation of capitalism's contradictions: "You reproach us, therefore, with intending to do away with a form of property, the necessary condition for whose existence is the non-existence of any property for the immense majority of society." See Karl Marx, *The Communist Manifesto* (New York: Norton, 1988), 69–70.

35 This is only a representative sample. Also see Anne Applebaum, *Twilight of Democracy* (New York: Doubleday, 2020); Aviezer Tucker, *Democracy Against Liberalism* (Cambridge: Polity, 2022); David Runciman, *How Democracy Ends* (New York: Basic Books, 2018); Ruth Wodak, *The Politics of Fear* (London: Sage, 2021); and Cynthia Miller-Idriss, *The Extreme Gone Mainstream* (Princeton: Princeton University Press, 2017).

36 Helmut K. Anheier and Edward L. Knudsen, "The 21st Century Trust and Leadership Problem: Quoi Faire?" *Global Policy* 4, no. 1 (February 2023): 139–48; R. S. Foa, A. Klassen, D. Wenger, A. Rand, and M. Slade, *Youth and Satisfaction with Democracy: Reversing the Democratic Disconnect?* (Cambridge: Centre for the Future of Democracy, 2020), www.cam.ac.uk/system/files/youth_and_satisfaction_with_democracy.pdf; "6 in 10 Americans Say Democracy Is in Crisis as the 'Big Lie' Takes Root," www.npr.org/2022/01/03/1069764164/american-democracy-poll-jan-6; Stephan Haggard and Robert Kaufman, *Backsliding: Democratic Regress in the Contemporary World* (Cambridge: Cambridge University Press, 2021); Nick Corasaniti, Michael C. Bender, Ruth Igielnik, and Kristen Bayrakdarian, "Voters See Democracy in Peril, But Saving It Isn't a Priority," *New York Times*, October 18, 2022.

37 See V-Dem Institute Democracy Report 2023, "Defiance in the Face of Autocratization," www.v-dem.net/documents/29/V-dem_democracyreport2023_lowres.pdf; and M. Lewandowsky and M. Jankowski, "Sympathy for the Devil? Voter Support for Illiberal Politicians," *European Political Science Review* 15, no. 1 (2023): 39–56.

38 Cas Mudde has wisely cautioned scholars against the temptations of predicting the imminent demise of democracy or underestimating its strengths. For example, see "Three Decades of Populist Radical Right Parties in Europe: So What?" *European Journal of Political Research* 52 (2013): 1–19.
39 See Michael Fürstenau, *Deutsche Welle*, April 19, 2023, https://www.dw.com/en/germany-trust-in-democracy-still-strong-survey-finds/a-65451290. Democratic resilience is especially notable in the Czech Republic where a 2021 Eurobarometer survey found trust in government to be at the bottom of the 27-member European Union, https://brnodaily.com/2021/05/04/news/eurobarometer-2021-czech-confidence-in-the-government-lowest-in-the-eu/. On voter support for the far right in the Czech Republic, see Petra Mlejnková's analysis in Chapter 4.
40 Marlene Laruelle, "Illiberalism: A Conceptual Introduction," *East European Politics* 38, no. 2 (2022): 303–27.
41 Drinóczi and Bień-Kacała, *Rule of Law*.
42 Mark F. Plattner, "Liberalism and Democracy: Can't Have One Without the Other," *Foreign Affairs* 77, no. 2 (1998): 171–80.
43 See Nancy Bermeo's observations about democratic decline, "On Democratic Backsliding," *Journal of Democracy* 27, no. 1 (January 2016): 5–19.
44 On the curious personality, "Raw Egg Nationalist," see José Pedro Zúquete's description in Chapter 10 p. 192, 194, 199.

PART II
The Language of Liberalism

2
MASTERS OF CONTEMPORARY NEWSPEAK

Tucker Carlson, Marine Le Pen, and Jordan Peterson

A. James McAdams

Far-Right Newspeak is everywhere, but we must resist the temptation to throw those who use the idiom into the same box. Paradoxically, the arguments of the politicians, television personalities, and intellectuals who fall under this rubric are simultaneously strikingly similar and significantly different. On the one hand, there are easily identifiable similarities in these actors' pitches. They uniformly invoke liberal concepts—freedom, equality, tolerance, diversity, unalienable rights—to condemn the supposedly anti-democratic and discriminatory policies of political, cultural, and corporate elites. Moreover, they claim that they have special insight into returning their countries to their foundational principles. On the other hand, there are substantial differences in how these actors use this liberal vocabulary. This is understandable. Not only do they have different professional and personal agendas, they come from countries with distinctive political cultures and social norms. However, they do have one thing in common. Each seeks to open the Overton window to propagate views that could undermine their audiences' confidence in democratic institutions and the values that make these institutions possible.

My goal in this chapter is to shed light on both sides of this paradox by focusing on the use and abuse of liberal concepts by three prominent expositors of Far-Right Newspeak, the American cable TV pundit and "X" (formerly Twitter) commentator Tucker Carlson, the French politician Marine Le Pen, and—somewhat controversially—the Canadian psychologist and YouTube celebrity Jordan Peterson. In my view, the similarities and differences in these figures' positions are sufficient to meet the standard criteria for a meaningful comparison. All three have taken advantage of popular discontent over social and economic conditions to promote illiberal and even anti-liberal views. In the process, each has built an enormous following. Until his

DOI: 10.4324/9781003436737-4

dismissal from the American media giant Fox News in early 2023, Carlson was the most-watched cable news host in the United States, reaching millions of viewers every night and boasting over five million Twitter followers. Since 2011, when she took control of her party, the *Front National* (now called the *Rassemblement National*), and initiated the "de-demonization" (*dédiabolisation*) of her movement to improve its image in the public eye, Le Pen has proven to be a savvy politician and normalizer of far-right views. In 2022, she came close to winning the French presidency, garnering the support of more than 23 percent of voters in the election's first round and more than 41 percent in the second-round battle with President Emmanuel Macron. In 2023, psychologist Peterson had more that 7.3 million subscribers to his lectures on YouTube and 7.5 million Instagram subscribers.[1] He had also sold more than five million copies of his self-help book, *12 Rules for Life: An Antidote to Chaos* only two years after its release in 2018.[2]

Yet, Carlson, Le Pen, and Peterson have pursued notably different strategies in building their followings. In his past role at Fox and on his current "X" platform (@TuckerCarlson), Carlson presents himself as the "everyman" who wants nothing more than to encourage his viewers to speak truth to power. Although a majority of Carlson's followers are white, his appeal extends to all age groups, socioeconomic strata, and significant numbers of women. Testifying to the attraction of his provocative style, he even enjoyed a large viewership among self-identified Democrats in his days on Fox.[3] In contrast, Le Pen's focus has been on winning the support of specific constituencies. Presenting herself as an uncompromising leader who will defend the French nation against weak-willed domestic elites, anti-Christian immigrants, and predatory multinational corporations, she has won the support of low-income voters, the residents of rural communities, aggrieved young people, and as Sarah Shurts shows in Chapter 3, significant numbers of women. Peterson presents himself as both a liberal-minded critic of political correctness and a scientifically trained self-help guru. In the latter function, he has pointedly reached out to disaffected young, white males, many of whom are associated with extremist causes.

In making my argument, I shall focus on Carlson's, Le Pen's, and Peterson's approach to the challenge of reconciling two of the pillars of liberalism: the exercise of individual freedom and the promise of equality to all citizens. As I shall argue, there are significant differences between the three actors' views on this question and those of moderates on both sides of the political spectrum. Whereas the latter may disagree about how best to address the tension between these twin imperatives, they agree that their goal should be to find an optimal balance between them. In contrast, albeit in different ways, Carlson, Le Pen, and Peterson regard these ideals as potentially or even inevitably incompatible. On this basis, they advise their followers that when a choice must be made between these ideals, freedom should always trump equality. In fact, all three have espoused views on specific issues that lead one to wonder whether the presence of inequality and discrimination in their societies matters to them at all.

In accord with these attitudes, Carlson, Le Pen, and Peterson have aligned themselves with positions that will make it more difficult for less advantaged segments of their countries' populations, such as racial and ethnic minorities, immigrants, and adherents to non-Judeo-Christian faiths, to act on their convictions and, if they are citizens, to enjoy the benefits of being fully included in their societies. Carlson presents a "soft" approach, alerting his viewers to ongoing threats to the American dream and endorsing countermeasures that conveniently coincide with his personal cultural preferences. Tapping into her country's Gaullist legacy and a constitutional commitment to a strong presidency, Le Pen envisions a leader who by virtue of her or his election would be in the position to rationalize exclusionary policies by asserting the right to represent the "will of the majority." While claiming to have little interest in politics, Peterson prefers a world dominated by an enlightened elite that has risen to its appropriate station through a Darwinian struggle for survival with less deserving competitors. Whether this perspective is sufficient to characterize Peterson's views as truly far-right is open to debate. Some observers maintain that the thrust of his arguments remains within the vein of right-wing libertarianism. Others are concerned that his ideas could provide a rhetorical "gateway," in Steven Pittz's words, to far-right positions. I am more critical. I shall contend that the sum total of Peterson's views about human worth are properly categorized as far-right. In many ways, they are also incompatible with any form of democracy.

All in all, contrary to Carlson's, Le Pen's, and Peterson's professions of fidelity to liberal principles, each espouses positions that would justify making their societies less free, less equal, and ultimately less democratic. To understand the implications of their ideas, we must begin by asking what Carlson, Le Pen, and Peterson say and why millions of people have found their claims attractive and worthy of support.

What Do They Say? Why Do Their Audiences Like It?

It would be all too easy to attribute Carlson's, Le Pen's, and Peterson's success to an underlying current of extremist sentiment among large numbers of American, French, and Canadian citizens. Undeniably, there are unabashed racists, xenophobes, and bigots among these three figures' millions of supporters. However, it is unlikely that a majority of their followers secretly harbor extremist ideas or, at least, are aware of their influence on their thinking. The puzzle is why many who would once have been reluctant to throw their support to far-right politicians and ideologues should now feel comfortable doing so.

One explanation is style. For the most part, Carlson, Le Pen, and Peterson are careful about how they express their views. After all, they aspire to win the favor of the greatest number of people possible, not just the applause of fringe groups. As I have argued in Chapter 1, they would have little chance of currying the favor of populations who have experienced decades of enculturation in liberal-democratic norms if they gave the impression that they are enemies of democracy. Accordingly, when they share their most controversial perspectives, they often do so with a wink and a nod, posing rhetorical questions, making oblique references, and mustering coded language.

Nonetheless, words alone do not guarantee success. An even more important explanation for the appeal of far-right actors lies in their skill in molding their arguments to fit with their followers' tangible grievances. In the case of the three subjects in this chapter, these grievances are primarily driven by the divergence between citizens' expectations of their leaders and what they experience in their daily lives. It is crucial to recognize this point because it prevents us from characterizing the majority of the supporters of far-right politicians and movements as unsophisticated dupes or closeted racists. Democratic institutions and the capitalist economies that sustain them are destined to create both winners and losers, and no one wants to fall into the latter category. One must take these individuals' complaints seriously.

For this reason, even if one believes that government intervention in the lives of its citizens is necessary to address social and economic inequality—as both moderate liberals and moderate conservatives do—the preferential treatment of one segment of the population will inevitably cause some people to feel that they are unjustly being asked to pay the price for their leaders' preferences. Granting a special status to one segment of society is a recipe for conflict. Efforts to combat global warming by shutting down high-carbon-emitting factories and directing the state's resources to environment-friendly corporations can result in the loss of jobs and devastate small communities. The granting of legal authority to transnational institutions, such as the European Union, to counter discriminatory practices against some groups can lead to unpopular constraints on the free speech and religious practice of others.

Carlson is a master at exploiting these grievances. If one were to take his comments at face value, as many of his followers apparently do, one would think that he has no intention of voicing his personal opinions. "My job," he assures his audience, "is merely to note the things that we're already talking about, the obvious contradictions in people's arguments. The surface layer is what I deal with, so I'm not certain what the remedies are in a lot of cases, and I hope I never pretend that I am."[4] Just the same, Carlson certainly provides them with a tantalizingly simple frame of reference. In a folksy manner, he attributes their woes to the American ruling class's failure to fight for the principles that made the country great. As a result, "legacy Americans," as Carlson calls them, are the victims of their leaders' betrayal of trust.[5]

In particular, Carlson highlights the threat to freedom of speech. In his polemical book, *Ship of Fools*, he informs his readers that America's Founding Fathers knew exactly what they were doing when they put free speech at the top of the US Bill of Rights. "Free speech makes free thought possible. All other rights derive from it." In the best of times, Americans were willing to die for their fellow citizens' right to express their views. To illustrate this point, Carlson summons a surprising and, given his stand on matters of race and ethnicity that I shall describe momentarily, implausible cast of childhood heroes: César Chávez, Martin Luther King, Ralph Nader, and Betty Friedan. The extension of basic rights to all Americans, he advises, would have come to a halt if these courageous individuals had lacked the freedom to oppose racial segregation, economic injustice, and discrimination. Yet, one can no longer take these freedoms for granted. Now, it seems, politicians and corporate moguls are determined to subvert this right for the purpose of personal and financial gain. These elites are not interested in listening to the views of others. They are particularly irresponsible, it seems to Carlson, when it comes to addressing the American people's displeasure with letting large numbers of immigrants into the US. For those who oppose such policies, free speech is out. "Dare to complain [about the migration of immigrants to the US]," Carson tells his viewers, "and you'll be shouted down as a bigot, as if demanding that representation in a democracy were immoral."[6]

Adding to this gloomy picture, Carlson informs his viewers that another precious right has been compromised: the guarantee of equality of opportunity. Whereas Americans once had the chance to prove their worth through hard work and sacrifice, he explains, the political establishment has trampled on this right. Through discriminatory affirmative action programs and massive increases in welfare spending for the poor and indigent, the country's leaders have demonstrated, in Carlson's diagnosis, that they are intoxicated with the unattainable goal of absolute equality. Consequently, they no longer treat good Americans as thoughtful individuals who deserve an equal chance to improve their lives and contribute to the betterment of their communities. Instead, they judge their personal worth entirely on the basis of their association with specific racial, ethnic, and socioeconomic groups. Because of the ruling class's obsession with minorities, it has deprived the unlucky citizens in the majority—who, in Carlson's view, represent the best American traditions—of their right to reap the benefits they deserve.

At first glance, Le Pen's use of the language of liberalism may appear identical to Carlson's. In her 2022 campaign, Le Pen pledged to be the "president of French freedoms." Her use of the plural, she told voters, distinguished her party's objectives from the abstract and "empty" conception of freedom propagated by France's president, Emmanuel Macron. If elected, she would address the needs of every French citizen by championing "the concrete, real freedoms that everyone exercises on a daily basis." In a virtual potpourri of assurances that outside observers could have easily mistaken for the rhetoric of an American political campaign, Le Pen offered voters "vaccination freedom," the "freedom of women to move around in a skirt or dress," the freedom to start a family, and freedom from economic want.[7]

Le Pen has also echoed Carlson's words in portraying ordinary French citizens as the innocent victims of leftist politicians and social justice crusaders. She fills her speeches with references to the dangers of multiculturalism, gay rights, "Islamo-Leftism," and "wokeism" (*le wokisme*). The so-called progressivism of establishment politicians like Macron, she has maintained, "doesn't signify progress but instead deconstruction: it is a manifestation of wokeism and decolonialism, and it is contrary to national unity."[8] France's leaders have no intention of giving equal weight to the interests of all French citizens, or even to citizens at all. Instead, they have forced the majority to suffer the same fate as Carlson's legacy Americans. To justify giving favored treatment to minorities, and especially to migrants from other countries, they have insisted on viewing people solely in terms of their association with their respective corporate groups. By imposing this arbitrary standard, she asserts, the French elite has created artificial "communities that exist next to one another and," she adds, "sometimes against each other."[9]

However, Le Pen differs from Carlson in how she justifies these claims. Whereas Carlson seeks to win over his viewers by painting a picture of a halcyon past that has been distorted beyond all comprehension by liberal elites, Le Pen has the benefit of being able to latch on to a distinctively French understanding of individual rights. In this conception, which is shared by politicians across the political spectrum, including mainstream figures like Macron, the state embodies the collective will of the French people. It is the guardian of the nation. Hence, the individual is only truly free when he or she has an unmediated relationship with the state. Accordingly, any form of group identification, or *communautarisme*, that stands between the individual and the state is a potential assault on freedom. On these grounds, when Le Pen has been attacked for being a racist or extremist, she has readily fallen back on the argument that she is doing nothing more than defending her country's republican ideals. The government's favorable treatment of certain groups, and especially immigrants who know nothing about French culture and customs, is supposedly inconsistent with the nation's hallowed traditions.[10] This argument evidently carries significant weight among French voters. For example, in a survey conducted during her 2022 election campaign, only 40 percent of respondents agreed with the statement that Le Pen is a xenophobe.[11]

Finally, my third subject, Jordan Peterson, shares many of the same concerns as Carlson and Le Pen. In fact, he makes his case even more emphatically. Describing himself as a classical liberal in the tradition of John Locke and John Stuart Mill, Peterson revels in being perceived as an indefatigable defender of free speech. The right to speak one's mind, he informs his followers, is an essential component of democracy "because the entirety of society depends on, depends for [sic] its ability to adapt to the changing horizon of the future on the free thought of the individuals who compose it." In an open, free market of ideas, citizens of all backgrounds and beliefs can share their perspectives and decide how they will live together. Peterson admits that this is necessarily a messy enterprise. But, this is a good thing. Like his liberal forebears, and especially Mill, he emphasizes that we are richer for being in the position "to grapple stupidly with complexity." Out of this "stupid grappling, fraught grappling that's offensive and difficult and upsetting, we can grope towards the truth collectively before taking the steps to implement those truths before they've been tested."[12]

Capitalizing on the broad appeal of this liberal vocabulary, Peterson assiduously cultivates his image as a defender of equal opportunity, a standard he describes as the "true public good." This principle holds that

> no person should ever be denied an opportunity for progress in a productive direction for reasons that are unrelated to their competence or, to put it another way, that movement forward towards production of individual and social utility should ever be interfered with by arbitrary prejudice (which is discrimination that has nothing to do with the task at hand).[13]

In a YouTube series that catapulted him to fame in 2016, Peterson drew upon this definition of equality to condemn a proposed amendment to the Canadian Human Rights Act that would have prohibited discrimination on the basis of "gender identity and gender expression." Arguing—incorrectly, it would seem—that this bill required university professors to use gender-affirming pronouns in the classroom, he declared such demands were proof of the radical left's determination to replace the time-honored expectation that individuals should be judged on the basis of merit with an arbitrary ideology of "equity."[14]

On his subsequent path to fame, this theme has become Peterson's mantra. "The equity-pushers," he maintains, "assume axiomatically that if all positions at every level of hierarchy in every organization are not occupied by a proportion of the population that is precisely equivalent to that proportion in the general population that systemic prejudice (racism, sexism, homophobia, etc.) is definitely at play." Yet, Peterson emphasizes, there is no scientific evidence to support these assumptions. Quite the contrary, policies that automatically give one group unearned advantages over another erode public confidence in democracy. In this case, Peterson echoes Carlson. In the leftists' new world order, people are no longer asked to prove themselves worthy of their station in a free society. In fact, those who dare to challenge the equity doctrine's illegitimate conception of equality, as Peterson sees himself doing, face the prospect of being punished for their views.[15]

If one focuses solely on these aspects of Peterson's arguments, one can understand why even some of his critics are ambivalent about characterizing him as a far-right thinker. For his followers, his attacks on government overreach into citizens' professional and private lives seem perfectly sensible. In the next section, I shall explain why I think that the sum total of Peterson's arguments should be characterized as far-right, if not even more extreme. At this point, it is enough to say that he stretches the boundaries of a defensible conception of liberalism in two significant ways. First, one can reasonably ask whether Peterson takes seriously the fact that people must wrestle with the challenge of living together. In his ideal universe, the building block of humanity is nothing more than what he calls the "sovereign individual."[16] In a world that prizes this principle, every person will enjoy absolute autonomy in making decisions about how he or she will live and commune with others. For this reason, Peterson wants us to believe that diversity and inclusion programs are not merely unfair. When governments pursue social engineering projects and take into account engrained inequalities in making their decisions, they violate the individual's natural purpose.

When Peterson reaches this point in his argument, he then strains credulity by becoming hyperbolic. Rather than simply contending that the left's progressive policies violate his extreme characterization of classical liberalism, he predicts an ineluctable march toward totalitarianism. "The Soviets taught us that. The Maoists and the Khmer Rouge taught us that. The North Koreans, and the Cubans, and the Venezuelans continue to teach us in the same manner." Peterson admits that there are different views about why the left has entered this treacherous territory. But, he tells his enthusiasts, "I'm willing to stake my claim on the equity doctrine."[17]

Second, Peterson offers a sobering, but revealing, corollary to this hyperbole that takes him well beyond a conventional defense of equality of opportunity. In his ideal world of equally sovereign individuals, there is apparently no salvation for the person who makes the wrong choices or fails to live up to his or her potential. In an oft-cited section of *12 Rules for Life*, he makes this point in an unusual way by likening human beings to lobsters. In his portrayal, male lobsters live in natural hierarchies where only those who are ready to fight for their territory will be able to attract mates. When the battle for dominance is over, the less courageous will leave no progeny to lobster history. Predictably, Peterson argues that the same rules apply to humans. Since they, too, live in hierarchies, it is entirely up to each individual to take responsibility for his or her life. In particular, Peterson reaches out to young males. They have been emasculated by modern attitudes, especially those propagated by aggressive women. In this case, Peterson, the concerned father, has a personal message for these wounded souls. No matter how tough their lives may seem, they should stop feeling sorry for themselves. If they really want to get ahead (and, by implication, find the most desirable mates), they must "stand up straight with [their] shoulders back [and accept] the terrible responsibility of life, with eyes wide open." Should they fail to accept this challenge, they will presumably get the sorry fate they deserve.[18] On this ominous note, Peterson seems more like a devotee to Friedrich Nietzsche than to classical liberal thinkers like Locke and Mill.[19] This is an understanding of equality of opportunity in its bleakest form.

What Do They Really Mean? Why Should We Care?

Are Carlson's, Le Pen's, and Peterson's perspectives compatible with liberal democracy? If we were to ask them, not to mention their many supporters, all three would deem this question unfair. In unison, they would insist that their views are perfectly consistent with long-standing conservative and, in Peterson's case, libertarian critiques of big government and leftist progressivism. The only difference, they would proudly insist, is that they have the audacity to call attention to the perils of the establishment elite's attitudes about rights and freedom and its evisceration of age-old cultural values and traditions that other critics are too timid or self-interested to express.

In my view, however, there is a major difference between my three subjects' views and those of mainstream conservatives and libertarians about the challenge of reconciling the guarantee of individual freedom with the creation of conditions that give each citizen a chance to assert his or her views. In line with Leszek Kołakowski's argument about the "perpetual antimony" within liberalism, which I have outlined in Chapter 1, traditional conservatives and libertarians accept the proposition that liberalism requires one to take both objectives seriously. In the rough and tumble world of democratic politics, they would simply—and often passionately—disagree with their counterparts on the left about the appropriate way to respond to this obligation. What is the most desirable balance between these imperatives? To what extent should one allow the state to impinge upon the individual's freedom in order to guarantee equal access to the public realm? The important point is that moderates on the right, like their counterparts on the moderate left, do not regard freedom and equality as incompatible. They see them as complementary objectives. In their eyes, the pursuit of *both* ideals is a hallmark of a healthy democracy.

In stark contrast, Carlson, Le Pen, and Peterson regard this balancing act as far more harmful than salutary. Especially in Carlson's and Le Pen's cases, and potentially in Peterson's case, this is what makes their views far-right, and not simply right. Depending upon the circumstances and the issue at hand, each is inclined to regard freedom and equality as fundamentally antagonistic. In many cases, they would view the two ideals as "sworn and natural enemies" which, in the words of the popular historian, Will Durant, are more likely to tear society apart than to hold it together.[20] Predictably, each has different ideas about how or even whether it is desirable to preserve the peace between these principles. Yet, they share one inclination. Each has an unmistakable bias toward prioritizing one pole, freedom, over the other, equality. This factor, which has political ramifications that I shall explore in the next section of this chapter, makes all three figures highly problematic defenders of liberal democracy. If their respective remedies were put into practice, they would lead to the imposition of significant constraints on efforts to ensure that all citizens are treated as equals. As a result, those persons with the greatest resources to manipulate the levers of power would become even more powerful while those with the least would become even weaker and more vulnerable.

In Carlson's case, there is ample evidence that his claim to respect the equality of all persons is dubious indeed. In off-the-record remarks that have been made public over the years, he has expressed unquestionably racist, sexist, and homophobic views on numerous occasions.[21] However, if we judge Carlson on the basis of these revelations alone, we would miss the opportunity to understand how he manipulates the idea of equality to convey sanitized versions of these prejudices to his viewers and, in the process, positioned himself to turn anti-liberal ideas into acceptable public discourse.

There is no better example of Carlson's approach than his appropriation of the vocabulary of equal rights to persuade his viewers that white Americans, who constitute the majority of his followers, are the victims of policies that hold them to unacceptably higher standards than those that are applied to racial and ethnic minorities. "We [at Fox] don't think your skin color is the most important thing about you," Carlson informs his audience. "We think all people were created by God, and should therefore be judged by what they do, not by how they look."[22] Carlson finds his perfect foils in the proponents of critical race theory and race-conscious interpretations of American history, whom he misleadingly characterizes as representatives of the Democratic Party's mainstream. Supposedly, these ideas prove that these personalities are the true racists. "Only Nazis think your race defines you and we just don't believe there are a ton of people in this country even on the left who actually believe something that evil."[23] On the charitable assumption that no one, save for Nazis, wants to be perceived as evil, Carlson then leads his viewers to a seemingly logical conclusion: The only way to ensure that every American enjoys the blessing of equality is to oppose any steps, such as the promotion of diversity in corporations, that elevate the needs of racial and ethnic minorities over the interests of the white majority. After all, "being white . . . is not something you can control. Like any ethnicity, you're born with it. Which is why you shouldn't attack people for it, and yet the left does constantly—in case you haven't noticed."[24]

Carlson's characterization of true racism in the US would be problematic enough if he limited his complaints to the alleged victimization of white Americans. However, he takes his viewers one significant step further by maintaining that American greatness is at risk no matter what policies are adopted. Even if politicians were to stop giving minorities favored treatment, Carlson contends that his favored majority is already on the losing end for having to accommodate the interests of people with different backgrounds and cultures. As the majority suffers this indignity, so will all Americans.

At times, Carlson expresses this sentiment in a manner that seems more wistful than condemnatory. In one of his accounts of everyday life in America in *Ship of Fools*, he tells his readers a story about fishing on the Potomac that suggests that not everyone in the US has fully earned the right to be included in the American dream. In a chapter titled "They Don't Pick Up Trash Anymore," Carlson relates how he is usually the only American-born fisherman on the river. Everyone else, he says, is from Mexico or Central America. These people are always friendly, he notes. However, their arrival—if indeed they have just arrived, as Carlson claims—has coincided with a change in the river. "It's still pretty," he confides, "but no longer tidy. There's now trash everywhere along the banks, beer bottles and takeout chicken boxes and soiled diapers." Does this mean that these purportedly new arrivals from the South are responsible for this degradation of nature? Carlson acknowledges that homeless people—another pet peeve—may have done some of the damage. Still, it is notable that Carlson does not consider the possibility that his fellow fishermen might be American citizens. Or even if they aren't citizens, it's unclear why he blames them for the trash. Could it be their skin color that leads him to this conclusion? One way or another, Carlson would like his readers to believe that the favored group whom he calls "legacy Americans" "would never have tolerated this behavior."[25]

On other occasions, Carlson's depiction of ethnic and cultural outsiders unmistakably crosses the line between the controversial and the extreme. His most pronounced expression of the harder edge to his arguments is his unabashed application of the racist "Great Replacement Theory" to American conditions. Popularized by the French white nationalist author Renaud Camus in the early 2000s, this conspiracy theory holds that Western civilization is being destroyed by a cabal of progressive elites that seeks to replace rapidly declining white majority populations with non-white immigrants from Africa and the Middle East.[26] In Carlson's only somewhat sanitized version of this conspiracy, only the names have changed. The demographic threat to white America comes from places like Mexico, Guatemala, and Venezuela. The source of this evil is the Democratic Party.

In Carlson's telling, the Democrats are directly responsible for creating the problems that have led to an enormous demographic shift over the past six decades. Since the passage of the party's Immigration and Nationality Act of 1965, as Carlson tells the story, the US population exploded by 140 million people as of 2021. But, he asks, "who are [these people] and where did they come from?" "Well," he explains, "what you're seeing is not the kind of organic growth that you would see in a healthy society that's become more prosperous and welcoming of families." It turns out that Democratic politicians long ago "stopped trying to make the United States a hospitable place for American citizens, their constituents, to have their own families." Since the country is now "well under the so-called replacement level . . . eventually there will be no more native-born Americans."[27]

In addition, Carlson would have his viewers believe that the Democratic Party's readiness to replace home-grown Americans with millions of "brand-new people [who] broke our laws to get here, who don't speak our language, who have no idea what the US Constitution says and don't care" does not spring from any beneficent intentions. Rather, the Democrats have a deeply cynical plan to keep their members in office. By changing "the racial mix of the country," Carlson contends, they intend to "reduce the political power of people whose ancestors lived here, and dramatically increase the proportion of Americans newly arrived from the third world."[28] Naturally, Carlson assures his viewers that he has nothing against these migrating peoples; he is not a racist. Nonetheless, his suggestion that the loaded concept of "ancestral heritage" is somehow relevant to how one treats people does not bode well for the well-being of any racial or ethnic minorities, whether they are just arriving or are, like himself, simply ordinary citizens who call America their home.

Assessing Le Pen's manipulation of the language of freedom and equality presents a different type of challenge than in Carlson's case, because of both her direct engagement in politics and her appropriation of the uniquely French understanding of the terms. As a canny politician who has experienced the electoral benefits of portraying herself and her party in an appealing de-demonized light, Le Pen exercises great care in choosing her words. With only a few, but quite revealing, exceptions to which I shall return later, she has avoided making inflammatory statements about Muslims, North African and Middle Eastern immigrants, and other ethnic groups—*especially* if they already hold French citizenship. Gone are the days when Le Pen would unabashedly liken street prayers and the wearing of veils and burqas to the Nazi occupation of Paris during World War II, as she did in 2010.[29] Nevertheless, if Le Pen were to win office, her public statements indicate that she would readily take advantage of the conditionality of the French idea of equality to set a high bar for the inclusion of people who, in other countries, would fall under the category of ethnic and religious minorities. In a country where there is no room for intermediate bodies between the individual and the state—France officially has "no minorities"—there is good reason to think that this bar for Muslim immigrants would be insurmountable. Of even greater significance, there is equally good reason to think she would be open to applying the same bar to French citizens who happen to be Muslim.

It is easy to understand why Le Pen has chosen to single out the French government's favorable treatment of Muslim immigrants for her sharpest attacks. According to a Harris Interactive survey of voters conducted during her presidential campaign, more than six out of ten respondents agreed with the statement, "European, white and Christian populations are threatened with extinction as a result of Muslim immigration, from the Maghreb and black Africa."[30] In this context, Le Pen has enjoyed a straightforward opportunity to criticize the Macron government for welcoming people who, even if they come from France's former colonies, will never be able to live up to her narrow conception of what it means to be French. "Will France remain France," she asked potential supporters in 2021, "or be brushed aside by the massive uncontrolled torrent of immigration flows that will wipe out our culture, our values, our way of life?" In response to this rhetorical question, she promised that a President Le Pen would immediately hold a referendum to "drastically" reduce eligibility for French citizenship.[31]

Le Pen's even more consequential step has been to link this challenge to French identity with a theme that resonates well with a majority of French citizens: the purported threat of "Islamism."[32] In itself, there is nothing particularly controversial about this position. Given the fact that France has experienced repeated terrorist attacks in the name of a radicalized form of Islam, Le Pen simply comes off as a hardline, law-and-order politician who promises, in the words of her party's program, to prohibit "the exhibition and diffusion of Islamist ideology" and impose harsh penalties on offenders.[33] In fact, this stance has been a major factor in her electoral success. Still, Le Pen's blurring of the boundaries between Islamism and Islam has also opened the Overton window for her to normalize a new form of discriminatory politics. If it is Islam that makes immigrants a threat to the French nation—a statement with which over 60 percent of her country's population agrees—then French citizens who happen to be Muslims can be put in this category as well. Should Le Pen get what she wants, France's constitutional commitment to "the equality of all" will be significantly compromised.

During her presidential campaign, Le Pen provided a revealing indication of her intention to exploit this sentiment when she pledged to expand France's long-standing ban on wearing niqabs and burqas in public to include headscarves. If Macron had made this proposal, it would have seemed like an unusually extreme application of the French principle of strict secularism—*laïcité*—that allows the state to curb the expression of religious faith in public spaces. Headscarves are conventional attire for Muslim women—and of course, non-Muslim women wear headscarves as well and many of them are Christians. Still, in this hypothetical scenario, Macron would insist that this application of *laïcité* in no way prevents a Muslim from practicing her faith, let alone diminishes her status as a citizen. The striking difference in Le Pen's case is that she made a point of emphasizing that her pledge had nothing to do with *laïcité*. Instead, she justified the position in military terms, describing the headscarf as "an Islamist uniform." "It is a Muslim uniform," she declared, "and that makes all the difference. It is the uniform of an ideology, not of a religion." For this reason, she underscored, her proposed prohibition was "based on the battle against Islamist ideologies."[34] By implication, this stand would mean that any Muslim woman who wears a headscarf is an Islamist, and even a potential terrorist.

As if to rule out any ambiguity about her readiness to apply this standard to French citizens, Le Pen informed supporters at a campaign stop in 2019 that she would take her crusade to its logical conclusion. Her war was not only against Islamism but also against the practice of Islam itself. "We will eradicate," Le Pen declared, "all those, *Islamist or not*, who want to impose rules and ways of life on us that are not ours. Non-offenders will be put out of harm's way. . . . Offenders from France, in prison. The foreigners, on planes."[35] This is a remarkably revealing statement in that it would exceed the boundaries of *laïcité* and violate France's constitutional guarantee of religious choice. Moreover, her rationale could have even more extreme implications. It could provide an opening for Le Pen and other far-right personalities to deny equal treatment to any of their fellow citizens whose secular beliefs and personal choices they deem contrary to authentically French values.

Finally, contrary to his characterization of his arguments in terms of classical liberalism, Peterson provides a justification for preserving unequal social relations that goes beyond race and ethnicity. It includes all human beings. The key to understanding his position lies in the fact that his conception of natural hierarchy is as much a normative claim as an empirical one. For Peterson, the efforts of leftist radicals, feminists, and progressive politicians to address entrenched social inequalities are not only disturbing because they create conditions that are unfair to others (Carlson) or because they threaten cherished freedoms (Le Pen). Rather, the left's greatest offense is that it seeks to change what, in Peterson's view, cannot be changed. It is one thing, he maintains, to provide people with the opportunity to ascend to their appointed station in life. But, he adds, it is simply wrong to assume that the fundamentally hierarchical ordering of humanity can be altered.

This claim is undeniably problematic. True, it is impossible to eliminate all human hierarchies, but for good or bad, human beings have always taken steps to modify people's positions within them. However, Peterson generally prefers to sidestep this distinction. Instead, he conflates the unchangeable with the objectives of people whom he dislikes. "The problem with the radical left," Peterson underscores, "is that it assumes that all hierarchies are tyrannical, and that's an absolute catastrophe." Furthermore, Peterson suggests that even the attempt to distinguish the good from the bad and the changeable from the unchangeable is a perilous undertaking. To be sure, he recognizes that injustice is part of all hierarchies. For example, he admits, "there's plenty of sins on the conscience of the West as a civilization." Nonetheless, he advises his listeners to be content with what they have. "We can't throw the baby out with the bathwater and," he stresses, "there are far worse places."[36]

Were Peterson to stop at this point, this argument would arguably still lie within the bounds of a reasonable critique of the policies of the moderate left. However, Peterson takes his argument one major step further. He portrays any attempt to change the hierarchical structures that he personally prefers as a contributing factor in an apocalyptic struggle between the forces of "order" and "chaos." Naturally, Peterson reveres the former because of its time-tested success as "explored territory." "That's the hundreds-of-millions-of years-old hierarchy, position, and authority. . . . Order is tribe, religion, hearth, home, and country. . . . It's the flag of the nation, the greatness of tradition, the rows of desks in the classroom, the trains that leave on time." "In the domain of order," it seems, which includes the odd allusion to Mussolini's efficient trains, "things behave as God intended." Predictably, Peterson blames progressives for unleashing the forces of chaos. The new world lacks the familiarity and security of the old. Even relatively modest efforts to address issues, such as gender equality, fall under this category. When one challenges the forces of order, "the bottom drops out, and things fall apart, and you plunge through the ice." Chaos is "the foreigner, the stranger, the member of another gang, the rustle in the bushes in the night time, the monster under your bed, the hidden anger of your mother, and the sickness of your child."[37] Presumably, God did not intend for these aspects of the human condition to be released at all.

The result of this disruption of the natural order of things, Peterson emphasizes, has not been to foster equality or rectify injustice. Quite the contrary, the leftist do-gooders have merely succeeded in gutting the sense of certainty that people have always required to live up to their potential, regardless of their social status. "Modern people," he observed in a podcast with his daughter Mikhaila in 2017, "have been stripped of their archaic belief systems [which have been] exposed more completely to the possibility of a meaningless and painless existence with no superordinate meaning." If Peterson's listeners hoped he would provide them with a formula for reversing this destructive process, they would have been disappointed. "The advent of nihilism, our whole European culture," he declared, "is moving for some time now with a tension that is growing from decade to decade towards a catastrophe."[38]

In all of Peterson's claims, one cannot help but notice a striking irony. On the one hand, he goes to great lengths to convince his followers that he is the ultimate iconoclast and free thinker, someone who boldly acts on his freedom as a sovereign individual—and a self-confident lobster—to stand up to the repressive forces of political correctness and Woke ideology that surround him. This is the message he conveys to his young male readers about lobsterhood. On the other hand, Peterson seems just as intent upon defending his version of an acceptable state of order against anyone who dares to act on their own sovereignty to change it. In my view, this contradiction is why it makes sense to include Peterson in the company of far-right actors like Carlson and Le Pen. In the hands of a traditional conservative or libertarian, the solution would lie in recognizing the complexity of human relations and proposing solutions to social challenges that do not unduly impinge upon the exercise of individual freedom. Social hierarchies are real, but human beings are constantly at work trying to modify them in ways that serve the needs of others. Peterson will have none of this. As far as he is concerned, there is no dilemma at all. In his all-or-nothing understanding of humanity, it is enough to give each person the chance to rise to his or her appointed level in the human hierarchy. Once this opportunity has been provided, any requirement that others should sacrifice their well-ordered lives to help this person succeed constitutes an unjustifiable violation of their sovereign rights.

Will Their Words Matter?

What is the likelihood that Carlson's, Le Pen's, and Peterson's heavily one-sided interpretations of the contradictions between freedom and equality will have an impact on popular and elite attitudes about liberal democracy? Normally, this question would not be worth posing about pundits and intellectuals. Their voices may be heard but are rarely followed. Yet, given their enormous followings, opinion-makers like Carlson and Peterson are not normal cases. When Le Pen's political standing and continuing presidential aspirations are added to the mix, one can make a plausible case that the three individuals' diagnoses of their countries' ills and recommendations for their correction will have continuing relevance for public opinion. Whether they are directly involved or not, their success in normalizing far-right views about race, ethnicity, religious beliefs, and national identity will be attractive to many ambitious politicians and social influencers who are looking for every opportunity to aggrandize power.

As of 2024, Carlson's America has become a more hospitable place for extremist attitudes about race and ethnicity. The country has also become more hospitable to Carlson's most divisive claims. A public opinion survey sponsored by the Southern Poverty Law Center in 2022 found that two-thirds of self-identified Republicans either "strongly" or "somewhat" agreed with the substance of the Great Replacement narrative. The survey's findings included the belief that "the recent change in our national democratic makeup is not a natural change but has been motivated by progressive and liberal leaders actively trying to leverage political power by replacing more conservative white voters."[39] In the same survey, more than half of the Republican respondents "strongly" or "somewhat" agreed with the statement that these changes posed a "threat to white Americans and their culture and values."[40] Undoubtedly, Carlson helped to fertilize these convictions, having promoted the theme of replacement in over 400 episodes of his shows on Fox.[41] Given his insatiable desire to attract followers, it seems likely that he will continue to take advantage of opportunities to test the limits of acceptable political discourse, assuming his audiences are prepared to go along.

Additionally, while Carlson may never aspire to hold political office, one can expect that like-minded individuals who find themselves in influential positions will readily tap into his ideas in building their audiences. In the lead-up to the US presidential election of 2024, when a variety of both moderate and far-right think tanks devised plans to expand the executive authority of the White House in anticipation of a Trump victory, many echoed Carlson's arguments about restoring an authentically American understanding of freedom and democracy. Race was a recurrent theme in these organizations' appeals. Among them, the Center for Renewing America blamed leftist activists for perpetuating myths of "white dominant" power structures in order to foster a "totalitarian mindset." In promoting their progressive agenda, the Center's leaders claimed, these radicals had popularized an image of America that viewed "all of society through a racialized prism of identity groups, with minority groups being oppressed and white people serving as the oppressors." Only by strengthening the hand of the person in the Oval Office could the nation return to the Founders' ideal that "all men are created equal, endowed by their Creator with unalienable rights to life, liberty, and the pursuit of happiness."[42]

These efforts to create new instruments of political power are a model of politeness when compared to the expression of the even darker side of American politics in the storming of the US Capitol on January 6, 2021. In this context, Carlson's followers on the radical right can find inspiration in the ominous notes that sporadically pop up in his commentaries. One that stands out is the intimation in *Ship of Fools* that Americans should be prepared for dire consequences when whites become a minority population. "In a country where virtually every non-white group reaps advantages from being racially conscious and politically organized," Carlson observes, "how long before someone asks the obvious question: why can't white people organize and agitate along racial lines, too?" In this case, Carlson warns, "when white people become another interest group fighting for the spoils, America as we know it will be over."[43] In view of the widespread acceptance of the concept of racial replacement, Carlson's warning about an impending loss of power and social status could resonate with middle-of-the-road white voters as well.

Carlson's warnings become even more pointed when he addresses the ruling elites' failure to abide by their obligation to treat everyone according to his standard of equality. "In order to survive," he advises, "democracies must remain egalitarian." Otherwise voters will become "vengeful and reckless." Indeed, "if they continue to feel ignored, they will support increasingly radical leaders, who over time will destroy the ruling class, along with everything that made it prosperous." He concludes, "Left unattended, democracies self-destruct."[44] One cannot help but wonder what Carlson means by this path to destruction.

In contrast to Carlson, a President Le Pen would actually be in the position to shape her country's priorities directly. The French presidency is endowed with enormous power. Le Pen has never left any doubt about her intention to capitalize on the office. Revealingly, she frequently casts herself in the role of France's savior by identifying herself with Joan of Arc, France's patron saint who was called by God to defend her nation against English invasion. Despite her castigation of one religion, Le Pen has never hesitated to proclaim her own Catholic faith. Hence, it is easy for her to portray the fifteenth-century warrior as a spiritual ally and source of inspiration in defending French freedoms against the invading armies of secularism, immigrants, and Islam.[45]

To this end, Le Pen has championed the use of popular referenda as instruments of presidential power. The recourse to this populist form of agenda setting would allow her to maximize her influence over a panoply of divisive policy issues, such as compliance with EU directives and the extension of social benefits to immigrants. Her party's 2017 program provides a glimpse into her political objectives. If Le Pen were to be elected, these appeals to the "people's will" would allow her to make radical changes to the French constitution. Among its many institutional goals, the party program called for lengthening the term of the president, eliminating the legislature's control over constitutional amendments, reducing the number of parliamentary deputies by half, and inscribing new foundational principles in the constitutions to emphasize "our identity as a people" and fight "communitarianism."[46] Predictably, Le Pen has justified these proposals in the name of giving "the floor back to the people."[47] However, what she means by "the people" is the will of the majority, and not the representation of the diverse groups that comprise the French population. In a state that already entrusts the president with significant authority, one can easily imagine that Le Pen's idea of a rejuvenated France would look more like Viktor Orbán's Hungary than all preceding French governments, exceeding even the presidency of Charles de Gaulle.[48]

Finally, one should not be surprised that it is harder to assess the political implications of Peterson's arguments. Even if he were to be interested in influencing politics directly—an objective he strenuously denies—one could not be sure which Peterson would show up. Would it be the Peterson who advocates the vigorous expression of individual sovereignty or the one who recoils at the prospect of excessive exuberance? One way or another, there is an element in his overall argument that could present far-right actors with a rhetorical avenue to advocate positions that are even more extreme than those of Carlson and Le Pen. This is the "antidote to chaos" that the subtitle of *12 Rules for Life* promises to provide.

On the surface, Peterson's call to restore the sovereign rights of the individual seems to put him in line with classical liberalism. Yet, if we were to ask him why this right has been compromised, it is telling that he does not limit himself to the standard critique of government encroachments on essential freedoms. He goes much further, attributing the chaos of modern life to the left's destruction of the myths that have given meaning to people's lives for centuries and made it possible for them to live together peacefully within their natural hierarchies. Peterson's antidote to chaos lies in fashioning new forms of meaning. But, this raises an important question: Who should be charged with the daunting responsibility of living up to this challenge? As a purportedly disinterested observer of human behavior, Peterson would prefer to let others answer this question. Nonetheless, it is clear that he would not ask all segments of society to contribute to the task. Since people are unequal by virtue of their differences in biology, intelligence, and upbringing, this obligation must logically be shouldered by the gifted individuals at the top of the hierarchy. These people, among whom Peterson undoubtedly includes himself, are naturally equipped to identify what has been lost. On this basis, they will presumably then be best suited to decide what must be done to replace it.

Peterson's emphasis on restoring order to a chaotic world is ironic. As someone who implores his readers to take the lessons of Marxism, Maoism, and the Khmer Rouge to heart, one would expect him to avoid any hint that humanity should be governed according to the purported wisdom of the fittest. Nonetheless, the exhortation to excellence in a world in which, according to his argument, talents are unequally and irrevocably distributed is a recurring theme in his commentaries. If this principle were to be adopted by people of ill will who enjoy a monopoly in determining what is good for their fellow human beings, Peterson could end up with the totalitarian outcome that he claims to abhor.

Notes

I am grateful to Sam Piccolo, Steven Pittz, and Emma Schmidt for their many helpful comments on this chapter.
1 See https://socialcounts.org/youtube-live-subscriber-count/UCL_f53ZEJxp8TtlO kHwMV9Q; and www.instagram.com/jordan.b.peterson/guides/.
2 https://global.penguinrandomhouse.com/announcements/dr-jordan-b-peterson- announces-the-follow-up-to-his-global-bestseller-12-rules-of-life/.

3 https://ci-magazine.com/home/explaining-tucker-carlsons-democratic-demographic.
4 Matthew Rozsa, "Tucker Carlson Bashes Capitalism, Says He Might Vote for Elizabeth Warren," *Salon*, January 26, 2019, www.salon.com/2019/01/26/salon-interview-tucker-carlson-bashes-capitalism-says-he-might-vote-for-elizabeth-warren/.
5 www.adl.org/resources/blog/deplatform-tucker-carlson-and-great-replacement-theory.
6 Tucker Carlson, *Ship of Fools* (New York: Free Press, 2018), 12.
7 Marine Le Pen: "Je veux nationaliser les autoroutes et privatiser l'audiovisuel public," September 8, 2021, www.lefigaro.fr/elections/presidentielles/marine-le-pen-je-veux-nationaliser-les-autoroutes-et-privatiser-l-audiovisuel-public-20210908.
8 February 7, 2022, https://twitter.com/MLP_officiel/status/1490637838018359300.
9 CNBC interview with Le Pen, December 21, 2016, www.cnbc.com/2016/11/21/cnbc-transcript-french-presidential-candidate-national-front-party-leader-marine-le-pen-speaks-with-cnbcs-michelle-caruso-cabrera-today.html.
10 See Sudhir Hazareesingh, *How the French Think: An Affectionate Portrait of an Intellectual People* (New York: Basic Books, 2015).
11 Safaya Khan-Ruf, "Is Marine Le Pen Far Right? It Depends on Who You Talk To," *The Independent*, April 23, 2022, www.independent.co.uk/voices/marine-le-pen-far-right-french-elections-b2060754.html.
12 www.hoover.org/research/importance-being-ethical-jordan-peterson-1.
13 www.jordanbpeterson.com/political-correctness/equity-when-the-left-goes-too-far/.
14 Contrary to Peterson's claim, the Act's amendment did not even include the word "pronoun." See Ben Burgis and Matt McManus, *Jacobin*, April 20, 2020. https://jacobin.com/2020/04/jordan-peterson-capitalism-postmodernism-ideology.
15 For example, www.jordanbpeterson.com/political-correctness/equity-when-the-left-goes-too-far/.
16 "Psychologist Jordan Peterson Says Lobsters Help to Explain Why Human Hierarchies Exist—Do They?," *The Conversation*, January 24, 2018, https://theconversation.com/psychologist-jordan-peterson-says-lobsters-help-to-explain-why-human-hierarchies-exist-do-they-90489.
17 "Equity: When the Left Goes Too Far," March 23, 2019, www.jordanbpeterson.com/political-correctness/equity-when-the-left-goes-too-far/.
18 Jordan Peterson. *12 Rules for Life: An Antidote for Chaos* (Toronto: Random House Canada, 2018), 27.
19 I am grateful to Sam Piccolo for making this point.
20 https://fs.blog/will-durant-the-three-lessons-of-biological-history/.
21 For representative examples, see www.businessinsider.com/tucker-carlson-wont-apologize-for-bubba-the-love-sponge-tapes-2019-3; www.nytimes.com/2023/05/02/business/media/tucker-carlson-text-message-white-men.html.
22 "Tucker Carlson Tonight," *Fox News*, April 28, 2022.
23 Ibid.
24 Cited in Michael Edison Haydon, "It's OK to Be White: How Fox News Is Helping to Spread Neo-Nazi Propaganda," *Newsweek*, November 19, 2017, www.newsweek.com/neo-nazi-david-duke-backed-meme-was-reported-tucker-carlson-without-context-714655.
25 *Ship of Fools*, 237.
26 See Renaud Camus, *Le grand remplacement* (Paris: Reinharc, 2011).

27 Tucker Carlson, *Fox News*, July 19, 2022, www.foxnews.com/opinion/tucker-carlson-great-replacement-electoral-strategy.
28 Tucker Carlson, *Fox News*, September 21, 2021, www.foxnews.com/opinion/tucker-carlson-joe-biden-revealed-why-supports-illegal-immigration-2015-change-the-country.
29 www.rfi.fr/en/france/20101211-le-pen-daughter-compares-public-muslim-prayers-german-occupation.
30 https://harris-interactive.fr/opinion_polls/barometre-dintentions-de-vote-pour-lelection-presidentielle-de-2022-vague-18/.
31 Ania Nussbaum, "Le Pen Goes Back to Basics With Immigration Referendum," September 28, 2021, www.bloomberg.com/news/articles/2021-09-28/le-pen-joins-french-conservatives-seeking-immigration-referendum#xj4y7vzkg.
32 In an indication that the word "Islamism" is a code word for Islamic faith, a national survey in 2019 found that 61% of the population believed that Islam was "incompatible with the values of French society." www.ft.com/content/35a73fe7-53da-4fa1-be55-06b44169394a.
33 "Le programme de Marine Le Pen à la présidentielle 2022," www.lemonde.fr/politique/article/2022/02/14/le-programme-de-marine-le-pen-a-la-presidentielle-2022_6113605_823448.html.
34 www.nytimes.com/2022/04/17/world/europe/france-islam-le-pen-head-scarf.html.
35 The italics are mine. See Marine Le Pen, "Le voile n'est pas un bout de tissu anodin, c'est un marqueur de radicalité," www.dailymotion.com/video/x843zj9.
36 "Jordan Peterson Explains What Draws People to Socialism," April 8, 2019, www.heritage.org/progressivism/commentary/jordan-peterson-explains-what-draws-people-socialism.
37 *12 Rules of Life*, 36–38.
38 https://www.youtube.com/watch?v=4qZ3EsrKPsc.
39 An earlier survey conducted by the Associated Press in December 2021 found that nearly half of Republican respondents agreed that a "certain group of people in this country" was trying to replace "native-born Americans with immigrants." www.splcenter.org/news/2022/06/01/poll-finds-support-great-replacement-hard-right-ideas.
40 Ibid.
41 According to a *New York Times* analysis of his shows between 2016 and 2021. *New York Times*, May 15, 2022.
42 https://americarenewing.com/issue_topic/woke/.
43 *Ship of Fools*, 179.
44 Ibid., 240.
45 See Michel Eltchaninoff, *Inside the Mind of Marine Le Pen* (London: Hurst Publishers, 2018), and Daniel Rueda, "Is Populism a Political Strategy? A Critique of an Enduring Approach," *Political Studies* 69, no. 2 (2021): 167–84. https://doi.org/10.1177/0032321720962355.
46 See Théo Fournier, "A Constitutional Program Threatening the French Constitution," *Verfassungsblog*, March 2, 2017, https://verfassungsblog.de/marine-le-pen-a-constitutional-program-threatening-the-french-constitutional-regime/.
47 Ibid.
48 Not surprisingly, Le Pen is an avowed admirer of de Gaulle. See her book, *Pour que vive la France* (Escalons, Fr.: Grancher, 2012), 39, 104.

3

"WE ARE LOOKING FOR A NEW FEMINISM"

Marine Le Pen's Reappropriation of the Liberal Language of Women's Rights and Gender Equality

Sarah Shurts

In the 2012 presidential elections in France, Marine Le Pen won 17 percent of the first round of the vote and did not qualify for the second. Ten years later, in the 2022 presidential elections, she secured a shocking 41.5 percent of the vote in the second round. Such a jump indicates she has learned how to appeal to the mainstream voter despite warnings from many corners about her extreme, illiberal views on Islam and immigration. Of particular note is Le Pen's performance with women voters, which has been improving at a rapid rate each election cycle. Feminists on the left have been quick to protest Le Pen's inroads with women voters, accusing her of a false feminism and an abuse of the ideals of women's rights and equality. However, this claim of fraud is proving ineffective against a more powerful discursive tool crafted by Le Pen. Rather than directly assaulting liberalism and denigrating its key concepts of liberty, equality, and rights as some on the far right have chosen to do, Le Pen has developed a Far-Right Newspeak that infuses the traditional language of liberalism with right-wing values and meaning. She creates a potent combination of conservative and nationalist social and cultural values, some of which are very appealing to many women today, couched within the comforting language of liberalism. This couching is not a ruse or a façade, as some of her feminist critics will claim, but rather a reappropriation, a reinterpretation, and a revaluation of the old familiar concepts. Her approach to these concepts dear to liberals and feminists gives old words new meaning, yet it is meaning that is proclaimed an equally legitimate—or even as an older and therefore more legitimate—interpretation. By presenting far-right ideas as coexisting easily within the reassuring, republican concepts of liberty, equality, and women's rights, Le Pen's program resonates more effectively with an ever-broader circle of French women. The reinterpretation makes far-right policy, which might previously have made women hesitate, seem less extreme, less illiberal, more socially acceptable, and more morally defensible. In this way, her version of Far-Right Newspeak has allowed Le Pen to shift the direction of French political culture rightward without being seen as contradicting or challenging the liberal and republican values so essential to French concepts of identity.

Recognizing the power that women voters wield and their ability to shift the tide of the coming election in her favor, Le Pen published a "Lettre aux Françaises" on International Women's Day 2022 in which she claimed,

> Because I am a woman, I am, as you can imagine, particularly attached to the issues that concern us all. In general, I have integrated into my political campaign encouragement for women to take their place in our society. I hope to contribute to this by my own engagement at the forefront of public life.[1]

Political critics and pundits were quick to accuse Le Pen of insincerity and of abusing for political gain the feminist, liberal language of rights, freedom, and equality for women. According to these critics, her support for women's rights and equality in public life is a veneer, a ruse, or a Trojan horse to trick unwary women into voting for the true program of National Rally (*Rassemblement National*, or RN), formally National Front (FN): xenophobic and nationalist policies supporting an anti-immigrant and Islamophobic agenda. And so it may be. It is clear the RN and Le Pen prioritize a right-wing nationalist, anti-immigrant, and anti-Islam political platform. And, as with any political leader or pundit, there is no evidence that definitively proves Le Pen speaks the language of women, freedom, rights, and equality out of conviction rather than opportunism. But increasing numbers of women are voting for Le Pen, and continuing to argue that her use of the language of women's rights and equality is insincere is not preventing this shift or helping to understand its power. Despite their intent to provide dispassionate analysis from a distance, scholars sometimes fall into the same trap as these critics by asking if Le Pen is sincere in her campaign discourse. This is neither a useful question nor one we can feasibly answer. Instead, we should be asking how her reconceptualization of women's rights and roles using a reinterpreted, revalued language of freedom and equality could be resonating with women in democratic republics today and mobilizing them for the nationalist right.

This is a question with implications beyond France and Le Pen. Far-right women leaders are increasingly emerging in European politics: Marine Le Pen's niece Marion Maréchal in France; Alice Weidel of the AfD; Giorgia Meloni of the Brothers of Italy, who is Italy's first female prime minister; Rocío Monasterio, the president of Vox Madrid; and Pia Kjærsgaard, co-founder of the anti-immigrant Danish People's Party; while others like

Ellen Kositza have emerged in the cultural and intellectual sphere. As James McAdams points out in Chapter 1, even if we dislike these figures' arguments, we must still look closely at what they are saying and ask why their positions are appealing to their followers.[2] All of them have something to say about the rights of women, all of them model the role of professional women in the public sphere while simultaneously denouncing left-wing feminism, and all of them are building supportive audiences among politically mainstream European women. If we put aside for a moment the question of whether these far-right women politicians are disingenuously instrumentalizing liberal language as a smokescreen for a more sinister agenda, we can start asking instead how, in Western democratic states, the female leaders of the far right are reappropriating women's rights as a key plank in their campaign platforms. Le Pen, for example, is availing herself of a discourse of *liberté* and *egalité* with deep historical roots in the French Republic and revaluing both with far-right nationalist priorities. If we want to understand and even counter the phenomenon of women rejecting left-wing feminism and supporting the far right, we should stop dismissing the female right-wing politicians' discourse on women's rights as charlatanry and therefore their voters as easily duped. Instead we should try to understand their appeal as the spokeswoman for an alternative and far-right concept of women's rights, roles, desired freedoms, and perception of equality; a reinterpretation of the version that has been enshrined for decades by second-wave, liberal feminists.

Are Women's Equal Rights Incompatible With the Far Right?

"The extreme right is incompatible with the rights of women." This unflinching judgment by Osez le Féminisme! provided the introduction to a statement cosigned by 38 associations for women's rights on April 19, the eve of the second round of the 2022 French presidential election. They warned their readers, "When it comes to women's rights, the extreme right has one constant: that of fighting us, despising us and trampling on us." Therefore, it was incumbent on all women to vote, not for Le Pen to become the first female president of France, but rather for Macron, in order to "unreservedly block Ms. Le Pen in the second round of the presidential election."[3] This assessment of the Front National/National Rally as a masculine space unwelcoming and even hostile to women has long been supported by scholars of the French far right. This is not surprising since the far right, in all of its twentieth- and twenty-first-century transatlantic iterations, was perceived as a masculine space repressive and even hostile to women outside their traditional roles and spaces. The assessment that women's concerns are particularly irrelevant to Marine Le Pen's RN, despite having a woman at its head, is due in part to memory of the Front National under her father. The FN of Jean-Marie Le Pen from 1972 to 2011 was viewed as a repressive environment where celebration of masculine violence, descriptions of abortion as "anti-French genocide,"[4] and the claim that working mothers led to the delinquency and drug addiction of their children[5] corresponded to a dismally low rate of women voters. In the 1995 and 1997 elections, the FN was supported by only 12 percent of female voters and the gap between men and women FN supporters was 60 percent/40 percent. French women were actually more likely to be anti-immigrant than men and therefore were not avoiding the FN because they objected to its anti-immigrant program. Instead, in the 1990s, far-right parties like the FN simply "are not attractive to women" and "it would appear that in the case of the radical right, simply being female may make one less likely to vote for these parties."[6] The conclusion we must draw about the FN under Jean-Marie was that, as Fiammetta Venner wrote in 1999 of the party, "antifeminism is so unanimous in the extreme right that the submission of women is one of the foundations of its thought."[7]

However, since Marine Le Pen's accession to the presidency of the FN in 2011, elections have increasingly shown a decline in the gender gap and an increased percentage of female voters. In the second round of the 2017 presidential elections, the gap between male and female supporters of Le Pen actually inverted by .2 percent and the RN won 31.9 percent of the female voters age 18–26, up from 9 percent in 2007 under Jean-Marie.[8] Labeled the "Marine Le Pen effect,"[9] it reflects an effort by Marine to soften the image created by her father for the party, an effort she had termed *dédiabolisation* (de-demonization). Nonna Mayer found that in the 2012 presidential elections, "the personality of the new FN's leader made the difference and helped some women take the plunge" of voting for the far-right party.[10] Her study after the 2017 election confirmed it: "the decisive variable underpinning this gender-period effect would appear to be the replacement of Jean-Marie Le Pen as party leader by his daughter. Our results are in line with the hypothesis of a 'Marine Le Pen effect.'"[11] While other factors and voter's issues can certainly affect this shift, the party's core Islamophobic and anti-immigration platform has not changed dramatically, but a concerted effort to appeal to female voters has. This shift of female voters continued in 2022 when Le Pen won 41.5 percent of the total vote, and the Harris barometer of voting intentions in April showed Le Pen was expected to receive 26 percent of the female vote and 20 percent of male votes.[12]

This transfer of allegiance by female voters has not gone unnoticed by the liberal feminists who attribute Le Pen's rising popularity to co-opting women's issues and hijacking the liberal language of rights, freedoms, and equality for women that had been the hallmark of the feminist left. As early as 2007, when Marine was still only a regional councilor for the FN, Elsa Dorlin wrote an essay "Not in our name!: against the racist takeover of feminism by the French right." In it she warned, "making radical feminist engagement on the left a minority has allowed a masquerade of feminism to emerge on the right." The abuse of traditional feminism by the FN, she said, "aims to instrumentalize feminism within the framework of a rhetoric in the service of a more or less declared racist discourse."[13]

Since 2012, feminist organization leaders have increasingly rallied to speak out against her candidacy and denounce her use of the feminist language of women's rights as a hijacking, a co-opting and a double game, an instrumentalization and a pandering discursive strategy to broaden their appeal, and a manipulative façade. Leading up to the 2017 election, polls showed 20 percent of women voting for Le Pen, and analysts agreed her gender strategy and making inroads with women voters was key to her second-round finish.[14] In response, female scholars continued to present Le Pen's progressive discourse of women's rights as a ruse to soften the real priority of a xenophobic anti-migrant platform. Valérie Igounet, a historian of towns run by FN local politicians, claims, "Just as with other topics, when the Front National tackles the issue of women, it is really talking about immigration. It is immigration that underlies everything." Igounet concludes without hesitation, "the Front National is far from a party that is feminist and respects all rights of women."[15] Francesca Scrinzi agrees that right-wing politicians "have declared gender equality as a defining value of the French national identity" in order to contrast it more blatantly with the picture of "patriarchal 'cultures' attributed to migrants" and further their primary program of anti-immigration.[16] Rebecca Amsellem, founder of the feminist newsletter *Les Glorieuses*, warned 2017 voters, "Let's not kid ourselves. Marine Le Pen is no women's rights activist."[17]

By the eve of the first round of the 2022 election, Osez le féminisme! had created an online resource they called the féministomèter that ranked all of the first-round candidates on a scale from feminist to misogynist. Socialist and communist candidates all earned the feminist rank while both Le Pen and Éric Zemmour were the only misogynist candidates. In their summary assessment of Le Pen, the ranking said,

> Marine le Pen evokes the rights of women only when this will serve her racist political agenda. Her position stigmatizing the so-called "abortion of convenience," her longstanding support for masculinist leaders, and her program on immigration which would seriously harm foreign women living in France all create real danger for the rights of women.

Critiques of her policies included her lack of female representation on her campaign staff, opposition to extending legal abortion from 12 to 14 weeks, and "her obsession with forbidding the veil in public space" which though presented as a defense of the republican value of *laïcité* is actually about the control of the bodies of women.[18]

Given this reaction by feminists, should we preclude the nationalist far right from any discussion of women's rights, pro-women policies, or the concept of feminism? If we do, it is likely we will continue to misunderstand Le Pen's appeal with one in four French women voters. Linda Gordon claims the women of the KKK introduced a "white supremacist feminism" and reminds the skeptical reader, "there is a tendency for people to think of feminism as one coherent whole, which it has never been."[19] Ronnee Schreiber has argued that we can't simply dismiss American conservative women's movements like Independent Women's Forum (IWF) as being antiwomen or the dupe of conservative men. Instead, we need to see these right-wing women as articulating "alternative bases of understanding women's political interests."[20] Rather than seeing American conservative women leaders to have hijacked and abused liberal language to trick women, she proposes that they are using the language in new ways to appeal simultaneously to their conservative base and to a broader range of women voters, and attempting to merge those two identities into a comprehensive narrative. That means they must "reinterpret opposing or inconsistent values and beliefs through their own narratives and shift the meaning of issues to be more consistent with their views."[21] The product of this synthesis is something entirely distinct from both left-wing feminism and male conservatism. One of the contributors to this volume, George Hawley, has pointed out that American conservative women have begun to embrace feminism as a self-descriptor and to insist they are in fact "the real antiracists and feminists" since they often draw inspiration from nineteenth-century feminists like Elizabeth Cady Stanton and Susan B. Anthony.[22] This, Hawley says, raises the question of "what exactly it means to be a feminist and who can reasonably use the word as a self-description."[23] There is, therefore, room for women, women's rights, and even an alternative vision of feminism within the far right.

Le Pen and Feminism

Le Pen's ability to appeal to women using a revalued language of women's rights begins with her own self-identification as a woman and her advocacy of what she paints as a much older, traditional version of women's rights that the "neo-feminists" denature. In her 2011 autobiography she called herself a "quasi-feminist," simultaneously claiming the term and distancing herself from its dominant left-wing connotations.[24] For the next ten years, she cultivated a public image for herself of a female leader who was pro-woman as she defined it, not as it was defined by the prevailing feminist discourse.

By 2017 Le Pen had made her roles and experiences as a woman an intentional emphasis of her campaign. The FN mailed out four million copies of a four-page tract laid out like a glossy woman's magazine with the subtitle "I want to defend French women."[25] In it, headings like "A Woman of Heart:

Behind the Female Politician, the Mother, the Sister" and "In a World of Men: To Be a Woman in Politics Is an Asset Not a Disability," emphasized her roles and struggles as a woman. Under the heading "A True Legitimacy to Speak about Women," her plea to readers was predicated on her defense of women in both traditional and progressive roles: "Who better than a woman to speak about women, their difficulties, their real preoccupations, of the particular bond which links them to their children? Because she has lived it, Marine knows the difficulties and constraints of a professional life and their necessary involvement in family life."[26] The photos and stories laid out artistically in the pages highlighted her role as a working, single, twice-divorced mother of three children who understood the financial and emotional strain of the dual roles expected of the modern woman.

By February 2022, when asked directly in a televised interview if she was a feminist, she responded that she was a woman certainly but not a "neo-feminist" because "neo-feminism is a feminism of hate" where women fight against men and cause men to then fight against women, creating a cycle of hostility. With this single response, she claimed the possibility of multiple versions of feminism, rejected the dominant feminism as a "new" version harmful to women and their relationships, and legitimized her own program for women by recasting it as anterior to this "new" feminism. She draws her inspiration, she says, not from second-wave feminists but from women of France from Joan of Arc to Olympe de Gouges.[27] In a speech in 2015 celebrating Joan of Arc, she said, "In the National Front, we love Joan of Arc because she is a heroine who did not accept the fatalism of her condition. . . . She did not wait for gender equality to ride a horse and bear arms. She did not aspire for parity in order to command men and take over the leadership of an army."[28] This emphasis on traditional French heroines and especially women of the Revolution helps Le Pen tap into the long history of the republican tradition in France in order to better align herself with its traditional concepts of equality and liberty.

By March 2022, the same television interviewer asked, "One wonders what separates you from certain feminists even if you don't say that." Le Pen responded,

> It is just that I am not neo-feminist because I don't have any hatred toward men. I hear words that are sometimes violent against men in a general way as if all men were guilty and all women victims. I don't want to hear it, first, because it sends us systematically back to a victim position.[29]

She continued that society needs men and women and that since women can do everything simultaneously, and do it well, French women already know how incredible they are and don't need to be locked into permanent victimization. Portraying women as successful and capable, professionals and mothers, Joan of Arc–style heroines rather than victims of male repression and the patriarchy has great appeal to many women. According to Le Pen, her approach is more in line with the practical, real needs of women in today's generation than the left-wing neo-feminism preoccupied with fighting the abstract patrimony. Real women, Le Pen says,

> are juggling constantly between work, the grocery shopping, the kids and that damned feeling of guilt rooted in the heart of every mother who has to solve this equation every morning: "To bring them up, I have to earn a living; to earn a living, I need to work; if I work, someone else will have to bring them up."[30]

She claims it is with these real needs of women in mind, and the rights, freedoms, and equalities they require, that she has designed her presidential platform and legislative priorities. Her closing call in her 2017 tract for women emphasized the language of rights: "I say to women: I will not allow your liberties or your dignity to be called into question!"[31]

Le Pen's Reconceptualization of Equality, Freedom, and Rights

Le Pen's concept of equality for women is key to her stated rejection of liberal "neo-feminism." She says she is not "neo-feminist" because she sees men and women as equals rather than oppressors and oppressed and rejects the perception of women as victims. Instead, she promotes equality not as sameness but as a right to difference and complementarity of differences. While Marine has intentionally separated her approach to women from that of her father's FN, her conceptualization of equality as a right to difference and complementarity borrows heavily from the FN Women's council (CNFE) which produced publications from 1985 to 1995. A CNFE newsletter argued, "feminist movements consider relations between women and men as power relations. We think of them as complementary."[32] This complementarity and difference was exemplified by women's role as mothers and "transmitters of culture."[33] A complementary role for women as mothers was portrayed at all times as a vital service; they were the "social reproducers" of the nation and "repositories of national culture and identity"[34] and even of Western civilization as a whole. This revalorization and revaluing of motherhood was an appealing element of FN traditionalism for many women, and Marine Le Pen has adopted it as a central element of her understanding of women's right to difference.

Right-wing philosophies of complementarity and gender difference often come with an implied, if not explicit, hierarchy favoring men, but Le Pen's does not. In 2022 she called for schools to become centers for the transmission of French values, specifically "republican principles, like the equality of the sexes."[35] But within this equality, there is room for difference: "We have the right to be different—once again I am defending the fact that women can be different—I am not looking for men and women to be the same just because they are treated in the same way."[36] While Le Pen strongly supports working and professional women and highlights her own role as a working single mother, she also validates the work women do in the home and celebrates the fulfillment women can feel in their roles as mothers and wives. She argues that equal rights understood as a right to difference means women should have state financial support so that they can have the opportunity, if they choose, to focus on the role of mother and wife. But she clarifies that this must never confine women to these roles and instead says, "I call on them to defeat a form of reservation that is often unjustified in order to seek, by and for themselves, positions of responsibility" in all forms of public and professional life as she has for herself in politics.[37] However, it should be noted, many scholars argue complementarity is an abuse of the language of sexual liberty to surreptitiously reinforce traditionalist behaviors. Dietze and Roth argue, "almost all formations of the right-wing populist complex claim to stand for a 'new' and 'other' modernity" but say this is not true feminism, merely "modern window dressing [that] rearranges traditional 'values' in a new narrative."[38]

In 2022, Osez le féminisme's féministomèter claimed that Le Pen's conceptualization of equal rights as right to difference was misogynist, and that it was the reason that she spoke out in 2012 against the *parité* legislation passed in 2000 that requires equal numbers of male and female candidacies for political offices, an area where women had been historically underrepresented. But Le Pen argues her opposition to *parité* was in keeping with a long French republican history of *égalité* as opportunity. Le Pen and the RN have rejected of all forms of "positive discrimination" which she claims "inexorably eats away at the Republic" and calls instead for the older republican ideal of equality of opportunity and meritocracy.[39] However, in 2022 she acknowledged that *parité* had benefitted women. When an interviewer asked, "What explains this feminism in you? What has made you change?" she replied that it was not a reversal of a prior misogyny but rather a recognition that parity legislation allowed women to emerge in politics and helped them gain confidence, a change she celebrated despite its origins.[40] Unlike both the men of the far right and left-wing feminists, Le Pen uses the language of a woman's "right to difference" as a right-wing reconceptualization of the "equality of the sexes." And she proclaims equality of opportunity, not equality of outcome, to be the true heir of centuries-old French republican values of *égalité* and meritocracy.

Le Pen's concept of equality for women extends to other policy issues that can be surprisingly close to those of the left yet still show distinctive elements of right-wing ideals. Equal pay remains a cornerstone: "Is it still possible" she demanded in 2019, "that a woman be paid less than a man for the same job?"[41] Proposing increased financial support for single mothers, she asks, "is it decent that single mothers are not able to live? It is indispensable that the difficulties of single mothers be finally taken up in an energetic way: specific social aid, access to nursery schools, aid in finding housing."[42] She commiserated in a 2022 televised interview with single women saying she "knows it is hard to have children alone, both psychologically and financially"[43] and so proposes to double the social support payments for single mothers to 230 euros,[44] higher than Macron promised. She also supports increased salaries for teachers and nurses,[45] two professions with high numbers of women. Mothers would benefit also financially from the tax credit for the second child and an untaxed government loan for young families with all remaining debt forgiven after the birth of the third child.[46] Le Pen says these proposals are in no way intended to prevent women from working and force them to traditional roles as homemakers. Anyone who thinks this she dismisses as "totally disconnected from the economic and social reality of our country."[47] She says the reality is that "today the question posed by many women is not 'do I have the freedom to work?' but rather 'do I have the financial option not to work in order to stay home with my children?'"[48] It should be noted, however, that this social support is not offered to immigrants and is part of the broader nativist, natalist program of the RN.[49] Le Pen's defense of income equality for women is therefore in keeping with left-wing feminism, but it is also colored by right-wing values of natalism and nationalism.

Right-wing values also adulterate Le Pen's policies on women's reproductive health, which has become a signature element of her campaign where many policies align with those on the left. Right-wing natalism has traditionally extended to restrictions on abortion and birth control, but Marine Le Pen has increasingly evolved her views on these issues and transitioned the party toward women's reproductive rights. She has been critiqued by many feminists for saying she did not support "abortions of convenience," a phrase that many felt added a cruel stigma to those seeking an abortion, and for her unwillingness to expand abortion access from 12 to 14 weeks.[50] However, she does support protection of women's right to an abortion up to 12 weeks and in 2022 added government-reimbursed birth control for women beyond the current cut-off age of 25.[51] Women's rights to reproductive health care has also become a signature campaign promise for Le Pen, who has included the expansion of gynecological care, the training of new gynecologists, better salaries for midwives, and better recognition and treatment of diseases for women like endometriosis to her campaign platform as a basic right for all women.[52] Her proposals for women's rights to reproductive health care are therefore similar to those of feminists of the left but still retain conservative elements like an early limit to abortion access.

Le Pen has built a stronger platform of women's issues than she began with in 2012 and has revalued the liberal language of equality, protection of rights, and freedoms for women to mean a right to gender difference and a preference for meritocracy, albeit with a grudging respect for *parité*. These policy proposals are neither left-wing feminist nor right-wing traditionalist but instead a unique synthesis of the two. However, it is important to also include here the policies and proposals where Le Pen attempts to meld the liberal language of women's rights to the RN Islamophobic and anti-immigration tenets. This melding does not imply any deception of women voters nor insincerity in Le Pen's defense of women, as many scholars contend. Rather than using liberal language and women's rights as a smokescreen to hide a nationalist and xenophobic agenda, that agenda is an essential and highly visible element of Le Pen's program, constructed in the belief that opposition to Muslim immigrant men will resonate for women in France today. When asked once more if she was a feminist, Marine finally conceded, "she could consider herself as such to the extent that she defends women's rights, which are threatened by Islam."[53] One of the tropes that has been particularly successful in drawing both men and women to the RN is that of the "Islamist misogynist male immigrant." When asked what brought them to the far-right movements, many women describe being motivated by news reports of women being attacked or repressed by Muslim men.[54] Fear of "Islamism"—a concept often carefully distinguished by the RN from Islam—is expressed as a fight for liberation of fellow women from presumed repression, including patriarchal constraints of the home, forced marriages, clothing requirements and restrictions like the veil or burkinis on the beaches, separation in education, female circumcision, and gender-separate swimming. Le Pen has constructed a defense of women's freedom, using the liberal language of rights and republican concept of *liberté*, around a core of illiberal hostility toward immigration and Islam. It has yielded three main discourses: equality of treatment, freedom of dress, and rights to personal security.

Le Pen consistently invokes the long history of the French Republic's guarantee of *liberté* and *égalité* and marries it closely to her defense of women in her screed against Muslim immigrant communities. She writes of "Islamism" that it is an "offense to the Republic" that replaces "our values and laws with others which rest on the inequality between men and women."[55] In this way it is "incompatible with the rights, the liberties, and the principles recognized by the Constitution."[56] In 2019 she enumerated the many ways Muslim women were treated that violated French republican principles of equality and liberty, saying,

> Is it not disturbing that the ministry is obligated in France to launch plans against female circumcision or against forced marriage? These phenomena say much about the disquieting evolution of our country on the rights of

women. In French hospitals men refuse to be treated by a female doctor and refuse to let their wife be seen by a male doctor. Are we going to continue to comply with these demands from outsiders?[57]

By 2022 her list of abuses of women's equal treatment had expanded. "How, among other imported practices, are we not indignant to see arise in our country in the 21st century forced marriages, certificates of virginity, female circumcision, or crimes of honor?" she asked. These practices she declared both a violation of women's rights and French republican values, saying, "It is time to stop this turn toward barbarism. It is time to return France to order and reimpose, everywhere and for all, our values of civilization."[58] In this way, Le Pen presents the RN program as the defender of French values, women's rights, Muslim women victims, and Western civilization against the repressive male patrimony of fundamentalist Islam. Sara Farris has revealed that it is in this discourse of "the profound danger that Muslim males constitute for western European societies, due, above all, to their oppressive treatment of women" that far right, anti-immigrant, and anti-Islamist organizations have joined forces with some non-right-wing feminists who also reject Muslim communities as sexist and patriarchal.[59]

Opposition to Muslim girls wearing the veil has been one of the most public expressions of this intersection. In 2003, during the deliberation of the Stasi commission on implementing secularism in the schools, far-right objectors were joined in their demands for legislation banning the veil by 68 petitioners, including socialist minister for the rights of women Yvette Roudy and feminist philosopher Élisabeth Badinter. This unexpected alliance made an appeal to President Chirac published in *Elle* magazine, declaring the veil a "visible sign of female submission" in schools where there should be "strict equality between the sexes."[60] In her 2019 "French Women: Proud of Our Liberties!" Le Pen includes at the bottom of the cover page the question, "Tomorrow will French women be able to dress as they want?"[61] The complaint continues that French women's freedom to dress as they choose is curtailed by fundamentalism. "Is one able to admit that in France in 2019, under the pressure of Islamists, in certain quarters or schools the young girls are dissuaded from wearing a skirt or forced to veil themselves?" she asks. "Since the film the *Day of the Skirt* in 2009 posed this problem the situation has not been ameliorated. Numerous women submit to pressure on the choice of their clothes."[62] The RN calls for legislation to ban the veil and the burkini in the name of republican *laïcité*, particularly in the schools, and thus links freedom of dress to the long French tradition of secular republicanism and to equality of educational opportunity.

But the discourse on freedom of dress also evokes another far-right stereotype of the Muslim or Arab immigrant male as a sexual aggressor[63] by calling for protection of French non-Muslim women's right to wear shorts or skirts without being subject to harassment or sexual assault. The third discourse that ties women's rights to anti-immigration and Islamophobia invokes the republican promise of liberty, specifically a woman's right to freedom from assault and harassment. The perception that harassment of women in the street and even sexual assaults are more often committed by Muslim immigrant men has exacerbated this trend toward linking anti-Islamism and defense of women's rights. Such fear seemed substantiated when, on New Year's Eve 2015, over 1,200 women were harassed and sexually assaulted en masse in Cologne by gangs of men of predominantly Middle Eastern and North African ethnicity. The public was outraged, and "in response, right-wing extremist groups saw a surge in membership as they used the incident as proof that large numbers of Muslim refugees threaten the safety of women in public."[64]

Le Pen speaks to women of her understanding of their fears for their personal safety. "The freedom of women and young girls to move around without being hindered or menaced in a skirt or dress if they wear one at any hour of day or night in any quarter in any café will be reestablished," she promises in her 2022 publication on security.[65] She commiserates with the daily self-limitations of personal freedom women submit to in order to protect themselves, saying,

> In daily life we integrate, in an automatic way, strategies of avoidance like changing sidewalks, avoiding certain places like cafes, taking a taxi instead of public transport after a certain hour, not wearing a skirt in certain quarters. This is not the concept of liberty that we ought to accept.[66]

Therefore, she proposes more severe penalties for street harassment. "In addition to heavy criminal penalties," she pledges, "I will register street harassers as sex offenders and deport foreigners who engage in these outrageous practices."[67] After Cologne, Le Pen published an opinion piece in the French daily *L'Opinion*, saying, "I am revolted today by the unacceptable silence and, therefore, tacit consent of the French Left in the face of these fundamental attacks on the rights of women . . . the eternal moralizers are silent when, for once, the most central values of our Republic are flouted." Le Pen also explicitly appealed to Simon de Beauvoir, one of France's most famous feminist philosophers, to punctuate her point, quoting Beauvoir's exhortation to "'never forget that any political, economic, or religious crisis will suffice to call into question the rights of women,'" and saying that she was "scared that the migrant crisis signals the beginning of the end of women's rights."[68] Le Pen softened this by 2019 to language of protecting "civilization" rather than "migrant crisis," but the implications remained. Her rallying cry epitomizes the far-right conceptualization of women's rights she has constructed using the liberal language and long republican history of liberties, rights, and equality but with an underlying theme of anti-immigrant islamophobia:

> I am anxious about these silent attacks on women's rights. I want to move forward on this with you. In the European elections your choice will be a choice for your freedoms and those of your daughters and granddaughters. Behind the vote, there is a choice of civilization. ON MAY 26, 2019, FRENCH WOMEN, VOTE FOR YOUR FREEDOMS.[69]

Conclusion

Le Pen promotes many of the same general ideals of the left-wing feminists using the same liberal language: equality, rights, and freedoms, and she links these to a long history of French republican values. However, each of these concepts has been reappropriated and infused with new meaning so that it both operates within the liberal meaning of the word and simultaneously aligns with far-right values. Le Pen advocates gender equality, equal pay, and equal treatment and promotes women's professional and business leadership as the equals of men. But, Le Pen's equality promotes gender difference, complementarity, and equal opportunity, rather than what she claims is homogeneity and reverse discrimination.

Women's rights to gender-specific health care, abortion, and contraception are now firmly defended ideals of the RN just as they are for left-wing feminists. But Le Pen is reluctant to extend abortion beyond 12 weeks and has spoken against using it as a convenience. Paired with this is an unabashed natalist program that financially incentivizes homemaking and motherhood, but only for women who are French citizens. These financial programs support women who choose to work but also those who elect to stay home with their children, a traditionalist path seldom celebrated by left-wing feminism.

And finally, Le Pen claims to defend women's freedom to dress, escape oppression, and avoid sexual harassment or assault. Here in particular Le Pen's language and policies align with many feminists on the left. Yet this defense of women's freedom is more aligned with the nationalist right since it identifies these threats to women as primarily from Muslim immigrants. The RN version of protecting women from oppression, harassment, and assault is therefore tinged with the party's core: nationalism, anti-immigration, and Islamophobia.

Le Pen's reappropriation of the language of women's rights and republican ideals of liberty and equality to promote policies that are recalibrated to the far right has shown itself to be more than mere ruse. Increasing numbers of French women are turning to it, and not because it is a Trojan horse for anti-immigration, or obfuscation of islamophobia, or a hijacking and instrumentalization of the true feminism, or modern window-dressing on traditionalism. As we try to understand the success in closing the gender gap that the far right's reappropriation and revaluation of feminism in France is having, two scholars of Poland, Weronika Grzebalska and Elena Zacharenko, offer some insight: "labeling these proposals as 'anti-women' simply because they come from extremist actors does not help us understand women's support for them."[70]

> It is no longer feasible to ignore the empowering effects of participation in the right-wing project. In fact, it can be argued that women's support for right-wing projects can serve as an alternative model of empowerment and advancement for women who do not find the neoliberal feminist proposal appealing.[71]

Perhaps Nathalie Kosciusko-Morizet puts best the growing popularity of this approach: "We are looking for a new feminism. And Marine Le Pen has gotten inside this crevice, this lack inside the French political system."[72]

Notes

1. Marine Le Pen, "Lettre aux Françaises," *Le Figaro*, July 3, 2022, www.lefigaro.fr/vox/politique/marine-le-pen-lettre-aux-francaises-20220307.
2. See p. 4.
3. "Press Release," http://osezlefeminisme.fr/lextreme-droite-est-incompatible-avec-les-droits-des-femmes/.
4. Cécile Alduy, "Has Marine Le Pen Already Won the Battle for the Soul of France?" *The Nation*, March 5, 2014, www.thenation.com/article/archive/has-marine-le-pen-already-won-battle-soul-france/.
5. Fiammetta Venner, "L'extrême droite et l'antiféminisme," in *Un siècle d'antiféminisme*, edited by Christine Bard (Paris: Fayard, 1999), 419.
6. Terri E. Givens, "The Radical Right Gender Gap," *Comparative Political Studies* 37, no. 1 (February 2004): 304–05.
7. Venner, "L'extrême droite et l'antiféminisme," 417.
8. Abdelkarim Amengay, Anja Durovic, Nonna Mayer and Cadenza Academic Translations, "The Impact of Gender," *Revue française de science politique* (English Edition) 67, no. 6 (2017): viii, xiii.
9. Ibid., iv.
10. Nonna Mayer, "The Closing of the Radical Right Gender Gap in France?" *French Politics* 13, no. 4 (December 2015): 391–414.
11. Amengay, Durovic, and Mayer, "The Impact of Gender," xiv.
12. "Harris Barometer," https://harris-interactive.fr/opinion_polls/barometre-dintentions-de-vote-pour-lelection-presidentielle-de-2022-vague-40/.
13. Elsa Dorlin, "Pas en notre nom! Contre la récupération raciste du féminisme par la droite française," *L'autre campagne* (2007), http://lautrecampagne.labandepassante.org/article.php?id=132.
14. Joëlle Garrus, "Le Pen Woos Female Voters But Feminists Skeptical," *The Times of Israel*, May 5, 2017, www.timesofisrael.com/le-pen-woos-female-voters-but-

feminists-sceptical/ and Susan Chira, "Marine Le Pen's Canny Use of Gender in Her Campaign," *The New York Times*, May 4, 2017, www.nytimes.com/2017/05/04/world/europe/le-pens-campaign-strategy-shift-strong-but-soft.html.
15 Marine Le Pen, "Présentielle 2022: Les 8 candidats face aux Françaises," *Direct LCI Television Interview*, March 7, 2022, www.youtube.com/watch?v=OZtwG-qCBCA&t=3692s.
16 Francesca Scrinzi, "A 'New' National Front? Gender, Religion, Secularism and the French Populist Radical Right," in *Gender and Far Right Politics in Europe*, edited by M. Köttig et al. (Cham: Palgrave Macmillan, 2017), 129.
17 Garrus, "Le Pen Woos Female Voters."
18 "Osez le féminisme!," *Féministomètre*, March 7, 2022, https://osezlefeminisme.fr/feministometre/.
19 Jack Smith IV, "Why Women Have Always Been Essential to White Supremacist Movements," *MIC*, January 5, 2018, www.mic.com/articles/187223/why-women-have-always-been-essential-to-white-supremacist-movements.
20 Ronnee Schreiber, *Righting Feminism: Conservative Women and American Politics* (New York: Oxford University Press, 2008), 3.
21 Ibid., 9.
22 George Hawley, *Conservatism in a Divided America* (Notre Dame: University of Notre Dame Press, 2022), 156, 161.
23 Ibid., 155.
24 Marine Le Pen, *À Contre Flots* (Paris: Grancher, 2006), 188.
25 Marine Le Pen, *Au nom du people* (Rassemblement National, 2017).
26 Ibid.
27 Michael Eltchaninoff, *Inside the Mind of Marine Le Pen* (London: Hurst & Company, 2018), 46.
28 Christèle Marchand-Lagier, "Case Study of France," in *Triumph of the Women? The Female Face of the Far and Populist Right in Europe*, edited by Elisa Gutsche (Berlin: Friedrich Ebert Stiftung, 2018), 52.
29 Présentielle 2022: Les 8 Candidats.
30 Le Pen, *À Contre Flots*, 187.
31 Le Pen, *Au nom du people*.
32 Claudie Lesselier, "Far-Right Women in France: The Case of the National Front," in *Right-Wing Women: From Conservatives to Extremists Around the World*, edited by Paola Bacchetta and Margaret Power (New York: Routledge, 2002), 131.
33 Ibid., 140.
34 Scrinzi, "A 'New' National Front?" 134.
35 Marine Le Pen, *M L'école*, 2022, https://mlafrance.fr/pdfs/projet-l-ecole.pdf.
36 Présentielle 2022: Les 8 Candidats.
37 Le Pen, "Lettre aux Françaises."
38 Gabriele Dietze and Julia Roth, "Right-Wing Populism and Gender: A Preliminary Cartography of an Emergent Field of Research," in *Right-Wing Populism and Gender: European Perspectives and Beyond*, edited by Gabriele Dietze and Julia Roth (Bielefeld: Transcript Publishing, 2020), 12.
39 Marine Le Pen, *Pour que vive la France* (Paris: Jacques Grancher, 2012), 183.
40 Présentielle 2022: Les 8 Candidats.
41 *Femmes Françaises: Fières de nos libertés!*, publication of the Rassemblement National 2019.

42 Ibid.
43 Présentielle 2022: Les 8 Candidats.
44 Coline Baralon, Louise Besnard, and Mickael Raggi, *Présentielle 2022: Les programmes politiques au prisme de l'égalité des femmes et des hommes* (Paris: SciencesPo école d'affaires publiques, 2022), 22.
45 Osez le féminisme!, *Féministomètre*.
46 Marine Le Pen, M *La France: Mon Projet Présidentiel* (2022), 28, https://mlafrance.fr/pdfs/22-mesures-pour-2022.pdf.
47 Le Pen, *À Contre Flots*, 190.
48 Ibid.
49 Marine Le Pen, M *La Famille* (2022), 7, https://mlafrance.fr/pdfs/projet-la-famille.pdf.
50 Osez le féminisme!, *Féministomètre*.
51 Présentielle 2022: Les 8 Candidats.
52 "Avec Marine Le Pen, exigeons un retour de la sécurité pour les femmes françaises: soutenez nos propositions pour les défendre!" https://mlafrance.fr/petition/avec-marine-le-pen-exigeons-un-retour-de-la-securite-pour-les-femmes-francaises-soutenez-nos-propositions-pour-les-defendre and Présentielle 2022: Les 8 Candidats.
53 Sara R. Farris, *In the Name of Women's Rights: The Rise of Femonationalism* (Durham: Duke University Press, 2017), 36.
54 Anet McClintock, "The Woman Paradox: Misogyny and Women in the Far-Right," *Australian Outlook*, April 19, 2021, www.internationalaffairs.org.au/australianoutlook/the-woman-paradox-misogyny-and-women-in-the-far-right/.
55 Marine Le Pen, M *La Sécurité* (2022), 20, https://mlafrance.fr/pdfs/projet-la-securite.pdf.
56 Ibid., 21.
57 *Femmes Françaises: Fières de nos libertés!*
58 Le Pen, "Lettre aux Françaises."
59 Farris, *In the Name of Women's Rights*, 2.
60 Ibid., 47.
61 *Femmes Françaises: Fières de nos libertés!*
62 Ibid.
63 Todd Shepard, *Sex, France, and Arab Men: 1962–1979* (Chicago: The University of Chicago Press, 2017).
64 McClintock, "The Woman Paradox."
65 Le Pen, M *La Sécurité*, 13.
66 Le Pen, "Lettre aux Françaises."
67 Ibid.
68 Marine Le Pen, "Un référendum pour sortir de la crise migratoire," *L'Opinion*, January 13, 2016, www.lopinion.fr/politique/marine-le-pen-un-referendum-pour-sortir-de-la-crise-migratoire.
69 *Femmes Françaises: Fières de nos libertés!*
70 Weronika Grzebalska and Elena Zacharenko, "Country Case Study: Poland," in *Triumph of the Women? The Female Face of the Far and Populist Right in Europe*, edited by Elisa Gutsche (Berlin: Friedrich Ebert Stiftung, 2018), 89.
71 Ibid.
72 Chira, "Marine Le Pen's Canny Use of Gender."

4
FAR-RIGHT POLITICS IN THE CZECH REPUBLIC

Tomio Okamura's Liberal Language and Populist Playbook

Petra Mlejnková

Among the former Soviet satellite states of east-central Europe, far-right politics in Poland and Hungary have attracted the most attention. In contrast, in the Czech Republic, a country that was formed, along with Slovakia, when Czechoslovakia was divided into two countries in 1993, far-right parties and politicians have not enjoyed nearly as much success. However, this is not to say that they have been totally unsuccessful. In this chapter, I shall examine the views of a far-right politician, Tomio Okamura. Although his name is not well known outside of postcommunist Europe, Okamura has nevertheless left an important mark on Czech politics as the leader of two far-right parties. As I shall demonstrate, Okamura has been a master of using the liberal idiom of Far-Right Newspeak to portray himself and his party as the true heirs to his country's democratic traditions. In this respect, his ability to sell his ideas confirms George Orwell's warnings about the misuse and instrumentalization of the language of liberalism and democracy that James McAdams has described in Chapter 1. Despite the fact that Okamura is not as prominent as other far-right personalities, such as Viktor Orbán and Marine Le Pen, his ability to make himself heard in a country where there is overwhelming support for democratic values and institutions should not be understated. Using the political system's foundational language, he characterizes mainstream Czech liberalism as a defective ideology that has allowed a predatory power elite to curtail the Czech majority's rights and freedoms. He even characterizes the country's mainstream politicians as totalitarian. As an alternative, Okamura offers his supporters an appealing far-right package of solutions, such as nativism and illiberal politics. After providing some background on Okamura and the political circumstances in which he emerged, I shall seek to shed light on this strategy by focusing specifically on his use of the words "freedom" and "democracy."

Historical Background

With the fall of the communist regime in 1989, Czechoslovakia—and after 1992, the new states of the Czech Republic and Slovakia—entered a period of political, social, and economic transformation into a liberal-democratic system. The 1990s were a dynamic time for Czechs, full of significant changes, great expectations, and uncertainties and marked by an ongoing search for national identity. These events came after 40 long years in which Czechs and their fellow Slovaks were deprived of basic freedoms under the dictatorship of the Communist Party of Czechoslovakia. Even before these decades, Czechs had a mixed experience with democracy and enjoyed only one sustained period of significant freedom. Essentially, the only historical era that made sense for the leaders of the post-1992 Czech Republic to build upon was the period between 1918 and 1938, from the creation of an independent Czechoslovak state following the dissolution of the Habsburg monarchy at the end of World War I until the truncation of Czechoslovak territory by the Munich Agreement with Hitler's Germany just before the outbreak of World War II. With the exception of a brief return to democracy between 1945 and 1948, Czechs and Slovaks had only experienced unfreedom up to 1989, first under the control of Nazi Germany and subsequently the Soviet Union.

The 1990s were not only times of great expectations and excitement but also of significant uncertainty and disappointment. Although the process of building viable democratic institutions in the Czech Republic was peaceful and is generally seen as successful, the country's economic transformation negatively affected a significant segment of the population. Not long after the fall of the communist dictatorship, many Czechs felt that the promises of their newly established democratic parties had made their lives even more difficult. People struggled to adapt to the new sociopolitical situation. For many, the Communist Party remained a surprisingly popular alternative to the country's new democratic parties. After gaining 13 percent of the vote in Czechoslovakia's first free elections in 1990, the party continued to enjoy the support of no less than 10 percent of the Czech electorate for another 20 years. At the same time, popular dissatisfaction with the costs of the transition to democracy created space for non-communist protest movements as well, especially on the right side of the political spectrum. In particular, an extreme right party known as the Association for the Republic—Republican Party of Czechoslovakia (SPR—RSČ) quickly emerged.[1] Although the party initially failed to achieve success in the parliamentary elections of 1990, it entered Parliament with 6.2 percent of the votes in the 1992 elections and held significant weight in the legislature. It further strengthened its position in the 1996 elections, gaining 8 percent of the vote. The SPR—RSČ remained in Parliament until 1998 when it failed to receive a sufficient number of votes in the early elections.

During these years, the SPR—RSČ took the form of a classical protest party, drawing its support from those segments of the population that had been especially hard-hit by the course and consequences of the democratization process.[2] It was not alone. In the 1990s, populist parties on both sides of the political spectrum represented approximately one-fifth of the electorate. Surveys assessing satisfaction with the performance of the republic's first post-1989 government are indicative of the popular mood. Although the new liberal-democratic regime was still supported by a majority of the population, even as early in the transition from communism as 1991, 14 percent of Czechs did not perceive any change from the communist past, and 15 percent regarded the first democratic government, which lasted until 1992, as even worse than its communist predecessor.[3]

In this context, the far-right SPR—RSČ recognized the advantage of portraying itself as the true defender of democracy. Miroslav Sládek, the party's leader at the founding congress in 1990, declared, "the leading idea behind the establishment of the party [is] the awareness, in the current political situation, that the system is overloaded with parties of liberal-democratic-socialist orientation. Thus, it is necessary to build a truly radical right-wing party that will be the guardian of democracy."[4] In this spirit, Sládek warned voters of the danger that someone with dictatorial ambitions could take advantage of the country's uncertain conditions to divide society into two antagonistic groups—on the one side, those who were already suffering the effects of the transition and, on the other, the new class of politicians that had gained power by striking deals with the communists. To attract voters, the SPR—RSČ also used racist rhetoric.[5] It ethnicized social and criminal problems, attributing them primarily to the Roma population.[6] Nonetheless, following its defeat in 1998, the SPR—RSČ basically disappeared. For several years thereafter, there was an overall decline in the far right's fortunes.

However, it is important to recognize that the far right's decline was not due to a lack of popular support for its message. Rather, its weakness was largely due to the fact that specific leaders failed to seize political opportunities and offered no credible political alternatives to the policies of the major parties. This deficit was reversed by Okamura's emergence in 2012.

Okamura's entry into politics in 2012 coincided with a pivotal point in the Czech Republic's history. For 20 years, the country had been ruled by either a liberal conservative party or a social democratic party, and at one point by both. Popular passions were inflamed by repeated corruption scandals in these governments. Hence, the time was again ripe for populist politicians to claim that only they could be counted upon to end corruption, get rid of "political dinosaurs," as the mainstream elites were called, and usher the country into the twenty-first century.[7] Among the new parties, the most notable was ANO 2011 (short for "The Action of Dissatisfied Citizens"). The party was led by Andrej Babiš, a politician who combined populist rhetoric with a pragmatic pro-Western and pro-European Union stance. Benefiting from the party's success at the polls, Babiš became deputy prime minister and then minister of finance from 2014 to 2017, and subsequently prime minister from 2017 to 2021.

These conditions were also suited to Okamura's political style. While he would eventually make his name by advocating xenophobic and anti-EU policies, he was also adept at presenting himself as a multitalented personality. In developing his public profile, he capitalized upon his mixed heritage as the son of a Czech mother and a Japanese-Korean father to claim special expertise in issues related to immigration and the integration of foreigners into Czech society. Okamura also built a reputation in the business world as the vice president of the Association of Czech Travel Agencies and Travel Agents. At one point, he was a partner in an unusual travel agency that specialized in plush animal toys, organizing vacations in the Czech Republic for both its clients and their beloved companions on vacations.[8] In 2008, Okamura was appointed to the honorary position of Czech Ambassador for the European Year of Intercultural Dialogue, which was organized by the European Union.[9] Okamura continues to be involved in the tourist industry, as well as translation services and the sale of Japanese food products. In 2009, he made an appearance as one of the investors in the television reality show "Den D."[10] He even served as a member of the jury in the 2011 Miss Expat competition, which featured foreigners living in the Czech Republic.[11]

In 2013, Okamura finally turned his attention to politics, founding the far-right party Dawn of Direct Democracy (Úsvit přímé demokracie). He was also elected to the Chamber of Deputies of the Parliament of the Czech Republic in the same year. Despite this quick rise to political prominence, however, Okamura was expelled from the parliamentary group in 2015 in a dispute over party finances and was called upon to resign as party chairman. Not to be deterred, Okamura responded to this development in the same year by founding another far-right political party called Freedom and Direct Democracy, or SPD (Svoboda a přímá demokracie). Not surprisingly, the new party's electoral style and its programs were essentially the same as those of Dawn of Direct Democracy (which was dissolved in 2018). To this day, Okamura has remained the party's chairman.[12] Showing how much his style of leadership has mattered, the party has consistently received the support of around 10 percent of the electorate.

The SPD's main program is based on promoting the principle of direct democracy according to which ordinary people should be given as much direct power as possible in the making of key political decisions. This electoral strategy is consistent with the SPD's promotion of an "us" versus "them" dichotomy, where the supposedly honest efforts of ordinary people are mobilized to counteract the damage done by corrupt and self-serving elites. Hence, in framing itself as a defender of democracy, the party is aptly characterized as populist.[13] Under Okamura's leadership, the SPD has also adopted all of the trappings of a modern European far-right party. It presents itself as a model of nativism, protectionism, and Euroscepticism. In addition, it is noted for its anti-Islamic and anti-immigrant stances and for its highly conservative definitions of nation, family, and gender. During the migration crisis of peoples from non-European countries, such as Syria, Afghanistan, Iraq, and sub-Saharan Africa, to Europe, which peaked in 2015 and 2016, the SPD played a particularly prominent role in warning the Czech population about the supposed dangers of migration and the impending Islamization of Europe. Ironically, the numbers of refugees and asylum seekers from these regions were significantly lower than in western Europe, but this did not prevent Okamura and other leaders from successfully claiming that this influx was an imminent threat to European culture, its traditions, and social and economic systems, as well as the health, lives, and identity of the Czech people. In this way, the SPD's strategy has been to fuel hatred towards non-European immigrants, particularly Muslims, by portraying them as members of homogeneous groups that will never be successfully assimilated into Czech society.[14]

During the Covid-19 pandemic and following Russia's invasion of Ukraine in 2022, the SPD also intensified its efforts to win new voters by spreading disinformation and conspiracy theories.[15] As a result of these activities, the party attracted increased scrutiny by the Ministry of the Interior. Its name has become a recurrent feature of the ministry's reports on the role of extremist groups in spreading inflammatory rhetoric in Czech society.[16]

Okamura's Language of Freedom

Let us now have a deeper look at Okamura's use of the word "freedom," the theme that he has made the centerpiece of his efforts to present a positive image of the SPD's far-right orientation. After all, it is the first word in the name of his political party. Okamura's message to his supporters is that he represents the good face of Czech democracy by defending human rights and freedoms against the purported threats of a "totalitarian ideology" that was nurtured by a perverted form of liberal democracy. From a strategic perspective, this approach has made perfect sense because the country's commitment to democracy is regarded as incontestable by most of the population. According to the Freedom House's freedom rating in 2023, the Czech Republic scored 92 out of 100, placing it among the freest countries in the world.[17] Yet there also seems to be a "schizophrenic" side to Okamura's description of the SPD's stands. On the one hand, he has achieved notoriety for his condemnation of the government's policies. On the other hand, he has justified his attacks by calling for the regime's adherence to the EU Charter of Fundamental Rights and Freedoms, which is consistent with the constitutional order of the Czech Republic and inspired by the Universal Declaration of Human Rights. The Charter is notable for its sweeping commitment to human dignity, freedom of thought, conscience, and religion, a right to liberty and security, and the right to asylum.[18]

In particular, Okamura has put the Charter's guarantee of free expression at the center of his party's agenda. "The SPD firmly stands behind Article 17 of the Charter of Fundamental Rights and Freedoms," he has said, "which unequivocally states in Paragraph 3: 'Censorship is inadmissible.'"[19] In fact, he advocates for almost absolute freedom of speech, with only a few exceptions. He agrees that defamation, lying, spreading alarmist news, calls to violence, terrorism, and genocide should be punished. Nonetheless, he maintains that the regulation of any other form of free speech is illegitimate. Additionally, Okamura argues that even in those cases where regulation might seem justifiable, it should be applied only if someone feels threatened or is harmed. Such cases should be adjudicated under criminal and civil law. Under these conditions, it is possible that only calls for and in support of terrorism and genocide can be fully regulated. Thus, Okamura is highly critical of any other regulation, despite the fact that he claims to accept legitimate interference with freedom of speech according to existing laws and the Charter of Fundamental Rights and Freedoms.[20]

Okamura has had good reasons for focusing on this issue. The Charter of Fundamental Rights and Freedoms also specifies, "freedom of expression and the right to seek and disseminate information may be limited by law in the case of measures essential in a democratic society for protecting the rights and freedoms of others, the security of the State, public security, public health, and morality."[21] The limitations are also present in the Universal Declaration of Human Rights, on which the Charter is based. The Declaration states:

> Public authorities may restrict this right if they can demonstrate that their action is lawful, necessary, and proportionate in order to: protect national security, territorial integrity (the borders of the state), or public safety; prevent disorder or crime; protect health or morals; protect the rights and reputations of other people; prevent the disclosure of information received in confidence; maintain the authority and impartiality of judges.[22]

Moreover, the Criminal Code of the Czech Republic also provides significant room for applying these restrictions, defining acts as criminal in a variety of cases, including defamatory statements against national, ethnic, and racial groups and their beliefs; incitement of hatred against any group of people or the restriction of its rights and freedoms; spreading dangerous information; slander; the denial, questioning, approval, and justification of genocide, crimes against humanity, and war crimes; expression of sympathies towards movements aimed at suppressing human rights and freedoms. The Criminal Code also penalizes public expressions of racism, antisemitism, xenophobia, and the incitement of violence or hatred. In the European context, all of this behavior is contrary to the Universal Declaration of Human Rights.[23]

It is precisely in the context of punishing incitement to hatred where Okamura defines his position as the true defender of freedom of speech. In this case, he may seem to contradict himself when he simultaneously states that he accepts interference with freedom of speech according to existing laws and the Charter of Fundamental Rights and Freedoms. Yet, he then goes on to defend his own party by claiming that politicians who seek to apply restrictions on hate speech are only interested in limiting the free speech of critics of Islam, immigration, and the European Union.[24]

An example of Okamura's manipulative framing of the regulation of hate speech can be seen in an interview from 2021, where he relativizes the concept of "hate" to justify inflammatory language against immigrants and religious minorities. According to Okamura,

> Hate is a subjective concept. Hatred towards someone can be induced even by writing the truth about that person. When a journalist writes an article about a pedophile murderer, it will certainly cause many people to hate that pedophile murderer. When someone writes an article about Muslim immigrants gang-raping a girl, a lot of people will hate those Muslim immigrants.

But, Okamura adds, "the responsibility for the resulting hatred lies with these criminals, not those who provide information about it. And if the actions of these criminals cause hatred, it's no wonder."[25] In this way, Okamura denies that someone can actually incite hatred based on racist or xenophobic prejudices.

In manipulating the meaning of the word "hate," Okamura naturally sidesteps the many serious cases in which individuals have been attacked solely for belonging to a certain group. Rather than defend these victims, Okamura even goes so far as to say that punishment should be reserved for the mainstream media for deliberately inciting hatred against the SPD by lying and slandering the party. For the record, we should note that Okamura has never been above lying to get his way. Much of the reporting about his distortions of the truth is, in fact, well founded. To cite one example, on July 3, 2020, Okamura made the following comment in response to a video shared on social media: "Horrible. Immigrants attacked a woman in Lisbon, Portugal. We must not allow this in our country! The SPD movement says clearly—Stop immigration, stop violence!"[26] The video purportedly showed a woman being attacked by immigrants at a Lisbon train station. However, according to the Poligrafo website, the video was actually related to an incident where the alleged victim was the aggressor. The woman was intoxicated, behaving aggressively on the train, and attacking people. The video shows the intervention and immobilization of the woman until the arrival of the police.[27] Despite this fact, Okamura's penchant for spreading false information is evidenced by the fact that both the video and his comment remain available on his Facebook page.

Another example is a Facebook post from October 4, 2018, in which Okamura stated, "In recent days, rare cases of West Nile fever and monkey plague have appeared in European Union countries. Four people have died, including one Czech woman. These cases are undoubtedly related to illegal migration." Then, Okamura went on to praise the SPD, noting that his movement had been "warning for a long time that enormous health risks to the population of Europe are directly related to the EU's immigration policy. Health risks with an impact that is difficult to predict in advance." The SPD, he added, was "the only parliamentary force that unequivocally rejects the EU's migration policy."[28] Afterwards, Okamura's claims were contested by health experts who stated that there was no such thing as monkey plague, pointing out that Okamura may have confused the words with monkeypox. Furthermore, they stated that the occurrence of these cases had no connection to illegal migration.[29] Despite the misinformation, this post remains accessible as well.

Additionally, Okamura has frequently used his right to free speech to justify the rejection of "the other." This has allowed him to promote hatred, polarization, Islamophobia, and conspiratorial thinking, as well as to undermine the authority of the state. In this way, he utilizes the defense of free speech as a vehicle to justify what is actually offensive speech. The more Okamura has succeeded in normalizing this language, the more adept he has become in portraying illiberal and anti-liberal agendas in a positive light. Thus, the rights of the individual are ensured only if they fit within his ideological agenda. Consider the way Okamura twists the logic of free speech to undermine demands for gender equality. "The insane gender ideology promoted by political elites, journalists, and non-profit activists," he warns, "claims that gender is a social construct (and freely chosen and changeable), not a biological given. Social engineers then want boys to play with dolls, wear dresses and, in adulthood, to breastfeed or give birth to children. This is against nature and against common sense." Then, he uses this language to promote the SPD. "The SPD movement," he declares, "clearly defends traditional values and freedom of speech and the freedom to have one's opinion against such nonsense and against the new totalitarianism!"[30] In fact, the denigration of "the other" has deep roots in the SPD. One of the party's most incendiary claims can be found in an infamous Facebook post from 2015: "Guide to Protection against Islam." In the post, the party advised people to raise dogs and pigs and take them for walks around mosques and other places frequented by Muslims.[31]

As an example of the Czech government's supposed desire to punish anyone for exposing the truth about Islam, Okamura has cited the case of Karla Maříková, an SPD member of Parliament, who was investigated for her remarks about Muslim immigrants. In an inflammatory statement, Maříková had declared:

> It is prohibited to import invasive non-native species of plants and animals into the EU. Muslim immigrants are also not the original inhabitants of Europe and, like invasive species, they represent the unexpected spread and gradual displacement of Europe's original inhabitants. Therefore, they should also be banned from entering the EU.[32]

The investigation of this case was eventually dropped.

At the root of all of these claims is the politically opportunistic language of victimhood. In this portrayal of the supposed reality of Czech liberal democracy, Okamura contends that any dissent from mainstream narratives is grounds for punishment. According to him, even criticizing the EU is off limits. "Neo-Marxists, liberal democrats, and sunshiners," Okamura declares, "are full of talk about democracy, freedom, and tolerance, but when you don't support the European Union for eternity and instead defend the nation-state, patriotism, and traditional values, according to them, you are a Nazi or a racist who has no rights and needs to be eliminated."[33]

In 2022, the SPD's references to the topic of freedom of speech and censorship gained greater intensity in connection with Russia's invasion of Ukraine. At a time when both the Czech government and other European states were implementing measures to counteract the spread of disinformation by pro-Kremlin sources, the SPD spoke out against supplying weapons to Ukraine and campaigned to withhold financial support for the country. To justify their position, the party's representatives even expressed doubt about the massacres of civilians in Ukraine. On numerous occasions, Okamura himself downplayed the seriousness of the conflict, even incorrectly stating that it was only taking place in one part of the territory of Ukraine.[34] In this context, the SPD condemned the Czech government of suppressing free speech when it issued a controversial recommendation on February 25, 2022, to temporarily shut down the websites of media outlets that were spreading disinformation. Various NGOs and commercial companies immediately complied with the recommendation.[35] Selected Russian websites were blocked for three months. In addition, the European Council issued specific instructions to shut down RT and Sputnik News as official Russian propaganda channels. On these occasions, the SPD was joined by other political groups in denouncing these acts on the grounds that they lacked legal justification.

Going beyond denouncing these specific restrictions, Okamura has repeatedly manipulated the vocabulary of liberalism to condemn any steps to combat illegal and harmful media content, including disinformation. He has repeatedly labeled legislation created for this purpose at both the European level (primarily the Code of Principles for Combating Disinformation and the Digital Services Act) and similar national initiatives as violations of human rights and characterized them as tools to silence patriotic opinions and inconvenient facts.[36] In particular, he has accused the government of usurping the right to determine what can and cannot be said.[37]

It is easy to understand why Okamura and the SPD have felt an acute need to take these stands. All efforts to crack down on illegal and harmful content affect the SPD and its reach into the virtual space through disinformation media outlets and social networks. The definition of a disinformation media outlet is loose; it can be defined as any platform that creates false or manipulative content that either contradicts acceptable standards of journalism or that amplifies propaganda (in the Czech Republic it is dominantly pro-Kremlin propaganda). Because controversial positions of all kinds can be classified as harmful, the SPD has been joined in opposing these policies by communists and even Babiš's supporters who fear that they can be affected as well.

The SPD also has good reason to fear that its electoral chances could be impaired by these measures because it has a much better chance of reaching voters on these sites than if it were confined to using mainstream media. In fact, the data we have collected for 2019 clearly indicate that the followers of "disinformation media" sources tend to support populist and protest parties.[38] Ironically, despite the SPD's complaints, the owners of the media outlets it relies upon have never faced censorship or legal prosecution for their activities, except for those affected by the temporary shutdown at the onset of the war in Ukraine.

Okamura is particularly critical of social network providers. According to Okamura, there is no justification for limiting the dissemination of information and opinions on social networks, with the exception of cases involving terrorism and genocide. He criticizes Facebook and Google for deleting posts, arguing that this leads to unbalanced content and prevents citizens from forming their own opinions due to insufficient and misleading information.[39] However, his objections are ironic on two levels. First, social network algorithms are designed to serve different objectives than achieving balance and diversity of opinions. They actually have the effect of creating information bubbles. To keep users on their platforms for as long as possible, they provide content which they believe will be of interest to them based on their online activities. Interestingly, it seems that Okamura does not consider this particular aspect of these platforms problematic since he does not address it in the context of regulating social networks. Second, Okamura has made a concerted effort of his own to minimize discussion and suppress the expression of diverse opinions on his official Facebook page. Blocking users and hiding critical posts have given rise to a Facebook subculture known as "Tomio Okamura Banned Us."[40] It is worth mentioning that YouTube deleted Okamura's profile in 2020 after repeated violations of its rules, a step that he now uses to cement his claims to victimhood. For the same reason, Facebook has also threatened to close his account. However, none of his posts have ever been deleted, or at least he has never mentioned such a case.

Okamura's Instrumentalization of the "Totalitarian" Threat to Freedom and Democracy

In this section, I shall describe how Okamura's defense of free speech is undergirded by his argument that establishment politicians who claim to support liberal democracy in the Czech Republic are no different than Czechoslovakia's fascist and communist governments before 1989. I argue that this characterization of the past allows him to avoid the appearance that his claims are inconsistent. By describing Czech politicians as totalitarian, he can then monopolize the language of freedom and toleration. I will also show how this approach allows him to argue that democracy is exclusively instantiated by his political movement.

Framing the current state of freedom of speech in the Czech Republic as a deprivation of freedom and censorship has given Okamura the opportunity to maintain that any attempts to regulate illegal and harmful content in response to hostile actions by state and non-state actors amount to a return to the totalitarian practices of Czechoslovakia's pre-1989 communist dictatorship. His use of provocative words such as "snitching on the internet" or "squealing" evoke unpleasant memories for Czechs. Okamura has also provoked his followers with comments such as "it is incredible where we return" or "we return to the reality of the 1950s." The 1950s was a time of particularly harsh repression in Czechoslovakia, when many innocent people were sentenced to death in the communist regime's political trials. By employing this discourse, Okamura portrays the current democratic regime's efforts to prevent the spread of disinformation as a similar attempt to silence opposing opinions and impose censorship. Similarly, Okamura has also looked to a more distant past to justify his claims. He has described the Czech government's establishment of state bodies to combat disinformation or hate speech—such as the Ministry of the Interior's Center for Hybrid Threats and the National Headquarters against Terrorism, Extremism, and Cybercrime—as indicators of the return of fascism. In all these cases, Okamura's public message is straightforward: Although the country's previous totalitarian regimes have fallen, nothing has truly changed. Current politicians are simply continuing the policies of the past.

In addition, symbolism and demonization play a significant role in Okamura's rhetorical techniques.[41] He bolsters his warnings of a return to totalitarianism by utilizing terms such as "neo-Marxists," "Fascists," and the invocation of Adolf Hitler's name to amplify his message. "What is happening in the Czech Republic regarding the restriction of freedom of opinion," he has declared, "is a crystal-clear manifestation of totalitarianism and fascism, with power-hungry Euro-fascist boys tightening the screws on us more and more. We must fight for the remaining elements of freedom as much as we can."[42] Okamura assigns these labels to politicians in both the governing and opposition parties to emphasize who the real enemies of the people are. Naturally, he excludes the SPD, as the SPD is the only right choice for voters. To convey the seriousness of these supposed dangers, Okamura routinely cites examples of individuals who suffered under the repressive policies of the old communist dictatorship. For example, he has singled out the well-known case of Milada Horáková, a female victim of the political trials of the 1950s who was sentenced to death on the basis of fabricated charges of conspiracy and treason. Prominent figures in the West, including Albert Einstein, Eleanor Roosevelt, and Winston Churchill, petitioned for her life, but to no avail, and Horáková was executed by hanging in 1950. Incredibly, Okamura has then likened the victims of such political trials to the Czech government's investigation of the SPD parliamentarian, Karla Maříková, as well as the blocking of his personal YouTube channel.

Okamura's explanation for why the SPD is mentioned in the Ministry of Interior's annual reports on extremism is also evidence of a conspiratorial element in his thinking. Allegedly, the Ministry has taken this step simply to allow the intelligence services and the police to monitor the party.[43] All in all, Okamura contends, these actions prove that the current power elite is seeking to establish a totalitarian "New World Order" in the name of liberal democracy.[44]

Additionally, Okamura blames the Czech government for shaming the expositors of any opinions that do not align with its policies. Those who express controversial views are alleged to be racists, Nazis, or Fascists within liberal democracy. He even accuses the regime of engaging in mind control, indoctrination, and persecution. In this way, his arguments align with what the far-right thinker Aleksandr Dugin calls "totalitarian liberalism" or "liberalism 2.0."[45] Dugin contends that contemporary liberalism is incompatible with freedom since it is an ideology that aims to monopolize the truth, brainwashes citizens through its cultural policies, education, and media, and exhibits absolute intolerance towards other opinions. It punishes them accordingly. Dugin also argues, like Okamura, that liberalism's rejection of majority rule, freedom of speech and thought, religious choice, the right to have a family, and traditional gender relations is a new form of totalitarianism. The liberal-democratic state exhibits its power through political correctness, "cancel culture," and the shaming of anyone who does not accept liberal ideas.[46] Thus, for Dugin, as for Okamura, the promotion of illiberal policies represents the real fight for freedom.

Okamura shares with another prominent defender of illiberalism, Hungary's Prime Minister Viktor Orbán, the conviction that the nation-state is in danger. According to him, the Czech Republic's power elite is intent upon subordinating the country to a "European Union dictatorship" that will lead to an additional loss of freedom for Czech citizens. Under these circumstances, Czech national interests will become defined by the priorities of Western liberal democracies which, in Okamura's view, are Islamized and neo-Marxist.[47] Although the idea of a "national state" appears to be a crucial element in Okamura's thinking and is apparently linked to an ideology of nationalism, one must wait to see if he aligns with Orbán in providing a detailed vision of such a state that is based on the idea of illiberal democracy.[48]

On these bases, we can see how Okamura's claims about "totalitarian" threats to freedom in the Czech Republic are directly linked to his seemingly democratic calls for a redistribution of power. Under a political system that threatens to impose dictatorial rule, he argues, the ruling elite's decisions have nothing to do with the will of the people. Because the Czech Republic is a representative democracy, citizens have given up their mandate to act for themselves. As a result, politicians are free to act in the interest of maintaining their own power and financial well-being. This is what makes them democracy's greatest enemies. For this reason, Okamura reasons, the only sensible alternative is the adoption of "direct democracy." In this system, politicians at all levels of government will be directly elected, citizens will be able to recall them, and they will be given the opportunity to participate directly in the governance of their country. In particular, citizens will be able to propose laws and reject unfavorable laws through referenda.[49] Naturally, Okamura argues that only the SPD, which is specifically focused on direct democracy, can be relied upon to establish this authentic form of democracy.

In defense of the concept of direct democracy, Okamura employs unmistakably populist rhetoric when he claims that politicians pass laws that go against the will of most citizens. Furthermore, he argues that ordinary people are not adequately represented in Parliament because "it is full of intellectuals, elitists, and professional politicians." He adds, using a popular Czech expression, "Trying to find bakers, car mechanics, or farmers is about as fruitful as turning on a lamp at noon."[50] Whereas establishment politicians will only represent their own narrow interests, the representatives in a system of direct democracy would be plumbers, hairdressers, and so on. If such a transformation does not take place, Okamura warns, democracy will end and dictatorship will return.[51] At this point, Okamura returns to his familiar argument about the tyranny of liberal democracy.

Finally, Okamura seeks to assure doubters that the transition to direct democracy will not have any negative effect on the guarantee of minority rights and the representation of minority interests. According to him, direct democracy enables minorities to obtain rights and justice by definition. He emphasizes that the issue of representation is subject to constitutions and constitutional courts, and hence all decisions that are made by the people will be subject to judicial review. Therefore, it is the courts that are responsible for protecting minority rights. Under direct democracy, all citizens will continue to enjoy constitutional protection.[52] For this reason, Okamura concludes that there is no reason to devote special attention to the interests or needs of minorities.

Okamura's Threat to Freedom and Democracy

As we have seen, Okamura portrays liberal democracy in the Czech Republic as an oligarchical system in which power is concentrated in the hands of powerful elites. As an alternative, he offers voters an image of a potentially illiberal and populist democracy that is quite similar to the claims of other far-right politicians, like Viktor Orbán and Jarosław Kaczyński, whom Tímea Drinóczi and Agnieszka Bień-Kacała analyze in Chapter 5 of this volume.[53] On the surface, his claim to speak for an alternative form of political representation does not appear to be anti-democratic. Nonetheless, the consequence of this kind of representation can be the inability to reach political compromises, which are essential in a democracy.[54] Political scientist Takis Pappas has argued that where society is defined in terms of a single dividing line, such as in a populist vision of "the people" versus "the elite," it will ultimately become impossible for the two sides to work together. In such a regime, the majority will always prevail. Pappas argues that this kind of democratic illiberalism will not uphold two of the core elements of democracy: the rule of law and the protection of minorities.[55] Liberal democracy is based on the recognition of the pluralistic nature of society and offers conditions that ensure the peaceful coexistence of different interests and opinions through the rule of law and the protection of minority rights.

In this respect, the rejection of liberal democracy on a values level—which Okamura supports by criticizing liberalism for supposedly prioritizing minority demands, diluting traditional Western civilization values, and dismissing the importance of national, cultural, and religious identity—implies the rejection of the principles by which power is distributed within the state. It is liberal democracy that makes possible the principle of the separation of power according to checks and balances and that ensures that in every respect, citizens' rights will be respected. The application of rule-of-law principles through the court system provides the guarantees that both majorities and minorities will be treated equally. Liberal democracy also has other institutional mechanisms that reinforce this commitment. For example, it ensures that diverse views will be protected by guaranteeing that candidates who are defeated in elections are not removed from the public sphere.[56] In all of these respects, liberal democracy inherently prevents the abuse of political power, as no one can absolutize their group's wishes over those of another.

In contrast, Okamura's conspiratorial narrative about Czech politics, in which power has supposedly been usurped by oligarchic elites of politicians, judges, journalists, and capitalist profiteers who have no interest in reflecting the desires of ordinary people, will not provide any of the aforementioned guarantees. His absolutization of the concept of "the people" and his claim that "direct democracy" is the key to real democracy is flawed by definition. Without the adjective "liberal," the word democracy merely tells us where power is located. The protection of the rights of all people, and especially minority rights, cannot ultimately be guaranteed nor be a part of the regime if the liberal character of democracy, as the ideological source of this principle, is rejected. Without "liberal," democracy will simply degenerate into Alexis de Tocqueville's "tyranny of the majority." If we look at recent public opinion surveys, we can see that Okamura's form of Far-Right Newspeak continues to be attractive to some voters as a result of shifting popular moods in Czech society. In the early 1990s, as I stated at the beginning of this chapter, 15 percent of the Czech population was dissatisfied with developments in the country's post-1989 transition from communism. By 2021, this dissatisfaction had grown to a quarter of the population; these respondents considered the current political regime to be worse than its predecessors. Equally notable, the proportion of those who viewed the current regime as better decreased from a clear majority at the beginning of the 1990s (71 percent) to only a slight majority (58 percent).[57] Predictably, the SPD's voters perceive the current situation even more critically, with 67 percent convinced that the Czech Republic has moved in a negative direction since 1989.[58]

We can also observe a worsening trend in the evaluation of the Czech government's ability to safeguard basic freedoms, justice, and life opportunities. One interesting perspective has to do with how citizens feel about the toleration of free speech. A majority in Czech society believes that people are free to openly express their views on social problems and the shortcomings of government policy. Yet revealingly, a quarter of the population believes otherwise. SPD voters are nearly evenly divided. While 56 percent feel they can express themselves openly—and have other reasons for supporting the SPD, such as the party's opposition to EU policies and the belief that Czech interests should always come first—43 percent do not.[59] The existence of this high lack of confidence is politically significant because Czech society gravitates toward maximizing freedoms.[60] In fact, individual freedom is the most highly valued principle for Czechs. In the five years between 2017 and 2022, over 40 percent of the Czech population chose freedom as one of the country's three most important values, putting it into the same category as other popular values, such as the rule of law, human rights, and democracy. In comparison, the average freedom score across all European Union member states hovers around a modest 23 percent.[61]

The idea of "direct democracy" has the potential to become a major issue in Czech society. Populist appeals, like those made by Okamura, continue to resonate favorably throughout the country. Public opinion surveys indicate that more than half of the population agrees with the statement that ordinary people are more likely to agree with each other on politics and society than with politicians and elites (70 percent). Moreover, a majority of the Czech population (65 percent, with an additional 8 percent unsure) believes that "politicians and leaders have ruined most things in the past 30 years."[62] Only a minority (12 percent) is convinced that elected politicians should be able to decide important issues. Yet, Czechs are still undecided on the issue of holding popular referenda. Thirty-six percent believe that people, not elected politicians, should make the most important decisions, while 52 percent do not know. These findings demonstrate that there will continue to be significant space in Czech society for politicians like Okamura to capitalize on the topic of direct democracy.[63]

In this context, Okamura has found room to maneuver between the rhetoric of individual freedom and the reality of popular dissatisfaction with the record of liberal democracy. He has also had a significant advantage of not having to deal with the perpetual antinomy of democracy, which James McAdams describes in Chapter 1, of having to find a balance between the recognition of individual rights and the commitment to the common good. Despite his claims about the failures of establishment elites and his party's ability to save Czech democracy, he has never held any real responsibility for making political decisions in his entire career. Nonetheless, his views do provide useful insight into how a far-right Czech politician can claim to defend values like freedom and democracy while at the same time taking stands that undermine the liberal-democratic system that makes them possible.

Notes

1 The SPR—RSČ opposed the division of Czechoslovakia into separate states. Thus, it never replaced the words "Czechoslovakia" in its title with the name of the new state, the Czech Republic.
2 Miroslav Mareš, "Konstituování krajní pravice v českém stranicko-politickém systému," *Politologický časopis*, no. 2 (2000): 159.
3 STEM, "V Česku i na Slovensku převládá pocit nedostatečné spravedlnosti 2021," 2021.
4 Miroslav Sládek, "Hlavní referát přednesený předsedou strany Ph Dr. Miroslavem Sládkem," in *Sdružení pro Republiku—republikánská strana Československa:*

Materiály z ustavujícího sjezdu konaného dne 24. února 1990 v Praze, n.d., 2 in Mareš, "Konstituování krajní pravice," 161.
5 Josef Smolík, "Krajněpravicové politické strany v zemích V4: historie a současnost," *Sociológia*, no. 4 (2013): 396–97.
6 For example, the party proposed reducing criminal liability for Roma to the age of ten while maintaining the age of 18 for non-Roma.
7 Sean Hanley, "Dynamika utváření nových stran v České republice v letech 1996–2010: hledání možných příčin politického zemětřesení," *Czech Sociological Review*, no. 1 (2011): 115–36.
8 Sarah Gordon, "Bear Necessities: Czech Travel Agency Promises to Show Stuffed Toys the Sights of Prague," *Daily Mail*, February 26, 2010, www.dailymail.co.uk/travel/article-1253386/Czech-travel-agency-takes-teddy-bears-Prague-sightseeing-tour.html.
9 "About Me," *Tomio Okamura Official Webpage*, accessed May 23, 2023, https://tomio.cz/o-mne/.
10 This reality show provides entrepreneurs, inventors, and the creators of revolutionary ideas with the opportunity to present proposals to a panel of investors and attempt to secure funding to realize their business concepts. The show's format originally aired in Japan, lasting from 2001 to 2004. In 2005, the same format was broadcast by the British television network BBC under the title *Dragon's Den*. BBC1, *Dragon's Den*, www.bbc.co.uk/programmes/b006vq92.
11 Robert Muller and Jan Lopatka, "Far-Right Scores Surprise Success in Czech Election," *Reuters*, October 21, 2017, www.reuters.com/article/us-czech-election-farright-idUSKBN1CQ0T3.
12 Ian Willoughby, "Okamura Registers New Anti-Immigrant Party Freedom and Direct Democracy," *Radio Prague International*, June 16, 2015, https://english.radio.cz/okamura-registers-new-anti-immigrant-party-freedom-and-direct-democracy-8256951.
13 Kim Seongcheol, "Between Illiberalism and Hyper-Neoliberalism: Competing Populist Discourses in the Czech Republic," *European Politics and Society*, no. 5 (2020): 618–20. Petr Voda and Vlastimil Havlík, "The Rise of Populists and Decline of Others: Explanation of Changes in Party Support in the Czech Republic," *Problems of Post-Communism*, no. 4 (2021): 279–82.
14 Jakub Charvat, Denisa Charvatova, and Eva Niklesova, "Populism as a Communication Strategy: A Case Study of the Freedom and Direct Democracy Party and Tomio Okamura," *Communication Today*, no. 2 (2022): 106–08. Jonáš Suchánek and Jiří Hasman, "Nativist With(out) a Cause: A Geographical Analysis of the Populist Radical Right in the 2017 and 2021 Czech Parliamentary Elections," *Territory, Politics, Governance* (2022).
15 Seznam Zprávy, "'Nejúspěšnější' dezinformátoři v Česku: vyniká SPD i Ledecký," March 3, 2021, www.seznamzpravy.cz/clanek/zebricek-nejuspesnejsich-dezinformatoru-vede-spd-i-csakova-148558; "Tomio Okamura a jeho systematické šíření dezinformací," *Atlas vlivu*, accessed May 24, 2013, www.atlasvlivu.cz/kauza/tomio-okamura-a-jeho-sireni-proruskych-narativu.
16 Ministerstvo vnitra ČR, "Výroční zprávy o extremismu a koncepce boje proti extremismu," accessed May 24, 2023, www.mvcr.cz/clanek/extremismus-vyrocni-zpravy-o-extremismu-a-strategie-boje-proti-extremismu.aspx.
17 Freedom House, "Czech Republic," 2023, accessed May 23, 2023, https://freedomhouse.org/country/czech-republic/freedom-world/2023.

18 See Charter of Fundamental Rights, www.citizensinformation.ie/en/government-in-ireland/european-government/eu-law/charter-of-fundamental-rights.
19 "Tomio Okamura-SPD," *Facebook*, April 6, 2021, www.facebook.com/tomio.cz.
20 Tomio Okamura, "Je nepřípustné, aby sociální sítě a EU svévolně cenzurovaly svobodu projevu a porušovaly základní lidská práva daná ústavou," 2021, accessed May 24, 2023, www.spd.cz/je-nepripustne-aby-socialni-site-a-eu-svevolne-cenzurovaly-svobodu-projevu-a-porusovaly-zakladni-lidska-prava-dana-ustavou-3/.
21 Charter of Fundamental Rights and Freedoms, 1992, Article 17 (4), www.psp.cz/en/docs/laws/listina.html.
22 Universal Declaration of Human Rights, Article 10: Freedom of Expression, www.equalityhumanrights.com/human-rights/human-rights-act/article-10-freedom-expression.
23 Zpráva Komise Evropského parlamentu a Radě o provedení rámcového rozhodnutí Rady 2008/913/SVV, 2018, https://eur-lex.europa.eu/legal-content/CS/TXT/HTML/?uri=CELEX:52014DC0027&from=CS.
24 Tomio Okamura, "Okamura (SPD): Evropská unie svobodu slova a pluralitu potlačuje," *Parlamentní Listy*, November 29, 2020, www.parlamentnilisty.cz/politika/politici-volicum/Okamura-SPD-Evropska-unie-svobodu-slova-a-pluralitu-potlacuje-645618.
25 Tomio Okamura, "Můj dnešní rozhovor pro Parlamentní listy o aktuálním ohrožení svobody slova," *SPD*, June 30, 2021, www.spd.cz/tomio-okamura-v-rozhovoru-pro-parlamentni-listy-40/.
26 "Tomio Okamura-SPD," *Facebook*, July 3, 2020, www.facebook.com/tomio.cz.
27 Emanuel Monteiro, "Vídeo visto 1,6 milhões de vezes mostra migrantes a agredir uma mulher numa estação de comboios da linha de Sintra?," *Poligrafo*, June 21, 2020, https://poligrafo.sapo.pt/fact-check/video-visto-16-milhoes-de-vezes-mostra-migrantes-a-agredir-uma-mulher-numa-estacao-de-comboios-da-linha-de-sintra.
28 "Tomio Okamura-SPD," *Facebook*, October 4, 2018, www.facebook.com/tomio.cz.
29 Barbora Mašát Janáková, "Okamura varuje, že migranti šíří opičí mor. Nemoc neexistuje, je to dětská hra," *Deník N*, October 4, 2018, https://denikn.cz/2335/okamura-varuje-ze-migranti-siri-opici-mor-nemoc-neexistuje-je-to-detska-hra/. Jan Cemper, "Jak je to s tím 'opičím morem' Tomia Okamury?" *Manipulátoři*, October 9, 2018, https://manipulatori.cz/jak-je-to-s-tim-opicim-morem-tomia-okamury/.
30 "Tomio Okamura-SPD," *Facebook*, July 29, 2019, www.facebook.com/tomio.cz.
31 ČTK, "Choďte venčit prasata kolem mešit, vyzývá Okamura," *Aktuálně.cz*, January 3, 2015, https://zpravy.aktualne.cz/domaci/okamura-chodte-vencit-prasata-kolem-mesit-nekupujte-kebaby/r~4cd0f8a4935811e4a7d8002590604f2e/.
32 "Tomio Okamura-SPD," *Facebook*, March 6, 2020, www.facebook.com/tomio.cz.
33 "Sunshiners" are people who supposedly support immigration under all circumstances. "Tomio Okamura-SPD," *Facebook*, July 31, 2019, www.facebook.com/tomio.cz.
34 Martina Machová, "Zbraně Ukrajině ano, nebo ne? SPD se snaží vysvětlit změny názoru," *Seznam Zprávy*, March 12, 2022, www.seznamzpravy.cz/clanek/domaci-politika-zbrane-ukrajine-ano-nebo-ne-spd-se-snazi-vysvetlit-zmeny-nazoru-193104. Jan Wirnitzer, "Okamura: Na většině Ukrajiny není válka. Mapa:

Leda pokud za válku nepočítáme rakety a okupaci," *Deník N*, June 15, 2022, https://denikn.cz/900038/okamura-na-vetsine-ukrajiny-neni-valka-mapa-leda-pokud-za-valku-nepocitame-rakety-a-okupaci/.
35 Stella McGoldrick, "Vypnutí dezinformačních webů bude přechodné, to je jasné, míní Fiala," *iDnes.cz*, June 6, 2022, www.idnes.cz/zpravy/domaci/vlada-dezinformacni-web-opatreni-fiala.A220606_124231_domaci_iste.
36 Tomio Okamura, "Můj dnešní rozhovor." Okamura, "Hnutí SPD odmítá snahy eurokomisařky Jourové a Evropské komise cenzurovat sociální sítě," *SPD*, June 2, 2021, www.spd.cz/hnuti-spd-odmita-snahy-eurokomisarky-jourove-a-evropske-komise-cenzurovat-socialni-site/.
37 "Tomio Okamura-SPD," *Facebook*, April 24, 2022, www.facebook.com/tomio.cz.
38 Representative survey on the Czech population (N=1,000) using online panel of respondents (CAWI). The data were collected by the Data Collect agency in March 2019 for purposes of our research.
39 Okamura, "Je nepřípustné."
40 "Tomio Okamura nám dal BAN," *Facebook*, www.facebook.com/groups/1215511288852239.
41 Nicolas O'Shaughnessy, *Politics and Propaganda. Weapons of Mass Seduction* (Manchester: Manchester University Press, 2004).
42 "Tomio Okamura-SPD," *Facebook*, March 6, 2020, www.facebook.com/tomio.cz.
43 Zuzana Koulová, "Tomio Okamura povstává proti hnutí Black Lives Matter. Vyjmenoval největší dárce a má jasno, o co tu jde ve skutečnosti," *Parlamentní Listy*, July 19, 2020, www.parlamentnilisty.cz/arena/rozhovory/Tomio-Okamura-povstava-proti-hnuti-Black-Lives-Matter-Vyjmenoval-nejvetsi-darce-a-ma-jasno-o-co-tu-jde-ve-skutecnosti-630986.
44 "Tomio Okamura-SPD," *Facebook*, December 23, 2018, www.facebook.com/tomio.cz.
45 On Dugin, see McAdams, Chapter 1.
46 Aleksandr Dugin, "Proud to Be Illiberal," *The Fourth Political Theory*, accessed May 24, 2023, www.4pt.su/en/content/proud-be-illiberal. Alexander Dugin, "Liberalism 2.0," *The Fourth Political Theory*, accessed May 24, 2023, www.4pt.su/en/content/liberalism-20.
47 "Tomio Okamura-SPD," *Facebook*, June 25, 2022, www.facebook.com/tomio.cz.
48 On Orbán's illiberal vision, as well as that of Poland's Jarosław Kaczyński, see Tímea Drinóczi and Agnieszka Bień-Kacała's analysis in Chapter 5.
49 Tomio Okamura and Jaroslav Novák Večerníček, *Umění přímé demokracie* (Praha: Fragment, 2013), 4.
50 Ibid., 23.
51 Ibid., 32.
52 Ibid., 59 and 73.
53 For their arguments about the tangible implications of illiberal ideas, see pp. 89–102.
54 Hans J. Rindisbacher, "Direct Democracy, Populism, and the Rule of the Right People," *The European Legacy*, no. 6 (2022): 622–27, https://doi.org/10.1080/10848770.2021.1991655.
55 Takis S. Pappas, "Populists in Power," *Journal of Democracy*, no. 2 (2019): 70, https://doi.org/10.1353/jod.2019.0026.
56 Milan Dolejší, "Halík, Höschl a Kysela: Přímá demokracie by byla diktaturou většiny. Menšinám na úkor," *ČT24*, February 18, 2018, https://ct24.ceskatelevize.

cz/domaci/2394715-halik-hoschl-a-kysela-prima-demokracie-byla-diktaturou-vetsiny-mensinam-na-ukor.
57 STEM, "V Česku."
58 Český rozhlas, "Česká společnost 2019 — Rozdělená společnost," online data set, ver. 1.0. (Praha: Czech social science data archive, 2020), accessed November 30, 2022, https://doi.org/10.14473/CSDA00252.
59 Český rozhlas, "Česká společnost 2019."
60 CVVM, "Politická orientace českých občanů—září 2019," https://cvvm.soc.cas.cz/media/com_form2content/documents/c2/a5021/f9/po191024.pdf.
61 European Commission, Directorate-General for Communication, "Standard Eurobarometer STD97: Standard Eurobarometer 97 — Summer 2022," (v1.00), data set, 2022, http://data.europa.eu/88u/dataset/S2693_97_5_STD97_ENG.
European Commission, Directorate-General for Communication, "Standard Eurobarometer 95: Standard Eurobarometer 95 — Spring 2021," (v1.00), data set, 2021, http://data.europa.eu/88u/dataset/S2532_95_3_95_ENG.
European Commission, Directorate-General for Communication, "Standard Eurobarometer 92: Standard Eurobarometer 92," (v1.00), data set, 2020, http://data.europa.eu/88u/dataset/S2255_92_3_STD92_ENG.
European Commission, Directorate-General for Communication, "Standard Eurobarometer 88: Standard Eurobarometer 88," (v1.00), data set, 2018, http://data.europa.eu/88u/dataset/S2143_88_3_STD88_ENG.
62 Český rozhlas, "Česká společnost 2019."
63 STEM, "Česko společně," *Aktuálně.cz*, 2022, https://zpravy.aktualne.cz/domaci/cesko-spolecne-vsechna-dotazovana-temata/r~be30a9764aee11edbc030cc47ab5f122/.

PART III
Far-Right Newspeak in Practice

5

THE TRANSITION FROM LIBERAL TO ILLIBERAL CONSTITUTIONALISM IN POLAND AND HUNGARY

The Language of Rights and Equality

Tímea Drinóczi and Agnieszka Bień-Kacała

Introduction

Over the past decade, Hungary and Poland have been governed by illiberal autocrats. After their ascent to power in 2010 and 2015, respectively, Viktor Orbán and Jarosław Kaczyński created regimes that cannot be completely and fully understood without referring to the fact that they sometimes used the language of liberal constitutionalism to justify their policies while on other occasions simply used illiberal terms. Of particular note are their interpretations of constitutional guarantees of individual rights and equality. In keeping with the language of Far-Right Newspeak, Orbán and Kaczyński succeeded in redefining these terms and hollowing out the constitutional protections of these rights. Importantly, they realized their goals through legal means, using both a constitutionally and politically legitimate parliaments and constitutional courts to establish an essentially illiberal state.

Orbán has been a master of the kind of Far-Right Newspeak that we have seen in earlier chapters of this volume. In 2014, by which time Hungary could already be classified as an illiberal state, he used this language to justify the transition. An "illiberal state," Orbán argued, "does not deny foundational values of liberalism, as freedom, etc. But it does not make this ideology a central element of state organization, but applies a specific, national, particular approach in its stead."[1] Such a state, according to Orbán, would favor the state, nation, and family and interpret the status of the individual in the context of these communities. Within the realm of an illiberal state, therefore, the rights of the individual cannot be allowed to contradict these communities' values. Rather, these rights should serve the individual's communitarian identity. Because of this manipulation of the language of liberalism and democracy, we can see how Orbán and other Hungarian politicians have acquired the power to put their personal political narratives into practice. Their success has come at the cost of curtailing basic rights and freedoms.

Until the surprising defeat of his Law and Justice (PiS) party in the parliamentary elections on October 15, 2023, Kaczyński, too, presided over far-reaching changes in Poland's constitutional order. Even before his ascent to power, he had been impressed when Orbán's party, Fidesz, achieved its first constitutional majority in 2010. In addition, Kaczyński was fascinated with the constitution-making process in Hungary. After losing his parliamentary election in 2011, he pledged that he would one day bring the Budapest model to Warsaw. "I am deeply convinced that the day will come when we succeed, that we will have Budapest in Warsaw. Yes, ladies and gentlemen, sooner or later, we will win because we are simply right!"[2] Kaczyński achieved this goal four years later, in 2015, when the foundations of illiberal constitutionalism had already been laid in Hungary. Over the years leading up to the election, members of his party were already tilling the ground for similar organic changes.

In the making of an illiberal state, the differences in a country's systemic (e.g., a one- or two-chamber parliament), political (e.g., constitutional majority), and societal (e.g., religiosity) designs, which are apparent when we compare Poland and Hungary, are secondary to the ultimate goals: the creation of a fully developed illiberal constitutionalism and the realization of the "promises" of Far-Right Newspeak. Indeed, the abuse of the language of liberalism for illiberal ends is not an exclusively Hungarian or Polish phenomenon. Worldwide, far-right illiberal ideological movements and extreme right-wing political actors have adopted a variety of strategies and mechanisms for acquiring the space to influence the marketplace of public opinion and make arguments against progressive ideas. They have also used these arguments to defend their own privileges. Their understanding of individual rights and claims to equality has played a prominent role in these campaigns. In these respects, one can identify striking similarities in their appeals. Their aim is not to institute hard-core authoritarianism. Nor do all of them advocate all aspects of illiberal constitutionalism, let alone anti-liberalism. Still, most endorse a type of postliberal critique that "pushes back against liberalism after having experienced it."[3] It is this form of illiberalism that has resonated among both broad constituencies and the prevailing ruling majorities of Hungary and Poland. This approach is based on the reframing of the language of constitutional democracy through legislative and constitutional changes and specific interpretations by constitutional courts in both countries.

In this chapter, we will demonstrate how these actors used these changes to foster an atmosphere based upon the primacy of social homogeneity rather than social pluralism. In each case, they justified their arguments by emphasizing a uniform idea of the "good life." This approach represents a sharp break with the recognition of diverse conceptions of the good life that we would normally associate with liberalism. We will demonstrate how this approach has led to an environment that is different from the early years of the transition from communism. In this environment, some people, such as migrants and non-Christians, are deprived of basic rights because they do not fall neatly into the government's homogeneous definition of supposedly "true" and "good" Hungarians and "true" and "good" Poles.

Through two case studies, the first on the right to bodily autonomy and the second on the equal rights of LGBTQIA+ people, we shall show how the Orbán and Kaczyński regimes narrowed down the meaning of individual freedom (or liberty) and equal rights through a process of exclusion. At the same time, they replaced these rights with an excessive emphasis on majoritarian politics and social homogeneity. Finally, we shall show how these illiberal regimes used Far-Right Newspeak to foreclose the possibility of adapting the law to take the evolution of social norms and values into account. Their goal was primarily to keep their party's representatives in office and, by doing this, engineer their desired social changes. As we shall see, there are some notable differences in the positions of Orbán's and Kaczyński's governments on the issues of bodily autonomy and equal rights. This is not surprising. As James McAdams suggests in Chapter 1, the initiation of significant political change and the cultivation of popular support is always contingent upon multiple factors.[4] Nonetheless, both regimes shared the determination to create a constitutional culture that would be defined in terms of restrictive and exclusionary policies.

From Liberal Constitutionalism to Illiberal Constitutionalism and Illiberal Democracy

In Hungary and Poland until 2010 and 2015 respectively, liberal constitutionalism was understood as a substantive constitutional democracy in which the principles of the rule of law, democracy, and human rights protection were not only formally observed but also substantively. The leaders of the transitional postcommunist governments of the early 1990s regarded liberal constitutionalism and democracy as naturally complementary objectives. This disposition was reflected in the text of both countries' constitutions, which explicitly supplemented the phrase "rule of law" with the word "democracy" (demokratikus jogállam and demokratyczne państwo prawa). Both documents referred to the "democratic state of the rule of law," that is, a state in which all power stems from the people, which can exercise its power directly (through plebiscites) and indirectly through elections (democracy), and in which the exercise of power is constrained by law (the constitution and specific laws). Additionally, by acknowledging the guiding power of both the rule of law and democracy, the two countries' new constitutional systems provided the justification for the protection of human rights.

First and foremost, the rule of law means the need to constrain public power according to the principle that everybody is bound by the law. On both a supranational and international level, the rule of law has acquired a "thick" character. By this, we mean that the rule of law not only covers self-evident principles of lawmaking (i.e., a "thin" concept of the rule of law, such as respect for the hierarchy of norms, the prohibition of detrimental retroactive legislation, etc.) but also makes provisions for an independent and impartial judiciary and the ability to fight corruption. Relatedly, democracy is understood to mean more than rule by the people, such as through free, fair, and competitive multi-party elections (beyond the rare use of plebiscites). Democracy is also manifested in the lawmaking process. This latter function has at least two dimensions. First, it entails the citizens' meaningful involvement and participation, in both transparent and accessible ways, in the lawmaking processes of the different branches of government. Second, it means that all parliamentarians have the opportunity to be involved in the legislative process, including committee sessions and other forms of deliberation. If these conditions are met—and this was admittedly not always the case in the years preceding Hungary's Fidesz and Poland's PiS governments—they provide the groundwork for respecting the views and interests of minority groups and ensuring social diversity and pluralism.

The rule of law and democracy are thus intrinsically connected to the protection of human rights. In such a system, liberty is understood to be a political construct that protects people against the oppressive restrictions of rules. They will enjoy the opportunity to exercise self-determination and free will.[5] From a liberal standpoint, the guarantee of freedom impedes any attempts by the state to impose a single conception of the "good life" on its citizens.[6] In this sense, freedom entails the creation of conditions that allow for the expression of diverse conceptions of the "good life."

Similarly, a well-functioning democracy is meant to provide new resources for citizens to claim different types of rights. "Negative rights," for instance, entitle citizens to non-interference, especially freedoms from state interference in certain parts of life. "Active rights," meanwhile, provide citizens with the opportunity to engage in specific activities, such as voting or running for political office. "Positive rights," finally, offer citizens the provision of some good or service guaranteed by the state and its enforcement mechanisms, including the police, the judiciary, and electoral bodies. These positive rights can include social and cultural opportunities to practice an array of lifestyles, religions, and other desired expressions of personal identity. Crucially, we maintain that in liberal democracies, citizens' positive rights do not mean that the state can encourage or pursue a single conception of the "good life" for citizens. Positive rights merely require the proper protection and enforcement of rights and freedoms.

In human rights case law, rights are generally linked to the equality of all citizens. The classical concept of equality assumes that if two persons are considered equal in at least one relevant feature, these persons must be treated equally—and thus the state cannot encourage or discourage certain ways of life. Equality implies that the dignity of every person must be respected. In this context, true equality is guaranteed. No one is entitled to favorable treatment because they are supposedly nobler or superior to others.

In a general sense, we can speak of the existence of these guarantees of "liberal constitutionalism" during the first two decades of Hungary's and Poland's postcommunist transition. To be sure, if one looks closely, this was not always true across the board. Non-liberal values were present in both states' constitutional systems. One can point to numerous examples, such as the affirmative treatment of religious faith and the existence of limitation tests for fundamental rights, that have allowed courts to limit these rights based on other constitutional considerations, interests, values, and the way that the state's positive role is defined in the promotion of rights and liberties.

For example, the 1997 Polish Constitution itself may legitimately be labeled a mixed constitution since it juxtaposes liberal and non-liberal principles and institutions against each other. Thus, it affirms both liberal and individualistic values while at the same time providing for a more communitarian and illiberal vision of issues relating to the nation, the family, the Catholic Church, and religion in general.[7] Nonetheless, it is highly significant that pre-2015 Polish constitutionalism was at least based on a healthy balance between these provisions. This meant that the state was not in the position to dictate a particular definition of the "good life." This particular application of the need to ensure the rights of the individual and equality has not been removed from the text of the 1997 Constitution. Nonetheless, in the post-2015 era, more communitarian and paternalistic versions of constitutionalism have come to the fore. Most of these changes have been reflected in the interpretation of specific laws and the constitution itself. This shift has been largely due to the majority's electoral victories in 2015 and 2019. Yet, because it lacked the requisite number of seats to change the constitution, it was initially hampered in going any further. PiS also wanted to avoid any action that might suggest that it was seeking to undermine the formal rules of a democratic constitution. To resolve this problem, it packed the Polish Constitutional Tribunal with sympathetic judges. As a result, when it passed laws, it could count on turning them over to the Tribunal for review which would, in turn, declare the laws constitutional. In this way, Poland's liberal Constitution of 1997 was subject to more illiberal interpretations.[8]

Compared to its Polish counterpart, Hungary's ruling party, Fidesz, has been in a much more favorable position to implement changes given the parliamentary majority that it has enjoyed since 2010. As a result, it has largely gotten what it has wanted over these years. Through a non-inclusive and partisan process that has been marked by successive amendments, it has successfully funneled its illiberal views into Hungary's new constitution, the Fundamental Law of 2012. This has included the introduction of positive obligations of the state to act on its illiberal conception of human rights.

Poland's and Hungary's constitutional courts have been positioned to play the predominant role in creating and maintaining illiberal constitutionalism and advancing policies that serve these purposes. Together with their parliaments and ruling governments, they have shifted the balance between the liberal and illiberal elements of their constitutions. For their part, the Polish and Hungarian governments and their representatives in parliament have effected changes that have strengthened the communitarian elements at the expense of weakening those that support individualistic conceptions of human rights.

In these respects, Hungarian and Polish illiberalism has acquired the characteristics of a "thin ideology" which challenges liberal democracy in multiple ways. In the case of Hungary, we can see the emergence of a rudimentary, ideational core that undergirds a distinctively state-driven form of illiberalism. This illiberalism connects the political and legal arenas and defines the constitutional identity of both Hungary and Hungarian citizens in ways that support exclusionary policies, such as ethnonationalism and even nativism, chauvinistic understandings of national sovereignty, traditionalism, and heterosexual values. In Poland, we find a similar trend, aspects of which are likely to continue even after PiS's defeat. The culture and traditions of an artificially constructed, homogeneous nation have been used to justify new interpretations of individual freedom and national sovereignty at the expense of the rights of "the other."

These illiberal constitutional developments have been largely driven by two factors.

The first is the fact that Hungary's and Poland's populist autocrats were always opposed to "otherness." Since their respective parties' electoral victories, this disposition has been reflected in their use of words that dichotomize the relationship between the types of people they like and those whom they do not like. Thus, over the years, they consistently defended their policies by using words like "us," "friend," and "good" Hungarians and Poles to characterize their side. In contrast, the autocrats described "the other" by using words like "them," "the enemy," and "bad" Hungarians and Poles. In so doing, they put a variety of groups—migrants, people who do not lead their lives according to Catholic and Christian values, members of the LGBTQIA+ community, and anyone else who disagrees with them—into the unwelcome category. The second factor, which is linked to the first one, is embedded in a vision of society that combines some aspects of individualism with a much stronger emphasis on communitarian values. This communitarian vision is illiberal, anti-diversity and pro-uniformity, populistic, and formally Catholic and Christian. It manifests itself in exclusionary, intolerant, paternalistic, and misogynistic forms.

There are still some liberal remnants in both countries' constitutional and legal texts, as well as in their implementation. To a certain extent, there are also references to liberal conceptions of human rights. Nonetheless, in both Poland and Hungary, these elements have been undermined over the past decade. The changes have taken place through both explicit and implicit pressure on ordinary judges. In both cases, they have been possible because of their governments' success in packing their constitutional courts with their supporters.

In Poland, for example, the illiberal redefinition of human rights has taken two forms, both of which are considered natural and desirable in certain areas of life and legal regulation. The first is the emphasis on social hierarchies rather than individualism; the second is the emphasis on human inequality, as opposed to equality. By definition, each of these focuses narrows down the extent to which ideas of freedom and equal rights can be applied, while justifying the overemphasis on populist majoritarianism and homogeneity.

In both Poland and Hungary, the consequence of these steps is that their respective governments affirmed certain fundamental rights on a formal basis, while simultaneously whittling down other rights. As we shall demonstrate, this trend has been particularly pronounced in their focus on traditional and homogeneous conceptions of the family and gender roles, as well as their prioritization of communitarian rights.[9] The result has been the creation of societies divided between first and second-class citizens and first- and second-class human beings.[10]

Two Cases: The Right to Bodily Autonomy and LGBTQIA+ Rights

In contrast to what freedom means under liberalism, Hungary's and Poland's illiberal decision-makers have associated freedom with its positive ideal.[11] The positive ideal of freedom means that the state (i.e., politicians in their declarations, the legislative and the executive branches, and obedient constitutional courts) is entitled to pursue one of many competing concepts of the "good life." The illiberal concept of the "good life" includes an emphasis on traditional roles of men and women, especially those supported by Catholic and other Christian groups. This has reinforced an exclusionary approach to the LGBTQIA+ community, one that has coincided with the propagation of the idea of "real" and "good" Hungarians and Poles.[12] The position of women in illiberal settings is defined in terms of their traditional role in society. Women are largely perceived as caregivers and sometimes even reduced to their procreative function. This particular perspective is stronger in Poland, where the population is around 90 percent Roman Catholic and where the right to bodily autonomy has been considerably restricted since 2020. As we shall discuss later, the treatment of the LGBTIQAI+ community shows how conceptions of freedom and identity may be used against those who are not a part of the homogenous majority.

The Right to Bodily Autonomy

In Poland, women's roles are typically defined according to the traditional role of child-rearing. For this reason, it is not surprising that abortion played a significant role in the thinking of the PiS leaders during the years they were in power. Polish women have very limited freedom to abort unwanted pregnancies. However, the way Poland's highly restrictive laws came into effect is a story of paradoxes. PiS's governing majority had long expressed an interest in limiting abortions. Nonetheless, when the party came to power, it did not adopt—or, more precisely, did not push to adopt—the necessary legislation in the Polish parliament. Indeed, when the Catholic Church threw its support behind these restrictions and legislation was introduced into parliament in 2016—a measure that sparked cross-country protests on "Black Monday"—Kaczyński distanced PiS from these measures and said that the party favored smaller amendments to existing abortion access. "We will certainly not return to the ideas of the [anti-abortion] Ordo Iuris initiative," he insisted, "because we consider them disastrous."[13] "I wouldn't support that," Kaczyński went on, "regardless of Black Monday. It goes against my view of what line the state can't cross when it comes to intervening in people's lives." He added, "there is still a matter of some solutions . . . within the framework of the current law, allowing abortion due to the condition of the fetus, particularly in the case of Down Syndrome." Kaczyński noted that he hoped that abortions would soon be prohibited in such cases. Amending the abortion law was his government's goal. "We will strive to ensure that there are much fewer abortions in Poland than at present." These restrictions would apply "even in cases of very difficult pregnancies, when the child is doomed to death, severely deformed, end in childbirth, so that the child is baptized when it is buried and has a name."[14]

Some PiS members, however, were more candid than Kaczyński about what they actually thought. In October 2016, Krystyna Pawłowicz, a prominent former PiS parliamentarian and since 2019 a Polish Constitutional Tribunal judge, announced, "PiS will soon present its own bill excluding 90 percent of current abortions and penalizing women, and providing for shelters for women in vulnerable situations."[15] Nonetheless, such an initiative was never submitted.

As a result, it was not PiS's legislation but the judiciary that ultimately provided the foundations for abortion restrictions, albeit at the request of the governing coalition. In 2020, the Polish Constitutional Tribunal (with Pawłowicz in the panel) effectively banned abortion in Poland in a highly criticized and unprecedented decision (K 1/20 of October 22, 2020). Poland now has one of the strictest abortion legislations in Europe.[16] Since then, abortion is allowed only in two cases: when the pregnancy poses a threat to the life or health of a woman or when it has resulted from a prohibited act. As a result, abortion is banned in cases when there is a high probability of severe and irreversible impairment of the fetus or an incurable life-threatening disease. In its decision, the Tribunal interpreted the 1997 Constitution to mean that abortion was incompatible with the constitutional principles governing the dignity of the human being, the legal protection of human life, and the principle of proportionality.

We maintain—along with most liberal constitutional scholars—that the Tribunal did not properly balance competing constitutional rights and completely disregarded women's dignity, self-determination, and right to bodily autonomy. The Tribunal considered the well-being of the woman as a socioeconomic concern rather than a matter of constitutional liberty. It also prioritized the philosophical–ethical value of the fetus, adding arguments about the dignity of the "unborn child" to its repertoire. These considerations led the Tribunal to conclude that the dignity of the "unborn child" was a paramount constitutional value and, as such, should be protected to the fullest extent possible. This is a very high threshold, which a more permissive piece of legislation could not meet: No future elected representatives of the people could surpass this strict constitutional barrier.[17]

The Polish Constitutional Tribunal's decision led to mass protests even at a time when assemblies were banned during the Covid-19 pandemic and the protesters faced harsh police measures. Kaczyński downplayed the significance of the court's decision. "It is nonsense to say that abortion is prohibited. It is still allowed if the pregnancy is the result of a crime and if it threatens the woman's life or health." He pointed out that abortion was only prohibited in cases of Down and Turner syndromes. In making this case, Kaczyński was also intent upon emphasizing that "the Tribunal's decision [had] both a legal and moral dimension." The issue, he specified, could "be handled differently in practice." But, he added, "I believe that something will change in practice as well. I also know there are advertisements in the press that any person of average intelligence understands and can arrange such an abortion abroad, cheaply or expensively."[18]

At the same time that Kaczyński made these claims, the PiS government showed where it really stood by sending a diplomatic note to authorities in the Czech Republic, urging them not to adopt legislation that would enable Polish women to get abortions outside Poland.[19] The note acknowledged the Polish government's respect for Czech sovereignty. Yet, it also stated that it would be "unfortunate if legislative proposals legalizing commercial abortion tourism [were to be] openly justified out of a desire to circumvent Polish legislation protecting unborn human life, and if these proposals [were] intended to encourage Polish citizens to violate Polish law."

In contrast, Hungary has always had more permissive abortion laws, which it inherited from the socialist era. Unlike the Polish Constitution of 1997, neither the Hungarian Constitution, which was in effect before the enactment of the Fundamental Law, nor the Fundamental Law itself provides an expressed and unequivocal definition of human life or addresses the starting point of human life. Nonetheless, in one respect, the Fundamental Law is different from its predecessor. Article II stipulates both that "every human being shall have the right to life and human dignity" and that "the life of the fetus shall be protected from the moment of conception." Predictably, pro-choice advocates were concerned that this language would establish a constitutional foundation for restricting access to abortion. In the Hungarian Constitutional Court's first abortion decision in 1991, the Court had recognized the legislature's authority to decide on abortion. It justified its decision by referring to the need for clarity on whether fetuses are human beings and should therefore be entitled to human rights. The Court added two qualifications. If parliament were to decide that fetuses are not human beings and thereby do not enjoy human rights, the state would still need to meet its positive obligation to protect fundamental values, such as the protection of life. The Court also gave the parliament the freedom to decide that fetuses are human beings. On this basis, the legislature might stipulate that a subjective right to life exists.

Despite all of these qualifications, however, the content of the first abortion law of 1992 (Act on the Protection of Fetal Life) turned out to be permissive, allowing anyone to pursue their understanding of the "good life" and thereby allowing women to terminate pregnancies if they so desire. At the same time, this law, and especially its subsequent amendment in 1998, also took account of the Court's requirement to protect the abstract value of life. In its current form, the law requires pregnant women to justify their decision to have an abortion by addressing specific mental, physical, or social conditions that might endanger the healthy development of the fetus.

To be sure, the current Hungarian government and the Fidesz coalition have taken some symbolic steps against abortion. These have included adding the aforementioned constitutional provision, signing an international anti-abortion declaration in 2020,[20] and amending the implementation decree of the abortion law of 2012. We address this issue later in this chapter. However, the government has, as yet, implemented no significant restrictions on access to abortion.[21] Nor has there been substantial pressure on the government to change its policies. In fact, most of these pressures came from religious groups in the early years of Hungary's postcommunist transition, with the return of previously expelled religious orders, the opening of church-run schools, and the emergence of Pentecostal communities.[22] After this period, however, interest in religion has played a decreasing role in Hungarian politics.[23] In this context, faith-based pro-life initiatives have not enjoyed broad support in society. Indeed, 79 percent of Hungarians think that abortion should be permitted, at least under certain circumstances; there has been no change in this regard since 2014.[24] Given this support, we can see why the Orbán government has been reluctant to take any steps to create more restrictive abortion laws. The political price of taking such legislative steps would likely be too high. As a result, it is not surprising why this illiberal populist regime has taken no initiatives to implement a pro-life interpretation of the constitution's text.[25]

It is also interesting that the Hungarian government and Fidesz did not play an active role in promoting the changes in the implementation decree of the abortion law of 2012, which from this time onward has required doctors to provide "evidence of the fetus's vital functions" (in the form of an ultrasound image or cardiac activity). Although the government amended the implementing decree, it merely went along with the aims of the Mi Hazánk (Our Homeland) party, a far-right nativist, populist, and Eurosceptic political party which was formed after the 2018 election to fill the gap left by another nationalist party, Jobbik. Critics have condemned the provision, arguing that it puts unnecessary emotional and moral pressure on pregnant women. However, the supporters of the provision, which is known as the "heartbeat rule," contend that it is only meant to serve informational purposes. In the words of the party's representative, Dóra Dúró, the law is intended to give fetuses the chance "to say to the mother with the heartbeat: 'I am alive and feeling.'"[26] However, Dúró has also maintained, "it is also a delusion to believe that the woman has a right to self-determination or freedom of choice. She does not have them."[27]

In sum, in the case of the right to bodily autonomy, there have been changes in both Polish and Hungarian law, but much more so in the former case than in the latter. In Poland, political actors, including members of parliament and subsequently legal actors—in particularthe Polish Constitutional Tribunal—have used and abused the language of rights to sharply restrict a woman's control over her body. The message of the decision in the Polish case is very clear: In an illiberal democracy, women's rights are subject to the will of the state.[28] In this case, political decision-makers have simply circumvented the logic of representative democracy. They sought a friendly decision from an only formally independent constitutional court. And they got what they wanted by using the court to create a veneer of formal constitutional legitimacy to their wishes. The Polish Constitutional Tribunal did precisely what the ruling majority expected it to do. It created a constitutional interpretation to validate an illiberal vision of the "good life" according to which women's rights are reduced to the function of procreation and subordinated to the state's wishes. It also provided a constitutional justification for recognizing an additional right, the right of another, yet unborn, person, that is, the fetus.

In contrast, Hungary has not yet gone this far. Although some changes have occurred, they have been primarily initiated in the political arena and only symbolically in the field of the law. Still, the steps the country's autocratic leaders have taken could eventually be transformed from being merely symbolic gestures into actual law. At this time, it is more likely that access to abortion will become increasingly difficult for another reason. As a result of Hungary's deteriorating health care system due to a lack of doctors and nurses, women will find it harder to have abortions, especially if they are non-residents.

Equal Rights of LGBTQIA+ People

The constitutions of both Hungary and Poland see marriage as a bond between a man and a woman. In this way, both limit the equal rights and freedoms of LGBTQAI+ persons. For example, the Polish Constitution of 1997 holds that since marriage is a union between a man and a woman, this union should be placed under the protection and care of the Republic of Poland. Strictly speaking, from the legal point of view, the constitution does not contain a ban on same-sex marriages or prohibit the recognition of such unions made legally in another country. Nonetheless, the constitution's restrictive definition of marriage has made it easy for politicians and others to persuade their largely conservative population that such a ban exists.[29] During PiS's rule, the party's political positions were translated into legal argumentation in the Polish Constitutional Tribunal's decisions. Referring to the Tribunal's jurisprudence since 2017, Judge Mariusz Muszyński has noted, "the content of the family code, which is based upon the constitution's provisions for defining marriage exclusively in terms of a union between a man and a woman, is the result of a conscious and well-reasoned legislative decision." At the same time, the judge pointed out, "the constitution contains no provision that would oblige a legislator to recognize the institution of same-sex marriage."[30]

In contrast, in a 2022 decision on same-sex unions (II OSK 2376/19), the Polish Supreme Administrative Court (SAC) took a slightly different approach. On the one hand, the SAC acknowledged the open-endedness in the constitution in recognizing the rights claimed by the LGBTQAI+ community. On the other hand, it noted that the "recognition" of these rights would still require the legislature's affirmation. Given the fact that the former PiS government was skeptical about the existence of these rights, it is not surprising that the Polish parliament did not advance any legislation to clarify the situation. Therefore, the SAC could not recognize same-sex marriages or same-sex unions made in other countries because there were no legal grounds for doing so. Nonetheless, the Court's decision makes it clear that any legislation against the LGBTQAI+ community would be in direct conflict with the jurisprudence of the European Court of Human Rights (ECtHR). In the case of *Fedotova and Others v. Russia* (Decision of 13 July 2021, 40792/10, 30538/14, 43439/10), the ECtHR argued that the protection of the traditional family cannot be used to justify the absence of any form of legal recognition and protection for same-sex couples.

In this context, the citizens' initiative "Stop LGBT" provides a revealing picture of the illiberal orientation of a large segment of the Polish population. Submitted to parliament in 2021 and supported by Kaja Godek and Krzysztof Kasprzak, two prominent anti-abortion activists from the Life and Family Foundation, the initiative's aim was to restrict the freedom of assembly by limiting the topics that can be addressed at large gatherings. In particular, the proposed legislation would ban any discussions that question the definition of marriage as essentially heterosexual or otherwise advocated same-sex marriage and non-heterosexual relationships. The explanatory memorandum of the draft law has an unmistakably anti-LGBTQIA+ overtone, reflecting both Catholic attitudes and the attitudes of Poland's heterosexual majority. The initiative has been so controversial that the Prosecutor's office, at the request of a court, started an investigation to determine whether it was promoting values that would be typical of a totalitarian regime (II Kp 1035/22). In its request, the court stated that a totalitarian system is characterized by the imposition of stark limits on freedom and civil rights. In addition, it stated that an inherent feature of the fascist state is the subordination of all social relations to the state and the possibility of state intervention into all areas of human life, including even the most private dimensions. At the time of this writing, the legislative procedure involving the initiative remains open.

The intensification of hostility against transgender people may lead to this issue becoming a heated topic of future parliamentary debate. Kaczyński showed how inflammatory this sentiment can be when, in October 2022, he sarcastically described being transgender as no different from making a declaration: "For example, Mister Marshal says: from today onward, my name is Zosia [a female name]. One can say that this is against biology, against genetics, and against common sense and our Christian civilization."[31]

In Hungary, in contrast, the political status of such questions of sexuality is handled somewhat differently. For example, same-sex couples have had access to registered partnerships since 2008. Legally speaking, these partnerships are between a common law union and marriage, and in this realm Hungary recognizes the LGBTQIA+ rights claims more than Poland. Formal marriage, however, remains accessible only for heterosexual unions according to the jurisprudence of the Hungarian Constitutional Court (14/1995 [III. 13]) and the text of the Fundamental Law.

In other areas, LGBTQIA+ people in Hungary have experienced a diminution of their rights to self-determination. In some cases, this has involved the elimination of already acquired rights. For instance, name changes for the purpose of better expressing the individual's identity can no longer be requested. This change has taken place through formal constitutional procedures, and it has been justified on two major grounds: (1) to protect children and (2) to "provide the possibility of living a life in the fullest possible dignity for present and future generations."[32]

Unlike Hungary's first democratic constitution, which only stated that the Republic of Hungary would protect the institution of the family and marriage, the Fundamental Law—in its original text, which was further eroded by the Fourth (2013) and Ninth (2020) Amendments—gives a detailed account of what are constitutionally and therefore implicitly culturally acceptable interpersonal relations and forms of individual identity. The Fundamental Law defines marriage "as the union of one man and one woman" (2011), based on the interpretation of the word "marriage" by the Hungarian Constitutional Court in 1995. It defines the family as a unit "based on marriage or the relationship between parents and children" (2013). The latter provision was inserted into the Fundamental Law in reaction to a Constitutional Court decision in 2012 (43/2012 [XII. 20]) annulling the far more restrictive notion of family adopted by the Fidesz majority. It is important to note that in 2012 the Court was not yet completely occupied by judges who were selected by the ruling majority or biased in favor of the government.

Since 2020, Article L of the Fundamental Law has defined the sex of the father (the man) and mother (the woman) and constructed a "right of children to a self-identity corresponding to their sex at birth" (Art XVI [1]). Related subconstitutional rules were also changed. Henceforth, only married (thus heterosexual) couples may be adoptive parents; a single person, regardless of their sexual orientation and contrary to the previous rules, can adopt children only when the minister responsible for family matters grants a special permission. When providing this permission, the minister must consider new constitutional rules on the protection of the child. As a result, the previous loophole, which made it possible for gay couples to have a child based on the decision of a childcare officer, no longer exists. This course of action is clearly contrary to international court decisions, such as the *Coman* decision of the Court of Justice of the European Union from 2018 (C-673/16.). Another law which was passed in the summer of 2021 outlaws any depiction or discussion of diverse gender identities and sexual orientations in the public sphere, including schools and the media. To serve its advocates' purposes, the law limits or prohibits access to content that "propagates or portrays a divergence from self-identity corresponding to sex at birth, sex change or homosexuality" for individuals under 18 years of age.

What we find especially notable about these changes is not simply that they are legal instantiations of conservative ideas. Rather, their advocates use explicitly liberal language to defend the changes. On the basis of this form of Far-Right Newspeak, the Fundamental Law justifies restrictions on transgender identification by recognizing the right of individuals to identify with the gender of their birth, if they choose to do so. Just as liberals once defended the idea of freedom by saying that it was inalienable (e.g., one cannot consent to slavery), the Fundamental Law now states that the right to identify with the gender of one's birth is non-negotiable.

Especially after 2018, Hungary's constitutional and legislative changes have followed the logic of an exclusively populist and illiberal political narrative, one in which "you are either for us or against us." In May 2019, the Speaker of the Hungarian Parliament, László Kövér,[33] as well as the prime minister in October 2020,[34] labeled LGBTQIA+ people a danger to children, claiming, "there is no difference morally in the behavior of a pedophile and homosexuals who want to adopt." "'Normal homosexuals,'" Kövér argued, "try to adapt to the order of the world 'and don't consider themselves equal.'"[35] Since 2020, the Fidesz government has continued to fuel public discourse about the issues of gender identity, sexual orientation, and sexual education. It has also spread the claim that children need to be protected against Western gender propaganda and practices. In particular, Orbán himself has linked homosexuality with pedophilia.[36]

These attitudes were reflected in the questions contained in a proposed popular referendum on gender identity in April 2022. Though the laws that regulate the issue were already in place, this referendum included the following revealing questions: "Do you support allowing children in public schools to participate in sexual orientation classes without parental consent?" "Do you support giving children information about gender reassignment treatments?" "Are you in favor of allowing media content of a sexual nature that affects children's development to be presented to them without restrictions?" "Are you in favor of children being shown gender reassignment media content?" In order for such referenda to be successful, at least 50 percent of respondents must answer the same question in the same way, and at least 50 percent of eligible voters must cast their votes. This particular referendum did not meet these thresholds. Nevertheless, Orbán has used the referendum anyway to justify his opposition to "western gender ideology."

In sum, Orbán and Kaczyński clearly created a hostile environment for LGBTQAI+ people. The two leaders invoked Catholic and Christian culture to deny changing social conceptions of marriage and family rights. As a result, there is increasingly no place for these communities alongside Christian and heterosexual Hungarians and Poles. However, there are also notable differences between the two countries. While Hungarian constitution-making power has enabled the promoters of the idea of homogeneity to fill the Fundamental Law with provisions denying the rights claims of LGBTQAI+ people, PiS lacked the parliamentary votes to implement such changes. Moreover, there is ambiguity within Polish law about non-heterosexual forms of marriage.

It is still conceivable that the Polish constitution may serve as a basis to acknowledge such unions, though ordinary laws do not. Additionally, the Supreme Administrative Court has supported this interpretation of the law, without however suggesting ways to improve the situation of LGBTQAI+ people. Nonetheless, the Polish Constitutional Tribunal has supported the government's definition of marriage and foreclosed the use of constitutional provisions to address this issue. Notwithstanding these differences, Poland and Hungary are alike in one important respect. Neither state has respected the decisions of the Court of Justice of the European Union and the European Court of Human Rights that affirm the rights of members of the LGBTQAI+ community in both the private and family spheres. In this way, both Hungary and Poland limit their interpretations of individual freedom to the views of an imagined majority of citizens.

Conclusion

In this chapter, we have reviewed how the language of rights and freedoms that we associate with liberal constitutional democracy has been abused in Hungary and Poland and led to state-driven forms of illiberalism. The two countries' political and legal actors have realized their goals in two ways. They have shifted the constitutional balance between an individualistic concept of the public good toward a communitarian focus, and they have changed the balance between a liberal and pluralistic conception of human rights toward a focus that is primarily illiberal.

We have used two cases to demonstrate how Hungary's and Poland's leaders successfully reframed traditional understandings of freedom and equality. These are the right to bodily autonomy and the equal rights of LGBTQIA+ people. Through these examples, we have shown how the substantive aspects of the ideas of individual freedom and equality have been reduced to cover only those activities that are deemed to be "good" and favorable to the "majority." As a consequence, the terms that previously ensured the protection of the interests of many rights-holders ("everyone") have been replaced with exclusionary terms, such as "us," the "majority," and "good" and "real" Poles and Hungarians. The people in the "good" and "real" categories happen to be primarily white, heterosexual, and Catholic or Christian men.

This form of Far-Right Newspeak has been used as a justification for narrowing down the meaning of fundamental rights and then transforming it into law. These changes have been based on exclusionary policies and the replacement of the recognition of the interests of all Hungarians and all Poles with a heavy emphasis on populist majoritarianism and the idea of social homogeneity. These reframed and illiberal understandings of rights and equality, as they present themselves in Hungary and Poland, are not identical to conditions of "non-equality" and "non-freedom." However, we can recognize some of these characteristics in their application to specific groups of persons. Under these circumstances, the law can no longer be modified to account for new demands for equality, human dignity, and self-determination that arise as a result of changing social conditions. Instead, the law is now used for engineering changes in society that facilitate the interests of people in powerful positions.

Notes

1 Viktor Orbán, Tusványos, Orbán speech on July 26, 2014, https://budapest-beacon.com/full-text-of-viktor-orbans-speech-at-baile-tusnad-tusnadfurdo-of-26-july-2014/. In this speech, he uses illiberal state and non-liberal states as synonyms. In 2018, he used Christian democracy but, content-wise, he was still speaking of it as illiberal.
2 Jarosław Kaczyński speech, 2011, www.youtube.com/watch?v=tXlYsu17MqU.
3 Marlene Laruelle, "Illiberalism: A Conceptual Introduction," *East European Politics*, 38, no. 2, (2022): 303–27, https://doi.org/10.1080/21599165.2022.2037079.
4 See p. 15–18.
5 We note here that the Hungarian and Polish languages use one word ("szabadság" and "wolność") to express both liberty and freedom.
6 Katarzyna Eliasz and Wojciech Załuski, "Freedom," in *Encyclopedia of the Philosophy of Law and Social Philosophy*, edited by M. Sellers and S. Kirste (New York: Springer, 2023), https://doi.org/10.1007/978-94-007-6730-0_234-2.
7 B. Szlachta, "Aksjologia Konstytucji RP z 1997 roku. Perspektywa badacza myśli politycznej [The Axiology of the Constitution of the Republic of Poland of 1997: The Perspective of the Researcher of Political Thought]," *Przegląd Sejmowy* 6, no. 143 (2017): 125–50.
8 This has been particularly true in questions of judicial reform. See our book, *Illiberal Constitutionalism in Poland and Hungary: The Deterioration of Democracy, Misuse of Human Rights and Abuse of the Rule of Law* (London: Routledge, 2022), 161–63.
9 Marie-Luisa Frick, "Illiberalism and Human Rights," in *The Handbook of Illiberalism*, edited by A. Sajó, R. Uitz and S. Holmes (London: Routledge, 2022), 861–75. Frick equates illiberalism with communitarianism in regard to human rights.
10 M. Tushnet, "The Possibility of Illiberal Constitutionalism," *Florida Law Review* 69 (2017).
11 Eliasz and Załuski, "Freedom."
12 For a similar stance, see Laura K. Field's discussion of Adrian Vermeule's concept of common good constitutionalism in Chapter 8 of this volume.
13 We discuss this initiative later; see p. 95–96.
14 Interview with Jarosław Kaczyński, October 12, 2016, www.pap.pl/aktualnosci/news%2C671146%2Cwywiad-prezesa-pis-dla-polskiej-agencji-prasowej.html.

15 "Press Information on Pawłowicz Statement," www.rp.pl/polityka/art10898001-krystyna-pawlowicz-o-projekcie-pis-ws-aborcji.
16 A. Młynarska-Sobaczewska, "Unconstitutionality of Access to Abortion for Embryo-Pathological Reasons," *International Human Rights Law Review* 10 (2021): 168–79.
17 This constitutionalized protection of "unborn life" has a similar effect as the decision by the Supreme Court of the United States in *Thomas E. Dobbs, State Health Officer of the Mississippi Department of Health, et al. v. Jackson Women's Health Organization, et al.* Both decisions protect the life of the fetus at the expense of a woman's right to abortion.
18 Daniel Tilles, "There Is No Abortion Ban in Poland, Says Kaczyński. Women 'Can Arrange Abortions Abroad.'" *Notes from Poland*, May 25, 2021, https://notesfrompoland.com/2021/05/25/there-is-no-abortion-ban-in-poland-says-kaczynski-women-can-arrange-abortions-abroad/.
19 Daniel Tilles, "Poland Asked Czech Government to Prevent 'Abortion Tourism' by Polish Women," *Notes from Poland*, May 4, 2021, https://notesfrompoland.com/2021/05/04/poland-asked-czech-government-to-prevent-abortion-tourism-by-polish-women.
20 Geneva Consensus Declaration on Promoting Women's Health and Strengthening the Family; signed by 34 countries, including Poland, on October 22, 2020.
21 See I. Balogh, "'Reproductive Rights in Danger'?: Reflections From the Semi-Periphery," *Culture Wars Papers*, no. 23 (2022), www.illiberalism.org/reproductive-rights-in-danger-reflections-from-the-semi-periphery/.
22 M. Tomka, *Expanding Religion: Religious Revival in Post-Communist Central and Eastern Europe* (Berlin: De Gruyter, 2011).
23 G. Rosta and A. Hámori, "Declining Religiosity Among Hungarian Youth After the Turn of Millennium—Main Trends and Possible Explanations," in *Confessionality and University in the Modern World*, edited by E. Sepsi, P. Balla, and M. Csanády (Budapest: L'Harmattan, 2014).
24 "Ipsos: Global Views on Abortion in 2021," www.ipsos.com/sites/default/files/ct/news/documents/2021-09/Global-views-on-abortion-report-2021.pdf.
25 T. Drinóczi and L. Balogh, "Women, Sexual Orientation, Gender Identity and Constitutional Developments in Hungary" (forthcoming).
26 Dúró Dóra, Facebook, September 13, 2022.
27 https://24.hu/belfold/2022/09/13/duro-dora-abortusz-fidesz-magzat/#.
28 Tomasz Tadeusz Koncewicz, "When Legal Fundamentalism Meets Political Justice: The Case of Poland," *Israel Law Review* 55, no. 3 (2022): 302–59.
29 Michael Lipka and David Masci, "Where Europe Stands on Gay Marriage and Civil Unions," www.pewresearch.org/fact-tank/2019/10/28/where-europe-stands-on-gay-marriage-and-civil-unions/.
30 "Mariusz Muszyński: Co załatwił środowisku LGBT polski trybunał," 2023, www.rp.pl/opinie-prawne/art37823941-mariusz-muszynski-co-zalatwil-srodowisku-lgbt-polski-trybunal.
31 www.youtube.com/watch?v=eAjFUIm8_i4.
32 Explanatory Memorandum, 2020.
33 This sentence is a quotation from the news site Kafkadesk, "Hungarian Parliament Speaker's Homophobic Comments Spark Outrage," https://kafkadesk.org/2019/05/19/hungarian-parliament-speakers-homophobic-comments-spark-outrage/.

34 Nick Duffy, 2020. "Hungarian prime minister Viktor Orban demands gay people 'leave our children alone' in sinister attack on lesbian Cinderella book," https://www.pinknews.co.uk/2020/10/06/hungary-prime-minister-viktor-orban-gay-children-lesbian-cinderella-book.
35 Kafkadesk, "Hungarian Parliament Speaker's Homophobic Comments Spark Outrage."
36 Karina Cengel, "Orbán szerint vitatják, hogy pedofíliához vezet a homoszexualitás, a "szexuális szokások" elfogadása pedig a szülő joga. According to Orbán, "It Is Debatable Whether Homosexuality Leads to Pedophilia, and the Acceptance of Sexual 'Behaviours' Is the Right of Parents," https://merce.hu/2022/01/14/orban-szerint-vitatjak-hogy-pedofiliahoz-vezet-a-homoszexualitas-a-szexualis-szokasok-elfogadasa-pedig-a-szulo-joga.

6
WHEN LEGAL LANGUAGE MEETS APOCALYPSE ANXIETY

Democracy, Constitutional Scholars, and the Rise of the German Far Right After 2015

Frank Wolff

It is a common assumption that Justitia's "blindness" secures her nonpartisanship that then carries over to legal scholarship. Particularly during times of perceived crisis, constitutional scholars contribute to the public discourse by opining on complex questions, including on whose rights require special protection and on the possibilities, necessities, and boundaries of democracy and statehood. While these scholars defend their interpretations of the law by appealing to a disciplinary claim to neutrality based on a rational reading of the law, I argue that they are also implicated members of society.[1] Particularly when debating contested issues, this tension leads to academic diversity as well as to authoritative arguments for competing political groups.

But it can also lead to political controversy. In Germany, this climaxed in the wake of the so-called migration crisis of 2015 when the concept of the "rule of injustice" became the vehicle for expressing political paranoia dressed up in legal jargon. Most constitutional scholars have opposed this legal form of Far-Right Newspeak because of the sentiment behind it. However, a smaller group has actively used the term to accuse the German government of trying to subvert the rule of law and the will of the people.

This chapter will focus on this select yet influential group. Its representatives have developed certain interpretations of key terms in the German Constitution (Grundgesetz) to argue that Germany's migration policies are unconstitutional and thereby detrimental to democracy. Their main vehicle has been a type of legal jargon that has helped the German far right to fashion itself as both the voice of "concerned" citizens and a disruptive force against established civil and political structures. Of course, these interpretations have met scholarly critiques. But they have also garnered public praise and presented a valuable political opportunity for the country's most

DOI: 10.4324/9781003436737-9

prominent far-right party, Alternative for Germany (AfD), to benefit from popular anxiety while moving even further to the right.

How, then, has liberal legal language been used to advance far-right agendas in the heated atmosphere emerging in Germany after 2015? To date, few attempts have been made to examine the relationship between these legal scholars and the contemporary history of Germany's far-right movements.[2] This chapter does not approach the issue from a legal standpoint. From the position of contemporary history, I explore instead how the language of liberal law and scholarship has functioned in public debates as a catalyst for the normalization of far-right concepts on migration. In connection with the growing awareness of far-right tendencies in matters of jurisdiction and law enforcement,[3] I examine public perceptions of the role of constitutional scholars as impartial experts in rational matters, whose work has supposedly been confined to "the ghetto of specialized journals under the spell of the Constitutional Court."[4]

More generally, I aim to advance our understanding of the social role of legal expertise. Instead of presenting an overview of these questions, I concentrate on select yet connected cases in questioning the conceptual relevance of these scholars' arguments and choice of terms. In five steps, I explore different strands of constitutional scholars as public commentators on migration. In the first step, I outline the emergence of the concept of the "rule of injustice" before, second, briefly reflecting on academic certitudes in German public debates on migration. Third, I examine the connections between the language of leading political figures and that of legal scholars outside of the disciplinary establishment. In a fourth step, I focus on select views of established academic authorities on constitutional law, which during the so-called refugee crisis gained public attention in the twilight zone between conservatism and the far right. In a fifth and final step, I examine the ways in which these apparently separate strands of legal communication have intersected with the rise of the AfD after 2015.

An Influential Claim

The influence of specific forms of legal argumentation always depends on their context. In winter 2016, the atmosphere of political discourse in Germany was anything but cool. Like many other European countries, Germany had been contending with the mass arrival of primarily Syrian refugees since late summer 2015. At the same time, the terms of mainstream political debate were being challenged as a result of the AfD's transformation from a narrowly focused eurosceptic party into a significant representative of far-right positions across the board. It was a time, then, for myth-making.

Across the board, prominent politicians warned against the massive "illegal immigration" of supposedly uneducated persons into a social system that was already facing enormous strain. Even politicians within her own party accused Chancellor Angela Merkel of "opening" Germany's borders. On the far right, myths about the so-called replacement of Germans by migrants gained traction.

None of these claims were true, however. The newly arriving refugees were legally seeking shelter, particularly those from Syria whose level of education was, on average, higher than that of other groups of refugees arriving before 2015.[5] Contrary to the accusations of Merkel's critics, German border controls had already been abolished in 1985 following the Schengen Agreement and Convention. As a result, member states lack the practical and legal means to "close" their intra-European borders. There was never any plan to subvert German sovereignty. Both war and poverty (in particular, supply shortages in United Nations High Commissioner for Refugees [UNHCR] camps around Syria) were the actual causes of this mass migration. However, public opinion about the challenge the country faced was defined by what Nicholas de Genova has called the "border spectacle."[6]

In February 2016, in the midst of this combination of uncertainty and misrepresentation, Bavaria's prime minister Horst Seehofer raised the ante by claiming, "right now, we're not living under conditions of law and order. We are experiencing a rule of injustice [*Herrschaft des Unrechts*]."[7] Seehofer's choice of wording was remarkable. First, the word *Herrschaft* is typically associated with authoritarian rule; second, the literal translation of *Unrecht* is "un-law," and thus the opposite of the "rule of law"; third, *Unrecht* is closely connected to the concept of the *Unrechtsstaat*, a term usually reserved for the Nazi dictatorship.[8] Previously, only far-right movements, such as Patriotic Europeans Against the Islamisation of the Occident (Pegida), had gone beyond claiming that the policies of Merkel's governing Christian Democratic Union (CDU)—namely to move German democracy closer to the reality of being a country of immigration—were not only wrong but also illegal.

Now, though, the leader of the Bavarian Christian Social Union (CSU), the CDU's partner in the governing alliance that had sent Merkel to her fourth consecutive term in office, had described her chancellorship in such incendiary terms. While other party members and opposition politicians jumped to her defense in the ensuing tumult over Seehofer's remarks, his provocative language was meant to help win back right-wing voters by speaking their language. In a similar vein, Alexander Dobrindt, another prominent member of the CSU, called for a "conservative revolution by the people" to defend democracy against the "revolution" allegedly being propagated by left-wing elites.[9]

Sounding like the controversial constitutional theorist and supporter of National Socialism Carl Schmitt, Dobrindt's reference to a "conservative revolution" was connected to the far right's project of rewriting German history to serve its own purposes.[10] As the key figure in normalizing the conception of a "left-wing dictatorship"—ironically applied to a conservative politician like Merkel—the alleged "opening of the borders" was meant to justify the accusation that the government had brought about a state of legal disorder by breaching the rule of law. In this way, the expositors of this far-right language proclaimed that they were defending German democracy from a loss of self that would be otherwise inevitable. The so-called refugee crisis was, thus, at heart a crisis of legal language.

Scholarly Charisma

These politicians' largely moral complaints about the decline of German society and democracy were supported by jurists in high-ranking public positions. Among them were Thomas de Maizière, Germany's former interior minister, August Hanning, the former head of the Foreign Intelligence Service (Bundesnachrichtendienst), and Hans Georg Maaßen, the head of the Federal Office for the Protection of the Constitution (Bundesamt für Verfassungsschutz, BfV). All of these individuals were professional jurists, and one, Maaßen, was even the author of an authoritative commentary on German citizenship law.[11] Seehofer counted himself among them. Even though he never went to college, he nevertheless claimed such juridical authority by describing himself as a "jurist by experience." With that professional authority underpinning their credibility and argument, they thus presented scenarios of chaos and decline as legal facts.

In addition to these jurists in office, academics from different disciplines played a role in this political utilization of legal language too. As the news media tried to find its own point of orientation in this controversy—and sought to boost their ratings as well—they turned to scholars willing to share their views on the debate. Because of their academic status as scholars and professors, these commentators were often recruited regardless of their specific disciplinary expertise. Notable migration historians pointed to successful experiences in dealing with mass migration in the past.[12] But others—most prominently Jörg Baberowski, a prolific expert on Russian history without any track record of working on the subject of migration—gained instant attention by criticizing the German government's policies. In a widely publicized 2015 op-ed piece in the *Frankfurter Allgemeine Zeitung*, Baberowski argued that humanitarian voices did not even know the difference between migration and asylum and warned that "Germany [would] be deformed beyond recognition."[13]

Shortly thereafter, CSU leaders invited him to share his expertise at their "Symposium on Migration and Refugees." In the preceding months, Seehofer and his party had already begun to use public events to distance themselves from the chancellor. This included, via repeated media statements, the aforementioned symposium, or the invitation of Viktor Orbán as speaker and partner in designing modern migration policies. Seehofer's lament about the "rule of injustice" had brought these efforts to their climax.

Legal Language on the Margins: The Apocalypse as Juridical Diagnosis

The specific terminology Seehofer popularized had initially been advanced a few weeks earlier by a then little-known legal scholar, Ulrich Vosgerau, in an eponymous op-ed piece entitled "The Rule of Injustice." It appeared in *Cicero*, a mainstream monthly journal with a reputation for covering controversial subjects and publishing "edgy" opinions. Vosgerau's piece opened with the remarkable diagnosis that the German-Austrian border had become the site of a "breach of the law initiated by the state."[14] It alleged that the police had acted as human traffickers and accused the chancellor herself of being the head of an organized apparatus that was "illegally" bringing up to 10,000 persons into Germany every day.

Vosgerau's claims rested on the assumption that asylum was not an absolute right but conditioned by certain unspecified "reception capacities." Without defining the parameters, Vosgerau posited an undefined national "caveat of the possible" that supposedly superseded both German and international law. To the extent that Germany's "capacities" had been exceeded, European norms, as such, undermined legal German statehood. Vosgerau concluded that by granting protection to refugees in 2015, the government had, in consequence, acted illegally and was on the path to undermining the rule of law in Germany.

German legal scholars thoroughly reject this argumentation.[15] However, the interesting point here is that Vosgerau did not present his concerns as a contribution to a scholarly debate but rather as a political argument vis-à-vis legal language. *Cicero* is not a legal journal; it is geared, rather, toward an educated and conservative audience with an interest in cultural affairs. One can safely assume that only a select circle of its readers are sufficiently trained by profession to be able to develop an informed critique of his reading of the intersection between national and European law. The core of the article was thus not the legal position in itself but the presentation of a political judgment in legal terminology. It spoke to a sentiment shared between conservatives and the moderate right: Germany was providing a "service" to refugees without taking into account its capacity to integrate them. The article, however, went further. In columns filled with legal language, it claimed in naturalistic and extrajudicial metaphors that the government had decided to "flood" Germany and thus moved to destroy the basis for its own existence. The government was not only acting in a manner that was economically risky; it was violating, moreover, the Grundgesetz. Feeding on widespread anxiety about what the mass arrival of refugees would mean, as well as fears that it would last forever, Vosgerau closed his op-ed with a rhetorical question, asking his readers what constitutional norms the government would next undermine in dealing with the crisis at hand.

In contradiction to migration research and—as we can see in hindsight—the social reality of migration since 2015,[16] Vosgerau's spelling of doom relied on vaguely defined but reasonable-sounding concepts like "receptive capacity." These were deployed ultimately so as to claim an imaginary "right to no change." He used here, then, a legalistic form of Newspeak to set the stage for normalizing the far right's claims that Germany was "abolishing itself," in Thilo Sarrazin's words, through its migration policy.[17]

When viewed in isolation, Vosgerau's article was little more than a radical statement by a fringe legal scholar. What made it important, however, was its reception. Prominent politicians such as Wolfgang Bosbach, the then chairman of the Bundestag's Commission on Internal Affairs, recommended the op-ed on their homepages and even on public radio. While they were careful not to make open endorsements of the article given that Vosgerau was accusing their own party of criminal activity, they nevertheless described it as a "think piece" that was worthy of consideration. Then, Seehofer picked up on the article's themes.[18] Without referring to Vosgerau, he stated that the "rule of injustice" was a fact, thereby turning an incredible claim into a political diagnosis. Moreover, Vosgerau also provided the language to channel long-standing popular anxiety about so-called superalienation as a result of immigration and ongoing discontent among traditionally oriented conservatives with Merkel's course of modernizing conservative politics, by offering proof that the government had indeed breached the law.[19] By shifting the debate on migration from the realm of different policy opinions to the (counterfactual) claim of the illegality of refugee politics, it adopted the coded language of the far right—which ultimately treats the reality of migration as an illegal government policy undermining the German people.

While addressing a specific situation, the article and its reception were in fact responses to a longer process that had reshaped Germany's self-understanding into that of being an "immigration country."[20] Initially rejected by many conservative voters, the coalition of Social Democrats and the Green Party that had formed a government around the turn of the millennium would make this transition a key component of its political agenda. While in the following years this transition was finally—and then quickly—adopted by large segments of the CDU under Merkel's leadership, right-leaning conservative skeptics rebelled against it and called for the preservation of German national identity.

At that point, however, only far-right actors denounced such policies as illegal, and their voices went largely unheard. Nonetheless, their views gained momentum as a result of protests by supportive movements such as Pegida—which presented the ethno-nationalist rejection of a migration-defined Germany as the common-sense response of "concerned citizens."[21] After 2015, such far-right ethno-nationalist positions on migration were interlinked with conservative demands to maintain law and order. These developments shifted the focus from a conflict between multiculturalism and racism to one of upholding legal norms in the face of government misconduct and the alleged "left-green" self-abolition of democracy.

While rejected by scholars, those positions largely rested on the authority of academic titles. Vosgerau was introduced as a specialist on international law, when he was in fact an outlier in his discipline prone to radicalizing public interventions.[22] In the 1990s, one of his op-eds strongly rejected old right-wing elites' attacks on the first Wehrmacht Exhibition, who tried to denounce it as an attempt to attack German identity.[23] In a liberal tone, he wrote that the country had moved beyond those forms of identification and required a critical perspective on its own history. Then, from the first decade of the new millennium through the middle of the 2010s, he published irregularly, mostly on constitutional questions and jurisprudence—also completing his habilitation, which now developed an ethnic reading of "Germanness." At first sight, this might be seen as a contradiction to his former rejection of the right-wing romanticizing of the past. His emphasis on ethnicity as a constitutional factor in German and European law since the turn of the new century, however, fits very well with the "modern anti-modern" agenda of the far right—and particularly with the concept of ethnocentrism which was popularized by the French far-right movement, Nouvelle Droite, to characterize migration as the breaking point of Western civilization.

In 2015, these long-simmering undercurrents finally came to the fore. Despite his habilitation and a few entries in an encyclopedia being his single academic publications since then, Vosgerau started to write an increasing amount of op-eds and media articles of political content. After his piece in *Cicero*, he moved further to the right—making his name henceforth as a regular contributor to influential far-right periodicals like *Junge Freiheit* and *Tumult*, or in the German "Alt-right" blogosphere (e.g., *Tichys Einblick*). The article in *Cicero* thus marked a biographical rupture from being an erstwhile semi-productive scholar to now representing a juridical voice of the far right, one framing political opinion as legal conclusions and turning ethnocentric anxieties into "metapolitical facts."

This led to a monograph on the "rule of injustice" with *Kopp*,[24] a publisher known for books on esoteric self-help and far-right conspiracy ideologies. In it, Vosgerau argues that any legislation in Germany was subordinate to a "nation state's duty to maintain a certain degree of homogeneity."[25] This wording utilizes a major linguistic trick of Far-Right Newspeak: the pseudo-rational evocation of a gradual element ("certain degree") within an absolute concept ("homogeneity") that it then defines as the state's duty to uphold.

Linguistically, the argument pretends to evoke a foundational element of the rule of law, namely the obligation to proportionality, while de facto demanding the recognition of exclusive belonging as legal dogma.

In the monograph, Vosgerau goes on to claim that "national homogeneity in the constitutional state" rested on the "unity" of all citizens "as some form of a community by parentage" like a family.[26] In the German context, the idea of a community (and not a society) of the people, the reference to a family-like "Volk," and the presentation of ethnic homogeneity as an allegedly constitutional demand is peculiar. It echoes what historian Michael Wildt has called the far right's active confusion of "Volk" as an *ethnos* in the "völkisch" sense with "Volk" as *demos* according to the German Constitution.[27] In *Tumult*, Vosgerau subsequently posited a "constitutional right" to "maintain the ethnocultural identity of the German people."[28]

While presented in pseudo-rational legal language, Vosgerau's choice of terms reiterates the arguments outlined by lawyers for the NPD, a neo-Nazi party (now, Die Heimat), in the second NPD trial held before the German Constitutional Court in January 2017, where judges rejected their intentional misinterpretation of "identity" in the constitutional sense.[29] Vosgerau's latest writing, however, has never aimed at jurisdiction or legal experts. It, rather, speaks to far-right agendas by cloaking ethnonationalist thought in legal language.

On the one hand, this was also an act of scholarly self-marginalization; on the other, it connected with the far-right ecosystem of anti-establishment rhetoric, resting on propaganda against the alleged illegality of valid law and human rights, against an open society, and against diversity politics. In an exemplary statement, one Pegida protester would tell the media in an interview: "It is written in the constitution to prevent the German people from harm. And no one follows that anymore." This was closely connected to the statement: "I simply want us Saxons to stay just how we are."[30] Vosgerau's achievement, then, was to elevate such xenophobic sentiment into legal terminology in the mainstream media, ready to be picked up on by career-hungry politicians.

Authoritative Anxieties About Waning German Ethnicity

Other legal scholars like Karl Albrecht Schachtschneider, Emeritus Professor of Public Law at the University Erlangen-Nürnberg, would voice similar opinions.[31] There had previously been, however, a noticeable gap between those in proximity to the far right and the conservative camp within the academic legal establishment. In some parts, this boundary would crumble after 2015 when the "breach-of-law myth" led more legal scholars to now intervene.[32]

Following a conference convened on law and refugee policy, the academic publisher Schöningh issued a collection of essays called *The State in the*

Refugee Crisis as part of its jurisprudential series. The volume's two editors were highly established scholars: namely Otto Depenheuer, director of the Institute for State Philosophy and Legal Politics at the University of Cologne, one of Germany's oldest, and Christoph Grabenwarter, Professor of Law at the University of Vienna and current president of the Austrian Supreme Court. The book's subtitle "Between Good Will and Valid Law," however, indicated a message beyond strictly legal matters. For a scholarly collection, it has had an enormous public impact. Even the Austrian Federal Ministry of Defense's army magazine *Truppendienst* praised the publication by "two renowned legal scholars" as a "concise and comprehensive summary of the legal situation." *Truppendienst* concluded, "Prevailing law is neither applied nor enforced."[33]

This comment followed the edited volume's remarkable words: "The matter of the political is back on Germany's agenda."[34] This was a reference to the first lines of Carl Schmitt's "The Concept of the Political," which paved the way for his rise from being a conservative intellectual to the "Third Reich's crown jurist." In it, Schmitt tied legal thought to an existential struggle for survival between friend and foe—one he consequently defined in "völkisch" terms.[35] While for Schmitt Germanness and the German state were threatened by liberalism, international treaties, and Jews, the far right depicts migration and international law as the current nemeses. Referring to this in a 2016 scholarly publication was meant to bring that image of survival back onto the agenda. "In the context of the refugee wave," the editors wrote, "the state under the rule of law is about to dissipate because prevailing law is effectively suspended."[36] While, as such, the government ruled without constitutional control, the people were limited to standing by and must "silently witness the erosion of their collective identity."[37]

In German, "identity" has a number of possible meanings. In commonsense terms, it is often understood as an ethnopolitical concept of cultural unity and belonging.[38] While at first sight an inclusive notion, it is often characterized from a negative viewpoint as being threatened by migration and liberalism. That xenophobic "defense" against the erosion of identity forms the backbone of the "identitarian movement," namely for what A. James McAdams has described as the "second generation" of the far right.[39]

"Identity," however, also has a constitutional meaning that differs enormously from that first sense of the word. As a key term in Western German constitutional jurisdiction toward the end of the Cold War, "identity" was a demand articulated to maintain the unifying "bracket" of one German citizenship despite German division.[40] It meant cross-border inclusion in German citizenship regardless of East German statehood. In its groundbreaking *Teso* decision in 1987, the German Constitutional Court ruled nationalization—the acquisition of German citizenship for persons not born German—to be legitimate if it was performed based on GDR citizenship law and even though the law itself has never been accepted by West Germany. The goal here, then, was to maintain the "identity" of one German people across the Iron Curtain.[41]

In the first decade of the new millennium, meanwhile, far-right activists—from "sovereign citizens" to NPD members—rediscovered this ruling as a source of legal Newspeak to contest naturalization reforms that would open up German citizenship to long-term resident migrants and their children. By combining a culturalist understanding of "identity" with references to the *Teso* decision, this created a legal-sounding yet unconstitutional and racist differentiation between true "organic Germans" ("Bio-Deutsche") and false "Germans with a migration background."[42] In the earlier-mentioned second NPD trial before the Constitutional Court, the latter clearly rejected any race-based definition of the German people, underlining that the *Teso* decision rather "documents that exclusivity based on ethnic origin is absent from the definition of belonging to the German people."[43] As the German Constitution defines the German people as the entirety of "Germans," and a "German" as anyone who possesses German citizenship, neither the "dissipation" of the German people nor an "erosion of collective identity" are constitutional concepts. The dual pathway to citizenship via birth or naturalization means that the parameters of the "German people" are constantly changing, with no right or need to maintain a certain ethnic composition.

This takes us back to the edited volume by Depenheuer and Grabenwarter. Despite the excessive usage of "identity" throughout its pages, the point of reference here remains obscure. While authorship by legal scholars suggests a juridical reading, the book's first chapters instead connect the rule of law with ethnopolitical demands. Frank Schorkopf, for instance, argues that the "loss of control over the composition of the German population" was rooted not just in waning statehood along Europe's external borders and the lack of robustness in the Schengen zone, but more importantly constitutes the "intellectual mistake of society's elites, emerging from a romantic surplus in their political stance."[44] In other words, the elites' multicultural dreams harmed not only the ethnic composition of the German population but, far worse, the capacity of the state to defend itself against demographic change. In strikingly binary thinking, he positions the rationale of national self-protection—in light of limited capacities and a need for social cohesion—against the "romanticized" and "surprisingly authoritarian" ideas of openness reflected in Europeanization and human rights universalism.[45]

Other contributors to the volume would voice similar concerns. Despite writing as academics, they barely presented any instances of refined legal analysis but rather spoke to more abstract "values." Existing refugee politics, they argue in summary, not only happens outside of legal norms but, moreover, leads to the general erosion of the categories of belonging required for lawful statehood. In his lead contribution, Depenheuer diagnosed the advent of an "open statehood" in which "the differences between sex, parentage (Abstammung), race (Rasse), language, homeland (Heimat), origin and citizenship, belief and worldview (Weltanschauung) cease to matter."[46] While going unacknowledged, this was a (slightly warped) reference to the German Constitution—which in its third article explicitly states that those categories of belonging must not be sources of discrimination. Depenheuer's historical phrasing, however, suggests that until the advent of the "refugee crisis as the critical case of human rights universalism," categories like "parentage," "race," "origin," and "political or religious orientation" had been the foundational concepts of German statehood.

This tale of decline thus inverts the content of and legal-historical context to this "immutable" article in the German Constitution, introduced as a distinct response to both the Nazi past and the Declaration of Human Rights as a basis for the modern international order.[47] In a neo-Schmittian move, Depenheuer demands the reorganization of power for "preventive decision-making" to secure "the civilizational achievements of the modern state," which is now seemingly threatened by both the arrival of an endless stream of refugees as well as human rights universalism.[48]

The rewriting of history via the invocation of legal language and suggestive vocabulary becomes most evident in the contribution by Dietrich Murswiek, Professor Emeritus of Constitutional Law at the University of Freiburg and someone who has enjoyed a strong public presence during the last few decades. Murswiek's chapter revolves around a history lesson on Germany as "the national state of the Germans." Again, he is picking up here on the terminology of "identity." "The government must not," he writes, "structurally alter the identity of the people to which it owes its legitimacy." Realizing the need to clarify the term, he offers an organic concept in response: a state's character, he thus writes, is defined by "the historically grown identity of its communality [Gemeinwesen]."

Rejecting constructivist concepts like Jürgen Habermas' famous "constitutional patriotism," Murswiek continues by arguing that "identity" is an expression via which "the German people has manifested itself through society, culture, and language."[49] Instead of returning to a constitutional understanding of "identity," Murswiek refers to common-sense notions of German history—contradicting therein both general research on nationhood and its imagined nature, as well as the particularities of that collective experience.[50] By bending the complex and ruptured German past into a process of identity-forming self-manifestation, Murswiek's version of history as the source of legislative legitimacy pretends to center on belonging in Germany from "the past" until today, while neglecting the ambivalence and contingencies defining that shared trajectory.

Over the course of the last few decades and indeed centuries, nothing has been as contested and repeatedly redefined as the meaning of "German identity"—with dramatic and even genocidal consequences. While removed from historical scholarship, Murswiek's evocation of a tradition of ethnic commonality has an argumentative function. The perceived decline in statehood and Germanness is, accordingly, caused by migration, as leading to "a completely new ethnocultural structure of the constitutive people."[51] Under such a pretext, the German Constitution and subsequent law fail to achieve the goals to not only organize migration but rather maintain the sanctity of the legal system by pursuing extra-legal goals—above all, ensuring the preservation of the ethnic composition of the German people.

In such a diagnosis of erosion, the main question needing to be addressed is the source of this decline. The state, Murswiek thus writes, "must not aim at the substitution of the nation state by a multicultural society or even a multiethnic state." This invocation of a duty to maintain a certain ethnic composition is not only a critique of a laissez-faire migration policy that we could understand as ethnic pluralization by neglect. It is, rather, a complaint about an active policy of demographic alteration. As evidence, Murswiek cites *Time*'s choice of Merkel as "Person of the Year 2015" because she had implemented the process to "discard the old and agonizing national identity."[52] Citing the acceptance of Germany being an immigration country even by the majority of conservatives as the source of German statehood's dissolution, Murswiek warns against underestimating the threat from a majority of the population being "culturally not rooted here." He continues:

> If the birth rate of the Germans remains so low and that of immigrants so high, as it is in their countries of origin, the extreme case is becoming more and more likely. And if the borders remain open without a defined quota for total allowable immigrants, this case will definitely come to pass in the foreseeable future.[53]

A few months earlier, the leading far-right AfD-politician Björn Höcke stated at a Pegida rally in Dresden that the German people were "fundamentally threatened in their existence by the decline of the birth rate [and] mass immigration," demanding in response a "180-degree [turn] in memory politics."[54] Indeed, rewriting history as a narrative of pride and cohesion based on ethnic belonging is a recurring theme of the far right. While one caused a scandal and the other was perceived merely as a controversial scholarly statement, in a troubling way Höcke's speech and Murswiek's chapter seem to share terms and anxieties. While the latter has repeatedly uttered his sincere concerns about the unconstitutional nature of a Höcke-led AfD, Murswiek's tale of cultural German self-manifestation is nevertheless itself a "whitewashed" version of German history—thus one without "Kulturkampf," without anti-Semitism, genocide, and mass murder, without colonialism, without Europeanization, without long-standing immigration from Eastern and Southern Europe, and most importantly without reflection on the concept of "Volksgemeinschaft" being the historical antipode to modern German constitutionality.[55]

Using German history to imply a grown ethnic communality contradicts history as a contingent process of negotiating exclusion and inclusion (and in the German case, unspeakable violence). In short, history turns from attempts to understand the past to a tool of persuasion. By disguising memory politics as a legal tractate, this translates key concepts of the New Right—such as "replacement theory," the "völkisch" redefinition of Germanness, and the confusion of identity of citizenship with ethnic belonging—into legal language.

Parliamentary Junctions

While these contributions matched the tone and thought of the edited volume's introduction, they ultimately misrepresented its overall nature. A notable number of the other authors called for restrictive refugee policies but neither argued for ethnic homogeneity nor supported the thesis of a (fatally) eroding legal system. Reviewers later wondered why moderate voices agreed to be included in a volume lamenting the "dissolution" of the rule of law. The introduction also summarized them as "16 constitutional scholars concerned about these developments." This was not only the assurance of a unanimity of views that was absent in the volume; the wording also echoed the normalization of far-right protesters as "concerned citizens."[56]

We may explain this internal diversity and claimed homogeneity by way of the dual nature of the book (as well as of the series and its publisher). While some authors approached the volume as a place of scholarly debate, it was also a means of political communication. And it was received as such too, as for instance exemplified by book's endorsement in *Truppendienst*. It left reviewers in public legal journals like *Legal Tribune Online (LTO)* puzzled about how a "professorial analysis" could be "in part so surprisingly naïve."[57] Yet, if we look beyond the individual arguments and instead at their public function, these statements appear less poorly thought out and, rather, as well-conceived interventions.

Academically speaking, the scholars examined in this chapter can be organized into two different camps. On the one hand, we have "outcasts" like Vosgerau who dissociated themselves from disciplinary cohesion by moving toward the far-right sphere orbiting around *Junge Freiheit* and *Kopp*. Cloaking "völkisch" concepts in the language of Far-Right Newspeak, they have managed to introduce legal tropes and warped constitutional terminology into the intellectual ecosystem of the far right. On the other hand, meanwhile, "concerned" legal authorities have relied on their established positions in the course of presenting ethnopolitical arguments as legal diagnosis.

At first glance, the nexus of the two is merely in the eye of the observer. From a legal standpoint, both sides have little in common. Philosophically, though, they share a certain notion of historical Germanness, of a constitutional aim of ethnic belonging, and the perception of migration as an existential threat. To better understand their respective contributions to Far-Right Newspeak, however, we need to examine situations of practical overlap between these different camps. This junction is connected to the rise of the AfD as Germany's leading far-right party and its attacks on democracy as an unjust anachronism.

Neither Seehofer, after his diagnosis of the "rule of injustice," nor leading legal scholars like the former president of the German Constitutional Court Hans-Jürgen Papier, in the wake of complaining about "extralegal spaces in the security of the external borders," ultimately put their words into action.[58] They publicly used a language suggesting a decline into illiberalism but never went to court to defend liberalism. Harvesting the field Seehofer and others had cultivated, the AfD filed an "Organklage" in spring 2018—a legal action brought to the Constitutional Court against the government's decision to not reject refugees right at the border, thereby using the language of liberalism to bolster the party's illiberal agenda. The author of the complaint was one Ulrich Vosgerau. Presenting the petition, the AfD spokesperson and lawyer Stephan Brandner, a known representative of the "völkisch" section of the party around Höcke, opened the press conference with a reminder of the very failure just mentioned: "You know as well that in February 2016, Mr. Seehofer spoke of the rule of injustice in Germany. So, in fact, we're simply doing what Seehofer had announced without following through." Since Seehofer had become interior minister at this time, he could "end the rule of injustice instantly, with just one sentence, because he could restore the principle that the borders are closed and that it is dealt with as defined by the law of residence [Aufenthaltsgesetz] and the Asylum law."[59]

Vosgerau, wearing a tie with dominant red, black, and white colors, a combination best-known from the German Imperial Flag, functioned as the AfD's legal spokesman, discussing related concepts and formalities at length with an expert journalist. In a nutshell, his complaint represented his publications' earlier line of thinking, as underpinned with the ethnocentric arguments like those presented in the Depenheuer-Grabenwarter volume. He argued that the arrival of more than a million persons—"mostly men under 30 years of age, almost all of them from the Middle East, Africa, or other Muslim countries," and thus from a "rather foreign civilization [Kulturkreis]"—would "dramatically alter the composition of the population." Such an alteration, he said, would require a formal decision by the Bundestag. In other words, he argued that the allegedly ongoing "replacement" of Germans required a law.[60]

Similarly the AfD's legal advisor Brandner emphasized that the government had "no right to call the foundations of the German state into question by the mass migration of millions, at the cost of many billions, and to alter the complete system of society or at least, via gross neglect, to accept its alteration." When critically pressed by legal journalist Christian Rath about the function of international law and European norms, AfD spokesperson—and educated jurist—Jürgen Braun intervened before Vosgerau could answer, waving the volume published by Depenheuer and Grabenwarter in the air. "This would help you," he lectured, moving the introduction's claim to unanimity to the political stage: "Germany's essential constitutional scholars, and simply speaking the top scholars—and not those declared big by the media—those respected in scholarly literature have made their statement here and laid it down in brief sentences."[61] Accordingly, the party concluded, "the complaint cannot aim at abolishing the rule of injustice, because that is a mere statement of fact. All we want is to determine it officially."[62]

In a legal sense, the AfD failed. The court refused to process the complaint because the AfD had neither been harmed by the policy nor had it used its power to alter the situation by initiating a migration law.[63] Politically speaking, however, the party benefited from simply filing the appeal: While Seehofer only tried to capitalize from Vosgerau's term and "cockily announced a complaint; we are now, in essence, presenting this very complaint."[64] To the dismay of other observers, the court's ruling was a purely formal rejection, thus failing to take the opportunity to clarify the relationship between people and statehood in Germany's migration society.[65] Indeed, afterwards, Brandner tried to reinterpret the lack of a decision as a decision, stating, "Now, as ever, the Constitutional Court has not contradicted that the Merkel government and the traditional parties are responsible for a millionfold breach of law and the undermining of the constitutional state." And, regardless of any court decision, "also in the future we will leave nothing undone to completely restore the constitutional state."[66]

The complaint mainly served the aim of supporting the AfD's self-proclamation as the "party of the constitutional state" (Rechtstaatspartei).[67] In this way, the party particularly tried to resist being put under watch by the Federal Office for the Protection of the Constitution (BfV), which in the German parliamentary system and public budgeting carries acute disadvantages. The AfD hired Murswiek for an internal legal opinion. In the resulting remarkable document that was leaked by critical media, Murswiek first found that there were indeed indications that the BfV might come to the conclusion that the party is engaged in unconstitutional activities. This, he argued, was mostly connected to the issue of language. His opinion continued by defining complicated terminologies and by suggesting an alternative, less controversial vocabulary. To prevent the suspicion of unconstitutionality, the AfD should, for instance, stop referring to National Socialism as something positive, stop using terms like "superalienation" or "great replacement," and stop confessing to the prioritization "of the ethnically defined Volksgemeinschaft."[68]

Murswiek suggested, then, that the AfD needed to be more careful. The party needed to do this even though "without any right," the BfV nevertheless interprets as unconstitutional the "fundamental rejection of immigration" and the "demand to protect the national identity of the German people." After listing evidence that the party indeed acted unconstitutionally, he suggested presenting the same content in less problematic words. He tried to teach them Newspeak.

This worked well under the controversial BfV presidency of Maaßen, a constitutional scholar and author of influential comments on citizenship legislation. After his departure from office because of his lax stance on right-wing extremism and violence, Maaßen mainly assumed the limelight by complaining about "a red-green race theory" and "racisms against native Germans," against which "we would be protected in any other country of the world by the Geneva Refugee Convention."[69] Under its new head Thomas Haldenwang, the BfV finally categorized key sections of the AfD as "right-wing extremist." In this process, Murswiek stepped in, arguing that now even the Verfassungsschutz was hindering free democracy. While under Maaßen the BfV would have obeyed the law, its new director Haldenwang had instead bowed to political pressure and "acted in breach of the law."[70]

Conclusion

We like to think of constitutional scholars as engaged in meticulous debates about the meaning of terms and the interrelationship of norms on the national and international levels. Indeed, controversies here often occur around "dry" questions of procedure, the technicalities of law, and its application. From a historical standpoint, however, public function matters too. This is more a question of form than of content. For professional reasons, lawyers as much as legal scholars tend to present interpretations as conclusions. While fellow jurists can decode such statements, these claims and interpretations are often read as facts in the public and political eye. In times of crisis legal positions can inform the public debate, yet they can also help elevate certain positions by rendering political agendas as binding norms. Legal scholars become, in other words, political actors.

This became particularly evident in Germany in the aftermath of the mass arrival of refugees in 2015, a situation of great public confusion and collective anxiety about the fundamentals of society. The force of the perceived "refugee crisis" was reinforced by its presentation as a constitutional one too, supporting the unprecedented normalization of far-right concepts and terminologies. As this chapter has shown, legal language was used by authority figures to speak to these widespread anxieties, accentuating far-right notions like "replacement theory" and "the right to ethnic homogeneity" as constitutional categories. Based on the imagination of a "breach of the law" by the Merkel government, constitutional scholars provided the legal vernacular for imaginary social and political consequences—at worse, the demise of Germanness and the remaking of Germany per se.

This created a junction between the formerly marginalized far-right, allegedly impartial scholarly expertise, and controversial media trying to gain attention by putting spark to tinder. And, indeed, if Vosgerau's judgment that "Germany is experiencing a coup d'état from above" were true, one could hardly stand by idly (or even engage in refugee relief). Yet, as this notion proved wrong and as those conservative politicians who had first used such apocalyptic wording silently disregarded it, the legal language stuck. As self-fashioned Cassandras, constitutional scholars helped to transform controversial opinions and far-right concepts into what appeared to be constitutional requirements or mere "facts." This would have a tremendous impact on the public discourse, ultimately benefiting only the far right and the rise of the AfD.

Notes

1 On the concept of implication see Michael Rothberg, *The Implicated Subject: Beyond Victims and Perpetrators* (Stanford, CA: Stanford University Press, 2019), 12–22.
2 Thorsten Kingreen, "Mit gutem Willen und etwas Recht: Staatsrechtslehrer in der Flüchtlingskrise," *JuristenZeitung* 71, no. 18 (2016): 887–90; Stephan Detjen and Maximilian Steinbeis, *Die Zauberlehrlinge: Der Streit um die Flüchtlingspolitik und der Mythos vom Rechtsbruch* (Stuttgart: Klett-Cotta, 2019); Achilles Skordas, "A Very German Cultural War: Migrants and the Law," *ZaöRV* 79 (2019): 923–34; Maximilian Pichl and Eric von Dömming, "Autoritäre Inszenierung und Umdeutung—Die Rechtspolitik der "Alternative für Deutschland," *Kritische Justiz* 53, no. 3 (2020), 299–310.
3 Michael Stolleis, *Geschichte des öffentlichen Rechts in Deutschland, Vol. 3, Weimarer Republik und Nationalsozialismus 1914–1945* (München: C. H. Beck, 2002); Joachim Vogel, *Einflüsse des Nationalsozialismus auf das Strafrecht* (Berlin: Berliner Wissenschaftsverlag, 2004); Michael Stolleis, *Geschichte des öffentlichen Rechts in Deutschland, Vol. 4: Staats- und Verwaltungsrechtswissenschaft in West und Ost 1945–1990* (München: C. H. Beck, 2012), esp. 211–46; Heike Klefke and Matthias Meisner, eds., *Extreme Sicherheit: Rechtsradikale in Polizei, Verfassungsschutz, Bundeswehr und Justiz* (Freiburg: Herder, 2019); Joachim Wagner, *Rechte Richter: AfD-Richter, -Staatsanwälte und -Schöffen: eine Gefahr für den Rechtsstaat?* (Berlin: Berliner Wissenschafts-Verlag, 2021).
4 Bernhard Schlink, "Die Entthronung der Staatsrechtswissenschaft durch die Verfassungsgerichtsbarkeit," *Der Staat* 28, no. 2 (1989), 162.
5 Anna-Katharina Rich, "Asylerstantragsteller in Deutschland im Jahr 2015: Sozialstruktur, Qualifikationsniveau und Berufstätigkeit," *BAMF-Kurzanalyse* 3 (2016), 1–11.
6 Nicholas de Genova, "Migrant 'Illegality' and Deportability in Everyday Life," *Annual Review of Anthropology* 31 (2002), 419–47.

7 Cit. "Seehofer unterstellt Merkel 'Herrschaft des Unrechts,'" *Merkur*, February 9, 2016.
8 Including a debate about whether it could be applied to the German Democratic Republic (GDR), see Everhard Holtmann, "Die DDR—ein Unrechtsstaat?" *bpb.de*, May 11, 2020, www.bpb.de/themen/deutsche-einheit/lange-wege-der-deutschen-einheit/47560/die-ddr-ein-unrechtsstaat/.
9 "CSU-Landesgruppenchef: Dobrindt will 'konservative Revolution' unterstützen," *Der Tagesspiegel*, January 4, 2018.
10 Volker Weiß, "Die 'Konservative Revolution',", in *Erinnerungsorte der extremen Rechten*, edited by Martin Langebach and Michael Sturm (Wiesbaden: Springer Fachmedien, 2015), 101–20.
11 Kay Hailbronner et al., eds., *Staatsangehörigkeitsrecht*, 6. neu bearbeitete Auflage (München: C. H. Beck, 2017).
12 See, e.g., in comparison Jörg Baberowski, "Ungesteuerte Einwanderung: Europa ist gar keine Wertegemeinschaft," *FAZ*, September 14, 2015; Jannis Panagiotidis, "Heute und damals: Es waren einmal drei Millionen," *FAZ*, September 3, 2015; Jochen Oltmer, "'Weltvergessen' und 'geschichtsblind': Kritik am deutschen Blick auf Migration," *Deutschlandfunk*, March 5, 2017.
13 Baberowski, "Ungesteuerte Einwanderung."
14 Ulrich Vosgerau, "Herrschaft des Unrechts," *Cicero* 12 (2015): 92–98.
15 For instance the legal expert on migration Daniel Thym, "Der Rechtsbruch-Mythos und wie man ihn widerlegt," *Verfassungsblog*, May 2, 2018, https://verfassungsblog.de/der-rechtsbruch-mythos-und-wie-man-ihn-widerlegt/.
16 Marcel Berlinghoff, "Über die 'Grenzen der Aufnahmefähigkeit' hinaus," *Netzwerk Flüchtlingsforschung*, September 28, 2015, https://fluchtforschung.net/uber-die-grenzen-der-aufnahmefahigkeit-hinaus/; Michelle Ty, "The Myth of What We Can Take In: Global Migration and the 'Receptive Capacity' of the Nation-State," *Theory & Event* 22, no. 4 (2019): 869–90.
17 Thilo Sarrazin, *Deutschland schafft sich ab: Wie wir unser Land aufs Spiel setzen* (München: Deutsche Verlags-Anstalt, 2010).
18 Detjen and Steinbeis, *Die Zauberlehrlinge*, 28.
19 On early references to "superalienation," see Martin Wengeler, *Topos und Diskurs: Begründung einer argumentationsanalytischen Methode und ihre Anwendung auf den Migrationsdiskurs (1960–1985)* (Tübingen: Niemeyer, 2003).
20 Karl-Heinz Meier-Braun and Reinhold Weber, eds., *Deutschland Einwanderungsland: Begriffe—Fakten—Kontroversen* (Bonn: Bundeszentrale für politische Bildung, 2017).
21 Dietrich Thränhardt and Karin Weiss, "Die Einbeziehung des Islam in Deutschland zwischen Integrations- und Religionspolitik," in *Staat und Islam: Interdisziplinäre Perspektiven*, edited by Uwe Hunger and Nils Johann Schröder (Wiesbaden: Springer Fachmedien, 2016), 23–41.
22 Based on his list of publications available under Ulrich Vosgerau, "Veröffentlichungen," accessed August 8, 2023, www.ulrich-vosgerau.de/veroeffentlichungen/.
23 Ulrich Vosgerau, "Für Recht und Freiheit," *Die Zeit*, May 5, 1995.
24 Anna Hunger, "Gut vernetzt—Der Kopp-Verlag und die schillernde rechte Publizistenszene," in *Strategien der extremen Rechten: Hintergründe—Analysen—Antworten*, edited by Stephan Braun, Alexander Geisler, and Martin Gerster (Wiesbaden: Springer Fachmedien, 2016), 425–37.

25 Ulrich Vosgerau, *Die Herrschaft des Unrechts: die Asylkrise, die Krise des Verfassungsstaates und die Rolle der Massenmedien* (Rottenburg: Kopp, 2018), 94.
26 Ibid., 96.
27 Michael Wildt, *Die Ambivalenz des Volkes: Der Nationalsozialismus als Gesellschaftsgeschichte* (Berlin: Suhrkamp, 2019).
28 Ulrich Vosgerau, "Demokratie ohne Demos? Die ethnisch-kulturelle Identität des deutschen Volkes wahren zu wollen, ist nicht verfassungsfeindlich," *Tumult* 2 (2022): 78–82.
29 BVerfGE 2 BvB 1/13 (NPD II), 44.
30 Anna Reimann and Christina Hebel, "Die wirre Welt der Wohlstandsbürger," *Der Spiegel*, December 16, 2014.
31 Karl A. Schachtschneider, "Das Unrecht der Masseneinwanderung. Auszug aus der Verfassungsbeschwerde," November 4, 2017, www.kaschachtschneider.de/das-unrecht-der-masseneinwanderung/.
32 For an in-depth analysis, see Detjen and Steinbeis, *Die Zauberlehrlinge*.
33 SD, "Der Staat in der Flüchtlingskrise," *Truppendienst*, May 23, 2017, www.truppendienst.com/themen/beitraege/artikel/der-staat-in-der-fluechtlingskrise.
34 Otto Depenheuer and Christoph Grabenwarter, "Vorwort," in *Der Staat in der Flüchtlingskrise: Zwischen gutem Willen und geltendem Recht*, edited by Otto Depenheuer and Christoph Grabenwarter (Paderborn: Ferdinand Schöningh, 2016), 7.
35 Joseph Bendersky, "The Expendable Kronjurist: Carl Schmitt and National Socialism, 1933–36," *Journal of Contemporary History* 14, no. 2 (1979): 309–28.
36 Depenheuer and Grabenwarter, "Vorwort," 7.
37 Ibid.
38 For an early warning against the term's exclusionary power, see Lutz Niethammer, *Kollektive Identität: heimliche Quellen einer unheimlichen Konjunktur* (Reinbek bei Hamburg: Rowohlt, 2000).
39 A. James McAdams, "Making the Case for 'Difference': From the Nouvelle Droite to the Identitarians and the New Vanguardists," in *Contemporary Far-Right Thinkers and the Future of Liberal Democracy*, edited by A. James McAdams and Alejandro Castrillon (London and New York: Routledge, 2022), 85–102.
40 Wilhelm A. Kewenig, "Die Deutsche Staatsbürgerschaft—Klammer der Nation?," *Europa-Archiv* 42, no. 18 (1987): 517–22.
41 BVerfGE 77, 137 (Teso), 150, Ingo von Münch, *Die deutsche Staatsangehörigkeit: Vergangenheit, Gegenwart, Zukunft* (Berlin: Walter de Gruyter, 2007), 104–05; Frank Wolff, "Rechtsgeschichte als Gesellschaftsgeschichte? Die Staatsbürgerschaft der DDR als Kampfmittel im Kalten Krieg," *Kritische Justiz* 51, no. 4 (2018): 413–30.
42 See, for instance, VerwG München, 08. Mai 2019 — M 7 K 17.1385, and BVerfGE 2 BvB 1/13 (NPD II), 295.
43 BVerfGE 2 BvB 1/13 (NPD II), 693.
44 Frank Schorkopf, "Das Romantische und die Notwendigkeit eines normativen Realismus," in *Der Staat in der Flüchtlingskrise: Zwischen gutem Willen und geltendem Recht*, edited by Otto Depenheuer and Christoph Grabenwarter (Paderborn: Ferdinand Schöningh, 2016), 11.
45 Ibid., 14–16.
46 Otto Depenheuer, "Flüchtlingskrise als Ernstfall des menschenrechtlichen Universalismus," in *Der Staat in der Flüchtlingskrise: Zwischen gutem Willen und geltendem Recht*, edited by Otto Depenheuer and Christoph Grabenwarter, Bd. 5 (Paderborn: Ferdinand Schöningh, 2016), 19.

47 See Michael F. Feldkamp, *Der Parlamentarische Rat 1948–1949: Die Entstehung des Grundgesetzes* (Vandenhoeck & Ruprecht, 2019), 71–74; BVerfG 124, 300 (Wunsiedel), 327.
48 Depenheuer, "Flüchtlingskrise als Ernstfall," 21.
49 Dietrich Murswiek, "Nationalstaatlichkeit, Staatsvolk und Einwanderung," in *Der Staat in der Flüchtlingskrise: Zwischen gutem Willen und geltendem Recht*, edited by Otto Depenheuer and Christoph Grabenwarter (Paderborn: Ferdinand Schöningh, 2016), 125.
50 Benedict Anderson, *Imagined Communities. Reflections on the Origin and Spread of Nationalism* (London: Verso, 1983).
51 Murswiek, "Nationalstaatlichkeit, Staatsvolk und Einwanderung," 127.
52 Ibid., 133.
53 Ibid., 126.
54 *Dresdner Gespräche mit Björn Höcke* (Dresden: Compact TV, 2017), https://youtu.be/WDUWh1LfDeA.
55 See Michael Wildt, *Volk, Volksgemeinschaft, AfD* (Hamburg: Hamburger Edition HIS, 2017).
56 Depenheuer and Grabenwarter, "Vorwort," 7.
57 Martin Rath, "Staatsrechtslehrer unter Migrationsstress," *Legal Tribune Online*, March 27, 2016, www.lto.de/recht/feuilleton/f/depenheuer-grabenwarter-der-staat-in-der-fluechtlingskrise-rezension/.
58 Cit. "Ex-Verfassungsrichter: Papier rechnet mit deutscher Flüchtlingspolitik ab," *Die Welt*, January 12, 2016.
59 Quotes from the recording AfD-Fraktion im Bundestag and Ulrich Vosgerau, "Herrschaft des Unrechts: AfD-Fraktion klagt vor Verfassungsgericht!," *AfD-Fraktion Bundestag*, May 18, 2018, https://youtu.be/J7hvBe9tzb4.
60 Ulrich Vosgerau, *Organstreitverfahren der AfD-Fraktion im Bundestag* (Berlin: AfD-Fraktion im Bundestag, 2018), 85. This was in essence also the conclusion of Murswiek's contribution examined earlier.
61 See footnote 59.
62 Ibid.
63 BVerfG, 2 BvE 1/18, 23–26.
64 See footnote 59.
65 Maximilian Steinbeis, "Die AfD und ihr Rechtsbruch-Mythos: Im Felde unbesiegt," *Verfassungsblog*, December 18, 2018, https://verfassungsblog.de/die-afd-und-ihr-rechtsbruch-mythos-im-felde-unbesiegt/.
66 Cit. ibid.
67 A self-description favored by party leaders like Jörg Meuthen and Alexander Gauland, cit. Pichl and Dömming, "Autoritäre Inszenierung und Umdeutung," 299.
68 Roland Hartwig, "Auszüge aus dem Gutachten von Prof. Dr. Dieter Murswiek," *netzpolitik.org*, October 22, 2018, https://netzpolitik.org/2018/wir-veroeffentlichen-wie-sich-die-afd-ihre-eigene-verfassungsfeindlichkeit-bescheinigen-laesst/.
69 Hans-Georg Maaßen and Alexander Wallasch, "Nach grün-roter Rassenlehre sind Weiße eine minderwertige Rasse," *alexander-wallasch.de*, January 16, 2023, https://www.alexander-wallasch.de/gastbeitraege/nach-gruen-roter-rassenlehre-sind-weisse-eine-minderwertige-rasse.
70 "Viele Bewertungen beruhen auf einer falschen rechtlichen Grundlage," *AfD TV*, January 19, 2020, https://youtu.be/rmxtr8lG8hI.

7
FROM PRACTICAL CRITICS TO HATEFUL MALCONTENTS

The Rise and Fall of the Online "Manosphere"

George Hawley

Throughout this volume, the contributors have identified notable figures, such as Marine Le Pen, who have used the language of liberalism to advance causes that depart from traditional liberalism.[1] They have shown how the far right has effectively used liberal language as a Trojan horse, appropriating terms and arguments they personally reject to gain a seat at the political table. These findings seem to suggest that this is straightforward to do. That is, an illiberal or anti-liberal movement can easily make cynical use of liberal principles such as free speech, civil debate, and equality under the law to grow in strength, engaging in an Orwellian abuse of language and not showing its true colors until it seizes power and no longer needs to maintain a liberal façade. Furthermore, the contributors have demonstrated in these pages that there are ideological movements where this seems to be occurring, such as in Viktor Orbán's Hungary and the PiS party's Poland. This chapter is different. I examine a movement that has followed an inverse trajectory, one that shows that right-wing backlash movements do not necessarily have an easy time maintaining a persuasive, liberal framework when making their arguments.

The so-called manosphere, the online anti-feminist movement, has shown that it can be hard for a fringe right-wing movement to maintain the discipline needed to achieve long-term success in a society that still expects political actors to uphold liberal norms. The movement's decline in recent years, which will be difficult to reverse, shows that keeping a radical movement within the rhetorical and ideological boundaries needed to achieve real-world success in liberal democracies can be challenging. To maintain an effective liberal rhetorical framework, a movement must achieve a baseline of discipline, keeping the hateful rhetoric of its radical fringes in check. This is

DOI: 10.4324/9781003436737-10

especially difficult in the era of online social movements. Leaders of primarily online movements, to the extent that leaders even exist, have a difficult time policing the words and behaviors of their followers. Over time, the hateful and unhinged voices come to dominate, drowning out and repelling more persuasive and reasonable people.

Anti-feminist backlash movements are not new.[2] In the latter decades of the twentieth century, there was a growing "men's rights movement" that argued men were disadvantaged in the US compared to women. This movement achieved some notice from the mainstream media, but it never garnered more than a fraction of the attention achieved by the feminist movement. The arrival of the Internet allowed this movement to reach a much broader audience. However, in the twenty-first century, the nature of online discourse also led to people with an interest in men's rights to splinter off into multiple smaller online communities, some more reasonable than others.

Online forums and blogs committed to men's rights first emerged in the 1990s. Some of the writers at these sites simply changed the communication medium of earlier men's rights activists without altering their arguments, continuing to campaign against elements of modern politics and culture that they found unfair to men. This is especially true of writers and sites associated with the "father's rights movement," which generally eschewed the kind of vitriol that characterized the later manosphere. Some arguments were compelling, and for a time it seemed as though the "manosphere" might transition into a political force. Although controversial from the start, the first iterations of the men's rights movement operated largely within a liberal-democratic framework, making complaints that many people, even those outside the movement, found reasonable. They furthermore offered practical suggestions for how their concerns could be addressed.

The online manosphere enjoyed a surge of success in the early 2010s, including many popular writers and speakers in its ranks. The offline manosphere also remained intact, with men's rights activists giving speeches at large venues. This period of growth was short-lived. The manosphere has been in decline for some time. A key moment came in 2014, when a woman-hating young man named Elliot Rodger went on a rampage, murdering six people and injuring 14 more. Rodger brought national attention to an online subculture known as "incels"—short for "involuntary celibates." From that moment forward, the most violent and dangerous elements of the online anti-feminist community came to define the movement in the public eye.

In this chapter, I discuss the evolution of the manosphere online movement and its predecessors. The blogs and websites under this broad umbrella term were not all aligned with each other, and some subgroups and prominent figures disagreed with each other across a wide variety of issues. Opposition to contemporary feminism was their only truly shared theme. Within this ecosystem you can still find traditional "men's rights activists" (MRAs) who focus on issues of equity, arguing that misandry is at least as common and problematic as misogyny. There are also "pickup artists" (PUAs) who focus on helping men navigate modern dating, arguing that mainstream dating advice is wrong. Some websites and writers in this camp are apolitical, and instead just encourage men to cultivate masculine virtues they believe are undervalued in modern life. Toward the other side of the spectrum, we can find the "men going their own way" (MGTOW) movement, which contends that relations between the sexes are now so toxic that men must opt out of the system entirely, eschewing cohabitation and especially marriage. The incels have proven to be the most misogynistic and poisonous element within this larger online culture. Unlike promoters of MGTOW, incels have not personally chosen to abandon conventional dating and marriage, and unlike PUAs, they do not believe self-improvement and practice can improve their prospects for healthy relationships with women. They show little interest in the material concerns discussed by earlier men's rights activists. The incel movement is driven primarily by resentment, offering no hopeful vision for men attracted to its message.

Over the last decade, energy within the manosphere shifted away from those calling for improvements in the cultural and legal treatment of men in contemporary Western democracies and became increasingly dominated by the most hateful and bitter critics of both feminism as a movement and women overall. Like many other researchers, I am alarmed by this development. However, I argue that the latest iteration of the manosphere, compared to its earlier manifestations, is likely to be wholly counterproductive—neither helping frustrated men at an individual level, nor moving the culture in their direction. Instead of a movement with a compelling real-world agenda, it became a morose network of message boards that spread a depressing and demoralizing message to lonely men, spurring some of them to violence.

In the early years of the manosphere, readers could find copious amounts of overt misogyny. However, it also often made arguments within a liberal framework. It used the language of rights and fairness. This was, not coincidentally, also the period when the movement was most persuasive and raised important issues that are worthy of discussion. By abandoning the broad liberal framework accepted by most mainstream ideologies, the manosphere pursued a path of self-marginalization. I conclude by suggesting that, despite its problems and failures, the manosphere may have made a long-term impact on American discussions of sex and gender, given that certain conservative commentators have picked up and promoted several of its major themes.

Men's Rights Before the Internet

The genealogy of men's rights activists can be confusing. Decades ago, the phrase "men's liberation" was associated with feminism and was not considered misogynistic or even conservative. As feminist ideas became more prominent in American life in the latter decades of the twentieth century, and a growing number of women were casting off traditional gender roles, some men, engaging with feminist literature, began to question whether they, too, were stifled by societal expectations surrounding gender. The concept of men's liberation within a feminist framework was somewhat tricky, however, as most feminists wanted to emphasize that society continued to uphold a system of male privilege.

In the early 1970s, groups of men, for the most part aligned with feminists and their goals, began calling for men's liberation, which they claimed would free men from rigid gender roles.[3] Similar to feminists' quest to free women from societal expectations about femininity, some men wanted to be free from elements of traditional masculinity they found oppressive. Just as women should be allowed to be strong and exhibit leadership qualities, these figures argued men should be allowed to cry, be nurturing, and otherwise act in ways not traditionally associated with masculinity.

The men's liberation movement as a branch within feminism was short-lived. Many feminists rejected the idea that men and women were equally oppressed by traditional gender roles, and they wanted to maintain focus on the ways women are uniquely oppressed.[4] Some men continued to focus on the special challenges men face, a few suggesting that men suffered more than women because of societal expectations.[5]

Over time, some of the men associated with the men's liberation movement broke with modern feminism entirely and began to use the language of "men's rights." The men's rights movement soon became a backlash movement, fighting against many of the claims made by feminism. Their cause was aided by the fact that many of their most important claims were factually correct. Many of the things they pointed out are well documented. Men, on average, have shorter lives and suffer more health problems than women. Men commit suicide at higher rates than women. Men are more likely to be employed in more dangerous professions and suffer more frequent workplace accidents. Men are typically disadvantaged in divorce courts, where judges often award custody of children and hefty child-support payments to mothers by default, without regard for the specifics of individual cases. Men are more likely to be homeless. Men are more likely to have problems with drug and alcohol addiction. Although many men writing in this genre acknowledged rape as a problem, they wanted recognition of the existence of false rape accusations, which can easily ruin lives and even lead to suicide among men who did nothing wrong. They insisted that they were not calling for renewed subjugation of women, only that a basic standard of fairness be achieved.

Proponents of the men's rights cause also pointed out negative portrayals of men in popular culture. For example, they argued that men are increasingly portrayed as unrealistically malevolent in movies and television shows, painting an exaggerated picture of how dangerous the typical man is. In comedies and commercials, men have long been portrayed as bumbling fools, in constant need of rescue by the wise, hardworking women that surround them. The media constantly noted the unrealistic body expectations for women set by film, television, and magazines, apparently oblivious to the fact that leading men in Hollywood also set unrealistic standards for men. One could argue that the men's rights activists were wrong about these cultural developments, or that they were blind to the many ways that women remain victims of problematic portrayals in various forms of media, but their complaints were not meritless.

Throughout the 1990s, men's rights activists proliferated. They created groups, wrote articles, and published books promoting their cause. However, a new medium of communication, the Internet, arrived on the scene during that decade, a development that dramatically increased the audience for this material. It also, eventually, led to a much darker tone among many anti-feminists and, eventually, spawned alienated and dangerous online subcultures.

The Manosphere

The arrival of the Internet was a boon for social movements, especially those not closely connected to powerful, real-world institutions such as labor unions, churches, or political parties.[6] Radical movements, such as anti-feminist movements, which lack the capital to make their presence well known on traditional forms of media, were suddenly accessible to millions of people. In part because the Internet makes it easier for smaller, niche movements and cultures to form, the men's rights movement began to develop different subcategories, focusing on different issues they considered important to men. We can include several different groups under the broader umbrella term "manosphere." Some of these groups dropped the language of fairness and equality that had once been a staple of discourse on the subject of men's rights, instead embracing pernicious anti-liberal and misogynistic arguments.

The impulse to divide men into discrete categories based on their success with women was a theme common across various subgroups in the manosphere.[7] The figure that every man should aspire toward is the "alpha." The alpha male has easy access to sex and love from women. This status is often associated with traditional markers of social success (wealth, power, fame, etc.) but does not require it. An unattractive, non-wealthy man could potentially achieve alpha status if he has sufficient charisma. Below the alpha is the beta male. The beta male is defined by a mindset: that women's affection must be bought, either in a literal sense by providing easy lives for them or via constant affection, affirmation, and devotion. Beta males can succeed with women, but their mindset limits their odds of success and increases the odds of future infidelity. Some writers also discuss the omega male: the man who is so repulsive to women that only a massive overhaul of many of his traits could provide an opportunity for any kind of romantic success.

The use of terms like alpha and beta when discussing hierarchies of men intentionally suggests the hierarchies of wolf packs and other groups of predatory mammals. A common idea across multiple groups in the manosphere is that human beings still possess the primal brains of our hunter-gatherer ancestors. Men desire women primarily for sex, though when thinking long-term they may also desire affection and loyalty. Women desire men for the resources they can provide and want to pair with the most high-status man they can obtain. Essays by writers in the manosphere often include lengthy discussions about evolutionary psychology, giving them a veneer of scientific reasoning, though one that often veered into conspiracy theory, a category Steven Pittz describes in his contribution to this volume.

Some writers in the manosphere simply picked up the torch of earlier men's rights advocates. The website A Voice for Men, founded in 2009, became the most significant website in this part of the manosphere—though many of the articles on that site were unquestionably more misogynistic than what one would read from a mainstream men's rights activist of a previous generation. Paul Elam, who founded A Voice for Men, while unquestionably a controversial figure,[8] long managed to engage with mainstream media figures, participating in many high-profile television interviews. Indeed, one feminist critic of Elam argued, "What makes the [men's rights activists] particularly insidious is their canny co-optation of social-justice lingo."[9]

Initially, the online manosphere was largely made up of bloggers or authors of short essays posted on established websites (as well as people writing in the comment sections of those posts and essays). Over time, the movement became increasingly centered on online forums, often anonymous, many with little or no moderation. This created a new dynamic, one where discussions increasingly lacked even basic standards of civility and coherence.

The men's rights movement did not receive glowing descriptions when it was discussed in the mainstream media, even when it was still, overall, largely working as a conventional social movement. Yet its treatment in the media was not entirely negative. A well-produced documentary, *The Red Pill*, was directed by a woman who was slowly convinced that the men's rights movement was correct on many of its key issues.[10] Men's rights activists also received fair but critical coverage from progressive media outlets.[11] A major publishing house released a book expressing sympathy for the movement.[12] Beyond the men's rights activists, other elements of the manosphere were also experiencing a surge in popularity throughout this period. New anti-feminist online subcultures began placing a particular emphasis on issues of sex, dating, and marriage.

Pickup Artists

Although they are counted as an important element of the online manosphere, the pickup artist community is not necessarily political. As the name suggests, PUAs write primarily about how to successfully pursue women. Some of these writings are aimed at men specifically looking for relationships and eventually marriage. More frequently, however, these writers and speakers discuss methods for securing a one-night stand or brief fling.

As a general concept, the basic premise of PUAs is not inherently misogynistic. People of both genders have always sought advice in areas of sex and love, and there are also feminist discourses that encourage casual sexual relationships. There are a few common themes among contemporary PUAs that feminists find objectionable, however. The PUA emphasis on sex alone, for example, seems to treat women as disposable objects—on this front, both progressive feminists and conservative traditionalists would reject the PUA message.

The idea of the pickup artist is not new, nor is the idea that men can learn certain esoteric truths about women from gurus. Even after the Internet was easily accessible, writers in this genre published successful books and others continued hosting real-world seminars. Books such as *The Game* and *The Mystery Method* were popular among young men, and a PUA guru was famously depicted—if with a critical edge—by Tom Cruise in the film *Magnolia*.[13] The Internet, however, was the first place many men looked for this kind of advice.

The means by which many of these writers suggest men should pursue women may seem demeaning and even dehumanizing. A common theme among PUAs is that the kind of advice men and boys receive from society about women is entirely wrong. According to their theories, women do not want to be complimented. In fact, you are more likely to secure their interest if you insult them (what is called "negging" by the PUA community). This, the theory goes, makes a man look more confident and simultaneously lowers a woman's self-esteem, making her more compliant. Men should not reassure women of their faithfulness. Instead, they should never miss an opportunity to make a woman jealous; as one popular PUA blogger put it, "Women will never admit this but jealousy excites them. The thought of you turning on another woman will arouse her sexually. No girl wants a man that no other woman wants. The partner who harnesses the gale storm of jealousy controls the direction of the relationship."[14] Critics of the PUAs have noted that these writers encourage men to engage in cruel manipulation to influence women's attitudes and behaviors.

Although feminists have understandable problems with the ideas PUAs spread about women, PUAs have an ultimately optimistic message for men: By mastering these skills, you can find sex and companionship. One can argue that their understanding of women's psychology is flawed and that their ideas are ultimately demeaning to women, but they do nonetheless offer hope for even low-status men, suggesting they can achieve their relationship goals through self-improvement and persuasion. In this regard, PUA discourse is qualitatively different from the radically misogynistic and sometimes violent ideas promoted by other anti-feminists.

Voluntarily Giving Up on Women: The MGTOW Movement

The leading voices of the men's rights movement argued that many of the problems men face are the result of public policies or cultural norms that could be changed. The pickup artists mostly accepted the cultural and legal status quo, but they gave advice on how men could navigate it successfully and have positive experiences with women. In the 2010s, however, a new online movement sprang up, arguing that the problem was with the very nature of modern women, and there was little hope of ever changing them. This group instead called for men to abandon a dating market that was rigged against them. The term they settled on was "men going their own way" (MGTOW). The development of MGTOW as a concept and movement represented the manosphere's turn toward a particularly hostile brand of misogyny.

The MGTOW movement argued that contemporary gender relations are now so dysfunctional that men simply need to opt out of relations with women entirely—and the problem can furthermore not be resolved by policy changes. Instead, men should go on strike. With the deck so stacked against them, men should simply refuse to give any woman love, commitment, or support. The chances that any marriage would ultimately end with the woman's infidelity, divorce, and the man's poverty via alimony and child support are too high. Men should therefore opt out of the entire process, and if they cannot bear celibacy, they should fulfill their sexual needs via one-night stands or prostitutes.

Voices on MGTOW forums emphasized that their withdrawal from dating and marriage is a conscious choice. That is, they insist that they could date and marry women but choose not to do so because the risks outweigh the potential rewards.[15] MGTOW has also been called "going Galt," a reference to the hero of Ayn Rand's libertarian novel *Atlas Shrugged*.[16] As a movement, it emphasizes men's agency and their ability to overcome a system that works against them by voluntarily and peacefully opting out.

Permanently giving up on sex and romance is a difficult thing to do, however. As the best example of this problem, the MGTOW community was dealt a blow in 2013 when one of its thought leaders, Mark Minter, violated his own principles and got married.[17] The response from the broader manosphere to that decision was unsurprisingly vitriolic. However, his experience demonstrates the challenges faced by any movement espousing a message like MGTOW. If even one of the most intensely anti-nuptial voices on the Internet could himself get married, how will those with only a passing interest in these ideas maintain the discipline the movement requires?

When someone associated with MGTOW decides to form a long-term relationship with a woman or even get married, it also raises questions about how committed the movement's members really are to a set of principles. Perhaps most of them are simply unable to form meaningful relationships with the opposite sex, for whatever reason, and they delude themselves by insisting that their lifestyle represents a personal decision that they could revisit at any time. Eventually, a new anti-feminist subculture began to attract adherents, one that did not claim that its members were perpetually single as a choice.

Involuntarily Giving Up on Women . . . and Hating Them: The Incel Movement

All the aforementioned groups presented a message with at least a hint of empowerment. According to the men's rights movement, men can organize and demand fair treatment in the courts and culture. Via self-improvement and seduction techniques, pickup artists argue most men have a shot at sex and love. Even the MGTOWs believe they are pointing toward a brighter future, one where men will reclaim their rightful place in society via peaceful withdrawal from the contemporary dating market. These elements of the manosphere have received deserved criticism, and some of their leading figures could be accurately described as far right, but their basic themes were not inherently anti-liberal. The incel movement has proven very different, both more dangerous than its predecessors and completely devoid of a practical political or social agenda.

The PUAs and MGTOWs at least suggested men had some control over their romantic lives. The PUAs said every man can improve his odds of success with women. The MGTOWs may have rejected meaningful relationships, but they at least suggested this was their choice. The incels promote a very different attitude. These are men who have no success with women, and they resent women and the men who do have romantic relationships. They furthermore hold out little hope that their fortunes will reverse. Their only solution, to the extent that they offer a solution at all, is a total reorganization of society that denies women basic rights and freedoms. It is an agenda with negligible popular support and infinitesimal odds of success.

Like men's rights, the concept of involuntary celibacy has followed a complicated trajectory. Although the term is now associated with young men, when it was coined more than 20 years ago it was not associated with a specific gender. In fact, the term was first created by a woman, and although the community that is associated with the term was, almost by definition, lonely and romantically unsatisfied, it was not initially connected to hatred and violent threats.[18]

For many years, the online incel community was largely ignored. Indeed, they were all but invisible to the rest of society. As was the case for the men's rights movement, the incels were reacting to a real phenomenon. The share of the population that rarely or never has sexual encounters is on the rise.[19] And to be clear, most celibate people, voluntarily celibate or not, are not dangerous. Nor are they especially conservative—a recent study of incels found that they are more likely to be left-wing than right-wing in their politics.[20] The incel movement is largely defined by its low feelings of efficacy—in both the personal lives of individual incels and their collective ability to shape society. Lacking any belief in their own ability to create societal changes they would consider salutary, they have also dropped the mainstream, generally liberal style of argumentation that characterized earlier men's rights activists. Instead of productive collective action, the incel movement has inspired extremism and violence from a small subset of its adherents.

Although not everyone associated with the incel culture believes the same things, there are common themes in their discourse. They make the seemingly paradoxical argument that sexual liberation and female promiscuity have resulted in a growing number of sexless men. Their general claim is that women are naturally attracted to dominant men, and they will always prefer sex with men of high status. The concept of "hypergamy," which suggests that women will always try to pair with the most high-status men they can obtain, is pervasive on incel discussion forums. In an earlier era, according to this view, even the most attractive men were limited to just one or a few sexual partners because of the expectation that people would pair up and marry early, maintaining monogamy for the rest of their lives. Because of revolutionary changes in norms surrounding marriage and sex, however, some men have sexual access to a much larger percentage of women than they would have in the past. Furthermore, they say, because the female drive to mate with alpha males is so strong, they will prefer to be part of an "alpha male's" unofficial harem indefinitely, rather than marry a man of lower status. On incel forums it is common to see unrealistic estimates of how sex is distributed across the population. One common claim is that 20 percent of American men are having 80 percent of the sex—a claim that is not founded on any credible data sets.[21]

These arguments about the nature of women are not novel. The PUAs often make similar claims. The difference is that incels reject the PUA argument that charisma (what they call "game") can raise their status enough to achieve sexual success. Incels instead despise the small number of "Chads" in the world who enjoy unlimited access to promiscuous "Stacys"—the latter being a group they view as simultaneously too "slutty" to be worthy of respect and too picky when it comes to sexual partners. Women were often referred to in demeaning language—"femoids," short for female humanoid, is a common term indicating that they do not consider women fully human.

On incel forums, anger at the PUA blogosphere is not as common as anger at women as a category, but it is a consistent theme. In fact, one of the more vitriolic incel forums (now defunct) was titled "PUAhate." Incels have made many critiques of PUAs, some understandable. Some PUA writers imply that, via carefully scripted pickup lines, well-timed physical touches, and a consistent cocky attitude, women can be almost hypnotized into sex, even by physically unattractive men with low social status. When men find that this advice fails to have its intended effects, and perhaps even leads to their embarrassment, they become disillusioned and even angrier than they were before.

The period in which the online incel movement's existence was mostly unknown and ignored by the broader society was short-lived. It quickly gained global infamy when people associated with the community engaged in shocking acts of brutal violence. The most infamous act of incel violence in the US occurred in 2014, when 22-year-old Elliot Rodger murdered six people in a rampage in Isla Vista, CA. Before the attack, Rodger wrote a long manifesto and posted videos on YouTube explaining his motivations. In his final video, he declared, "Well now I will be a god compared to you. You will all be animals. You are animals and I will slaughter you like animals."[22]

One notable element of Rodger's final video and subsequent actions was the lack of any kind of concrete political agenda. In this sense, these murders seem distinct from other varieties of terrorism. Rodger made no demands, and he offered no suggestions for how the world could be improved for people like him. Despite the heinousness of his crimes, Rodger was hailed as a hero on some of the more extreme incel forums. He was also cited as an inspiration by subsequent incel killers, including Alek Minassian, who killed ten people in Toronto, Canada,[23] and Scott Paul Beierle, who killed two people in Tallahassee, Florida.[24] The incel movement has now been identified as a terrorist threat, and many of its most popular message boards have been shut down.

Some media discussions of incels as a category unfortunately paint with too broad a brush.[25] Part of the problem is that incel is both a literal description of tens of millions of people and the name for a very small, angry, misogynistic online community. It would be a mistake to stigmatize people simply for failing to achieve romantic success. An unfortunate consequence of incel violence is that many lonely people who have done nothing wrong are now included in a category associated with hatred and violence.

The Manosphere's Demise: A Consequence of Illiberal, Uncivil Discourse

Whereas other groups discussed in this volume have learned to appropriate the language of liberalism to promote an illiberal agenda, the "manosphere" went in the opposite direction. Exceptions of course remain, but in general, the online world of anti-feminism devolved from debatable critique to nihilistic rage. The people in some of these online subcultures have no serious intention of creating activist groups or lobbying for any kind of political action, nor is it even clear what that would even theoretically entail. It is only a matter of time before someone involved in these online forums again lashes out in a violent manner.

The manosphere, at least as it existed in the early 2010s, is now mostly defunct. Many of the most active voices in the movement have changed the focus of their writings or stopped writing entirely. Some people who were once influential figures in the movement concur that its moment has come and gone. Daryush "Roosh" Valizadeh, who ran the popular and influential manosphere site, Return of Kings, stopped adding new material to the site and even took the archive offline. Valizadeh explained that his recent conversion to Christianity prompted this decision.[26]

Quantitative social scientists have examined the evolution of the manosphere, tracking the migration of users across multiple manosphere communities. They found that the less toxic elements of the manosphere, such as the men's rights activists and pickup artists, have lost ground to the more bitterly misogynistic communities, such as MGTOW and incels.[27]

The manosphere's most recent popular forums, especially those associated with the incel movement, have largely abandoned the forms of argumentation that are persuasive to broad segments of the American public. Despite concerns about democratic backsliding in the US, the American political culture still places a high value on individual rights and fairness.[28] This was the focus of the early men's rights movement, and with continued effort, they might have had some success. Feminists and others opposed to their agenda understandably pushed back against many of their claims and demands, but they were working within the established liberal framework. They made a case about culture and policy that could have received a fair hearing in the public arena. A movement motivated primarily by misogynistic rage and morose fatalism has no chance at creating societal change; it can only inspire depression and, occasionally, acts of terror.

The acts of incel violence did not only make their movement infamous. The negative publicity spilled over and caused harm to other elements of the manosphere. Despite maintaining a very different approach to women than incels, the PUA community was also harmed by the negative publicity all anti-feminists received because of the attacks. That movement was already in decline, with many of its leading figures moving on to other projects, and those that remain have apparently experienced a serious decrease in readers and paying customers for seminars and online products. Feminists had been painting them as dangerous misogynists for some time, and even their tangential relationship with incel thinking was sufficient to render them unappealing to a massive percentage of the population.[29] There are still writers promising men that they can succeed with women by following their advice, but the peak of PUAs as a large online community has clearly passed.

With the rise of extreme right movements on the Internet in recent years, which has occurred in tandem with the decline of older sources of information (newspapers, print magazines, network news, etc.), many people have reasonably lamented the decline of traditional gatekeepers.[30] For all their faults, older sources of information were expected to maintain certain standards. Newspapers employed fact checkers, and journalists were expected to maintain some element of objectivity. The fact that there were fewer sources of information in the past further helped maintain at least some kind of national consensus about basic facts and a semi-coherent, widely shared political culture. The decline of traditional media has fractured American political discourse, as ideological and partisan tribes retreat into information silos that align with their prejudices.

All those concerns are valid, but the evolution of the manosphere and the concept of men's rights more generally demonstrates that the decline of gatekeepers can also hurt the cause of backlash movements. Most early proponents of men's rights, even when they were overtly anti-feminist, remained in the broad liberal family. Although some of their claims were questionable, most of them were nonetheless worthy of consideration. Men's rights activists such as Paul Elam may not have achieved their goals, but they were at least engaged in the kind of political and cultural work that has the capacity to move the Overton window. This is not true of incels.

My point in this chapter is not to praise earlier iterations of the men's rights movement. The movement was controversial from its inception for a reason, and many people have raised legitimate objections to its arguments. However, it mostly behaved like a normal political or social movement, following the usual norms of US politics.

The manosphere was made irrelevant, in part, by the movement's total democratization. It became an angry online mob, marinating in its own sense of helplessness. More reasonable voices, calling for self-improvement, better social skills, and concrete political and social goals that could be achieved through organizing and peaceful collective action were drowned out, replaced by anonymous forums dominated by hate-filled posts attacking all women.

Other authors in this volume have pointed out that far-right movements achieved success by appropriating the language of liberalism into their arguments, even when they sought to accomplish illiberal goals. Their points are valid. However, the experience of the manosphere suggests maintaining that framework is not inevitable for right-wing movements, and with the Internet's democratization of social movements, it is not necessarily easy. In the world of anonymous online forums, especially in the case of forums associated with right-wing backlash movements, the most angry and toxic voices tend to push out more reasonable thinkers. The extreme misogyny of both MGTOW and the incels is furthermore not relatable to a massive percentage of men who might have been sympathetic to the men's rights cause but who have not had similar, entirely negative experiences with women. The result has been a negative spiral for the movement, diminishing its appeal to people who do not already accept all their premises.

Did the Manosphere Succeed Despite Itself?

Although the manosphere's days as even a loosely organized movement are in the past, the issues it focused on have not gone away. In fact, certain ideas that were originally developed by people directly or indirectly connected to the manosphere have gone mainstream within conservative politics. For example, the psychologist Jordan Peterson has written and spoken extensively on issues related to gender and masculinity, typically from a traditionalist perspective. Although I have not seen credible evidence that he was directly influenced by the online figures discussed in this chapter, his views on gender essentialism are congruent with what leading figures in the manosphere were writing a decade ago. However, as James McAdams emphasizes in Chapter 2, Peterson has vastly more reach and influence than does any of the figures I discussed earlier in this chapter.[31]

Peterson is not a unique figure in this regard. In recent years, we have witnessed the rise of new conservative figures, working primarily online, echoing themes from the manosphere. A new breed of right-wing body builders and other influencers have attracted a sizable audience. Andrew Tate, a misogynist social media personality, made headlines when he was arrested for human trafficking.[32] Perhaps more shocking than the crime itself was the fact that Tate had a massive following of young men who viewed him as a kind of role model or aspirational figure. Although he is one of the better-known figures in his milieu, there is no shortage of right-wing social media influencers focusing their energy on issues related to masculinity.

Themes that were once mostly found in the manosphere have since been embraced by certain voices in the mainstream conservative movement. For example, Tucker Carlson, formerly of Fox News, recently interviewed an anonymous social media influencer who uses the name "Raw Egg Nationalist" (REN), who has promoted various claims about the emasculating nature of the modern world, both in the sense that US culture now devalues traditional masculinity and in the literal sense that the typical American diet is loaded with phytoestrogens, making men more feminine.[33] Carlson also interviewed Tate on his new program on Twitter.[34]

Does this mean that, despite falling apart, the manosphere nonetheless made important metapolitical gains? Possibly. On the other hand, the new breed of online writers, podcasters, and social media influencers creating content related to men's rights and masculinity tend to be even less political than their manosphere predecessors, critiquing modern cultural trends but not promoting a coherent political or policy agenda. Tuning out of mainstream culture, lifting weights, avoiding soy and seed oils, eating raw eggs, and sunbathing your scrotum (which REN promoted on Carlson's program) may make sense for certain individuals, but these are not inherently political acts.

Despite seeming to have made at least some impact on conservative discourse in the US, the collapse of men's rights as even an inchoate movement is significant because organized groups are essential to the success of a political cause. The manosphere's turn toward hate and illiberalism, and its inability to control the behavior of its most anti-social elements, unquestionably hindered the movement's ability to act as a force for political or cultural change, turning it into an insular club of malcontents, unlikely to engage in successful or substantive collective action.

Notes

1 In Chapter 3 of this volume, Sarah Shurts discusses Le Pen's efforts to create a far-right feminist vocabulary.
2 For an introduction to backlash movements as a concept, I recommend Karen J. Alter and Michael Zürn, "Theorising Backlash Politics," *The British Journal of Politics and International Relations* 22 (2020): 739–52.
3 Several influential texts promoting these ideas were published in this era, such as Warren Ferrell, *The Liberated Man* (New York: Random House, 1974); Jack Nichols, *Men's Liberation: A New Definition of Masculinity* (New York: Penguin, 1975); Marc Fiegen Fasteau, *The Male Machine* (New York: McGraw-Hill, 1974).
4 Michael A. Messner, "The Limits of 'The Male Sex Role': An Analysis of the Men's Liberation Movement and the Men's Rights Movements' Discourse," *Gender and Society* 12 (1998): 255–76.
5 See, for example, Herb Goldberg, *The Hazards of Being Male: Surviving the Myth of Masculine Privilege* (New York: Signet, 1976).
6 In this chapter, I am defining "social movement" very broadly. In particular, I am leaning on Mario Diani's definition. Mario Diani, "The Concept of a Social Movement," *The Sociological Review* 40 (1992): 1–25.
7 Michael Vallerga and Eileen L. Zurbriggen, "Hegemonic Masculinities in the 'Manosphere': A Thematic Analysis of Beliefs About Men and Women on The Red Pill and Incel," *Analyses of Social Issues and Public Policies* 22 (2022): 602–25.
8 Adam Serwer and Katie J. M. Baker, "How Men's Rights Leader Paul Elam Turned Being a Deadbeat Dad Into a Moneymaking Movement," *Buzzfeed*, February

5, 2015, www.buzzfeed.com/adamserwer/how-mens-rights-leader-paul-elam-turned-being-a-deadbeat-dad.
9 Jaclyn Friedman, "A Look Inside the 'Men's Rights' Movement That Helped Fuel California Alleged Killer Elliot Rodger," *The American Prospect*, October 24, 2013.
10 Cassie Jaye, director. *The Red Pill*. Gravitas Ventures, 2016. 1 hr., 27 minutes. https://www.amazon.com/Red-Pill-Cassie-Jaye/dp/B06XGW2F9M.
11 For a relatively recent example, see Emmett Rensin, "The Internet Is Full of Men Who Hate Feminism. Here's What They're Like in Person," Vox, August 18, 2015, www.vox.com/2015/2/5/7942623/mens-rights-movement.
12 Helen Smith, *Men on Strike: Why Men Are Boycotting Marriage, Fatherhood, and the American Dream—And Why It Matters* (New York: Encounter Books, 2013).
13 Neil Strauss, *The Game: Penetrating the Secret Society of Pickup Artists* (New York: Harper Collins, 2005); Mystery, Lovedrop, and Chris Odom, *The Mystery Method: How to Get Beautiful Women Into Bed* (New York: St. Martin's Press, 2007).
14 "The Sixteen Commandments of Poon," *Chateau Heartiste*, May 19, 2019, https://heartiste.org/the-sixteen-commandments-of-poon/.
15 Jie Liang Lin, "Anti-Feminism Online. MGTOW (Men Going Their Own Way)," In *Digital Environments: Ethnographic Perspectives Across Global Online and Offline Spaces*, edited by Urte Undine Frömming, Steffen Köhn, Samantha Fox, and Mike Terry (Bielefeld: Transcript Verlag, 2017), 77–96.
16 In the plot of that novel, John Galt leads a strike of the world's capitalist leaders, leaving only parasitic government bureaucrats in charge. Without the best minds and most disciplined people, society quickly collapses. Ayn Rand, *Atlas Shrugged* (New York: Signet, 1957).
17 Daryush Valizadeh, "Mark Minter Is a Phony," *Return of Kings*, July 28, 2013, https://web.archive.org/web/20131216064923/www.returnofkings.com/14846/mark-minter-is-a-phony.
18 Ben Zimmer, "How 'Incel' Got Hijacked," *Politico*, May 8, 2018, www.politico.com/magazine/story/2018/05/08/intel-involuntary-celibate-movement-218324/.
19 Christopher Ingraham, "The Share of Americans Not Having Sex Has Reached a Record High," *The Washington Post*, March 19, 2019, www.washingtonpost.com/business/2019/03/29/share-americans-not-having-sex-has-reached-record-high/.
20 William Costello, Vania Rolon, Andrew G. Thomas, and David Schmitt, "Levels of Well-Being Among Men Who Are Incel (Involuntarily Celibate)," *Evolutionary Psychological Science* 8 (2022): 375–90.
21 Lyman Stone, "Male Sexlessness Is Rising but Not for the Reasons Incels Claim," *Institute for Family Studies*, May 14, 2018, https://ifstudies.org/blog/male-sexlessness-is-rising-but-not-for-the-reasons-incels-claim.
22 "Transcript of Video Linked to Santa Barbara Mass Shooting," *CNN*, May 28, 2014, https://edition.cnn.com/2014/05/24/us/elliot-rodger-video-transcript/index.html.
23 E. J. Dickson, "How the Toronto Van Attack Suspect Was Radicalized by Incels," *Rolling Stone*, September 27, 2019, www.rollingstone.com/culture/culture-news/alek-minassian-toronto-van-attack-incels-891678/.
24 Tom Porter, "Scott Beierle: Florida Yoga Studio Gunman Likened Himself to 'Incel' Killer Elliott Rodger," *Newsweek*, November 4, 2018, www.newsweek.com/florida-yoga-studio-gunman-likened-himself-incel-killer-elliott-rodger-1200452.

25 For example, see Camilla Long, "A Cult With Warped Beliefs Spawning Mass Murderers. I'd Say Incels Are Terrorists," *The Times*, August 15, 2021, www.thetimes.co.uk/article/a-cult-with-warped-beliefs-spawning-mass-murderers-id-say-incels-are-terrorists-hpx3kwl2t.
26 Daryush Valizadeh, "Permanent Closure of Return of Kings," *Return of Kings*, December 21, 2022, https://web.archive.org/web/20221229170458/https://www.returnofkings.com/index.html.
27 Manoel Horta Ribeiro, Jeremy Blackburn, Barry Bradlyn, Emiliano De Cristofaro, Gianluca Stringhini, Summer Long, Stephanie Greenberg, and Savvas Zannettou, "The Evolution of the Manosphere Across the Web," *Proceedings of the International AAAI Conference on Web and Social Media* 15 (2021): 196–207.
28 For an example of this, we can look to the Christian right, which has had more success using the language of rights (the right to life, religious liberty, etc.) than the language of theocracy. For an excellent treatment of this issue, I recommend Andrew R. Lewis, *The Rights Turn in Conservative Christian Politics* (New York: Cambridge University Press, 2017).
29 Charlie Powell, "The Death of the PUA Community," *Return of Kings*, March 11, 2018, https://web.archive.org/web/20221216000536/https://www.returnofkings.com/159286/the-death-of-the-pua-community.
30 George Hawley, *Making Sense of the Alt-Right* (New York: Columbia University Press, 2017).
31 Nellie Bowles, "Jordan Peterson, Custodian of the Patriarchy," *The New York Times*, March 18, 2018, www.nytimes.com/2018/05/18/style/jordan-peterson-12-rules-for-life.html.
32 Rebeca Jennings, "The Arrest of Misogynist Influencer Andrew Tate, Explained," *Vox*, January 4, 2023, www.vox.com/culture/2023/1/4/23539528/andrew-tate-arrest-jail-rape-human-trafficking.
33 "'The End of Men': Tucker Carlson Originals Investigates the 'Collapse' of American Males' Testosterone Levels," *Fox News*, October 11, 2022, www.foxnews.com/video/6313315096112. On "Raw Egg Nationalist"'s other views, see José Pedro Zúquete's analysis in Chapter 10.
34 Shweta Sharma, "Anger as Tucker Carlson Drops Lengthy Interview With Sex Trafficking Suspect Andrew Tate," *The Independent*, July 12, 2023, www.independent.co.uk/news/world/americas/us-politics/tucker-carlson-andrew-tate-interview-b2373698.html.

PART IV
The Ambiguities of a Concept

8
FORCED TO BE FREE? AMERICA'S "POSTLIBERALS" ON FREEDOM AND LIBERTY

Laura K. Field

This chapter is about high-profile American "postliberals," with a focus on Professor Patrick Deneen of the University of Notre Dame and Professor Adrian Vermeule of Harvard Law School. "Postliberalism" is a philosophical movement that explicitly rejects social and economic liberalism, in favor of a more communitarian outlook and an embrace of strong, even autocratic, government, but without fully jettisoning the language of modern liberal democracy and modern democratic constitutionalism. Deneen and Vermeule only fit uneasily in the category of "far-right" thinker and would likely bristle at the characterization insofar as they present themselves as nonpartisan actors who are willing, in theory, to collaborate with the left. But this theoretical collaboration extends only to economic matters. I argue in this chapter that the American postliberals, like the other thinkers under consideration in this volume, fit neatly into Marlene Laruelle's definition of illiberalism. They each seek to "restore the authority of traditional institutions, to use these institutions to propagate alternative values to classical liberalism, and to turn their followers' sense of victimhood into a source of political power."[1] Deneen and Vermeule have each demonstrated populist (or rather "Aristopopulist") tendencies and sympathies with the American "New Right."

The idea of Orwellian "Newspeak" is also a contentious descriptor for Deneen and Vermeule's approach, since postliberalism is, obviously, explicit about its rejection of liberalism. In this respect, postliberals are more extreme than other far-right thinkers but might also be considered more direct and honest. And yet, if we define Far-Right Newspeak as a form of rhetoric or distortion that exploits the language of liberalism to provide a permission structure for illiberal change, as A. James McAdams suggests in Chapter 1, then postliberals remain squarely in a gray zone. In this chapter I show that,

DOI: 10.4324/9781003436737-12

while Deneen and Vermeule reject the concept of liberalism, they continue to embrace key liberal-democratic concepts, like liberty and constitutionalism, in ways that are vague and/or ambiguous and/or misleading.

My particular emphasis in this chapter is the ways in which these two scholars discuss freedom and liberty. I focus on the work of academics because, as American conservatives have proclaimed for generations now, "ideas have consequences."[2] Further, as Frank Wolff has shown in Chapter 6 of this volume, the unwieldy deployment of language on the part of intellectuals and scholars can have an outsized impact on civil discourse, especially in times of social flux or perceived crisis.

In what follows, though, I begin with a discussion of former attorney general Bill Barr: someone whose rhetoric has tilted in a post- or anti-liberal direction, but whose actions demonstrate that he remains, however uncomfortably, in the liberal, democratic constitutional camp. From there, I turn to Deneen and Vermeule. I follow the trajectory of their recent work, beginning with Deneen's 2018 book *Why Liberalism Failed*, to Vermeule's semi-critical review of that work, to Vermeule's 2022 book *Common Good Constitutionalism*, and then Deneen's 2023 book, *Regime Change*. I argue that this trajectory is one of dramatic radicalization and increasingly overt illiberalism.

I contend that both thinkers work to repurpose the concept of liberty for the sake of their own very different and illiberal political vision. Deneen squarely rejects traditional liberal conceptions of freedom in favor of "positive" and ancient ideals of liberty that he considers to be more genuine. The problem here, with regard to Newspeak, is that Deneen does not provide a full accounting for the political forms or structures (i.e., the limits on political authority) that he hopes to install in place of those older forms; he wants to jettison liberal freedom but does not explain what that portends for traditional liberal limits on governmental power. Vermeule takes a different approach. He works to suppress and diminish the status of freedom relative to other ideals from America's constitutional past—including especially his own particular conception of "the common good"—but in order to do this he has to flatten and falsify a complicated and contentious tradition. Both Deneen and Vermeule reject what political theorists call negative liberty— including its emphasis on limiting state coercion—and embrace positive, virtue-based liberty, but without the traditional emphasis on republican and democratic engagement. This revamp of liberty makes ample room for expansive state action and is arguably an important tool in efforts to erect illiberal political forms.

What is more, when it comes to actual politics, both thinkers have shown a taste for illiberal and anti-democratic ideas. The postliberals show a keen admiration for Viktor Orbán's Hungary. As Tímea Drinóczi and Agnieszka Bień-Kacała have convincingly argued in Chapter 5 of this volume, Hungary now exists as an illiberal constitutional regime, and is on a clear path of democratic backsliding into authoritarianism.[3] The reappropriation and reorientation of the language of liberty and freedom are a major part of this new effort, at least as concerns intellectuals and civil society. In the next part of this chapter, I turn briefly to consider the postliberals' trajectory as activists and public intellectuals, alongside one of their key collaborators, Gladden Pappin of the University of Dallas, who has moved to Hungary and is now directing a think tank that advises Orbán on foreign policy.

None of these figures have totally abandoned the concepts of liberty or freedom (I use the two terms interchangeably), but they openly and intentionally depart from traditional liberal understandings of these words. The postliberals have worked in various ways to effect a semantic overhaul of the language of liberalism, which in turn creates conceptual space for more expansive forms of state action. There is also—especially in the work of Adrian Vermeule—a concerted effort to suppress the import of freedom in the American context.

Viewed sympathetically, these efforts could be seen as a much-needed corrective to stale and/or confused ideas about the nature of freedom and its relationship to state action in late modern liberal democracies, and the postliberals likely view themselves as correcting the liberal co-optation of these terms from the classical tradition. As Sarah Shurts argues in Chapter 3 of this volume, right-wing thinking can sometimes reveal genuine vulnerabilities and inconsistencies in liberal practices. But, given how stridently American postliberal thinkers oppose modern liberalism, and judging from their political behavior, the postliberal views of freedom are better understood as an effort to replace modern liberal conceptions of freedom with older views that are much less sympathetic to individual rights and liberties, and much more tolerant of state oppression (Vermeule in particular is an especially strong proponent of the administrative state, a distinctly unclassical institution). The linguistic moves taken by American postliberals fit neatly with the political maneuvers taken by populist leaders in the new illiberal regimes of Central Europe—actions that expand state power while seizing control of electoral institutions and diminishing the options for recourse on the part of individual citizens. This raises real questions about the term "postliberalism" and the concept of Newspeak—questions I take up by way of conclusion.

William Barr's Constitutionalism

On Friday, October 11, 2019, Attorney General William P. Barr gave a closed-door speech at the University of Notre Dame on religious liberty. The speech attracted national attention for its unprecedented partisanship. Among other things, Barr spoke of "progressives" and "militant secularists" engaged in an "uncompromising assault" on religion and traditional values.

At one point he struck a conspiratorial tone: "This is not decay; it is organized destruction." Barr's speech told a vivid story of steep social and political decline, caused in large part by liberal moral relativism.

If the foreground purpose of Barr's speech was to chart and describe the alleged secular liberal attack on traditional Judeo-Christian religious expression, a secondary intention was to revive an older, more conservative conception of freedom—one that has little to do with limits on state authority, or with liberal autonomy, or with republican civics, and everything to do with moral self-regulation and life lived within the bounds of traditional faith. Barr's speech offered a glimpse of how America's postliberal conservatives are redefining and reappropriating the concept of liberty for a postliberal future.

The Notre Dame speech had three parts.[4]

The opening had originalist elements and sought to establish the importance of religion to the American founders and to their conception of republican life. Barr argued that, for the framers, religious experience and political liberty were mutually constitutive and deeply interconnected. The founders believed religious faith and discipline—and the Judeo-Christian belief system in particular—to be the only sound basis for republican self-rule. Barr argued further that, for the framers, liberty had less to do with political mechanisms and electoral processes and more to do with "the capacity of each individual to restrain and govern themselves." With this, Barr attributed to the founders a conception of liberty that was more personal and moral than distinctly political. The core question for the framers was "whether the citizens in such a free society could maintain the moral discipline and virtue necessary for the survival of free institutions." The answer given by his speech was that the framers counted on "the Judeo-Christian moral system" to undergird the system by providing the necessary moral guidance and "the right rules to live by."

In the second part of the speech, Barr took a more aggressive turn. This is where he charted the decline of the American social order, tracing it directly to the decay of traditional religion:

> I think we all recognize that over the past 50 years religion has been under increasing attack. On the one hand, we have seen the steady erosion of our traditional Judeo-Christian moral system and a comprehensive effort to drive it from the public square. On the other hand, we see the growing ascendancy of secularism and the doctrine of moral relativism. By any honest assessment, the consequences of this moral upheaval have been grim. Virtually every measure of social pathology continues to gain ground.

According to Barr, the rise of moral relativism—which might more charitably be called moral or religious pluralism, or even liberal religious freedom—is causally related not only to the decline in traditional religion, but also to the increase in "virtually every measure of social pathology." The culmination of Barr's argument was that liberals and secularists, in addition to being licentious and immoral, have also become fanatical and oppressive: "The problem is not that religion is being forced on others. The problem is that irreligion and secular values are being forced on people of faith." This is presumably what Barr meant with his claims about "organized destruction." As Steven Pittz observes in Chapter 9 of this volume, such conspiratorial claims are often rhetorically effective.

If we step back from Barr's specific claims, it is striking how cleanly Barr breaks with any standard *political* conception of American liberty. The concept of the separation between church and state is implied in Barr's critique of overreaching secularists, but otherwise goes unmentioned. The notion that Americans have a right to choose freely among different religions (or irreligion) is absent, despite its being a bedrock of American constitutionalism; instead, Barr implies that the founders all agreed to the primacy of the Christian outlook, despite contestation around this issue at the time of the founding and the passing of the Bill of Rights.[5] And when Barr presents moral self-discipline as the core of freedom and emphasizes the founders' attachment to Judeo-Christian values, he neglects what was arguably even more important to them, as demonstrated by their revolutionary actions and the Declaration of Independence—namely, political liberty, and the ideal of collective self-rule within the confines of a formal constitution.

In the conclusion to his speech, however, Barr struck a more moderate tone, and in his recommendations for the future was careful to stay within the bounds of the liberal constitutional order. Despite the grave threats that he had outlined, Barr recommended that conservatives work towards renewal by abiding by their faith, educating their children in the faith, and being active in the legal struggles being waged against religion. These are all entirely legitimate means that fit squarely within modern liberal constitutional conventions.

Barr's speech was in violation of conventional norms that govern actors in the Department of Justice, but he kept within the bounds of the liberal constitutional order insofar as he respected the fundamental importance of concepts such as the rule of law, democratic accountability, human rights, and the separation of powers. He did not argue that the judiciary should start ruling in favor of conservative political interests in the face of constitutional restraints, for example, and he did not imply that conservatives would be warranted in breaking or changing election laws to gain power. When, in late 2020, President Trump denied the results of the 2020 presidential election and spouted falsehoods about election fraud and "the big steal," Barr resigned from the administration—a move that constituted a strong rebuke to the president and a strong signal of support for the constitutional order, including electoral forms. In his resignation letter on December 14, 2020, Barr began with a statement about the importance of doing "all we can to assure the integrity of elections and promote public confidence in their outcome."[6] The message of constitutional restraint and support for civic health and basic democratic practices was front and center. After January 6, Barr also spoke out repeatedly and consistently against President Trump's actions.[7] This sort of practical restraint is not characteristic of the postliberal theorists Patrick Deneen and Adrian Vermeule.

Barr's views on religious liberty are hardly anomalous. Rather, his speech at Notre Dame reflected a pre-existing strain of radical thought on the American right that flattens the theological complexity of the founding into one straightforward narrative. The speech foreshadowed a dramatic reorientation towards explicit anti-liberalism on the New Right in subsequent years, including the rejection of the liberal dimensions of the American founding. When it comes to questions of religious liberty, Deneen and Vermeule are on the same page as Barr. In the language of political theorists, we might say that they reject "negative" liberty, or "freedom from" state coercion, and seek to renew more classical or "positive" understanding of freedom—but without the traditional emphasis on republican power-sharing, democratic political engagement, and the tradition of fundamental rights and liberties that goes back to the Declaration of Independence, Revolutionary War, and Constitution.

But both Deneen and Vermeule go much further than Barr, and together demonstrate the postliberal trajectory towards illiberalism and extremism. As we will see in what follows, the postliberals don't just raise interesting questions about the nature of freedom, they also seek to use the government to effect change and sometimes explicitly endorse the use of questionable, illiberal means.

Patrick Deneen and the Postliberal Reduction of Liberty

Deneen provided a fuller and more substantive discussion of freedom, fully consonant with Barr's outlook, in his 2018 bestselling book, *Why Liberalism Failed*.[8] Deneen is arguably the most influential member of the newly emergent postliberal right, and so his thinking about liberal freedom and liberty vis-à-vis traditional conservative conceptions is key to understanding how freedom is being reconceived within the broader movement. Deneen rejects liberal conceptions of freedom wholesale, including the idea of individual rights protections guaranteed by the state; he embraces a virtue-based, positive form of liberty in its place.

The centrality of the issue of liberal freedom to Deneen's project cannot be overstated because Deneen makes it one of two defining characteristics of liberalism—and so one of the two main causal forces behind liberalism's supposed failure. The core claim of *Why Liberalism Failed* is that liberalism contains the seeds of its own demise, and that its (alleged) collapse has been brought about, paradoxically, by its terrific success. In particular, an excess of liberal individualism has been liberalism's undoing: It has undermined traditional faith communities, laid waste to familial life, and given unbridled appetite full reign in the economy. Deneen's characterization of how liberal freedom has destroyed traditional education is characteristic of the broader argument: "The collapse of the liberal arts in this nation follows closely upon the *redefinition* of liberty, away from its ancient and Christian understanding of self-rule and disciplined self-command, in favor of *an understanding of liberty as the absence of restraints upon one's desires.*"[9]

Deneen presents liberal freedom in terms similar to Isaiah Berlin's "negative liberty" as presented in the famous 1958 speech, "Two Concepts of Liberty" and that largely coincide with the use of the term "liberal" throughout this volume.[10] By Deneen's lights, liberal freedom is unlimited and fundamentally ignoble. He asserts. "Liberty, as defined by the originators of modern liberalism, was the condition in which humans were *completely free to pursue whatever they desired.*"[11] He describes liberalism as the "titanic wager that ancient norms of behavior could be lifted in the name of a new form of liberation and that conquering nature would supply the fuel to permit nearly infinite choices."[12] Since Deneen argues that the essence of liberal democracy is the rejection of restraints in favor of endless personal choice and autonomy, he takes liberalism to signify an attack on all traditional cultures and institutions. A society simply can't have this understanding of freedom and sustain healthy institutions. Deneen does not discuss how this modern conception of liberty corresponds to a clear set of rights and expectations for citizens vis-à-vis their governments. In standard liberal conceptions of political freedom, governments exist to protect individual rights and choices—and this means that they are limited in key respects.[13] They cannot oblige a citizen to partake in a specific religious ritual, for example. Like Barr, then, Deneen focuses squarely on the social/cultural or nonpolitical dimensions of modern freedom.

In place of the liberal understanding of freedom, in *Why Liberalism Failed* Deneen seeks to rehabilitate what he takes to be a truer, more traditional understanding—one that is more closely related to Berlin's notion of "positive liberty." For Deneen, real freedom consists of the capacity to overcome and/or control one's desires. He writes that positive freedom involves "choosing the right and virtuous course" or "higher faculties of reason and spirit through the cultivation of virtue."[14] And he often focuses narrowly on private virtues and bodily self-control. "Liberty comes through habituation, training, and education—particularly the discipline of self-command," he writes.[15] In contrast to negative liberty, this has more to do with what Plato described as the correct ordering of the soul, with reason ruling over the spirit and the appetites and/or with the spiritual capacity to choose faith and grace over sin. Kant's moral idea of the freedom involved in moral decisions also resonates with what Deneen has in mind. The point is that in the positive conception, freedom doesn't just consist of the absence of external restraints or the practical liberty that an individual might have to do whatever they please. It also has an internal moral element: True freedom is something that individuals cultivate from within and that responsible communities should actively foster, too.

In *Why Liberalism Failed*, Deneen is dismissive of the limits that liberalism places on the government's role, especially when it comes to shaping morality (Deneen argues rather that the liberal state imposes a morality of its own). But he also gives short shrift to distinctly political extensions of positive moral virtue and self-control—which is to say, it gives short shrift to civic liberty of the kind so highly prized by the ancient Greeks and Romans (and arguably embraced, at least in part, by early modern liberals like John Locke). The apolitical, private nature of Deneen's preferred conception of liberty is perhaps most evident in his description of the purposes of liberal education. According to him, a traditional liberal education teaches "hard-won self-control through the discipline of virtue" and involves an "ethic of restraint"; it teaches us to be free from "the tyranny of internal appetite and desire"; the great books teach how to use liberty well, according to Deneen, and offer a special focus on "how to govern appetites that seemed inherently insatiable."[16] Here, he evinces little interest in those parts of classical liberal education that are concerned with civic ambition and political rule (not to mention other liberatory concerns—going back to Plato—that involve moving beyond or escaping convention).

Deneen is also highly ambiguous about the political gains achieved by modern liberalism. His basic practical recommendation in *Why Liberalism Failed* is that modern peoples should focus on their own selves and local communities, but toward the end of the book there is a passage that suggests that he is fundamentally uninterested in the liberal practice of guarding individual rights and liberties by delimiting state action. Having advocated for a retreat to a kind of thick, normative localism, Deneen refuses to address the possibility of autocratic (local) government overreach. Here is the passage I have in mind:

> Calls for restoration of culture and the liberal arts, restraints upon individualism and statism, and limits upon liberalism's technology will no doubt prompt suspicious questions. Demands will be made for comprehensive assurances that inequalities and injustice arising from racial, sexual, and ethnic prejudice be preemptively forestalled and that local autocracies or theocracies be legally prevented. Such demands have always contributed to the extension of liberal hegemony, accompanied by simultaneous

self-congratulation that we are freer and more equal than ever, even as we are more subject to the expansion of both the state and market, and less in control of our fate.[17]

In the American context the problem of local autocracy isn't an abstraction. It was the historical status quo for millions of Black and Indigenous people, and for other minorities too, until quite recently.[18] Deneen anticipates the liberal argument against autocratic local governments and heavy-handed communal norms, and rather than addressing such concerns directly, he mocks and dismisses them.

Adrian Vermeule, the Suppression of American Liberty, and Postliberal Extremism

After the publication of *Why Liberalism Failed*, a whole intellectual community emerged around Deneen's notion that it was time to move on from liberal democracy. One of the focal points for the group is a Substack newsletter and group blog called Postliberal Order, and there Deneen's main intellectual counterpart is Adrian Vermeule, the Ralph S. Tyler Professor of Constitutional Law at Harvard Law School.[19]

Vermeule was not well known outside of scholarly circles until he published a polemical essay with *The Atlantic* in March 2020. That essay was called "Common Good Constitutionalism" (or "Beyond Originalism") and in it Vermeule outlined a bold argument about the nature of constitutionalism that challenged standard legal practices and traditions on both sides of the American partisan divide.[20] In 2022, Vermeule published a book by the same title, *Common Good Constitutionalism*, in which he provided a vivid, theoretically elaborate, and ambitious framework for an American politics after liberalism.[21] Couched in the modest language of legal interpretation, Vermeule's book signifies a much more thorough displacement and replacement of American liberties and freedoms (as traditionally conceived) than did *Why Liberalism Failed*. Deneen's book condemned liberal notions of freedom and revived a positivist conception of moral liberty. Vermeule shares Deneen's frustrations with what he sees as contemporary libertinism, but he is less interested in redefining freedom, or reviving different conceptions of it, and more interested in diminishing its general relevance as an ideal or value of American jurisprudence.

Vermeule was explicit about the fact that, for him, Deneen's localist hopes for American renewal did not go nearly far enough. In a review of *Why Liberalism Failed* from February 2018, published in the journal *American Affairs* and entitled "Integralism From Within," Vermeule offered very high praise to Deneen's book, but also contended that Deneen lacked ambition. "An outstanding work might have been a masterpiece," he wrote.[22]

Vermeule's argument was that, by concluding with an open-ended and explicit retreat from theory and ideology and by petitioning for a return to localism, Deneen relapsed into a kind of inherent dependency on the pluralistic liberal order. Just as liberals worried that Deneen's localist communities will infringe on hard-earned rights and liberties, Vermeule (with reason) worries that "localist communities after Deneen's fashion must tremble indefinitely under the [liberal] axe." In other words, the local communities that Deneen favors might still be subject to liberal rights, protections, and norms. In his review of Deneen's book, Vermeule is explicit about the need to undermine liberal democracy more radically.

The title of the review, "Integralism From Within," was revealing. Integralism is a Catholic intellectual movement, of which Vermeule is a vocal participant, that rejects the traditional liberal separation of church and state and instead posits that the state and its various constituencies should be subject to Catholic spiritual authority and that man's "temporal end is subordinated to his eternal end."[23] Vermeule posits one way in which this transformation might be achieved: "The vast bureaucracy created by liberalism in pursuit of a mirage of depoliticized governance may, by the invisible hand of Providence, be turned to new ends, becoming the great instrument with which to restore a substantive politics of the good." Leon Wieseltier, in a powerful article that takes the integralists to task for their extraordinary willingness to whitewash the complexities (including the atrocities and oppression of the Jews) of premodernity and medieval Europe, memorably calls this Vermeule's method of "sacred subversion."

Liberal freedom, according to one of the main leaders of the movement, Edmund Waldstein, a Cistercian monk in Austria, is the root cause of many social problems today. He likens modern freedom to slavery, quoting scripture ("every one who commits sin is a slave to sin," John 8:34), and asserts that he "is therefore convinced that we should oppose the modern view of freedom by every possible means. The most important means of opposition is the revival of the traditional and true account of freedom."[24] There is nothing in Deneen's or Vermeule's work, that I have seen, that challenges what Waldstein said in this essay.[25] And Vermeule's review of Deneen's book includes a reimagining of the ending of *Why Liberalism Failed* whereby, rather than a retreat into localism, anti-liberals co-opt the power of the state to undo liberal freedoms. Listing several prominent religious figures who were able to rework political life by attaining positions of influence within the system, Vermeule speaks approvingly of a "determination to co-opt and transform the decaying regime from within its own core." He goes so far as to suggest that the vast bureaucracy created by liberalism might "by the invisible hand of Providence, be turned to new ends, becoming the great instrument with which to restore a substantive politics of the good."

Vermeule concludes the review with a frank plea for the destruction of liberalism. Just as Deneen anticipated and dismissed liberal concerns about the rights and freedoms of minorities, Vermeule concludes by dismissing liberal concerns about state coercion. The concluding passage is worth quoting in full:

> It is a useless exercise to debate whether or not this shaping from above is best understood as coercive, or rather as an appeal to the "true" underlying preferences of the governed. Instead it is a matter of finding a strategic position from which to sear the liberal faith with hot irons, to defeat and capture the hearts and minds of liberal agents, to take over the institutions of the old order that liberalism has itself prepared and to turn them to the promotion of human dignity and the common good. In my view, only in this way will liberalism well and truly fall victim to its own success. And this line of approach would make straight the crooked turn at the end of Deneen's near-masterpiece.

Where Deneen remained cautious and hedging, Vermeule was excitable and, from the perspective of mainstream American conservatism or liberalism, highly unorthodox.[26] Catholic integralism was not an explicit theme of Vermeule's *Atlantic* article or of his 2022 book. In both places Vermeule took pains to argue that his outlook could have broad, even secular, appeal.[27] But at bottom, what he advocated for in *Common Good Constitutionalism* was the rejection of liberal pluralism and freedoms and their replacement with a system of constitutional interpretation that posits a monolithic set of guiding values that together constitute what he terms "The Common Good," but which actually point towards distinctly Catholic values. Most importantly for our purposes, in both his definition of the common good and in the story he tells about the history of American constitutionalism, Vermeule removes freedom—liberal or otherwise—as a serious guiding principle or value. Whereas Deneen sought to redefine freedom, Vermeule works to demote it. This is a challenging task, especially in an American context.

So how does Vermeule define "The Common Good"? Vermeule treats it as relatively straightforward. As a general matter, the common good is, "for the purposes of the constitutional lawyer, the flourishing of a well-ordered political community."[28] He adds that the common good is "unitary and indivisible" rather than something that could be understood in the aggregate.[29] When getting more specific, Vermeule asserts that the common good consists of what he calls the classical "famous trinity" or "triptych" of *justice*, *peace*, and *abundance*, and then later adds the "modern triptych" of health, safety, and security.[30] Throughout the work Vermeule treats these six ends—justice, peace, abundance, health, safety, and security—as the straightforward objective aims of all healthy political life. The list of ends that constitute Vermeule's objective set excludes freedom and liberty.

According to Vermeule, the common good is the true end or aim of all law, and so too of all jurisprudence. He calls the tradition whose laws and norms aim at the ends that form the common good "The Classical Legal Tradition," and contrasts it with the liberal system. As he asserts towards the end of his introduction, "The largest point of the [classical legal] tradition is that public authority is both natural and legitimate—rather than intrinsically suspect, as one might infer from certain strands of the liberal tradition."[31] In other words, the classical legal tradition, unlike the liberal one, does not distrust authority or seek to delimit governmental power, but instead trusts the regime to act on behalf of the common good.

Vermeule further argues—and this is where his work becomes highly controversial—that the classical legal tradition he advocates in *Common Good Constitutionalism* is the long-forgotten jurisprudential doctrine that has always undergirded American jurisprudence. Vermeule presented *Common Good Constitutionalism* as a project of radical recovery, against a background of what he calls "our legal culture's amnesia."[32] Vermeule's claim is that American legal actors used to abide by common good constitutionalism and the classical legal tradition, but over time that tradition was lost and forgotten and replaced with the imposter theories of originalism and living constitutionalism. His claim is that the traditional American understanding is the same as his own—it's the classical legal understanding that excludes liberal freedom from its set of first principles.

This is a blatant form of historical revisionism that is impossible to reconcile with the historical record. Freedom plays a central role in the Declaration of Independence, the Constitutional Preamble, the Gettysburg Address, and so forth. Vermeule nevertheless works to make the case that freedom is better understood as a secondary value in the American pantheon of ideals.[33] Vermeule's explicit injunction to "sear the liberal faith with hot irons" is an example of explicit reactionary extremism. His subversive, revisionist diminishment of liberal freedom constitutes a clear example of Far-Right Newspeak.

In 2023, Patrick Deneen released a new book, titled *Regime Change*, in which he joins Vermeule in the project of "integralism from within." The title alone is dramatic and revealing and implies a total repudiation of liberal democracy. Here again Deneen elevates the supposed premodern conception of liberty and rejects liberal freedom (which supposedly does away with traditional "guardrails"), while saying little about the limits or guardrails—especially those having to do with spiritual matters—that modern liberalism seeks to place on government.[34] In this book Deneen, following Vermeule, advocates for "common-good conservatism," and the final chapter of the book is titled "Toward Integration." He coyly advocates for the transformation or "replacement" of today's elites with a new and more virtuous kind of truly aristocratic elite (a "genuine aristoi").[35] And he repeatedly (and in the first instance in bold characters no less) justifies the deployment of **Machiavellian means towards Aristotelian ends** as a central part of his new vision, at one point approvingly citing a particularly dramatic passage from Machiavelli that approvingly refers to mobs in the senate and the streets and "shops boarded up."[36] Elsewhere Deneen says that his regime change should involve "the peaceful but vigorous overthrow of a corrupt and corrupting liberal ruling class," but it is hard to read his citation of Machiavelli as anything other than an open flirt with the idea of violent action. Ironically, whereas Machiavelli was writing in defense of republican freedoms and the discords that these inevitably involve, Deneen's tumults would be on behalf of a postliberal movement that tends to denigrate political freedom and values order extremely highly.[37] While *Regime Change* is full of interesting theoretical observations about the old Aristotelian idea of a mixed constitution and contains some valuable recommendations about policy changes that could help revitalize American democracy, it is also an incredibly radical tract. In *Regime Change*, Deneen walks a fine line between cagey Far-Right Newspeak and outright right-wing extremism and autocracy.

Postliberalism in Practice

Patrick Deneen and Adrian Vermeule are both scholars whose work is highly abstract. What are some more concrete real-world applications of their ideas? It's worth noting that in the aftermath of Joe Biden's 2020 victory and the events of January, Vermeule was subject to a campaign by several Harvard Law School organizations who sought reprimands for his online posting, which they characterized as being "harmful to democracy." As reported in the Harvard *Crimson*, "The statement urges Law School administrators to condemn Vermeule's 'spread of inaccurate conspiracy theories about the election.'"[38] In addition, both Deneen and Vermeule have found affinities in Central Europe, in the relatively homogenous postcommunist regimes of Poland and Hungary, where right-wing populism and "illiberal democracy" have gained ascendance.

Adrian Vermeule gave a speech in Poland in 2018, at the invitation of the consul-general and in honor of the Polish intellectual Ryszard Legutko, in which he took on some of the controversies there concerning Polish sovereignty and a 2017 judicial reform there that gave the executive control over the country's court nominations (thereby consolidating the power of the ruling Law and Justice Party and eroding the principle of judicial independence).[39] Vermeule in no way denied that these actions on the part of the Polish government were illiberal and violated liberal principles; rather he implied that they were legitimate, having been enacted by elected representatives and according to constitutional procedures.[40] The implicit argument of the speech was that it is not possible to violate constitutional principles by way of democratic or constitutional procedures—a highly contestable claim—and, on the flipside, that anything an elected/popular ruler does is legitimate. This is a politically incoherent and unstable position insofar as it leans on the idea of electoral legitimacy while at the same time critiquing the processes and norms that guarantee fairness in elections.[41]

In Poland in 2018, Vermeule also called the controversial right-wing Brexit politician and major Trump backer Nigel Farage "the defining mind of our era."

In 2022, Vermeule and Deneen made another appearance in Warsaw, again for an event in honor of Legutko.[42] At that event, Vermeule praised Central Europe's embrace of "the European tradition in the broadest sense. . . . Which stands upon the three pillars of Greek philosophy, Roman law, and Catholic faith." He also expressed excitement about the New Right revival of "the European tradition" in the United States, praising the New Right movement for being "unafraid to use public authority in the service of the common good where necessary."

Deneen expressed a similar sentiment during a visit to Hungary in 2021.[43] In an interview at the Mathias Corvinus Collegium in Budapest, alongside conservative blogger Rod Dreher, Deneen was asked what main thoughts he would take back to the United States from Hungary. In his response, Deneen explained that American conservatives had a lot to learn from Hungary about the use of the laws to support economic and social security. He continued:

> In other words, in an age that fragments, that shatters, and that destabilizes, the only likely source for at least the practical everyday experience of human beings is going to come from the laws. It will also come from places like the churches and the communities, but in order to protect those spaces, we're going to need the help of the laws. And this runs contrary to a deep-seated sense of what it is to be an American: that to be free means that we have to be free of the government.
>
> I think we have a lot to learn about what will be the best protector of freedom, a kind of genuine freedom in a world in which you could say that the arrangements of the world are the deepest threats to a genuine kind of human flourishing, which I think is the deepest form of freedom that we can experience.

Here Deneen sounded a good deal like Bill Barr in his critique of the modern age, but in contrast to Barr, he argued for the active involvement of the country's legal and political institutions—with the aim of defending "genuine freedom" and "the deepest form of freedom." It is not difficult to imagine a future attorney general of the United States using such a rationale to defend illiberal and/or unconstitutional actions.

The postliberals' admiration for Viktor Orbán's Hungary is also well documented in their Substack publication, *Postliberal Order*. In August 2022, Patrick Deneen and Gladden Pappin published a "Dispatch From Budapest" that entailed their "Notes on a Conversation With Hungary's Viktor Orbán."[44] The post begins with high praise for the Hungarian prime minister. Deneen and Pappin write of Orbán's "remarkable candor," his "remarkable analytic and even philosophical depth." They claimed to have witnessed a "genuine tour de force of political analysis and vision, a quality almost wholly absent in today's American political class."

The post culminates in a description of Orbán's thoughts about how "conservative leadership can win, lead, and shape the next generation." And they claim, "Without question, Hungary is a singular example of such success in recent years." Orbán emphasized the importance of speaking directly to the people (this includes media "work-arounds" and conservative ownership of media), "shaping universities to promote a conservative worldview," promoting international cooperation among right-wing groups, focusing on youth leadership, and, finally, "Christianity and the management of society."

In their discussion of this final point, Deneen and Pappin wrote:

> The prime minister observed that, at root, the western European elite have lost the ability to manage their societies. Liberalism does not explain, justify or preserve the countries it takes over. True freedom, by contrast, rests on fundamental Christian commitments as well as a context of order.

Deneen and Pappin further praised Orbán's turn away from the "liberal conception" of freedom and his return to a Christian "framework for understanding the bedrock commitments needed for good politics." Orbán has been explicit in other contexts about his redefinition of liberty. In an interview from 2020 at a National Conservatism conference in Rome, he said, "We developed a new theory, a new approach: that is Christian Democracy. And instead of liberal freedom we use Christian liberty, so we have a wording how we describe the system we have built up."[45] The postliberals' praise for Orbán, and their invocation of postliberal freedom, is something of a gamble, because—as even they sometimes acknowledge—it presents a real mismatch with America's liberal-democratic traditions and with traditional American conceptions of freedom and liberty. There is a boldness to their initiative—in their willingness to claim that true freedom is something radically different and quite detached from America's political inheritances. And they are nothing if not sincere. Pappin moved from Dallas to Budapest with his family in 2021 to join the Mathias Corvinus Collegium as a visiting fellow, and in 2023 he took a job as president of the Hungarian Institute of Foreign Affairs—a job that involves advising Orbán directly.[46]

One major question is how any of these ideas would play out in an American context, given its vastly different history and social constitution—its more fully entrenched history of liberal-democratic constitutionalism, its diversity relative to Poland and Hungary, and the power of liberal notions of freedom in the American public imagination. On the other hand, Poland and Hungary are both part of the European Union and so subject to a measure of external pressure to act within the legal parameters of that institution.[47] In the United States, state actors are restrained in a similar way, at least to an extent; there are no such limits on America's national actors.

Conclusion

During his speech at Notre Dame, Bill Barr asked, "What is it that can fill the spiritual void in the hearts of the individual person? And what is a system of values that can sustain human social life?" He concluded, "The fact is that no secular creed has emerged capable of performing the role of religion." Bill Barr was right, in a way: There is no unifying liberal creed that has taken up the role of traditional religion in the modern world.

The postliberals blame liberalism and modern conceptions of freedom for modern spiritual malaise and supposed cultural atrophy. Patrick Deneen and Gladden Pappin write, "Liberalism is premised on the idea that we are naturally *free individuals*, autonomous beings that can construct from our free choices how we exist in the world, how we relate with other humans, our relationship to the natural world, how we understand religion and even God." They go on: "Nothing works so fast to dissolve the rich tapestry of human civilization as liberalism does."[48] Their solution is to work on behalf of a world after liberalism, and this includes a radical reorientation towards the concepts of liberty and freedom.

The postliberal intellectuals are not post-liberty, but their relationship to traditional American conceptions of liberty is highly fraught. In Deneen's case it is distorted and partial, like Far-Right Newspeak, and in Vermeule's account it is suppressed in the name of "constitutionalism"; for him, "constitutionalism" is the word being manipulated. In both cases, though, the less that liberal freedoms and liberties matter, the more the state has room to operate with impunity. And the idea of positive moral freedom and virtue formation (all in the service of their very own conception of the "Common Good") gives distinctive shape to potential postliberal governmental action. For the postliberals, the time has clearly come for modern governments to take a much stronger hand in shaping modern moral life and directing human action. If postliberalism has a future, it is because it is drawing on meaningful traditions besides liberalism to contend with some of liberalism's genuine vulnerabilities.

The problem, of course, is that there are real problems, risks, and potential losses here.

Postliberals critique multiculturalism (and the freedom to choose one's cultural and moral forms) as inherently destructive. But theirs is an odd and all-or-nothing conception of culture and one that contradicts the mixed-up and dynamic cultural and religious history of every place everywhere. The postliberals' work implies that only monolithic, traditional cultures count as real (though, as Wieseltier points out, no such thing has ever existed), and, furthermore, that the moment individuals are given cultural options and spiritual choices—that is, the moment they are granted liberal freedoms—they will choose not to take part in cultural life at all. That seems to deny the possibility of hybrid cultures and cultural innovation—that is, to deny so much of what empirically exists and flourishes in the contemporary, pluralistic world. The postliberals seem totally uninterested in even acknowledging the dynamism and hybridity that has been such a major part of their own Church history.

When the postliberals deny the value of liberal freedoms, they are also denying the spiritual value of individual autonomous action. One of the most compelling arguments in the liberal tradition (which is also there in the "classical" tradition as I understand it, going back to Plato and Aristotle) is that conscious moral deliberation and decision-making are an important part of what constitute our humanity—especially when it comes to essential matters like religion and politics. This is an important point of liberal pushback against postliberal conceptions of freedom and politics, and one way in which liberals might improve their own use of the language of liberalism. Liberal freedom isn't merely negative: It can be active and constitutive, too.

Liberals would also be wise to become more proactive about promoting community and cultural enrichment, as well as providing cultural and religious accommodations, within the strictures of liberal constitutionalism. If liberal society can make more room for citizens' faith and cultural traditions, including in public spaces and including traditional faiths, then the complaints of cultural disintegration and rampant secularism on the part of postliberals and other conservatives will be less persuasive.

But the most obvious risk that comes with postliberalism is a descent into authoritarianism, by way of something like illiberal constitutionalism or Caesarism. Hungary appears to be well on its way along this trajectory, which has involved manipulation of the electoral system, the judiciary and the separation of powers, state capture, laws that criminalize assistance to refugees, policies that exclude the LGBTQ community, the manipulation of media, "patrimonialism and clientelism," and increased state control of universities. It is not hard to see how such transformations could set the stage for far more oppressive forms of state action and indoctrination; indeed, it is difficult to conceive of anything that might limit such "Machiavellian means," apart from the particular beliefs and desires of those in power.[49]

The postliberals seek above all to establish cultural stability and order, but, to me, their political vision appears highly destabilizing. It is, after all, cynical about basic democratic forms—and such cynicism undermines existing institutions and the rule of law. It is dismissive, or contemptuous, of hard-fought liberal rights—and that could, of course, lead directly to abuses and unrest.[50] It is sloppy in its rhetoric, speaking breezily about "searing with hot irons," "Machiavellian means," and elite "replacement." And left unchecked, postliberalism would leave people at the mercy of the state—which is to say, coerced and unfree, including in core matters of faith and conscience. Dressed up in anodyne language of "genuine freedom," "genuine aristoi," and "Common Good Constitutionalism," upon analysis the postliberal future looks repressive, undemocratic, and narrow-minded. As far as Far-Right Newspeak goes, "postliberalism" might be one of the most Orwellian words of all.

Notes

1 See Marlene Laruelle, "Illiberalism: A Conceptual Introduction." *East European Politics* 38, no. 2 (2022): 303–27.
2 See especially Richard M. Weaver, *Ideas Have Consequences* (Chicago: University of Chicago Press, 1948).
3 Tímea Drinóczi and Agnieszka Bień-Kacała, "Illiberal Constitutionalism: The Case of Hungary and Poland," *German Law Journal*, no. 20 (2019): 1140–66. https://doi.org/10.1017/glj.2019.83. Also see Chapter 5 in this volume.
4 "Attorney General William P. Barr Delivers Remarks to the Law School and the de Nicola Center for Ethics and Culture at the University of Notre Dame," South Bend, IN. Friday, October 11, 2019, www.justice.gov/opa/speech/attorney-general-william-p-barr-delivers-remarks-law-school-and-de-nicola-center-ethics.
5 There is good evidence for the claim that America was a Christian nation at the time of the founding, but the idea that it was founded *as* a Christian nation is highly contested because several state constitutions precluded religious establishment, as does, of course, the First Amendment. And of course America has become much more pluralistic and spiritually diverse over the course of the past few centuries.
6 William P. Barr to President Donald J. Trump, December 14, 2020. See www.documentcloud.org/documents/20424018-attorney-general-william-barr-resignation-letter.
7 For example, see Barr's appearance on CNN in the immediate aftermath of Trump's third indictment. "Barr Says He Believes Trump 'Knew Well He Lost the Election,'" *CNN*, August 3, 2021, www.youtube.com/watch?v=X6m72ZQRBh8.
8 Patrick Deneen, *Why Liberalism Failed* (New Haven: Yale University Press, 2018).

9 Ibid., 116, emphasis added. For a fuller assessment and critique of this book, some of which is reasserted in this chapter, see Laura K. Field, "Revisiting Why Liberalism Failed," *Niskanen Center*, December 21, 2020, www.niskanencenter.org/revisiting-why-liberalism-failed-a-five-part-series/.
10 Isaiah Berlin, "Two Concepts of Liberty," in *Liberty* (Oxford: Oxford University Press, 2002), 166–217.
11 Deneen, *Why Liberalism Failed*, 100. See also Benjamin Constant, "The Liberty of the Ancients Compared With That of the Moderns," An Important Speech from 1819 that Influenced Berlin, https://oll.libertyfund.org/title/constant-the-liberty-of-ancients-compared-with-that-of-moderns-1819.
12 Deneen, *Why Liberalism Failed*, 41.
13 Constant, in "The Liberty of the Ancients Compared With That of the Moderns," is excellent on this point.
14 Deneen, *Why Liberalism Failed*, 100 and 113.
15 Ibid., 113.
16 Ibid., 114–15.
17 Ibid., 196–97.
18 For a powerful account of how twentieth-century European fascism paralleled, and was even anticipated by, the culture, practices, and legacy of American slavery, see Sarah Churchwell, "American Fascism: It Has Happened Here," *NYRB*, June 22, 2020, www.nybooks.com/online/2020/06/22/american-fascism-it-has-happened-here/.
19 https://postliberalorder.substack.com/, the other two regular contributors are Chad Pecknold of Catholic University and Gladden Pappin.
20 Adrian Vermeule, "Common Good Constitutionalism," *The Atlantic*, March 31, 2020, www.theatlantic.com/ideas/archive/2020/03/common-good-constitutionalism/609037/.
21 Adrian Vermeule, *Common Good Constitutionalism* (Cambridge: Polity Press, 2022).
22 Vermeule, "Integralism From Within," *American Affairs*, Spring 2018, https://americanaffairsjournal.org/2018/02/integration-from-within/.
23 The quote here comes from a website called The Josias, which is a good resource for understanding the contemporary Integralist movement (see https://thejosias.com/about/). See Edmund Waldstein, "Integralism in Three Sentences," October 17, 2016, https://thejosias.com/2016/10/17/integralism-in-three-sentences/. Vermeule converted to Catholicism in 2016 and has several entries on the Josias site.
24 Edmund Waldstein, "Contrasting Concepts of Freedom," *The Josias*, November 11, 2016, https://thejosias.com/2016/11/11/contrasting-concepts-of-freedom/. Vermeule cites this essay in his book (note 89, p. 198).
25 The best response to the rise of the integralists that I have seen is Leon Wieseltier's essay "Christianism," *Liberties*, Spring 2022, https://libertiesjournal.com/articles/christianism/.
26 In his review of Deneen, Vermeule acknowledges that among Western countries, the United States "best approximates a self-consciously liberal constitutional polity," and with this concedes the radical and anti-conservative nature of his own project.
27 For more on the religious underpinnings of Vermeule's work, see Micah Schwartzman and Richard Schwagger's review of his book in *The American*

Prospect ("What Common Good?" July 2022, https://prospect.org/culture/books/what-common-good-vermeule-review/).
28 Vermeule, *Common Good Constitutionalism*, 7.
29 With this assertion Vermeule glosses over some major questions of political philosophy dating back to Plato and Aristotle. Both classical Greek philosophers explored the question of common versus the individual good in depth in their major political works; though they each defended something like a common good approach to political existence, they never treat the matter as simple or settled.
30 See Vermeule, *Common Good Constitutionalism*, 7 and 59; see also 134, 138. Vermeule staunchly rejects other progressive values and developments as historical impositions on objective principles.
31 Vermeule, *Common Good Constitutionalism*, 7.
32 See Vermeule, *Common Good Constitutionalism*, 54 and 180.
33 Vermeule's sleight of hand vis-à-vis American history is most evident in a subsection of Chapter 1 titled "Moral Readings of the Constitution" (*Common Good Constitutionalism*, 38–43).
34 Patrick Deneen, *Regime Change* (New York: Sentinel Press, 2023). On various conceptions of freedom, see 4–6, 79–81, 197–98, and 228–29.
35 See *Regime Change*, 153–57, 185.
36 Ibid., 165, quoting Machiavelli's *Discourses on Livy*, Book 1, Chapter 4.
37 See introduction, xiii–xiv: "What is needed—and what most ordinary people instinctively seek—is stability, order, continuity, and a sense of gratitude for the past and obligation toward the future. What they want, without knowing the word for it, is a conservatism that conserves."
38 See Emmy Cho and Isabella Cho, "Harvard Law School Organizations Petition to Denounce Professor Adrian Vermeule's 'Highly Offensive' Online Rhetoric," *The Crimson*, January 13, 2021, www.thecrimson.com/article/2021/1/13/harvard-law-school-petition-vermeule/. For further discussion of conspiracism among intellectuals on the American New Right, see Laura K. Field, "On the Highbrow Conspiracism of the New Intellectual Right: A Sampling From the Trump Years," *Niskanen Center*, April 2021. www.niskanencenter.org/the-highbrow-conspiracism-of-the-new-intellectual-right-a-sampling-from-the-trump-years/.
39 See Adrian Vermeule, "Liberalism's Fear," *The Josias*, May 9, 2018, https://thejosias.com/2018/05/09/liberalisms-fear/.
40 Vermeule's outlook is consistent with the idea of "political constitutionalism" as discussed by Drinóczi and Bień-Kacała, "Illiberal Constitutionalism: The Case of Hungary and Poland," *German Law Journal*, no. 20 (2019): 1140–66. https://doi.org/10.1017/glj.2019.83.
41 At one point in the speech Vermeule claims that under liberalism, "Democracy is reduced to a periodic ceremony of privatized voting by secret ballot for one or another essentially liberal party, safely within a *cordon sanitaire*." He also argued that liberals are the ones who manipulate language.
42 See Adrian Vermeule, "In Honor of Ryszard Legutko," *Postliberal Order Substack*, June 20, 2022. www.postliberalorder.com/p/in-honor-of-ryszard-legutko.
43 See www.facebook.com/watch/live/?v=158843492853549&ref=watch_permalink; this quote comes from towards the end of the interview, at minute 1:09 or so. I have lightly edited Deneen's words for clarity.

44 See Patrick Deneen and Gladden Pappin, "Dispatch From Budapest: Notes on a Conversation With Hungary's Viktor Orbán," *Postliberal Order Substack*, August 5 2022. https://postliberalorder.substack.com/p/dispatch-from-budapest.
45 See "Prime Minister Viktor Orbán: Interview With Chris DeMuth," *NatCon Rome 2020*, https://youtu.be/9WP8xzxH7YY.
46 See Gladden Pappin, "Within the West, Hungary Has Set the Standard for a Reasonable Approach," *Postliberal Order Substack*, April 14 2023. https://postliberalorder.substack.com/p/within-the-west-hungary-has-set-the; see also "The Hungarian Institute of International Affairs Is Reorganized," https://kki.hu/en/the-hungarian-institute-of-international-affairs-is-reorganized/.
47 See Drinóczi and Bień-Kacała, "Illiberal Constitutionalism: The Case of Hungary and Poland," *German Law Journal*, no. 20 (2019): 1140–66, 1148, 1150. https://doi.org/10.1017/glj.2019.83.
48 See Patrick Deneen and Gladden Pappin, "Dispatch From Budapest: Notes on a Conversation With Hungary's Viktor Orbán," *Postliberal Order Substack*, August 5 2022. https://postliberalorder.substack.com/p/dispatch-from-budapest.
49 For elaboration on the mechanisms used to transform Poland and Hungary, see Drinóczi and Bień-Kacała, 2019; Robert Sata and Pawel Karolewsk, "Caesarean Politics in Hungary and Poland," *East European Politics* 36, no. 2 (2020): 206–25. https://doi.org/10.1080/21599165.2019.1703694; Kim Lane Scheppele, "How Viktor Orbán Wins," *Journal of Democracy* (July 2022): 45–61, www.journalofdemocracy.org/articles/how-viktor-orban-wins/; and Zach Beauchamp, "It Happened There: How Democracy Died in Hungary," *Vox*, September 13, 2018, www.vox.com/policy-and-politics/2018/9/13/17823488/hungary-democracy-authoritarianism-trump.
50 Both Deneen and Vermeule have been outspoken critics of gay marriage and *Obergefell v. Hodges* (2015), the US Supreme Court ruling that recognized the right to homosexual marriage. See Vermeule, *Common Good Constitutionalism*, 118–19, 120–23, and 131–33. In a set of 2015 reflections on *Obergefell* for the journal *First Things*, Deneen wrote, "While many have pointed to the 1973 decision of *Roe v. Wade* as an obvious historical analogue for the *Obergefell* decision, to my mind, the insistence that *all must conform* to the new, official definition of marriage that no civilization has ever endorsed until yesterday seems to be more aptly compared to life under Communism." See Patrick Deneen, "After Obergefell: A Symposium," *First Things*, June 27, 2015, www.firstthings.com/web-exclusives/2015/06/after-obergefell-a-first-things-symposium.

9
SHINE A LIGHT OR BURN IT DOWN? CONSPIRACISM AND LIBERAL IDEAS

Steven Pittz

In January 2022, legendary rock star Neil Young issued an ultimatum to the streaming service Spotify: "Joe Rogan, or me." Young threatened to pull his music from Spotify because Rogan, who hosts the wildly popular show "The Joe Rogan Experience," had interviewed Dr. Robert Malone. Malone is a virologist who researched mRNA Covid-19 vaccines but grew skeptical of them, and used his appearance on Rogan's show to air his critiques of the vaccines, critiques that Rogan entertained without entirely endorsing. Spotify chose Rogan, and listeners must look elsewhere to find "Heart of Gold," "Harvest Moon," or Young's other classic songs.

But the dispute brought Rogan even more into the public eye, as major media outlets and politicians alike joined Young in attacking him for interviewing Malone. Rogan was charged with abusing the idea of free speech to spread misinformation, and many suggested that he was allowing conspiracy theories to spread. Indeed, this volume has detailed how figures on the far right—which Rogan is alleged to be by some—have used the liberal principles of free speech and association to defend their ideas and challenge liberal regimes. In this light, Rogan may be charged with engaging in Far-Right Newspeak. At the same time, figures on the right allege that narratives offered by liberal political powers are untrue, engaging in conspiratorial thinking—what I call conspiracism—that purports to be more honest. While these two phenomena may appear at odds, in this chapter I show how they are connected. I make a distinction between "pragmatic" and "systemic" conspiracism. While pragmatic conspiracism can reflect the liberal virtues of questioning authority, checking the influence of powerful people and institutions, and civic participation—that is, *shining a light*, systemic conspiracism tends to undermine liberal democracy altogether, that is, *burning it down*. In essence, I suggest that pragmatic conspiracism is not Far-Right Newspeak, while systemic conspiracism may be.

First, I look at popular media through the podcasts of Joe Rogan and Russell Brand, interrogating their use of liberal ideas and language. I focus specifically on their use of conspiracism as a rhetorical device to counter the power of government and mainstream media outlets. I argue that while Brand's use of liberal language does not avoid systemic conspiracism, Rogan's tends to be more subtle. I suggest that Rogan may indeed occupy the middle ground of "pragmatic conspiracism," where liberal language is altered but not entirely abandoned. Second, I move from media to politics, where I evaluate how conspiracism and evolving interpretations of liberal ideas are affecting current libertarian parties. By investigating recent changes to the agenda of libertarian parties, I show how changes in liberal language begin to percolate into party politics. I end with a broader assessment of the relation between liberal language and conspiracism through these new uses of liberal ideas—when their use is appropriate or aligned with classical liberal theory and when they are abused to promote illiberal ends.

Conspiracism

Conspiracism is not typically associated with liberal language. Famous American conspiracy theories insist that Lee Harvey Oswald alone did not kill John Kennedy, the moon landings were faked, and that the public account of the 9/11 attacks conceals a deeper truth—"jet fuel can't melt steel beams." Conspiracy theorists tend not to be concerned with correspondence to the world and are so far outside the mainstream that they do not appear concerned with convincing others in great numbers. Conspiracy theory generally involves detailed, complicated reinterpretations of the world. Yet at the same time, there are certain liberal virtues that are practiced in the process of developing conspiracies, namely a skepticism of authority, open access to information, and active participation by citizens in debate oriented toward understanding our shared political world. After all, a free press is considered integral to liberal democracies. Journalists employed these conspiratorial virtues in uncovering the Watergate scandal, the Pentagon Papers, the roots of the 2008 financial crisis, and other conspiracies that figures in authority would have been happy to remain unknown. In this chapter, then, I distinguish between pragmatic and systemic conspiracism. I suggest that while systemic conspiracism can lead to anti-democratic conspiracy theories that seek to *burn it all down*, pragmatic conspiracism can reflect those liberal virtues that allow citizens to *shine a light* on powerful people and institutions.

Increased attempts to challenge establishment views have wrought a growth in conspiratorial thinking. Conspiratorial ideas, particularly in online spaces, trafficked primarily—but not exclusively—by those on the right, have led to what recent scholars have labeled "conspiracism."[1] Conspiracism is less sophisticated than the typical conspiracy theorizing. The latter is often quite complex and marshals substantial evidence to arrive at a compelling, but alternative, explanation of events (for example, the sophisticated conspiracy surrounding the assassination of JFK). They are to some extent science- or knowledge-based, presenting an alternative narrative while using facts similar to those employed in the dominant narrative. Conspiracism, on the other hand, is memetic and repetitive. It propagates through "coded" words and loose ideas. The apparent simplicity of conspiracism is a major reason for its success—it doesn't require extensive knowledge of a situation to be used.

At first glance, conspiracism seems simply dangerous, an assault on truth and something that must be rooted out. Upon closer inspection, however, conspiracism is more complex, particularly as it exists in liberal democracies, where great emphasis is placed on citizen involvement, government accountability, and democratic deliberation. I want to suggest here that conspiracism is not simply anti-liberal or anti-democratic, as its attributes can either exemplify or pervert liberal values. A sensible way to distinguish between them is offered by Nadia Urbaniti, who observes a difference between "pragmatic" conspiracism and "systemic" conspiracism. The former can coexist with, and even represent, liberal-democratic life. Pragmatic conspiracism brings to light issues that would otherwise remain in the dark.

> This unveiling process is an important part of political life. We would not say that democracy requires or is equivalent to conspiracy, but undeniably, most of the actions connected to this kind of conspiracy are an expression of democratic politics because they are an attempt to establish the priority of publicity in political competition.[2]

There are democratic virtues present in pragmatic conspiracism: It can hold leaders to account, increase publicity and transparency, and increase political engagement and the rhetorical power of average citizens.

We do not find similar virtues in systemic conspiracism. Here we see not a "detective-style search"[3] to uncover truths kept hidden by those in power, but instead a full-scale assault on the dominant narrative, irrespective of facts that may be concealed. Employed through bare assertion and repetition, systemic conspiracism seeks to delegitimate all authority, disorient those who encounter it, and distort reality in order to sow doubt in fellow citizens. It also tends toward dogmatic and authoritarian claims, frequently without evidence. The prevailing attitude in pragmatic conspiracism is skepticism of authority, which is fundamentally a liberal virtue. In systemic conspiracism, the prevailing attitude is the dogmatism that authority is corrupt. One can also observe conspiracism devolving from pragmatic to systemic. What begins as a good faith exploration of alternative ideas can end in a bad faith attempt to distort reality and destroy one's enemies. Indeed, George Hawley charts a similar sort of devolution in the online "Manosphere" in Chapter 7 of this volume.[4]

Evaluating the use of conspiracism is, then, a difficult but ineluctable task. Alternative media has created a political environment ripe for conspiratorial thinking. On the one hand, new avenues for generating conspiracism are freer than ever. On the other hand, conspiracism has often become more authoritarian in its content. If we can distinguish between the more liberal, democratic, pragmatic variety and the more authoritarian, systemic variety, we can better assess the impact of conspiracism. We can also decipher which instances of conspiracism can be left alone, in order to benefit from their virtues, and which need to be combatted to neutralize their vices. We should also be on our guard for those conspiracists who "speak the language of liberalism." Indeed, conspiracism of the pragmatic variety can be a liberal virtue. But systemic conspiracism is indubitably a "liberal" vice, and those that use liberal language to promote or defend the illiberal ends of systemic conspiracism must be challenged.

We cannot expect, however, that these dangers will discourage conspiracists. The rhetorical power of conspiracism is quite evident to its users, and with new media forms that facilitate its generation, we can plausibly expect conspiracism to maintain, even increase, its role in shaping political discourse. The immense popularity of the likes of Rogan and Brand is evidence of this, and there is no shortage of figures emulating them. Moreover, conspiracism is a genuinely global phenomenon. It is substantially aimed at global elites and domestic actors perceived to benefit from economic globalization, or even the more encompassing idea of "globalism." Backlash against the "Great Reset" and "rootless cosmopolitan elites" is often a theme of conspiracists, an issue considered by José Pedro Zúquete in Chapter 10.[5]

Podcasts and Free Speech

In recent years, podcasts have become a preferred media format for right-wing pundits, journalists, and intellectuals. Much like the rise of conservative talk radio pioneered by Rush Limbaugh in the 1980s to counter a left-wing-dominated network media, the world of podcasting has emerged as a contemporary right-wing response to what is perceived as continued left-wing domination of major media outlets and public radio. Among these podcasts are two with uncommon influence, *The Joe Rogan Experience* in the United States and *Stay Free With Russell Brand* in the United Kingdom. In this section, by analyzing their use of liberal language to articulate alternatives to mainstream narratives, I illuminate the widespread discursive changes this volume seeks to understand and explain.

For anyone who pays attention to politics, Joe Rogan needs little introduction. Formerly a mixed-martial artist and stand-up comedian, Rogan started his podcast in 2009. It is immensely popular, as it is downloaded nearly 200 million times a month[6] and dominates standard cable news outlets like CNN and MSNBC in sheer viewing numbers. Rogan attracts 11 million viewers per episode. CNN prime time anchor Anderson Cooper, by contrast, draws 238,000. Even NBC Nightly news with Lester Holt has lower viewership than a Rogan podcast.[7] Politicians, industry titans, academics, athletes, entertainers, and others have become wise to Rogan's influence. The impact of appearing on his show can be immense: take, for example, the rapid political ascension of Andrew Yang, whose campaign manager (Zach Graumann) credits an appearance on the *Joe Rogan Experience* for putting Yang on the debate stage in the 2020 presidential election.[8] Rogan had Bernie Sanders as a guest and later endorsed him. Reps. Tulsi Gabbard and Ben Crenshaw have sat across from Rogan on multiple occasions. Mark Zuckerberg appeared on Rogan to drum up interest for his new Metaverse, and Elon Musk has appeared multiple times. Musk infamously smoked cannabis with Rogan on an appearance in 2018, and Tesla's stock dropped nine percent in the immediate aftermath—another testament to the power of the podcast.[9]

Though many of Rogan's guests are uncontroversial and unrelated to politics, his show has given airtime to some fringe political figures, most notably Alex Jones—who was recently more or less bankrupted by lawsuits related to his false claims that the Sandy Hook school shooting was a false flag event. Rogan's podcast also sparked controversy over the Covid vaccine, particularly over the effectiveness of the drug Ivermectin as a possible treatment option. Bret Weinstein—a professor turned podcaster after leaving Evergreen College—claimed on the podcast, "Ivermectin alone is capable of driving this pathogen to extinction."[10] Later, Rogan hosted the virologist Robert Malone to discuss the vaccines. Dr. Malone had been banned by Twitter for violating "Covid misinformation policies" and was widely considered by the medical establishment to be spreading misinformation. On Rogan's show, Malone presented the dangers of the Covid vaccine, claiming that those who get vaccinated after already having had the virus are at a greater risk of adverse side effects.[11] Rogan also repeatedly recommended that young people should focus on improving the overall health of their immune systems rather than take the vaccine.[12] Rogan's stance on Covid vaccination garnered a substantial response from mainstream outlets, and even resulted in musician Neil Young demanding that Spotify (which owns the rights to *The Joe Rogan Experience*) either cut ties with Rogan or remove all Young's music from the platform.[13]

Russell Brand is also an influential podcaster, albeit not at the level of Rogan. Based in the UK, Brand enjoys a healthy six million subscribers, and an average episode garners approximately 750,000 viewers[14] (compared to Rogan's 13 and 11 million, respectively). Such statistics are sufficient to make Brand the #4 ranked politics podcast in the United States and #9 in the UK.[15] While Brand does bring in guests to interview on his YouTube channel, his primary means of reaching his audience is through 10- to 15-minute monologues. Whereas Rogan only creates long-form interviews, Brand employs short videos highlighting his own reactions to political and cultural events and trends. Throughout his career as a pundit, Brand has been a vocal and open advocate for progressive causes, particularly the issue of income inequality. He is also, however, a vocal supporter of free speech and a critic of censorship in all its forms. Not coincidentally, he named his podcast "*Stay Free With Russell Brand*," and he promises to engage with heterodox views and to hold political, media, and cultural elites to account. In September of 2022, Brand was censored by YouTube for (like Rogan) misinformation regarding Covid policies. Brand also touted the efficacy of Ivermectin, and for this any content related to the subject was taken down from YouTube. While Brand conceded that he must do a better job ensuring the accuracy of information presented on his podcast and even apologized for the airing of imperfect information, YouTube refused to put the videos back up. This resulted in Brand leaving YouTube for Rumble, where he now hosts his podcast.[16] Such a move may seem strange for a progressive, as Rumble is considered a conservative platform that hosts the likes of Donald Trump Jr. and Alex Jones. For Brand, however, the move was driven by a desire for free speech and a lack of censorship—"Rumble claims to be a platform that is 'immune to cancel culture' and aims to 'protect a free and open internet.'"[17]

What unites Rogan and Brand—along with many other lesser-known right-wing media personalities—is their self-portrayal as truth-tellers and defenders of democracy and freedom. They see the government and mainstream media—the "Establishment"—as enemies of free thought. It is up to them, and other alternative media, to create a space for heterodox views that are ignored or covered up by those with more power to shape political discourse. As a result, they are also a platform for conspiracism, or the propagation of alternative narratives on current events. We now turn to a discussion of this phenomenon.

Rogan and Brand as Conspiracists

I now move to assessing our chosen right-wing actors, applying the theoretical framework I outlined in the preceding section. In focusing on Rogan and Brand, there are three crucial questions we must answer: To what extent do we see conspiracism employed in this case? Is said conspiracism of the pragmatic or systemic variety? How are liberal ideas used, how do they speak the language of liberalism to protect and facilitate their conspiracism?

To recap, many similarities exist in the approaches of Rogan and Brand. Both entertain heterodox and often conspiratorial ideas, both consider the issue of censorship and the value of free speech to be major challenges of contemporary media, and both reach substantial audiences. Their skepticism of mainstream media and elite political and cultural discourse is perhaps one of the reasons for their large followings. Liberal openness, buttressed by free speech, is essential to their craft, and they both make statements that reflect recognition of this fact.[18] Their skepticism, however, also leads to frequent conspiracism. The size of their platforms and their reach renders Rogan and Brand as important purveyors of conspiratorial ideas. Indeed, both engender impassioned responses among those who see such conspiracism as dangerous. I weigh this danger to liberal society by applying the categories of pragmatic and systemic conspiracism. Where might we place Brand and Rogan, and are their respective approaches significantly different?

Let's begin from the position that neither podcaster pushes a cynical agenda or harbors malicious intent when platforming heterodox, out-of-the-mainstream, conspiratorial ideas. In most cases, they do appear interested in getting at the truth rather than furthering a certain agenda. Nonetheless, I think Rogan does a much better job of facilitating genuinely liberal and open conversations, fit for a liberal society that prizes democratic deliberation. Despite the controversy surrounding the *Joe Rogan Experience*, there is much that is liberal about the podcaster's approach. While he entertains conspiratorial ideas, he always does so by way of a long-form conversation. He generally gives a full hearing to opposing viewpoints, trying to understand the position of his guest before asking questions. He defends free speech for those with whom he agrees and disagrees. He often seeks to book guests on different sides of the same issue, and in most cases treats those guests in like fashion, first allowing the guest to thoroughly present their position.

Moreover, he rarely claims definitive knowledge of the subjects discussed. The Covid controversy is a case in point. After receiving substantial backlash for "giving a platform" to vaccine skeptics and for discussion of alternative treatments, Rogan clarified that he is "not an anti-vax person" and also repeatedly insisted, "I'm not a doctor" or a "respected source of information."[19] He did maintain, however, his stance that young people should skip the vaccine and consider natural immunity. In order to give the same platform to the mainstream view of Covid and its treatment, Rogan invited CNN chief medical correspondent Sanjay Gupta in for a three-hour interview. The case for vaccination had its hearing, and Gupta wrote later about the openness of the conversation, even if he was ultimately unable to completely change Rogan's mind.[20] Whatever conspiratorial positions are taken on the *Joe Rogan Experience*, their presentation is essentially pragmatic. The end is to explore all possible explanations (within reason and a three-hour time window) to get at the truth, and the means is one of liberal, open conversation.[21]

For interviewing one scientist skeptical of the mainstream account about Covid vaccines and one who promoted these claims, Rogan has been critiqued for implying a false equivalency about the prominence of skeptical positions in the scientific community. Yet there is nothing illiberal about suggesting that the validity of arguments is not wholly dependent on the number of "experts" who defend them. One hundred years ago, a majority of doctors would not have said that cigarettes were harmful; that only a small minority objected does not mean that any newspaper that elevated that minority's argument in dialogue with the majority was being illiberal. Indeed, though the claims of Rogan's most vaccine-skeptical guests have not been vindicated, as more time passes it becomes clear that much of the popular wisdom propagated about Covid vaccines—such as that vaccination makes one a "dead-end" for the virus—was not entirely true. As Samuel Piccolo suggests in the concluding chapter to this volume, liberal democracies can weaken trust among citizens when heavy-handed efforts to control information popularize narratives that turn out not to be fully true. Liberal democrats might find that the virtue of genuine skepticism, which at his best Rogan practices, could strengthen public trust.

Brand's approach cannot be so easily defended. While Brand does exercise, and consciously model, free speech as a means of questioning authority, the sheer frequency and volume of his attacks on "elites" makes it hard to label him a pragmatic conspiracist. A simple enumeration of Brand's podcast titles is enough to demonstrate the point. We need only look at titles from recent months to observe the tactics and trends, say from September to November 2022. Here is a small sample:

"Hang On, Now They Want Your BLOOD!?"; "THIS Is How US Has LIED About Ukraine War"; "Midterms: They Don't Want You To Know THIS"; "Pfizer Didn't Expect THIS To Be EXPOSED"; "So THIS Is Why They Didn't Want Him To Have It" [On Elon Musk acquiring Twitter]; "Holy Sh*t, Trump Was About To Reveal THIS"; "The Queen's Funeral— The HIDDEN Truth THAT NOBODY IS TALKING ABOUT"; "This is F*cking Dangerous"; "It's Official. . . . They Lied"; "Bill Gates Has WHAT Under All His Properties?!"; "So, It's All Bullsh*t"; "Come On. . . . They Can't Be Serious!"[22]

What should we make of such titles? Of course, content creators are nearly all culpable of using "clickbait" titles to draw in viewers. This practice is morally dubious in itself, but Brand is certainly not alone in using it. What is striking, however, is how often Brand seeks to plant the seeds of doubt about anyone in a position of authority. Brand routinely seeks to delegitimate those in power, often through suggesting malicious intent amongst leaders of all sorts—political, cultural, industrial, and so on. Notice, for example, how frequently he employs the pronoun "they" to identify who is behind something fishy. If one watches enough of Brand's podcast, it becomes evident that "they" almost always refers to "elites," or those who hold institutional power in politics, media, industry, or culture. "They" always seem to be conspiring in some way, and their conspiracy is never to the benefit of "regular" citizens.

Brand is not a merely pragmatic conspiracist, seeking only to shed light on ideas, facts, or theories that are potential alternatives to the mainstream narrative. His approach is aimed also, if not primarily, at inculcating wholesale disaffection and distrust with both elites and the political system itself. In other words, the aim is to burn the system down rather than to shine a light on particular issues. Recalling our earlier definition of systemic conspiracism, we see a full-scale assault on the dominant narrative, irrespective of facts that may be concealed. He seeks often to delegitimate all authority, disorient those who encounter it, and distort reality in order to sow doubt in fellow citizens. In Brand's monologues we also see greater prevalence of dogmatic and authoritarian claims, often with scant evidence. This tendency is exacerbated by Brand's format—brief and punchy *monologues*—which cannot be challenged in any way, in real time. They are also more likely to result in the dogmatic and authoritarian claims of the systemic conspiracist. This "burn-it-down" approach is common in far-right discourse and is compatible with authoritarian or even fascist political movements. Once institutions are successfully diagnosed as in terminal decline, and widely perceived as thoroughly corrupted and irredeemable, reforms to them are similarly perceived as impossible. Instead of incremental changes achieved through a democratic process, a call for a revolution—coming from the right—to recover an uncorrupted past seems the only way forward. Josh Vandiver discusses a similar notion of "political death" in Chapter 11 of this volume.[23]

Rogan, on the other hand, entertains conspiratorial ideas but approaches them in a much more skeptical way. Rogan's format—a three-hour *dialogue*—invites much more questioning of conspiratorial ideas themselves. A dialogue is also fundamentally democratic in nature. Rogan's is a "shine-a-light" approach. Indeed, Rogan's conspiracism is closer to the pragmatic version, whereas Brand's leans towards the systemic, with the caveat that neither assessment can be considered categorical. The analysis requires measuring the degree to which specific content conforms to either type of conspiracism, so a blanket label around all their respective content is inappropriate. Nevertheless, the distinction between the two is critical. Liberal democracy requires openness and deliberation, which not only allow shared governance but also bolster the legitimacy of those doing the governing. Pragmatic conspiracism, like Rogan's, is fundamentally liberal in nature. Rogan both speaks the language of liberalism and models a form of democratic deliberation. This does not mean that Rogan always comes to a conclusion that traditional liberal democrats will agree with, but his use of liberal language is not generally an abuse. Brand may often claim a liberal approach—particularly in his defense of free speech—but his systemic conspiracism is hardly a useful tool for the construction and maintenance of a liberal-democratic regime. Both "speak the language of liberalism," but only Rogan can be considered an ambassador of the liberal-democratic ideal.

The Libertarian Party (LP)

Next, I would like to turn to a second case study on the Libertarian Party (LP) in the USA, the largest "third" party in American politics.[24] Changes to the party in recent years reflect the changing meanings and usages of many classical liberal ideas. Moreover, the party has moved in a direction that appears more comfortable entertaining conspiracies to gain adherents. Here we explore the evolving meaning of liberal ideas in the LP, that is, how liberalism is "spoken" differently now, but first we require a brief history of libertarianism. For starters, older libertarian platforms emphasized the classic liberal ideals of individual rights, maximal freedom, free market economics, and property rights. They supported freedom of movement and were pro-immigration. In the past and today, however, these platforms saw the inclusion of other ideas as well. Libertarians merged these classically liberal ideas (or reinterpreted them) with populist or paleoconservative ideas. Populism and paleoconservatism became central to the libertarian platform in 2017, after the election of Donald Trump. They remain so in the Mises Caucus wing of the party, which currently holds the most institutional power, at least in terms of positions in party offices. The intellectual seeds of this growth, however, were planted earlier by the Mises Institute, via Murray Rothbard and Lew Rockwell.

Beginning in the 1990s, Rothbard and Rockwell advocated for the adoption of "paleo-libertarianism," which married classical liberal ideals with a more traditional, right-wing approach. This was done primarily through the Ron Paul newsletters, which were largely ghostwritten by Rockwell. Both Rothbard and Rockwell were interested in bringing libertarianism to the middle classes and reducing the power of "elite" libertarians in Washington, DC. Rockwell accused Beltway libertarians of "hatred of Western culture" and of promoting the degeneration of American culture.[25] He further argued, "the family, the free market . . . the individual, private property rights, the very concept of freedom—are all products of our religious culture."[26] In a famous letter in 1992, Rothbard added a "Right-Wing Populist Program" to the libertarian agenda, which included a defense of traditional family values, an "America First" foreign policy outlook, and abandonment of "the absurd left-atheist interpretation of the First Amendment" in favor of supporting public displays of Christian religion.[27] All of these reforms were aimed at garnering support of the middle classes at the expense of the elites and to apply libertarian ideas in ways that pit the middle class against the state.

Such changes to the classical liberal libertarian agenda are strange on the level of principle. Historically, libertarianism was quite consistent in its resistance to authority, whether emanating from the state or from cultural institutions within society. While classical liberalism was not openly hostile to religious tradition, it took pains to separate church and state and to emphasize freedom of conscience. The "live and let live" mantra of libertarianism ought to the promotion of certain values, certain religions, and certain nations. Rothbard precisely does promote these things, and the reasons are political: the fusion of classical liberal libertarians and paleo-libertarians' attempts to extend the reach of libertarianism by highlighting what the two camps share. As Andy Craig and John Hudak note, both groups are anti-elite and anti-establishment, and both want to radically alter the state.[28] As a testament to this partnership, in 2016 Rockwell encouraged libertarians to cast a vote not for libertarian candidate Gary Johnson but for Donald Trump. Northwestern law professor Andrew Koppelman charts the change in libertarianism in a recent book, arguing that, following Hayek, the libertarianism of the twentieth century was focused on a free market correction to the follies of central planning. In the twenty-first, however, it has focused, following Rothbard, on an extreme anti-statism (unsurprising given Rothbard's self-declared anarcho-capitalism).[29]

In short, the notion is that libertarianism needs populism to clear the path for a libertarian revolution. Populists combat the power of elites, strip power from the state, and thereby allow for the possibility of implementing libertarian ideas and policies. Populism links with conspiracism, and if one studies Rothbard's 1977 draft essay, "Toward a Theory of Libertarian Social Change," the connection becomes apparent. Interrogating the motives of elites is an essential activity of both populists and conspiracists. Moreover, Rothbard does not shy away from the need to delegitimate those in authority to pave the way for libertarians' ideas. "Most people," Rothbard argues,

> have neither the time, interest, or ability to be experts in every area important to their lives and concerns; they therefore *have* to rely on expert authorities to form their judgments in these areas—from politics to morals to economics to medicine. But since, in most of these areas, authorities are in the well-paid service of the State, it becomes vital for libertarians to *desanctify*, to delegitimate these alleged authorities in the eyes of the deluded public.[30]

And Rothbard realizes that this truth-telling will be labeled conspiracist by the Establishment itself: "This sort of analysis, of course, is commonly countered—particularly by Establishment liberals and conservatives—with the charge that it is merely an exercise in 'the conspiracy theory of history,' 'paranoia.'"[31] In short, anyone who seeks revolutionary change via attacks on the Establishment should expect to be labeled a conspiracist.[32]

Both the paleo/populist strategy and the conspiracist tactics of Rothbardian libertarianism continue with the Mises wing of the LP today. In a 2017 speech for the Mises Institute, Hans-Hermann Hoppe (a direct intellectual descendent of Rothbard) made the case for the compatibility of libertarianism and the Alt-right. This is a continuation of the paleo-libertarian approach, albeit in modified form. The subtitle of his talk was "In Search of a Libertarian Strategy for Social Change," recalling Rothbard's 1977 essay. Remarkably, its form mirrors that of Rothbard's 1992 letter. Hoppe's recommendations have been accepted, to a large extent, by the Mises Caucus of today's American LP, which actively courts disaffected citizens (mostly young and online) who are not drawn primarily to liberal ideas but to Alt-right frustrations with establishment elites.[33] The Mises Caucus finds traditional libertarian outlets like the CATO Institute and *Reason* magazine much too conciliatory to elite agendas, and has sought—and gained—power in the LP by appealing to issues, or at least not rejecting issues, favored by social conservatives and those on the Alt-right. The Caucus made a concerted effort to appeal to Trump voters and to bring ideas from the MAGA platform into the libertarian "Overton window." As James McAdams discusses in the Introduction, the "Overton window" refers to the range of acceptable ideas in political discourse, and was originally politicized by a libertarian think tank.[34] With this new agenda, the Mises Caucus swept into power in May of 2022, gaining all the leadership positions in the LP, highlighted by the election of Angela McArdle as National Committee Chairperson.[35]

Much of this success can be attributed to the Mises Caucus's use of conspiracism and the language of liberalism to further their agenda via a number of avenues. First, the Caucus used free speech to appeal to the fringe. Libertarianism has always been a fringe ideology, and there is a sense in which those personally attracted to libertarianism continually seek the outer bounds of what is politically acceptable.[36] Put differently, libertarians tend to seek out alternative viewpoints and positions, which put them in tension with both the dominant narratives and the culture of political correctness. The Mises Caucus has affirmed the value of free speech, and its critics say it relies on this strident affirmation to challenge language norms and say controversial things. Justin Amash, who in 2020 became the first member of the LP to ever serve in the US Congress, worries that the Mises Caucus often resorts to making "outrageous statements just to get attention."[37] To the contrary, Mises Caucus founder Michael Heise claims that the previous LP administration tried in vain to appeal to the "middle," effectively eliminating what was different about the LP. Not only was bolder messaging required, Heise also claimed, "we need to push forward our own culture, our own vision, our own language, our own narrative."[38]

This attitude appeals to the Alt-right, hence it is not difficult to divine why those on the Alt-right sought a home in the Libertarian Party. For the contemporary LP and the Alt-right generally, freedom of speech means something closer to fearless speech (the Greek *parrhesia* or the notion of speaking truth to power). Fearless speech is, of course, an important component of the right to free speech, but it can also mean something closer to saying provocative and offensive things to prove one's freedom. Petra Mlejnková describes a similar situation in Chapter 4 on the Czech Republic, where defending free speech is a "vehicle to justify what is actually offensive speech characterized by intolerance and harmful rhetoric."[39] While *parrhesia* is a protected form of speech, it is not the only way to conceive of freedom of speech. A more holistic, and classically liberal, interpretation of free speech views it as a fundamental right that protects individuals from government propaganda, facilitates democratic deliberation, and promotes shared governance. Thus, while the LP and Alt-right emphasize the liberal value of free speech, they do not do so in the most liberal way. The goal is not to bolster the practice of liberal democracy, but often to boldly assert their contempt for democratic practices.[40] Coupled with Rothbardian anti-statism, the policy positions and the rhetoric adopted by the Mises Caucus skew more towards a systemic conspiracist approach than a liberal, pragmatic approach.

Take, for example, the reinterpretation of classical liberal ideas by the Mises Caucus. They use concepts like property rights and freedom of association to justify anti-immigration and a generally exclusionary politics. From Locke's Second Treatise to the present, property rights have dominated classical liberal and libertarian theory. Private property protects other basic rights and was traditionally predicated on a concept of self-ownership, since for Locke property meant "life, liberty, and estate." Belief in self-ownership and individual autonomy, then, was historically linked with the justification for property rights. In recent years, however, this link has been severed, or at least stretched, by some libertarians. Today, libertarianism may be split between those that make self-ownership or autonomy the basis of libertarian philosophy and those who identify the basis as private property rights.[41] This split mirrors the division between left-libertarians and paleo-libertarians, or right-wing populists. The latter group ties property rights to freedom of association, with an emphasis on that freedom's exclusionary character. We are free to associate with whom we choose, which comes with the contrary freedom to choose whom we will not associate with. On the property we own, this right to exclude is absolute.

Much as in the case of free speech, we see a liberal value—freedom of association—interpreted or "spoken" in an illiberal way. The right to exclude becomes the basis for merging the right-wing populist anti-immigration effort with libertarianism. Perhaps the most influential purveyor of this agenda is the aforementioned Hoppe, who attempted to lay out the new libertarian strategy in a 2017 speech. In his enumeration of ten "specifics of a populist strategy for libertarian change," Hoppe places "Stop mass immigration" in the first spot, claiming it of "the greatest urgency."[42] Recall that in this speech Hoppe is updating and modifying his mentor Rothbard's 1992 strategy. In the 1992 letter, Rothbard identifies eight crucial goals for right-wing populism. In 2017, Hoppe identifies ten for a libertarian–Alt-right partnership, five of which directly replicate Rothbard's list.

The primary divergence of Hoppe's strategy is, however, the focus on immigration. Relying on freedom of association and the right to exclude, Hoppe argues,

> no one is against immigration and immigrants per se. But immigration must be by invitation only. All immigrants must be productive people and hence, be barred from all domestic welfare payments. To ensure this, they or their inviting party must place a bond with the community in which they are to settle, and which is to be forfeited and lead to the immigrant's deportation should he ever become a public burden.[43]

Hoppe recognizes that the anti-immigrant stance is anathema to many, if not most, libertarians, who support immigration and freedom of movement. To those he has a message:

> To all open-border and liberallala libertarians, who will surely label this, you guessed it, "fascist": In a fully privatized libertarian order there exists no such thing as a right to free immigration. Private property implies borders and the owner's right to exclude at will. And "public property" has borders as well. It is not unowned. It is the property of domestic taxpayers and most definitely not the property of foreigners.[44]

This position is shared by the Mises Caucus, who once in power deleted a commitment to open borders in the LP charter.[45]

Property-owning citizens and states alike have the right to exclude those who are not of benefit to them, and this sense of property rights becomes a new or revived basis for libertarianism. Again, as in the case of free speech, we observe liberal ideas or values (freedom of association mediated through property rights) put forward to justify what most would consider an illiberal end (closed borders and heavily regulated immigration). We see libertarians, at least those of the Mises Caucus, speaking the language of liberalism in a new way. The classical liberalism of Locke, Mill, and Hayek has been transformed into more illiberal Rothbardian and Hoppean libertarianism.

When considering the presence of systemic conspiracism in American libertarianism, we ought to consider the historical connection between Ludwig von Mises and the John Birch Society (JBS). The JBS is an American right-wing political advocacy group that has often been accused of promoting conspiracy theories. Mises, the libertarian philosopher after whom both the Mises Institute and Mises Caucus are named, served on the editorial advisory board of the JBS magazine. Ever since, there have been strong ties between at least certain parts of the LP and the JBS. Fred Koch, father of David and Charles Koch, was a founding member of JBS.[46] In the early 1960s, Charles Koch opened a John Birch Society bookstore with a friend of his father, Bob Love.[47] Charles did, however, distance himself from JBS in the 1970s, partly due to skepticism of the group's connection to "far-fetched conspiracy theories, which included a belief that many prominent Americans, including President Dwight D. Eisenhower, were communist agents."[48] When founding the Cato Institute and the Center for Libertarian Studies (CLS) in NYC in the late 1970s, Charles' feelings about JBS were ambivalent. While he continued to fault the JBS's "obsession" with conspiracies, he acknowledged the group's successes. In a paper presented to stakeholders of the CLS, he

> methodically analyzed the strengths and weaknesses of a group he knew intimately, the John Birch Society, as a model for his budding movement's future enterprise. His assessment was clear and businesslike. He pointed out that despite the fringe group's shortcomings, it boasted 90,000 members, 240 paid staffers and a $7 million annual budget.[49]

He also admired JBS's ability to remain outside of view, and "argued in favor of copying the John Birch Society's secrecy." He remarked, "in order to avoid undesirable criticism, how the organization is controlled and directed should not be widely advertised."[50]

The extent to which the LP, through the Mises Caucus, is connected to the JBS is open for debate. Even Rothbard, who acknowledged the need for conspiracist thinking to usher in real social change (or, rather, thinking that will be labeled as conspiracist by those with institutional power), deemed the JBS a failed organization.[51] Nonetheless, as investigative journalist Dave Troy reports, there are accusations on Twitter that the Mises Caucus is perfectly aligned with JBS and Trumpism as well.[52] This would mean that the LP is very much in the conspiracy business, just like JBS, and has moved further away from organizations like the Cato Institute. Indeed, there is a battle for the soul of the LP ongoing, but it is much too early to tell what the outcome will be.[53] Moreover, there is no extant credible evidence for the aforementioned accusations of the Mises Caucus being "perfectly aligned" with the JBS, and we can only point to the connections between the LP today and the JBS as well as the historical emergence of these groups.

We can also acknowledge that challenging dominant narratives, questioning who in the Establishment benefits from certain narratives or policies, and suggesting or asserting foul play on the part of elites are all tactics likely to elicit a conspiracist label. To some extent, Libertarians are always and everywhere likely to challenge government institutions—particularly in challenging government overreach in the market economy, through regulation and taxes. Yet surely such attempts tend toward the pragmatic approach. Many Mises Caucus tactics, however, invite scrutiny as to whether they tend towards systemic conspiracism. For example, popular libertarian commentator and potential 2024 LP presidential candidate Dave Smith has often questioned election results, including the 2020 presidential vote.[54] He has also argued that anyone who dismisses allegations of election fraud outright (as "the big lie") is part of or beholden to a brainwashed corporate media.[55] Moreover, NC chairperson McArdle has gestured towards conspiracies such as "German New Medicine"[56] and others in the Mises Caucus have parroted Russian propaganda in their denunciation of American involvement in the Ukraine war.[57] In this chapter I do not have the space to consider the truth or fiction of these claims. But they are evidence that the current LP is comfortable with actively promoting alternative theories, will deliberately embrace controversy and provocative messaging to garner more attention, and has shifted from a Hayekian limited government approach to one that favors Rothbardian anti-statism. In these ways, the LP is "speaking the language of liber(tarianism)" in a new way.

Conclusion

The cases of Rogan, Brand, and the Libertarian Party illuminate the strategy and tactics of many contemporary far-right actors. Strategically, they adopt the position of free thinkers and truth-tellers who seek to defend free speech and promote democratic discourse. Concomitantly, they consistently portray the government and mainstream media outlets as enemies of free thought who seek to dominate democratic discourse with well-crafted narratives that only a "conspiracist" would question. It should be no surprise, then, that part of the tactical approach of these actors is to entertain and propagate conspiracism.

This chapter has explored two phenomena: first, how these actors use liberal ideas like free speech and democratic discourse to promote their ideas. Second, how the use of conspiracism supports these efforts. Presupposing that these phenomena are here to stay, I have also provided a preliminary framework for evaluating these strategies and tactics. In many cases, I contend that they are compatible with liberal-democratic society, namely when they hew towards a pragmatic rather than a systemic conspiracism. In others, they abuse liberal ideas and pose real challenges to liberal-democratic life.

Thus, serious and honest observers of contemporary political discourse in the West cannot simply dismiss conspiracism, or far-right populism, out of hand. There must be a concerted effort to understand the strategies, tactics, and values of these actors and those who are attracted to them.

Notes

1. Russell Muirhead and Nancy L. Rosenblum, "Introduction," in *A Lot of People Are Saying: The New Conspiracism and the Assault on Democracy* (Princeton: Princeton University Press, 2019).
2. Nadia Urbinati, "For a Tripartite Model of Conspiracy" in "Conspiracism and Delegitimation," *Contemporary Political Theory* 19 (2020): 142–74, https://doi.org/10.1057/s41296-019-00372-6.
3. Ibid.
4. George Hawley, "From Practical Critics to Hateful Malcontents: The Rise and Fall of the Online 'Manosphere.'" in *Far-Right Newspeak and the Future of Liberal Democracy*, edited by A. James McAdams and Samuel Piccolo (London: Routledge, 2024).
5. José Pedro Zúquete, "Against the Global Prison-Society: The Opposition to the Great Reset," in *Far-Right Newspeak and the Future of Liberal Democracy*, edited by A. James McAdams and Samuel Piccolo (London: Routledge, 2024).
6. Aubrey Marcus, "Choosing Your Struggle With Joe Rogan," *Aubrey Marcus Podcast*, April 17, 2019, produced by Aubrey Marcus, podcast, MP3 audio, 60:14, https://luminarypodcasts.com/listen/onnit-336/aubrey-marcus-podcast/200-choose-your-struggle-with-joe-rogan/?country=US.
7. Richard Markosian, "Joe Rogan vs. CNN," *Utah Stories*, February 1, 2022, https://utahstories.com/2022/02/joe-rogan-vs-cnn/.
8. Sam Stein and Will Sommer, "How Little Known Andrew Yang May End Up on the 2020 Debate Stage by Gaming the System," *The Daily Beast*, March 6, 2019, www.thedailybeast.com/how-little-known-andrew-yang-may-end-up-on-the-2020-debate-stage-by-gaming-the-system.
9. Justin Peters, "Joe Rogan's Galaxy Brain," *Slate*, March 21, 2019, https://slate.com/culture/2019/03/joe-rogans-podcast-is-an-essential-platform-for-free thinkers-who-hate-the-left.html.
10. "Joe Rogan: Four Claims From His Spotify Podcast Fact-Checked," *BBC News*, January 31, 2022, www.bbc.com/news/60199614.
11. Ibid.
12. Mark Savage, "Neil Young Wants to Quit Spotify Over Joe Rogan's Vaccine Misinformation," *BBC News*, January 25, 2022, www.bbc.com/news/entertainment-arts-60124003.
13. Andy Greene, "Neil Young Demands Spotify Remove His Music Over 'False Information About Vaccines'," *Rolling Stone*, January 24, 2022, www.rollingstone.com/music/music-news/neil-young-demands-spotify-remove-music-vaccine-disinformation-1290020/.
14. HypeAuditor, "Youtube Stats & Analytics for Russell Brand (@RussellBrand)," accessed January 20, 2023, https://hypeauditor.com/youtube/russell_brand-UCswH8ovgUp5Bdg-0_JTYFNw/.

15 Ibid.
16 Emma Mayer, "Russell Brand, Once Seen as Progressive, Moves to Conservative Platform," *Culture*, September 28, 2022, www.newsweek.com/russell-brand-once-progressive-moves-conservative-platform-1747130.
17 Sam Ramadan, "The Real Reason Russell Brand Decided to Quit YouTube," *Bustle*, September 20, 2022, www.bustle.com/entertainment/russell-brand-youtube-controversy-censorship-rumble-platform.
18 Foundation for Individual Rights and Expression, "Russell Brand Breaks Down the Difference Between 'Free' Speech and 'Me' Speech," *Youtube Video*, 0:21, April 20, 2022, www.youtube.com/watch?v=Gm3HrNF6itI; Jonathan Turley, "Can Joe Rogan Save Free Speech?" *The Hill*, February 1, 2022, https://thehill.com/opinion/technology/592240-can-joe-rogan-save-free-speech; Aja Romano, "How Do You Solve a Problem Like Joe Rogan?" *Vox*, February 23, 2022, www.vox.com/culture/22945864/joe-rogan-politics-spotify-controversy.
19 Mark Savage, "Neil Young Wants to Quit Spotify Over Joe Rogan's Vaccine Misinformation," *BBC News*, January 25, 2022, www.bbc.com/news/entertainment-arts-60124003.
20 Sanjay Gupta, "Dr. Sanjay Gupta: Why Joe Rogan and I Sat Down and Talked—for More Than 3 Hours," *CNN News*, October 14, 2021, www.cnn.com/2021/10/13/health/sanjay-gupta-joe-rogan-experience/index.html.
21 This description of Rogan from *New Yorker* writer Lawrence Wright is representative: "Rogan is five feet eight, but his shoulders are about as wide as he is high. He's dauntingly muscular and tattooed, but despite his formidable physical presentation he's friendly and amusing. The experience of being on his podcast is like having a curious fellow pull up a barstool next to you; three hours later, you've unloaded your life story. Before the interview, we got our nostrils swabbed for a mandatory covid test—which was interesting, given that Rogan had been strongly criticized for giving air time to vaccine skeptics." Lawrence Wright, "The Astonishing Transformation of Austin," *The New Yorker*, February 6, 2023, www.newyorker.com/magazine/2023/02/13/the-astonishing-transformation-of-austin.
22 Russell Brand, n.d., accessed January 15, 2023, https://www.youtube.com/c/RussellBrand/videos.
23 Josh Vandiver, "Hard Men, Hard Money, Hardening Right: Bitcoin, Peter Thiel, and Schmittian States of Exception," in *Far-Right Newspeak and the Future of Liberal Democracy*, edited by A. James McAdams & Samuel Piccolo (London: Routledge, 2024).
24 www.libertarianism.org/articles/libertarian-movement-and-libertarian-party.
25 https://encyclopedia.pub/entry/30814.
26 Ibid., 37.
27 Murray N. Rothbard, "Right-Wing Populism: A Strategy for the Paleo Movement," *Rothbard-Rockwell Report*, January 1992.
28 Aaron Ross Powell, Andy Craig, and John Hudak, "How Libertarianism Went Off the Rails (w/ John Hudak and Andy Craig)," *Reimagining Liberty*, May 4, 2022, produced by Landry Ayres, podcast, MP3 audio, 57:39, https://reimagininglibrary.com/episodes/how-libertarianism-went-off-the-rails-w-john-hudak-and-andy-craig.
29 Andrew Koppelman, *Burning Down the House: How Libertarian Philosophy Was Corrupted by Delusion and Greed* (New York: Saint Martin's Press, 2022).

30 Murray N. Rothbard, "Toward a Strategy for Libertarian Social Change," April 1977, 46. http://www.davidmhart.com/liberty/AmericanLibertarians/Rothbard/Strategy/1977TowardStrategyLibertarianSocialChange.html.
31 Ibid., 47.
32 For evidence of the revolutionary nature of Rothbard's approach in this essay, consider that he draws his principal inspiration from Vladimir Lenin and explicitly rejects "gradualism" in effecting change in favor of swift and decisive action. "But this means that libertarians must not adopt gradualism as part of their goal; they must wish to achieve liberty as early and as rapidly as possible. Otherwise, they would be ratifying the continuation of injustice." Ibid., 5.
33 Amanda Griffiths (UCLA), interview by author, August 10, 2022.
34 The Mackinac Center for Public Policy. See McAdams Introduction, footnote 6.
35 *LPedia*, s.v. "National Convention 2022," https://lpedia.org/wiki/National_Convention_2022.
36 Aaron Ross Powell (Founder of Cato Institute's Libertarianism.org), interview by author, July 15, 2022.
37 Nick Gillespie and Zach Weissmueller, "Inside the Mises Caucus Takeover of the Libertarian Party," *Youtube Video*, 30:42, June 15, 2022, www.youtube.com/watch?v=NsgFdPqOAhk.
38 Ibid.
39 Petra Mlejnková, "Far-Right Politics in the Czech Republic: Tomio Okamura's Liberal Language and Populist Playbook," in *Far-Right Newspeak and the Future of Liberal Democracy*, edited by A. James McAdams & Samuel Piccolo (London: Routledge, 2024).
40 In this volume it is worth noting that this distinction also tracks what we would expect from the pragmatic vs. systematic use of conspiracist speech.
41 Aaron Ross Powell, Andy Craig, and John Hudak, "How Libertarianism Went Off the Rails (w/John Hudak and Andy Craig)," *Reimagining Liberty*, May 4, 2022, produced by Landry Ayres, podcast, MP3 audio, 57:39, https://reimagininingliberty.com/episodes/how-libertarianism-went-off-the-rails-w-john-hudak-and-andy-craig.
42 Hans-Hermann Hoppe, "Libertarianism and the Alt-Right: In Search of a Libertarian Strategy for Social Change" (speech from Property and Freedom Society meeting in Bodrum, Turkey, September 17, 2017), *Free Life*, https://libertarianism.uk/2017/10/20/libertarianism-and-the-alt-right-hoppe-speech-2017/.
43 Ibid.
44 Ibid.
45 Nick Gillespie and Zach Weissmueller, "Inside the Mises Caucus Takeover of the Libertarian Party," *Youtube Video*, 30:42, June 15, 2022, www.youtube.com/watch?v=NsgFdPqOAhk.
46 "About Us," *The John Birch Society's Official Website*, accessed April 22, 2023, https://jbs.org/significant-figures/fred-koch/.
47 Lisa Graves, "The Koch Cartel: Their Reach, Their Reactionary Agenda, and Their Record," *The Progressive* 78, no. 7–8 (July 2014), https://ia903106.us.archive.org/33/items/6240399-2015-Lisa-Graves-Koch-Cartel-Article/6240399-2015-Lisa-Graves-Koch-Cartel-Article.pdf.
48 Jane Mayer, "The Secrets of Charles Koch's Political Ascent," *Politico*, January 18, 2016, www.politico.com/magazine/story/2016/01/charles-koch-political-ascent-jane-mayer-213541/.

49 Ibid.
50 Ibid.
51 "The failure of the John Birch Society is surely due to its sole dependence on the limitations of one man, Robert Welch, so that his lack of knowledge in many areas and his paranoid outlook have necessarily been stamped upon the Birch Society, to its grave and permanent detriment." Rothbard, "Toward a Strategy for Libertarian Social Change," 61–62.
52 Dave Troy (@davetroy), "Let's Be Really Clear: Mises PAC = Libertarian Party = John Birch Society = Trump = Putin. Messaging Is Fully Aligned," *Twitter*, October 18, 2022, 10:08 a.m., https://twitter.com/davetroy/status/1582403188636135424?lang=en.
53 From a recent *Reason Magazine* article: "The Libertarian Party has always been fractious, but its infighting has intensified since the Mises Caucus, a faction opposed to 'wokeism,' took control of the organization. Many of the party's more socially liberal members have exited since the takeover—and in some cases, they're trying to take the party's state affiliates with them." Jesse Walker, "How Third Parties Die," *Reason*, February 2023, https://reason.com/2023/01/24/the-life-cycle-of-a-third-party/.
54 Dave Smith (@ComicDaveSmith), "Some Stuff Seems Incredibly Shady in the Election, But I Don't Know. I Do Know That It's Hilarious to See Some Libertarians Laughing Off the Idea of Fraud," *Twitter*, November 5, 2020, 8:23 p.m., https://twitter.com/ComicDaveSmith/status/1324553000707366914.
55 Dave Smith (@ComicDaveSmith), "I Have Never Been Convinced that the 2020 Election Was Stolen Through Voter Fraud. That Said, If You Use the Phrase 'Big Lie' You Are Brainwashed by the Corporate . . ." *Twitter*, August 17, 2022, 5:20 p.m., https://twitter.com/ComicDaveSmith/status/1560043868971753474.
56 Fakertarians (@fakertarians), "Last Night, LP Chair Angela McArdle Told Timcast Viewers to Look into a Crackpot Theory Called 'German New Medicine.' It Was Thought Up by Ryke Geerd Hamer, Who . . . " *Twitter*, March 17, 2023, 2:58 p.m., https://twitter.com/fakertarians/status/1636834430969937921.
57 Aaron Ross Powell (Founder of Cato Institute's Libertarianism.org), interview by author, May 5, 2023. Powell also directed me to Twitter handle "fakertarians," where much documenting of LP conspiracism occurs.

PART V
Beyond Far-Right Newspeak

10
AGAINST THE GLOBAL PRISON-SOCIETY

The Far Right's Language of the Opposition to the Great Reset

José Pedro Zúquete

Since the emergence of Covid-19 in 2020, the World Economic Forum (WEF) has promoted a "Great Reset" as a new beginning for the global economy and humanity. Proponents of the Great Reset argue that it takes advantage of the pandemic to reorganize societies in better ways than before. But critics identify the WEF's proposal as nothing short of a sinister global plot by power-grabbing elites to rule the world. Behind nice-sounding slogans, they argue that a sinister, absolutist, dictatorial force is at play, plotting essentially to remake the world and subject it to the control of a global technocratic and authoritarian elite. The New World Order that would result from the Great Reset would entail a nefarious transformation of human beings economically, politically, and culturally. Technology would be employed, critics allege, to alter human nature not only in the domains mentioned earlier but biologically as well. A small class of elite oppressors would entail the superclass that would oppress the underclass—the overwhelming majority of humanity. The Great Resist (GR)—as this diffuse sociocultural movement of anti-Great Reset opponents sometimes calls itself—is diverse. Although it is more dominant among the far right, it finds a base too on the far left. Its support is in fact quite broad and includes social critics not easily ideologically pigeonholed. Fleshing out the dominant anti-Great Reset narratives from this vast array of different groups and individuals—and covering all its manifestations—is a task that exceeds the scope of this chapter.

My more restricted focus here is on the ways that some voices within this wide ecosystem of resistance and dissidence engage with—and perceive themselves to be crusaders for—two key dimensions that we associate today with liberalism: freedom and democracy. In short, I argue that opponents of the Great Reset interpret and promote their activism as combat over the

DOI: 10.4324/9781003436737-15

very meaning of individual and collective freedom, since they believe a global power elite is engaged in an authoritarian takeover and clamping down on popular sovereignty. They maintain that proponents of the Great Reset are the ones engaged in a "Newspeak" of their own, one that seeks to redefine terms like freedom, democracy, and transparency. In contrast, the opponents of the Great Reset see themselves as the defenders of these values.

To illustrate this point, I shall single out a few far-right Great Resist promoters. My subjects include politicians such as Thierry Baudet, the leader of the Dutch political party Forum for Democracy, and Nick Griffin, the former leader of the British National Party; social movement leaders and activists such as Martin Sellner, one of the founders of the Austrian identitarian movement; and social media influencers such as the anonymous British author Raw Egg Nationalist. This of course does not preclude references throughout this chapter to other examples of anti-Great Reset activism. The primary sources underpinning the chapter are taken from digital sources—especially alt-tech platforms, personal interviews, and more traditional outputs such as documents and books. The Great Resist cause is taken up both by popular individuals and activists operating within larger organizations and by lesser-known activists on podcasts, video-sharing platforms, and messaging apps. Moreover, it draws advocates from a wide range of professional backgrounds: current and former politicians, media personalities, bloggers, self-identified dissident individuals and groups, social media influencers, and content creators. Geographically, anti-Great Reset activism is concentrated in the Global North, especially North America and western Europe, although its narratives have a wider worldwide reach and support. The attractiveness of anti-Great Reset activism to a wide range of people indicates, as Samuel Piccolo suggests in the concluding chapter of this volume, that mainline liberal democrats have lost considerable credibility in their claims to champion liberal-democratic values.[1]

The Great Reset: The Deep Roots

The opposition to the Great Reset is the latest incarnation of a longer history of anti-globalism.[2] Accordingly, the Great Reset is viewed by critics as a rebranding of a New World Order agenda. This rejection can be voiced in varying degrees of conspiracism, a concept that Steven Pittz has explored in Chapter 9, and can be more or less apocalyptic—as a metahistorical struggle against the forces of evil and of light against darkness—but is always framed by different individuals and groups as a showdown against powerful, rootless cosmopolitan elites hell-bent on world domination.

What triggered this latest incarnation of an old theme was the Great Reset initiative, a project launched in 2020 by the WEF and promoted on the Forum's website with a phrase by Klaus Schwab, its German founder and executive chairman: "The pandemic represents a rare but narrow window of opportunity to reflect, reimagine, and reset our world."[3] As stated in the Introduction to *The Great Narrative* (2022), his follow-up to *COVID-19: The Great Reset*, which he co-wrote with the French economist Thierry Mallet in 2020, "We can't predict the future. However, we can imagine it and even design it."[4]

Although the WEF, notwithstanding its dreams of supranational policymaking, is not a decision-making body—it more resembles a "talking shop for elites," as some observers have argued[5]—it is a place of power and networking where, in the eyes of critics, policies are devised that have real impact in people's lives. Renaud Camus, the French writer known for coining and popularizing polemical terms, calls it Davocracy—or "the direct management of the human park by the banks, the stateless financiers, and the multinationals"[6]—in a reference to the Swiss Alps town of Davos where the Forum's annual meetings take place.

If the thrust for a world government predates the Great Reset in the eyes of many opponents, what distinguishes it is that its proponents "say the quiet part out loud"—they not only announce that they have a plan to control peoples and nations, but openly advertise it as a positive and inevitable development in the name of the greater good, global public interest, and humanity. Other than that—together with the unprecedented technology that elites have at their disposal to ensnare the masses and enforce social control—the Great Reset is only but the last episode of a series of developments.

The Great Reset's ultimate roots vary according to its critics. David Engels, a Belgian historian of the ancient world and the president of the Oswald Spengler Society, sees it as

> only the latest update of a social programme that we already find in the anti-Christian and Enlightenment circles of the 18th century. The basis is a fundamentally anti-traditional view of the world and the human being. Instead of understanding the human being as part of numerous complex solidarity communities—gender, family, village, faith, profession, nation, language, culture and so on—like the European tradition, those self-declared "humanists" preach a radical individualism that is no longer willing to accept any other community between the individual and the whole of humanity (except for the all-familiar and allegedly persecuted "minorities," of course).[7]

One of the co-founders of the Austrian youth movement, Generation Identity, retraces the Great Reset's origins to ancient atomism and the explanation of phenomena in terms of indivisible atoms:

> From the perspective of history of ideas, this process started with Atomist philosophy in Antiquity, went through Scholasticism, Humanism, modern natural sciences, Individualism, and then gave birth to Liberalism, Capitalism, and Enlightenment, before it has begotten Globalism at the "end of history" after the conclusion of the Cold war.

With a nod to the present, he adds,

> since Globalism is failing—the failed color revolutions and wars in the Middle East, against Russia and China, the rise of Populism in Europe and the US are no victories of Globalism—the Great Reset is a desperate undertaking in order to restart Globalization anew in a new kind of quality.[8]

In *Democracy in America*, Alexis de Tocqueville warned that people should be on the lookout for the rise of what he called "administrative despotism"—a form of government that "reduces each nation to being nothing more than a flock of timid and industrious animals, of which the government is the shepherd." In this way, de Tocqueville, too, foresaw the current despotism of a global technocratic elite. At least, this is the interpretation of de Tocqueville put forth by the Dutch politician Thierry Baudet. The same is true, Baudet said in an address to the Dutch Parliament, of the predictions by political theorist James Burnham about the excessive power of a superclass of technocratic elites in governments and corporations: "Big government and big businesses are merging, going hand in hand, as [Burnham] foresaw sixty years ago. . . . Total government control. Unlimited possibilities for an omnipotent state."[9]

The influencer Raw Egg Nationalism (REN), who is very active in social media and alt-tech platforms, takes these arguments further. He believes that combat against the Great Reset must ultimately liberate food supply and production from corporate control. "We can't understand the great reset without understanding the way that the globalists want us to eat in 2030," he said in a podcast, arguing that the relationship between food and social control is a very ancient theme. Plato's *Republic*—where vegetarianism is prescribed for good citizenship not out of concern for animals but as a tool of social control—corroborates this point: "the ideal Republic would have to be a vegetarian Republic and if the workers were allowed to eat meat that would lead to all sorts of conflicts within society and it would no longer be harmonious."[10] REN then added, "you got this striking and ancient notion that you can transform the totality of a society, and the way that everybody behaves in that society, by changing their diet." Repeatedly, he warns "globalists want to change what we eat and as a result change the way that we live" in order to have a food-dependent, and thus more domesticated, population.[11]

Disaster Capitalism Unleashed

In its self-proclaimed mission to beat despotism and fight for freedom, the anti-Great Reset camp frequently refers to both the concept of "disaster capitalism" and, to Naomi Klein's chagrin,[12] the "shock doctrine"—or the way that elites capitalize on chaos and brutally explore crises to advance agendas. This notion that elites profit from collective shocks and turmoil is a central master-frame of the Great Resist. C. J. Hopkins, playwright and self-described "weird leftist," explains the "totalitarian method" that drives the alleged elite-driven push for Global Tyranny: "If you scare the living shit out of people you can control them . . . it's an ancient instinct we all have."[13] The recipe for success, Hopkins elaborates further, requires that GloboCap (global capitalism) totalitarianism cannot present itself as such: "In order to exist, it must not exist . . . it must appear to us as an essentially beneficent response to whatever 'global crisis' GloboCap thinks will terrorize the masses into a mindless, order-following hysteria."[14]

Examples of this weaponization of crises are part and parcel of Great Reset narratives and are akin to the reaction to the "financial state of emergency" after 2008, as Josh Vandiver describes in Chapter 11. The response to the Covid-19 pandemic—including lockdowns, vaccine passports, and digital certificates—is viewed as little more than a test run by elites to implement radical policies of wider control of populations. The far-right French intellectual Alain Soral—who made a series of podcasts dedicated to the Great Reset—argues that the West is heading toward a global oligarchic dictatorship, identifying Islamic terrorism, climate change, and the pandemic as the dominant strategies of submission by terror. These topics, he argues, have been weaponized to facilitate and deepen elite social control.[15] Baudet takes a similar position. In the same way that the response to 9/11 gave rise to a wide and invasive infrastructure of surveillance "that never went away,"[16] he contends that the same will happen to Covid-response infrastructures and digital tools that will be further used to induce herd behavior and manipulate the masses. "Coronavirus is the alibi, the pretext, the inducement, to realize the new world order that had been prepared and desired for a long time," Baudet says. The spreading of digital identity will pave the way to a QR society, barcoded and scanned, and to a social credit system (with China as the model) where "good behavior is rewarded by access to social-societal life, and bad behavior is punished with a scanner turning red."[17] Meanwhile, the American right-wing media personality Glenn Beck has identified the Great Reset as a driving force behind the growing use by companies and banks of ESG scores—"environmental, social and governance" social credit—in the evaluation of individuals and businesses.[18]

Nick Griffin has joined these critics. After leading the BNP and joining the Knights Templar International, a group that emulates the medieval military order, he noted in a podcast talk about his book *Deus Vult: The Great Reset Resistance*, that Covid (which he views as "an excuse to remodel our world") is intimately bound to the "climate change hoax." Griffin railed against "the same group of criminals and the same collaborators in the media, in major political parties, who are involved in both."[19] Whether crises are manufactured, exploited, or both—the opinion varies according to each foe—it is not the most important thing for the anti-Great Reset narrative. What anti-Great Reset theorists and activists are most concerned with is the idea that every crisis leads to further seizure of power by global elites. In one of his "Templar Reports," broadcast in the video streaming platform Purged. TV ("home of the deplatformed, home of the truth"), Griffin predicted, "first they [globalists] used Covid as an excuse for a power grab over us, individually and collectively, and now climate change is being used as an excuse for a huge power grab over food supply."[20]

In the anti-Great Reset narrative, everything is connected. The Covid crisis, the climate crisis, the energy crisis, and even future global crises that may arise are viewed as pieces of a puzzle. These episodes legitimize putting in place a series of "states of exception"—that withdraw liberties and entitlements of the population—which with each passing crisis become less and less exceptional and more and more a permanent feature of Western societies. All of these crises, and the ways they are managed, are stepping-stones toward an endpoint: the concentration of power in the hands of the few, the global oligarchic class, at the expense of the liberties and self-determination of the many.

One of the areas on which anti-Great Reset opponents focus to denounce this trend is gastropolitics. When in 2016 the WEF announced its "8 predictions for 2030," it included one about how "you will eat much less meat—an occasional treat, not a staple. For the good of the environment and our health."[21] Anti-Great Reset opponents perceive this prediction as yet more evidence of a conspiracy that is hidden in plain sight to control people's behavior and ways of life. Campaigns to reduce livestock herds or hailing the benefits of edible bugs are not benign ways of helping to "save the planet," but instead advance a much more self-serving and cynical elitist globalist agenda. Raw Egg Nationalist connects this push to reduce meat consumption with the weaponization of inflation. The 2021–22 inflation surge serves the globalists' purpose: "Inflation making meat expensive is a good thing from their perspective—that's a way to get people to stop eating meat" while easing the way for the widespread use of genetically modified organisms (patented by corporations) and novel forms of protein (plant-based and insect-based) that can also be patented and controlled by corporations.[22]

Griffin argues that "[t]he impact of [the ongoing] destruction of the farming and cattle industry, the fertilizer shortages, the diesel fuel price increases, the diesel exhaust fluid shortage catastrophe just around the corner [worsening supply chain disruption]," will mean that regular people cannot buy meat. Further, he suggests that the "global elite" will use this crisis to say "'meat is expensive and very bad for the planet' so you're going to eat bugs and bacteria from our industrial farms—that is where they are going."[23] Raw Egg Nationalist similarly identifies a "broader plan to control agriculture, to squeeze the little man out, so that we are totally dependent on corporations for everything we need, including food—you can call it a coup."[24]

Even though this shock doctrine logic is applied to many areas, the anti-Great Reset camp is broad enough to include divergences of analysis. One prime example concerns geopolitics. Just before the breakout of the war in Ukraine, Baudet warned, "the Covid plan to make the Great Reset is failing so the plan B is ready: war with Russia."[25] Around the same time, Griffin identified the "genius idea" of the Great Reset elite "to provoke Russia into actions which would allow them to impose the sanctions which will achieve the next stage of their 'Great Reset.' Because the real target of sanctions isn't Vladimir Putin—it's YOU!"[26] Even though the global energy crisis exacerbated by the war has seemed to advance their designs, not everyone agrees with the real impact of the war on the globalists' plans. Martin Sellner, who ranks as the most popular leader of the identitarian movement in the German-speaking world, is adamant that "the avant-garde of the Great Reset will use every crisis and scarcity to further their goals of global population control and technocracy." However, "a war, as it is a return of 'the political' as the German legal theorist Carl Schmitt described it, might also endanger their plan. A real political enemy might further the trend of deglobalization and create a neo-imperial world order, in which national identity is key again."[27] If Covid marked the opening of the current Great Reset, war could deal it a final blow.

Total Control: The Technological Reset

The French author Lucien Cerise—who has written extensively on what he calls "government by chaos," or the way that elites capitalize on crises and disorder to further social engineering projects—says that the Great Reset, which he sees as belonging to the utopian tradition, is a way to foster and deepen biopolitics: "[B]iopower, which is only an update of the notion of eugenics, is therefore characterized by an ever-increasing intrusion into people's physical intimacy in order to modify it and above all to control it."[28] The growing impact of digitalization on society and people's lives is an integral element of this process, as "the goal of power remains to place us in an increasing dependence on information technology for every act and gesture of everyday life."[29] According to this narrative, the logic behind the elites' push for a cashless society where physical money is replaced by digital currency is that central banks will gain total control over economic transactions—which they can use to switch off accounts of dissenters and make daily life impossible for non-aligned citizens.

The unprecedented digital power of control and surveillance will extend far beyond financial transactions. Technology will be used increasingly as a tool for total control in the hands of a minority of overlords. Many opponents view transhumanism as the end goal of the Great Reset. According to a former Austrian identitarian leader, "Globalist elites like Bill Gates and Klaus Schwab push a transhumanist agenda, in order to gain control over our bodies." The new Covid vaccines were just the beginning, he says, because "the aim of this new stage of globalization is the abolishment of man itself and the progress to transhumanism, which strives for the merging of man with machine."[30]

A new era of the Internet of Bodies (IoB) based on the fusion of technology and biology arises: Internet-connected devices that monitor the human body and collect personal biometric data, which means that everything can be tracked, will lead to a future of absolute control over humans. The criticism is not that the fourth industrial revolution, or 4IR, *can* be turned against humans but that *it will* be turned against humans. Critics of the Great Reset sound the alarm about a dystopian society in the making, where common people are monitored for every piece of information that they have, tracked through devices that are commonplace, and controlled through those devices.

The development of human enhancement technologies (the transition from human 1.0 to human 2.0) will invest elites with a terrible and limitless power over humanity. According to Baudet,

> The elite ruling class is strongly convinced that human freedom is dangerous. Human nature is dangerous. Human nature should be changed—humanity remade. That is why they push transhumanism. They find human nature unsatisfactory, and believe human intellect and planners like them can improve it . . . they believe in humanity 2.0. Their hatred for individual freedom is inextricably linked to it. They hate humanity 1.0—real people.[31]

These technologies will also put an end to the quest for human equality. If the Great Reset, according to the Irish nationalist influencer Keith Woods, consolidates the power of corporate oligarchy and gives rise to the next stage of capitalism as a kind of neo-feudalism—a system divided between super wealthy oligarchs and the peasantry[32]—the coming transhumanist society will further fortify this caste system in the near future as a regime where a superior caste of artificial intelligence/human hybrids rules over the masses, with society itself divided between the enhanced and the unenhanced. In this way, the merger of technology and biology will be the final nail in the coffin of popular rule and democracy.

Griffin embraced this spirit in a tweet: "The global corporate elite #covid power & wealth grab is so blatant & dangerous that building #Resistance outweighs ALL other divisions, differences & quarrels." The stakes have been made starkly clear: "Either we get rid of them, or they'll make us all serfs in a twisted #transhumanist feudalism. #byallmeansnecessary."[33]

The Great Reset and the Great Replacement: Means of Domination

The "taming of humans," which Peter Sloterdijk discusses in *Rules for the Human Zoo*, will supposedly soon be complete. In the eyes of many of its foes, the Great Reset will naturally lead to a stage of the complete domestication of humans, facilitated and made fully achievable by technology with which globalists have de-potentiated them, made them manipulable elements of a herd, and shepherded them into subjugation.

Anti-Great Reset sentiment is often bound with and inextricable from anti-Great Replacement activism. The elimination of differences between peoples through mass immigration, diversity, and multiculturalism; the erosion of ethnic and cultural identities of peoples; the treatment all peoples as a global mass that is undifferentiated—all of these dynamics serve to blur distinctiveness, enforce sameness, and result in a global populace that is detached from primal identities, rootless, and therefore more easily controlled and dealt with by the global overlords. In the words of one identitarian leader,

> Of course, there's a link between the restart of globalization proclaimed by the Great Reset and the ongoing mass migration. The globalist elites favor mass migration, since they need it as "human capital" in the West in order to strengthen their profits and divide the population inside the West. Furthermore, they also want to weaken the global south economically and destroy not only the identity of the Europeans, but also the identity of the peoples from Africa, Asia, and Latin America. Their final aim and the goal of transhumanism is to "liberate" man from all forms of collective identity.[34]

Sellner has a similar view. Both the Great Reset and the Great Replacement, he maintains, "are part of a 'trans-agenda,' that is universalistic transnationalist, transsexual, and transhumanist, and therefore anti-identitarian."[35] The "health dictatorship" (related to the far-reaching anti-pandemic rules, from Covid to future ones), policies of "eco-dictatorship," as well as replacement migration and neo-Malthusian policies of depopulation (promoted especially in the West), are recurrently tied up in the anti-Great Reset camp as essential features of the ongoing bio-political governance of global elites.

These assessments have led to a question that is a source of contention among theorists and activists: Which anti-GR combat should be prioritized, that against the Great *Reset* or that against a related theme, the Great *Replacement*? The White nationalist author Greg Johnson argues in favor of the latter: "Are the Great Reset and the Great Replacement connected? Yes and no. Aside from the word 'great,' not really. Pretty much the same types are pushing both, but the Great Reset is more of a short-term gambit, whereas the Great Replacement is a long-term plan." Unlike the unparalleled magnitude and meticulousness behind the Great Replacement—which "has been in operation for more than half a century"—Johnson discounts any sort of originality to the Great Reset: "Utopian zealots and social planners welcome disasters as opportunities to reshape society according to their schemes. It is a sinister phenomenon, but nothing really new."[36]

In contrast, Cerise argues, "until 2020, the urgency in Europe was to fight against the Great Replacement of Europeans by non-Europeans," but the situation has changed since "the launch of the global health dictatorship [because] the problem has become even larger, and we must fight against the replacement of the human by the machine and the post-human." To Cerise, "the issue of migration is now only part of the fight against the transhumanist Great Reset. For Europeans, and for whites in general, it is therefore necessary to support white nationalism against the other supremacisms already mentioned, black, Jewish, Islamic, but above all [against] technoscientific supremacism."[37] Even close allies, such as the Austrian metapolitical thinker Martin Lichtmesz and Sellner, diverge on the issue. They co-wrote the book *Bevölkerungsaustausch und Great Reset* ("Population Replacement and Great Reset") and debated which of the two is the greatest threat to the future. "If [the Great Reset] succeeds," Lichtmesz contended, "fighting for any dissident cause will become extremely difficult, if not impossible, and that includes opposition to demographic replacement."[38] Since then, in contrast, Sellner has argued, "population replacement is more dangerous, because it destroys the body politic and the populus [ethnic people], which otherwise can defend itself against other acts of national and international tyranny."[39]

In any case, an either/or framework does not seem to be a valid perspective for Great Reset opponents. As Frodi Midjord, the European Alt-right entrepreneur,[40] stated, "the issues are not disconnected, they are part of the same problem—current elites are destroying the world where we can feel at home and they're creating a dystopia where we are completely alienated."[41]

"The Great Revolt"

In the Great Reset opponents' view, the Covid pandemic will inevitably slide into the rearview mirror. But its symbolic power as a watershed moment in a takeover bid by global elites to reset the world anew and remake it according to its plans will nevertheless endure. The anti-Great Reset narrative will outlive the pandemic and remain as a master-frame that both provides the key to interpreting current and future events and also serves to energize and mobilize the opposition. This narrative identifies targets, exposes causality, and connects a wide range of events by integrating them into a common and familiar setting. In short, it provides a total explanation.

And it ignites the fire of an additional reaction: The "Great Revolt" against all perceived attempts by "globalists" to coercively administrate the life and ways of life of populations, in the name of health, in the name of security, in the name of sustainability, in the name of the market, or in the name of human enhancement and transhumanism. In this case, national protests, such as popular unrest and demonstrations against governmental policies, are viewed within a broader anti-New World Order frame. Examples include demonstrations against pandemic rules and lockdowns, Canada's trucker protests against pandemic restrictions and vaccine mandates, Netherlands' farmer protests (which have spread to other European countries) against government climate plans to cut livestock and reduce farming, and even mass protests in places like Sri Lanka against food, electricity, and fuel shortages. These protests trigger showings of a global unified eruption of "Freedom Fights" against global tyranny, as well as symptoms of the Great Revolt. As a former Austrian identitarian leader argues, "I definitely see all anti-covid protests and the populist movements as part of the freedom fight against global biopolitics, since they reject globalization and the Great Reset as such."[42]

In this narrative, there is the idea that under the banner of the "Great Revolt," new convergences between right and left are necessary. That opposition must cut across the ideological spectrum. Martin Lichtmetz says, "solidarity and alliances with other opponents of this policy who are not 'from the right' should be considered."[43] These calls for a united front are made notwithstanding the recurrent critique, within the right-wing side of the anti-Great Reset camp, that most of the left is now fully aligned with the dominant goals of the ruling globalist class and that the left-wing anti-corporate globalization movement from the turn of the century is now a thing of the past. There are many examples of this criticism. Raw Egg Nationalist declares,

> A lot of the things we're saying now sound almost like what the hippies and leftist environmentalists were saying in the 1970s—it's very noticeable that now health and the broader physical health of the population is not a concern for the left at all. The left has come down very firmly on the side of corporations.

He adds, "For some reason the left that once upon a time was the sworn enemy of corporations—certainly up until Occupy Wall Street—I think something very strange happened."[44] Glenn Beck says, in regard to the New World Order agenda, "we [on the right] were wrong. We thought it would come as, you know, some sort of communist Marxist thing [but] this is coming through our corporations." Adding, "They [the left] knew all this stuff. We mocked them. And now we're standing where they were and we are like 'guys, you were right. I mean, can't you see this?'"[45]

"What happened to the left?" asks Paul Cudenec, an activist and writer who runs the anarchist collective Winter Oak and a prominent anti-Great Reset voice, who blasts what he sees as the "abject historical failure of the left at the hour of our greatest need."[46] Cudenec blames this failure on identity politics, on the postmodernist tendency that pours "scorn on simplistic old-fashioned concepts such as class struggle or opposing state-corporate power," as well as "the funding and/or infiltration of left/anarchist organizations by various billionaire-linked foundations and networks." Cudenec also sees the potential for new alliances:

> Today, the ground has shifted and the dividing line is no longer the old left-right one. People who oppose a future of techno-totalitarian global corporate dictatorship have found themselves standing together on one particular side of a new political dividing line based around decentralization versus centralization, freedom versus authority, values against profiteering. This should be an encouraging moment for anarchists, who have every reason to participate in this embryonic "movement" and help to shape its future evolution.[47]

Interestingly, we find a similar stance in the far-left French collective "The Invisible Committee," which has assigned itself the task of imagining a new form of opposition to the system: "The joy of conspiring is that of meeting, of discovering brothers and sisters where we least expected it. . . . It is in practice, in the test, that we know with whom we can arrange and who must be kept away." As they write in the *Manifeste Conspirationniste*, "the righteous hideouts don't wear badges."[48]

Freedom, Democracy, and the Coming Dystopia

Critics of the Great Reset warn that if its march is left unimpeded, it will lead to a global prison society based on technological might, mass surveillance, and total subjugation of the many to the few: an authoritarian system that is the antithesis of any sort of democracy. "The ultimate consequence of this 'brave new world,' however, is not, as naïve or ignorant voters might imagine, a free, democratic and classless society," says David Engels, "but rather a strictly regulated and soulless collective, which is to be ruled by a finely delineated, strictly hierarchical global elite, which will only give itself a halfway democratic façade on the outside."[49] This is the dark, dystopian reality—the black pill worldview that pervades the thought of the anti-Great Reset bloc.

As to their views on liberalism itself, anti-Great Resetters are not of one mind. Alexander Dugin, author of *The Great Awakening vs. The Great Reset*, equates the Great Reset with what he calls "liberalism 2.0" (left-wing, as opposed to the right-wing liberalism 1.0). Keith Woods says that what drives the global elites is a utopian impulse, a fanatical, but sincere, push for an Open Society that must overcome all natural barriers. "The consensus of these people [Davos types] is very much in line with the post-war liberal consensus," he says, "and although they may be increasingly willing to commandeer state power for their objectives, it is all in service of the ideal of The Open Society." Although the "minoritarian liberalism" that Woods identifies at the heart of the Great Reset elitism "is certainly conflicting with the rights of the individual that were traditionally held dear by liberals," he argues, "the elites' contempt for individual liberty" was not driving their promotion of the Great Reset.[50]

However, Dugin's and Wood's positions are contested by other voices within the anti-Great Reset field. They argue that, at its heart, the Great Reset is not liberal at all. Such is the view of Martin Lichtmesz, for whom authoritarian and proto-totalitarian forms of rule are being enforced under the Great Reset banner. In Lichtmesz's view, these forces are in direct opposition "to what so far has been understood by liberalism: the rule of law, freedom of opinion, ideological pluralism, protection of the citizen against encroachments by the state, 'government by discussion,' etc." Furthermore, even "democracy, understood as 'the rule of the people,' of the majority which announces its will in free elections, and which must be carried out by governments, is being undermined. It is now seen as fascistoid 'populism.'" And "while the limits to free speech are set by 'experts' and 'fact-checkers,' governments guard against the election of any party that fundamentally challenges the status quo." The Great Reset is thus the driver of a tyrannical society, and liberalism itself stands as the last best hope to survive it:

> Today we are witnessing a rapid collectivization and conformity of society. As a result of the Great Reset, the western world is also becoming less and less liberal and less and less individualistic day by day. For this reason alone, the idea of a "Great Awakening Against the Great Reset" movement operating under anti-liberal and anti-individualist auspices is utterly absurd. We cannot outdo this monster when it comes to illiberality and anti-individualism. What is left of liberalism and individualism is now *the only weapon* we have against totalitarian globalism's outright takeover.[51]

From this standpoint, we can flesh out three major connections of the wider anti-Great-Reset movement with some foundational principles of liberalism. This movement aims for three Great Escapes.

The first escape would be the escape from existence under the shadow of the Leviathan. In this case, the escape connects with anti-absolutism, which entails the rejection of absolute and arbitrary power and is a foundational principle of liberalism. It deals with the idea that a global plan, or world government, clashes with the liberal principle of a constitutional/limited government focused on advancing the rights of individuals to life, liberty, and property, and clashes with the idea that power is—and must be—limited, not unlimited. Power must be bounded, not boundless.

The second escape is from the watchful eye of totalitarian surveillance. This escape is connected with the classical liberal right to privacy. In the New World Order being accelerated by global elites, personal data will be technologically controlled by superior powers such as corporations and governments. This control will lead to the erasure of the border between public and private—a hallmark of totalitarianism.

The third escape is the escape from serfdom. In this it connects with the basic liberal tenet of the freedom of the individual. Anti-Great Reset theorists and activists promote the idea that the world being advanced and forced upon humanity spells the end of individual freedom at the hands of a world technocracy, a small clique of power-grabbing elites that monitors and controls others through corporations and governments. The end result is a state of permanent subjugation, or slavery. The opposite of slavery is freedom.

Notes

1 See Chapter 12.
2 See, for example, Daniel John Smith, "*The False Song of Globalism*": *Anti-Globalist Politics and Ideology in the United States From 1945 to 2000*. Doctoral Thesis, Dept. Politics and International Studies (Girton College, University of Cambridge, November 2021).
3 World Economic Forum, "The Great Reset," https://www.weforum.org/videos/series/the-great-reset-863c8ea2d4/.
4 Klaus Schwab and Thierry Malleret, *The Great Narrative for a Better Future* (Geneva, Switzerland: Forum Publishing, 2022), 9.
5 CTV News, "Truth Tracker: Analyzing the World Economic Forum 'Great Reset' Conspiracy Theory," May 28, 2022, www.ctvnews.ca/canada/truth-tracker-analyzing-the-world-economic-forum-great-reset-conspiracy-theory-1.5922314.
6 Grégoire Canlorbe, "A Conversation With French Writer Renaud Camus," July 5, 2018, www.gatestoneinstitute.org/12604/renaud-camus-interview.
7 David Engels, E-mail communication with author, August 13, 2022.
8 E-mail communication from a former Austrian identitarian leader, October 16, 2022.
9 Thierry Baudet, "Thierry Baudet's Speech in Dutch Parliament about the Agenda Behind Covid-19," October 21, 2021. CTV News, "Truth Tracker: Analyzing the World Economic Forum 'Great Reset' Conspiracy Theory," May 28, 2022, www.ctvnews.ca/canada/truth-tracker-analyzing-the-world-economic-forum-great-reset-conspiracy-theory-1.5922314.
10 Noor Bin Ladin Calls . . . Raw Egg Nationalist #2, September 19, 2022, https://noorbinladincalls.podbean.com/e/noor-bin-ladin-calls-raw-egg-nationalist-2/.
11 Ibid.
12 Naomi Klein, "The Great Reset Conspiracy Smoothie," December 8, 2020, https://theintercept.com/2020/12/08/great-reset-conspiracy/.

13 Geopolitics & Empire Podcast, "C. J. Hopkins: The Virus of Mass Destruction & Brave New Totalitarian Normal," July 25, 2020, https://american-podcasts.com/podcast/podcast-geopolitics-empire/c-j-hopkins-the-virus-of-mass-destruction-brave-ne.
14 Margaret Anna Alice, "Dissident Dialogues: C. J. Hopkins," August 8, 2022, https://margaretannaalice.substack.com/p/dissident-dialogues-cj-hopkins.
15 "Le Grand Reset . . . ou Le grand ménage?" # 5 *Great Reset et Moeurs*, May 14, 2022, https://podcasts.apple.com/us/podcast/le-grand-reset-ou-le-grand-m%C3%A9nage/id1624596805.
16 Mark Granza, "Thierry Baudet: Europe's Hopeful Pessimist," June 15, 2021, https://im1776.com/2021/06/22/interview-thierry-baudet/.
17 Thierry Baudet, "Thierry Baudet's Speech in Dutch Parliament About the Agenda Behind Covid-19," October 21, 2021. CTV News, "Truth Tracker: Analyzing the World Economic Forum 'Great Reset' Conspiracy Theory," May 28, 2022, www.ctvnews.ca/canada/truth-tracker-analyzing-the-world-economic-forum-great-reset-conspiracy-theory-1.5922314.
18 BlazeTV Staff, "ESG Scores EXPLAINED: This Is Why Companies Are Going Woke," January 25, 2022, www.glennbeck.com/esg-the-great-reset.
19 Live Stream | Nick Griffin Live—The Great Reset, May 6, 2021, www.purged.tv/l/3206212459/8pm-Live-Stream-Nick-Griffin-Live-The-Great-Reset-6-5-21.
20 *Templar Report*, July 16, 2022, www.purged.tv/l/3453444824/Templar-Report-July-26-2022.
21 WEF, "8 Predictions for the World in 2030," https://www.facebook.com/watch/?v=10153920524981479.
22 Noor Bin Ladin Calls . . . Raw Egg Nationalist #2, September 19, 2022, https://noorbinladincalls.podbean.com/e/noor-bin-ladin-calls-raw-egg-nationalist-2/.
23 Templar Report, July 16, 2022, www.purged.tv/l/3453444824/Templar-Report-July-26-2022.
24 Noor Bin Ladin Calls . . . Raw Egg Nationalist #2, September 19, 2022, https://noorbinladincalls.podbean.com/e/noor-bin-ladin-calls-raw-egg-nationalist-2/.
25 Thierry Baudet, "Het COVID-Plan," January 14, 2022, https://twitter.com/thierrybaudet/status/1482072174118719489?lang=en.
26 Nick Griffin, February 25, 2022, https://vk.com/wall292118168_1648.
27 Martin Sellner, E-mail communication with author, May 6, 2022.
28 Rebellion, "Entretien Avec Lucien Cerise," May 6, 2020, https://rebellion-sre.fr/entretien-avec-lucien-cerise-face-au-biopouvoir-nous-navons-pas-le-capital-economique-mais-nous-avons-le-capital-humain/.
29 Strategika, "La plus grave menace de tous les temps—entretien avec Lucien Cerise," March 9, 2022, https://strategika.fr/2022/03/09/la-plus-grave-menace-de-tous-les-temps-culture-populaire-sentretient-avec-lucien-cerise/.
30 E-mail communication from a former Austrian identitarian leader, October 16, 2022.
31 Thierry Baudet, "The Speech That Shook Parliament," September 26, 2022, https://fvdinternational.com/article/the-speech-that-shook-parliament.
32 Keith Woods, "The Truth About the World Economic Forum," April 4, 2021, www.youtube.com/watch?v=LXIwnlAcUqQ.
33 Nick Griffin, November 20, 2021, https://twitter.com/NickGriffinBU/status/1462081473087946772.

34 E-mail communication from a former Austrian identitarian leader, October 16, 2022.
35 Martin Sellner, E-mail communication with author, May 6, 2022.
36 Greg Johnson, E-mail communication with author, September 1, 2022.
37 Breizh-info, "Lucien Cerise: Les Blancs n'ont pas le droit d'avoir une conscience raciale," October 5, 2021, www.breizh-info.com/2021/10/05/171735/lucien-cerise-blancs-conscience-raciale/.
38 Martin Lichtmesz, E-mail communication with author, August 3, 2022.
39 Martin Sellner, E-mail communication with author, August 2, 2022.
40 See José Pedro Zúquete, "Beyond America: The Rise of the European Alt-Right," in *Contemporary Far-Right Thinkers and the Future of Liberal Democracy*, edited by A. James McAdams and Alejandro Castrillon (London: Routledge, 2021), 207–22.
41 Kulchur Lodge Radio, "'Only a God Can Save Us'—Morgoth on the Plan for a Metaverse Tech-Dystopia," *Kulchur Lodge Radio #35*, February 10, 2022, https://podcastaddict.com/episode/135310411.
42 E-mail communication from a former Austrian identitarian leader, October 16, 2022.
43 Martin Lichtmesz, E-mail communication with author, August 3, 2022.
44 Raw Egg Nationalist, "The Great Reset Agenda to Be Weak and Effeminate EXPOSED [raw egg nationalist]" October 17, 2022, https://theinfowar.tv/watch?id=634cb96866c27b0d30d5439e.
45 Rubin Report, "Why the Great Reset Is No Longer a Conspiracy Theory | Glenn Beck | POLITICS," February 6, 2022, www.youtube.com/watch?v=pwVjlPJTxV8.
46 Paul Cudenec, "Our Insurrection Will Be Impure!" February 17, 2022, https://network23.org/paulcudenec/2022/02/17/our-insurrection-will-be-impure/.
47 Paul Cudenec, E-mail communication with author, September 16, 2022.
48 *Manifeste Conspirationniste* (Paris: Seuil, 2022), 311–12, https://www.fnac.com/a16372086/Anonyme-Manifeste-conspirationniste.
49 David Engels, E-mail communication with author, August 13, 2022.
50 Keith Woods, E-mail communication with author, November 1, 2022.
51 Martin Lichtmesz, "Dugins "Das Große Erwachen gegen den Great Reset" (4/5)," March 21, 2022, https://sezession.de/65577/dugins-das-grosse-erwachen-gegen-den-great-reset-4-5 [emphasis in original].

11
HARD MEN, HARD MONEY, HARDENING RIGHT

Bitcoin, Peter Thiel, and Schmittian States of Exception

Josh Vandiver

Much right-wing and far-right discontent in Western liberal democracies is fueled by perceptions that they are failing in their promise to *be* liberal or democratic. In the United States, the Stop the Steal movement, which culminated in the 2021 Capitol storming on January 6, was motivated by fears of an unconstitutional and undemocratic conspiracy: first, to manipulate the vote in the 2020 election and, second, to foreclose judicial exposure and prosecution of such manipulation. In Canada, the Freedom Convoy, which culminated in a 2022 blockade of Ottawa, was motivated by fears of an illiberal assertion of power by the Canadian state in mandating lockdowns during the coronavirus pandemic. Neither appealed to the stridently illiberal and anti-democratic language of the interwar and postwar far right.[1] Stop the Steal and Freedom Convoy dissidents often spoke the languages of liberalism and democracy, which they viewed to be under threat and in desperate need of defenders. Most chapters in this volume focus upon how far-right figures speak, and especially how they use liberal-democratic terms for their own purposes to create a form of Newspeak. José Pedro Zúquete and Steven Pittz, for instance, detail figures who claim that liberal states are using technology to repress individual freedoms.[2] This chapter takes a different approach: It turns to capabilities—the tools right-wing figures are building and what they are trying to concretely accomplish within or on behalf of liberal democracy. Focusing on these efforts to develop capabilities is especially important when considering how the right will be significant in the decades to come and how these figures will react when liberal democracy faces new crises.

I approach this question by focusing on what I call the *tech right*. Members of the tech right, far from being neo-reactionaries who look to premodernity for ideal politics, are enthusiastic about the potential for technology to solve political problems. My argument is that in the West we are witnessing the emergence of a *hardening right* in the technological sphere. By this, I do not mean "hard right" in the sense of ideological extremists who are intent on resisting or overthrowing liberal-democratic republics like the United States, Germany, and France. The hardening right is less interested in ideology or political language than other figures in this book. The hardening right is interested in capabilities that enable *action* within an existential "Machiavellian moment" in the life of a state, as understood in the constitutional tradition of republicanism, the classical and modern precursor to liberal democracy.[3] As formulated by J. G. A. Pocock, arguably the most influential historian of republicanism in the twentieth century:

> [The Machiavellian moment] is a name for the moment in conceptualized time in which the republic was seen as confronting its own temporal finitude, as attempting to remain morally and politically stable in a stream of irrational events conceived as essentially destructive of all systems of secular stability.[4]

In this chapter, I focus upon two networks on the hardening right, each responding to distinct Machiavellian moments or crises in the life of the American republic. Both invest in and enthuse over new technologies, from financial innovations like Bitcoin and other cryptocurrencies to cutting-edge military, surveillance, and counter-surveillance technologies. Each expresses deep frustration with contemporary liberal-democratic constitutionalism in moments of national security or financial crisis. One network is more statist and nationalist in its envisioned responses to such Machiavellian moments, whereas the other is anti-statist and comparatively unconcerned with nationality.

The first network clusters around the German-born, South African-raised Peter Thiel, a billionaire venture capitalist and key figure in American right-wing politics over four decades.[5] While he has often self-identified as libertarian, Thiel increasingly appears keen to cultivate *hard men* capable of preserving or reforming liberal-democratic states in times of existential crisis. Thiel possesses formal academic training in philosophy and interests in various forms of political thought including libertarianism but also, most recently, that of the "national conservatism" conferences and the Nietzschean "masculinist right."[6] Since the early 2000s, Thiel has formulated critiques of liberal-democratic constitutionalism in the global war on terror and, more broadly, national security emergencies. I focus especially upon his 2007 essay, "The Straussian Moment," which emerged at the nadir of the neo-conservative-supported Iraq war. "The modern West has lost faith in itself," the war on terror reveals to Thiel, and he calls for the "Christian statesman" to act within an "exceptional framework" in such moments of existential crisis—his last phrase references Carl Schmitt's theory of the "state of exception," a space or time in which law is absent, inadequate, or suspended. As "America's constitutional machinery" of checks and balances "prevents any single ambitious person from reconstructing the old Republic," the statesman must now contemplate forms of republican extra-constitutionality.[7]

The second network clusters around the "Bitcoin bros," coding and cryptography adepts keen to cultivate technological rivals to state-issued currencies and established financial institutions. These men seek cryptographically secured alternatives to the ongoing monetary debasement and surveillance pursued by contemporary state institutions and quasi-state organizations like the Federal Reserve and commercial banks deemed "too big to fail."[8] While often characterized, including by themselves, as cyberlibertarian, their Machiavellian moments include the global financial crisis of 2007–08 and, more broadly, the numerous financial and monetary emergencies of the last few decades. For Bitcoin bros, such emergencies have become not only perennial but also perpetual, as the responses of state policymakers create permanent financial states of exception and vitiate liberal-democratic constitutionalism meant to secure bourgeois freedoms and rights, especially of property and contract. In reaction, Bitcoin bros seek not to cultivate the exceptional agency of a republican statesman, Christian or otherwise, but to develop capabilities for moving beyond the state: They are building a "blockchain democracy" in which the "sovereign individual" possesses *hard money* on blockchains like Bitcoin and secures bourgeois liberal freedoms through such cryptographically secured technologies, all developed outside and against the state under the maxim "code is law."[9] Bitcoin bros believe code itself is language—as of course it is—and indeed the most important one in politics today.

In my penultimate section, I touch upon a third network which I call *cryptopartisans*: figures and movements identified not by shared beliefs but by shared experiences of exclusion and by a turn *out of necessity* to Bitcoin and other cryptographically secured technologies. They include many participants in the 2017 Alt-right rally in Charlottesville, Virginia; in the 2021 storming of the Capitol; and in the 2022 Canadian Freedom Convoys—but they need not be far-right or even particularly right-wing. Cryptopartisans turn to crypto not out of cyberlibertarian zeal or technological fascination but due to their exclusion from mainstream platforms and services in contemporary liberal democracies: for instance, following their deplatforming from banks and other financial intermediaries after events like those noted earlier.[10] Unlike Bitcoin bros—who have no nation save cyberspace and who believe code can replace constitutional and other forms of law, cryptopartisans seek to defend national territories and liberal-democratic constitutions they see as theirs and threatened by the tyrannical power of governmental and quasi-state, often corporate, elites whom they believe to be oppressing the common people.[11] Cryptopartisans fuse Thiel's interest in hard men capable of acting *through* constitutional states of exception with the Bitcoin bros' interest in hard money and technologies capable of functioning *beyond* financial states of exception. Put more simply, cryptopartisans make the surprising turn to decentralized, denationalized technologies in their attempts to defend and reclaim their nation-states and constitutions from hostile "elites."

Together, these three networks constitute a hardening right concerned with cultivating certain capabilities that will enable them to act not to undermine liberal democracy, but to reclaim or reform it according to their own visions. While it is always possible they are masters of Far-Right Newspeak, thereby masking other intentions, most members of these networks do not present themselves as opponents of liberal democracy or the "modern bourgeois, Rechtsstaat," the "type of constitution to which the majority of today's constitutions conform."[12] In the Euro-Atlantic, almost all states claim to adhere to this constitutional form—with the exception of Russia, Belarus, and, in different respects, Hungary and Poland.[13] The challenge posed by such anomalies appears confined, at least rhetorically, to one-half of the liberal-democratic hybrid: they challenge the legitimacy of *liberalism*, not democracy, as in the case of the "illiberal democracy" constructed by Victor Orbán that has attracted trans-Atlantic admirers like the self-styled "post-liberals."[14] Thiel is more multifaceted in his critiques. He castigates certain forms of liberalism for contributing to the modern West's loss of faith in itself and he critiques certain forms of liberal constitutionalism for constraining statesmanlike action in times of crisis. He also has harsh words for contemporary democracy when it upends the delicate balance with liberalism: "I no longer believe that freedom and democracy are compatible," he states in 2009, defending liberalism *against* certain forms of democracy.[15] Bitcoin bros present themselves as staunch defenders of the bourgeois individualism and freedoms at the root of "classical" liberalism and stern critics of undemocratic financial institutions and monetary policymaking.[16] Cryptopartisans typically have no problem with liberal democracy per se, provided it can be reclaimed by and for those they deem the true people.

The Thielian Network

Before considering Thiel's political thought regarding contemporary crises facing liberal-democratic republics, which I do in the next section, I wish to note his centrality within a wide network of political and technological figures and innovations. Although he will later take a statist turn, his early networks overlap with precursors to those of the Bitcoin bros. In the 1990s in Palo Alto, California, alongside Elon Musk and experts in cryptography, Thiel helped create one of the online payment platforms that merged into PayPal in 2000. Challenging numerous financial and commercial intermediaries,

PayPal grew out of several movements within the broader "Californian Ideology" of Silicon Valley—including cryptoanarchism, cyberlibertarianism, and the cypherpunks—all heralds of the "long predicted convergence of the media, computing, and telecommunications in hypermedia."[17] These movements helped generate the ideological and technological milieux that would later birth Bitcoin.[18]

PayPal was to be a platform for "the creation of a new world currency, free from all government control and dilution—the end of monetary sovereignty," as Thiel later characterized it.[19] According to the Australian digital economist Jack Parkin, an expert on Bitcoin, the PayPal mission statement crafted by then-CEO Thiel evinced a deep "distrust in fiat currency" that "revolved around its vulnerability to nation-state corruption."[20] Such distrust of the nation-state stands within long-standing debates in Western political theory between decentralized and centralized forms of power. As another scholar puts it, the technologists in this "political revolution" generally side against the early modern philosophy of Thomas Hobbes and favor that of John Locke, rejecting "the power of the state versus the rights of the individual; the knowledge of the elite versus the wisdom of the masses; the decisiveness of a king versus the deliberation of the parliament."[21] Distrust also suffuses the republican tradition, with the crucial concept being *corruption*, as seen in the prior statement about Thiel.

Pocock shows how elite corruption and constitutional decay are inevitable, according to republicans. Republicans trust in the classical theory of constitutional cycles as revived by the Renaissance theorist Niccolò Machiavelli: Singular events of "renovation" effected through statesmanly *virtù*, including the judicious exercise of political violence, can renew a constitution.[22] In terms of early American debates on decentralizing power, one can point to the republicanism of Thomas Jefferson—which venerates the yeoman farmer and opposes projects like a national bank—or the populism of Andrew Jackson (a president to whom Donald Trump is often likened). Indeed, such historical touchstones continue to inform contemporary cyberlibertarianism. As characterized by the theorists Richard Barbrook and Andy Cameron, believers in the Californian Ideology are "passionate advocates of what appears to be an impeccably libertarian form of politics—they want information technologies to be used to create a new 'Jeffersonian democracy' where all individuals will be able to express themselves freely within cyberspace."[23]

Hard-core advocates for decentralization came to see PayPal as a failed attempt to achieve this vision of Jeffersonian democracy, becoming over time a highly centralized corporation just as likely to surveil and censor its users as other established financial intermediaries. Thiel's proximity to such visions did not end with his departure from PayPal, however. Years later, after the invention of Bitcoin by the pseudonymous Satoshi Nakamoto, the most brilliant and prolific early promoter of Bitcoin was the Russian-born Canadian

Vitalik Buterin, a coder who wrote for *Bitcoin Magazine*. One of Thiel's most high-profile projects is his Thiel Fellowship, which provides $100,000 to each fellow to pursue entrepreneurial projects, provided they delay or leave college for two years. Buterin was one of the first Thiel Fellows. He would go on to develop the code for Ethereum, the second-largest crypto network after Bitcoin, and the ether cryptocurrency, the second largest after Bitcoin.[24] Thiel and his venture capital Founders Fund have invested in Bitcoin and many other crypto projects.

Ironically, given that cryptoanarchists, cyberlibertarians, and cypherpunks harshly critique establishment banks and other financial intermediaries—as do the later Bitcoin bros—it can appear they merely propose capitalist solutions to capitalist corruption. Is that really a road to decentralized Jeffersonian democracy in cyberspace? The clear emphasis in these milieux is the critique of *state* corruption, for them the dominant and most pernicious kind. Republicans like Jefferson and Jackson specifically opposed federal state projects like a national bank. Similar critiques had originated in England in the eighteenth century, when new forms of state financing were opposed to the classical republican concept of civic virtue:

> The confrontation of "virtue" with "corruption" is shown to have been a vital problem . . . during that era, and its humanist and Machiavellian vocabulary is shown to have been the vehicle of a basically hostile perception of early modern capitalism, grounded in awareness of the elaborate conventions of public credit rather than of the more direct interchanges of the market.[25]

Over several centuries republicans and other advocates for decentralization—like contemporary cyberlibertarians—have increasingly felt that state-controlled financial instruments, from public credit to paper currencies, are avenues of corruption. Yet most republicans, *unlike* most cyberlibertarians, do not believe in escaping to an economic state of nature as a solution to such corruption.

In the 2000s, Thiel moved away from his libertarian and cyberlibertarian roots, shifting from the Californian Ideology towards a kind of republicanism more interested in state power, constitutionalism, and civic virtue. Earlier, I referred to Machiavelli's vision of statesmanly *virtù* as a counter to state corruption and constitutional decay. Republican virtue is highly gendered: *virtus* in classical Roman republican language stands for civic virtue in the sense of civic *manliness*.[26] As Pocock puts it, republicanism is built on "concepts of balanced government, dynamic *virtù*, and the role of arms and property in shaping the civic personality."[27] In his 2007 essay, as we will see, Thiel essentially says contemporary liberal democracies are obsessed with property and thereby neglect other elements of a flourishing republic, including the hard men (and arms) needed to defend it and republican freedom. Perhaps this growing awareness informed his next major corporate venture and, more recently, undergirds his interest in the masculinist right.

Thiel's second success as a corporate founder was Palantir, a predictive analytics and surveillance firm founded in 2003 in Silicon Valley and later relocated to Denver, Colorado. Now a public corporation, Palantir has held numerous US government contracts, beginning with the Central Intelligence Agency (CIA), which initially supported Palantir as a start-up through its strategic investment firm, In-Q-Tel (IQT).[28] Subsequent contracts include the National Security Agency (NSA), Special Operations Command (SOCOM), and Immigration and Customs Enforcement (ICE).[29] The firm is named after ancient, globular "seeing stones" in J. R. R. Tolkien's *The Lord of the Rings*—a fantasy favorite also of the European right—which enable users to espy events and persons distantly across both space and time.[30]

One Palantir contract with the Department of Defense (DoD) involves the Algorithmic Warfare Cross-Functional Team, code-named Project Maven, integrating artificial intelligence (AI) and machine learning in DoD operations.[31] Project Maven is also supported by the defense corporation Anduril (a powerful sword in Tolkien's work) founded by Palmer Luckey—a Thiel Fellow and fellow Trump supporter. Critics have alleged Luckey was a "tacit supporter" of GamerGate, a media controversy and trolling campaign which Alt-right leaders credit with radicalizing young men and creating a pool of potential recruits.[32] Intriguingly, given Thiel's interest in Schmitt's theory of the friend–enemy distinction as the conceptual and existential core of the political, discussed in the next section, Luckey describes Project Maven as a technological extension of that distinction: "Practically speaking, in the future, I think soldiers are going to be superheroes who have the power of perfect omniscience over their area of operations, where they know where every enemy is, every friend is, every asset is."[33]

Thiel and his network are now deeply invested in technologies that enhance state power in the realms of surveillance and military technology—involving what Pocock calls "the role of arms" in republican states. His turn from libertarianism may also be seen in his proximities to the masculinist right obsessed with gendered conceptions of politics. In an April 2023 speech at a gala in his honor hosted by *The New Criterion*, Thiel references Nietzschean masculinists like Bronze Age Pervert (BAP) and what he calls their "strongman argument," that "the West may in fact be chauvinist, racist, sexist, and all the other things it's accused of being, but we should embrace that rather than apologize for it."[34] BAP, in turn, boasts on social media of insider knowledge regarding outlandish Thielian political projects.[35] Thiel is a longtime fellow-traveler of the Claremont Institute, based in Claremont, California. Institute publications like the print *Claremont Review of Books* and the webzine *American Mind* were among the first mainstream conservative venues to critically engage with masculinists like BAP.[36] Both *American Mind* and *IM—1776*, another webzine supported by Claremont, feature original contributions from other members of the masculinist right. While theirs is not exactly a classical republican vision of civic virtue, their centering of masculinity and politics often points in that direction—far more than the deracinated, desexed individualism of most forms of liberalism and libertarianism.

The Thielian Moment

Turning from Thiel's various political and technological proximities to his academic network, consider the results of the July 2004 conference he hosted at Stanford University, starring René Girard, his teacher while an undergraduate there. Thiel's contribution to the conference, as published in 2007, evinces an intense concern for political decisions and the necessity of centering them in the state. Thiel insists that current conditions call for statesmen capable of making fundamentally *sovereign* decisions within an "exceptional framework"—a framing which evokes Carl Schmitt, as we will see.

Many participants at this conference were trained political theorists, including Wolfgang Palaver, an editor at the erstwhile left-wing journal *Telos* who published there several of Schmitt's works, most for the first time in English. Participants devoted themselves to Girardian thought and to that of Schmitt, Leo Strauss, and Eric Voegelin—all amidst a "unipolar moment" dominated by the post-9/11 global war on terror, the war in Iraq, and the neoconservative foreign policy of the Bush administration.[37] In 2007, several conference papers appeared as chapters in *Politics and Apocalypse*.[38] The penultimate chapter is by Thiel himself.[39] A *tour de force*, the work surveys the post-9/11 intellectual and political landscape by way of Schmitt, Strauss, Girard, and writers ranging from Oswald Spengler to Alfred, Lord Tennyson.

Thiel emerges as a thinker of *the political* in the Schmittian sense, the realm of friend–enemy distinctions, states of exception, and the hard men who pursue the "hard questions" in an epoch when liberal-democratic Westerners are attempting to escape them, fleeing political decisions for the beguiling entertainments of the end of history.[40] Thiel lambasts efforts to reduce politics to economic decisions or expanded possibilities for individual expression. Thiel calls for the courage to face the existential challenges confronting the state, especially in Western liberal democracies, given the shifting nature of conflict and power in the contemporary global order. This is a classic Schmittian framing. The essay could be named "The Schmittian Moment," for it contains—from first lines to last—many covert allusions to the German thinker, a hidden dialogue extending well beyond the passages explicitly devoted to Schmittian thought.[41] Indeed, in light of Thiel's discussion of Leo

Strauss, famously a proponent of esoteric writing, one suspects Thiel is practicing what Strauss preaches: He writes "in that terse and lively style which is apt to arrest the attention of young men who love to think."[42]

Thiel begins with 9/11: "In those shocking hours, the entire political and military framework of the nineteenth and twentieth centuries, and indeed of the modern age, with its emphasis on deterrent armies, rational nation-states, public debates, and international diplomacy, was called into question."[43] While Thiel does not name the text, he describes precisely the "Westphalian" order Schmitt valorizes throughout his geopolitical *magnum opus*, *The Nomos of the Earth in the International Law of the Jus Publicum Europaeum* (1950), a work Palaver considers at length in his contribution.[44] He valorizes an order that "bracketed" war in Europe: Sovereign states treated other states as *just* enemies, not as inimical foes—evil or subhuman—in need of annihilation. Schmitt decries the decline of this *nomos* or "ordering order" in twentieth-century international law and international relations, especially under the corrupting influence of the United States.[45]

In contrast with earlier, more truly political epochs, Thiel is sharply critical of the predominance of economic and financial thinking and policymaking in the modern West, from John Locke, an initial investor in the Bank of England (for which he is also critiqued by Bitcoin bros, as contrary to his decentralized political philosophy), to Adam Smith and the international institutions of the World Bank and the International Monetary Fund (IMF)—an unsurprising stance for a billionaire whose fortune began with a platform that set out to radically disrupt the financial establishment. Liberal policymakers in the West have been "naïve" to think they could achieve the "containment of violence" through economic and financial programs after World War II targeted at the "wretched of the earth" (a reference to the famous anti-colonial book by Frantz Fanon).[46] Such reflections closely track those of Schmitt in *Nomos of the Earth*, in which he critiques all attempts, especially those of the Americans in the nineteenth and twentieth centuries, to evade political decisions by retreating into liberal economics.

The influence of Schmitt's thought in *Nomos of the Earth*, a thinking beyond liberalism, can also be seen in Thiel's starting question: "[H]ow could mere talking or even great force deter a handful of crazy, determined, and suicidal persons who seemingly operated outside of all the norms of the liberal West?" The post-Westphalian bracketing of war is not accepted by Europe's enemies. Thiel presents himself as a hard thinker of hard questions, one prepared to advance, out of necessity, serious critiques of contemporary liberal-democratic constitutionalism:

> The awareness of the West's vulnerability called for a new compromise, and this new compromise inexorably demanded more security at the expense of less freedom. On the narrow level of public policy, there needed to be

more x-ray machines at airports; more security guards on airplanes; more identification cards and invasions of privacy; and fewer rights for some of the accused. Overnight, the fundamentalist civil rights mantra of the American Civil Liberties Union (ACLU), which spoke in the language of inviolable individual rights, was rendered an unviable anachronism.[47]

But while constitutional compromises may be needed in the defense of liberal-democratic republics like the United States, Thiel firmly rejects anything like the neoconservative "crusade" against Islam or anything redolent of a return to religious fundamentalism in the West. Citing Schmitt on the friend–enemy distinction, Thiel warns: "[O]ne must choose one's enemies well, for one will soon be like them."[48] While framed at the end of his section on Schmitt (indeed, as a critique of Schmitt), this statement subtly alludes to his earlier quotation from Schmitt's postwar diaries: "The enemy is our own question as a figure."[49] Islamic extremists do not represent an enemy in that sense, as one who calls into question one's very identity—as opposed to one's existence.

While rejecting illiberal fundamentalisms abroad and at home, Thiel is not prepared to do away with political theology, even in the liberal-democratic West. He brings the essay to its culmination by declaring the necessity of sovereign decision: "Sovereign is he who decides on the exception," Schmitt famously begins his 1922 book *Political Theology*, a work in which he postulated, "All significant concepts of the modern theory of the state are secularized theological concepts."[50] The political theology of Schmitt (a sometime Catholic), the influence of Thiel's teacher Girard (likewise), or perhaps his own avowed Christian faith—each could explain why Thiel assigns this decisionistic role to the *Christian* statesman who knows "there cannot be a decision to avoid all decisions." Thiel's statesman is tasked with "determining the correct mixture of violence and peace" in the concrete "close case" that cannot be seen in advance, theorized in the abstract, or answered within the existing legal and normative order.[51]

Here is the Schmittian state of exception, a condition in which law or norms—be they constitutional, economic, juridical, or political—are suspended in the interest of preserving an overall order facing an existential threat. Only a theologico-political framing is appropriate in such moments. The statesman must exercise the secular equivalent of a miracle: the suspension of law, including certain constitutional laws, in the name of something higher—the constitutional order itself. Thiel no doubt knows Schmitt's 1921 *Dictatorship*: The Roman republic provided for a constitutional office, that of dictator, which can be invoked by the Senate and the people in an existential crisis.[52] The dictator operates in a constitutional state of exception. He can legitimately take extraordinary, and otherwise illegal, measures to contain and terminate the crisis. The American republic lacks such an office. But since states of exception always emerge in law and politics, Thiel suggests, extra-constitutional powers will be needed—as will the hard men who can wield them.

The Bitcoin Moment

I now turn to the Bitcoin bros and how they seek independence and sovereignty through a digital revolution, freedom from the arbitrary power of central banks in Western liberal democracies to debase state "fiat" currencies—from the US dollar and the euro to the British pound and Swedish krona—through monetary policy. This is an originary narrative of Bitcoin bros, their account of the decline of freedom *in*, and the simultaneous decline *of*, the Western liberal democracies. Bitcoin bros call for radical financial change and celebrate the fruits of the technological innovation, which has created, in their view, an avenue for change via a cryptographic and financial invention: Bitcoin.[53] By arguing that central bankers and other financial elites exercise tyrannical power at the expense of the lowly public, Bitcoin bros use terms that put them squarely in the languages of liberalism and democracy.

Bitcoin bros, in contrast to Thiel, present themselves as wholehearted defenders of liberal-democratic constitutionalism, or at least the modern bourgeois freedoms identified by Schmitt as at the root of modern constitutionalism: "personal freedom, private property, contractual liberty, and freedom of commerce and profession."[54] For Bitcoin bros, as for the modern bourgeoisie, the sphere of liberal freedom and rights is unlimited, while the state sphere should be clearly delineated and sharply limited. While this position is often labeled libertarian, primarily in American discourse, in historical terms it sits squarely within modern bourgeois constitutionalism.[55] Bitcoin bros staunchly critique financial institutions like central banks for being illiberal and undemocratic; they especially target the Federal Reserve, as well as international financial organizations like the Bank of International Settlements (BIS), the "central bank of central banks," based in Basel, Switzerland—a powerful institution which prefers to remain virtually unknown to the democratic public.[56] Why target such institutions? In Schmittian terms, central banks like the Federal Reserve and government agencies like the US Treasury are the concrete institutional sites where sovereignty is wielded within financial states of exception—when both law and constitutionalism are suspended. Again unlike Thiel, Bitcoin bros desire an end to all states of exception. They desire the uninterrupted implementation of the maxim "code is law": new forms of money and politics that eliminate the need for sovereign decisions by both statesmen *and* illiberal, undemocratic financial elites.

Money is a golden thread through the warp and weft of Western political thought. In high modernity, it becomes a central domain of elite interest and theory. Shaped by the state, money "speaks different languages and wears different national uniforms," as Marx posits. The cyberlibertarian Bitcoin bros agree with the communist theorist: Money changes tongues and clothes, and there is no need for it to speak or dress in *national* terms at all, thereby being "separated from the *universal* sphere of circulation in the commodity world by national boundaries."[57] Monetary theorist Nigel Dodd emphasizes, "the 'golden age' of state (and, especially, territorial) money was extremely short-lived—if, indeed, it ever really existed." Prior to the nineteenth century, he notes, "a mixture of domestic and foreign currencies was in use throughout Europe, and in the United States, silver coins from Mexico and Spain dominated the domestic money supply."[58] Up to WWI under the so-called gold standard, the paper currencies of most major nation-states, "state fiat money," were universally convertible to an underlying, globally valued commodity, principally gold. Even for Marx, "fiat money represented a material base, i.e., the state's gold reserves."[59]

Bitcoin bros believe bitcoin is *digital gold*—the fusion of money with cryptography and the Internet. They herald an anti-statist global turn to a "Bitcoin standard," the *denationalization* of money.[60] In contrast to state fiat currencies, which now (unlike in Marx's day) are unbacked by any rare and valued commodity like gold, Bitcoin bros advertise bitcoin as the "hardest of hard monies," by which they mean the least amenable to monetary expansion, as the supply of bitcoin is permanently capped, in the original code, at 21 million bitcoin. More gold, they argue, can always be mined and is subject thereby to monetary expansion. Indeed, in a futurist twist, the "Winklevii" brothers Cameron and Tyler Winklevoss—early bitcoin billionaires and Mark Zuckerberg's old nemeses—speculate gold will become effectively worthless once massive quantities can be mined from asteroids.

Bitcoin, and the turn to a new hard money, emerges in reaction to a financial state of exception, the global financial crisis of 2008, an *annus horribilis* in which the global economic and financial order appeared at risk and policymakers responded decisively. Such decisions came at high cost. On both left and right, from Occupy Wall Street to the American Tea Party, enormous populist discontent erupted over publicly funded bailouts for private banks deemed "too big to fail." The first, genesis block of the Bitcoin blockchain is inscribed with a headline from the London *Times*, "The Times 03/Jan/2009 Chancellor on brink of second bailout for banks," referencing policymaking by Alistair Darling, then UK Chancellor of the Exchequer. Bitcoin bros argue existing financial laws and norms would have allowed large banks to fail in 2008 like other businesses do when they make poor decisions. Yet policymakers across the West prevented these bank failures and claimed they saved the financial system—in Schmittian terms, they exercised the sovereign decision to deploy extraordinary powers during an economic state of emergency.[61]

In addition to flagging resistance to UK responses to the global financial crisis, Bitcoin is inscribed with other messages of populist resistance, each destined to immortality so long as Bitcoin itself endures. The "raw hex" of the third block in the Bitcoin blockchain is inscribed with the face of Ben Bernanke, chairman of the Federal Reserve Board of Governors from 2006 to 2014. In this role, Bernanke was central to many of the American (and international) policy discussions and decisions that followed the global financial crisis, including those that inflamed populists, libertarians, and classical liberals—that is, speakers of liberal-democratic languages. Indeed, it is difficult to overstate the extent of such discontents, which cross many political boundaries, some beyond the languages of liberalism and democracy: A decade later on the Nietzschean masculinist right—which generally does not focus upon economics, finance, or money—one finds the pseudonymous figure Bronze Age Pervert (BAP) declaring in his influential 2018 book, *Bronze Age Mindset*, that most modern women are "botched" dating and marriage partners because they have been "Bernankefied up the ass."[62] Bad monetary policy impacts even sexual relations, presumably by turning women from true womanhood (which masculinists rarely bother to define) towards debt-financed consumerism within the ephemeral world of increasingly debased state fiat currencies.

To return to Schmittian states of exception: Dodd, in *The Social Life of Money*, stresses the importance of Schmitt's thought to monetary theory.[63] His concepts and heuristics are indeed useful for understanding Bitcoin bros and their opposition to financial states of exception. Legal theorist William Scheuerman credits Schmitt's work as "unsurpassed" in its contribution to a theory of economic emergency, specifically. Empirical developments in liberal democracies since the nineteenth century make such a theory essential, he argues: "Initially a mere supplement to *wartime* emergency powers, executive-dominated emergency economic regulation now represents a more or less *permanent* feature of political life in many liberal democracies."[64]

Bitcoin bros believe financial states of exception are both illiberal and undemocratic. Believing "inflation is theft," the creation of new state fiat money unbacked by any commodity appears as perpetually illiberal monetary policy, directly harming the property interests of savers and creditors while benefiting debtors—chiefly large corporations and the US government itself. Furthermore, Bitcoin bros dilate on the undemocratic policymaking processes that have emerged in the governance of state fiat currencies. Executive-dominated wartime states of emergency in the American Civil War and World War I prompt multi-year suspensions of the convertibility of gold and fiat, enabling the creation of vast amounts of fiat money to fund war efforts far beyond what state finances would otherwise have been able to bear—thus prolonging and intensifying such wars, causing greater deaths among the democratic citizenry who fight in them.[65]

Furthermore, wartime states of emergency come to serve as models for economic states of exception in peacetime. Bitcoin bros dilate upon the 1933 banning of private ownership of gold by American citizens and the abrogation of gold clauses in private contracts and in federal bonds by Franklin Delano Roosevelt, both by executive decree followed by *post hoc* Congressional legitimation. A plurality of the Supreme Court—including justices typically supportive of the New Deal—ruled FDR's abrogation of the gold clause in Treasury bonds to be unconstitutional, although they denied relief to bondholders.[66] Such developments are not unique to the United States: "As early as 1931, Schmitt identified the widespread tendency within twentieth-century liberal democracy to equate economic and financial crises with military attacks and armed insurrections, thereby justifying executive recourse to sweeping emergency powers as a means of undertaking ambitious forms of economic management."[67] Indeed, as Dodd emphasizes, "the economic background for [Schmitt's] theory of the exception was the then-current hyperinflation, which might be called a state of economic emergency."[68]

Bitcoin bros also criticize the complete abandonment of gold as a material base for the US dollar in the administration of Richard Nixon, when spending on his predecessor's "Great Society" social welfare agenda and the ongoing Vietnam War threatened state finances. Nixon suddenly abandoned the gold standard on August 15, 1971—again followed by *post hoc* Congressional action—thereby enabling a major devaluation of the dollar relative to gold.[69] To such cases, and that of the global financial crisis, may be added the widespread monetary creation of 2020–21 prompted by the coronavirus pandemic.[70] Financial states of exception are damning cases of monetary malfeasance in the eyes of Bitcoin bros: proof positive that the state should not control money. In Schmittian terms, such developments move Western liberal democracies closer to permanent states of financial emergency.

In contrast, due to the workings of the gold standard, Bitcoin bros see the nineteenth and early twentieth centuries up to 1914—when the gold standard was suspended by the belligerents—as the high tide of liberal democracy and economic globalization. In these respects, they follow Austrian economists like Ludwig von Mises:

> The gold standard was the world standard of the age of capitalism, increasing welfare, liberty, and democracy, both political and economic. In the eyes of the free traders its main eminence was precisely the fact that it was an international standard as required by international trade and the transactions of the international money and capital markets. It was the medium of exchange by means of which Western industrialism and Western capital had borne Western civilization to the remotest parts of the earth's surface, everywhere destroying the fetters of age-old prejudices and superstitions, sowing the seeds of new life and new well-being, freeing minds and souls, and creating riches unheard of before. It accompanied

the triumphal unprecedented progress of Western liberalism ready to unite all nations into a community of free nations peacefully cooperating with one another.[71]

Bitcoin bros, clear-eyed, see through the mendacity of fiat currencies. Sporting unbounded brio and futural optimism—as all bros do—they seek no return to an earlier monetary epoch, the gold standard of their great-grandfathers. We now live in the Age of Tech, whose reigning deity is the Internet. Bitcoin bros do not shy from proclaiming themselves the true defenders of bourgeois freedom today, singular possessors of the truth of twenty-first-century geo-economics: All fiat currencies are debasing, their associated liberal democracies are going bankrupt, the currencies of the "Technopolar Moment" will be digital like bitcoin, and networks like Bitcoin will empower decentralized forms of freedom and sovereignty.[72]

In sum, according to Bitcoin bros, gold was unseated as the global reserve currency through the machinations of liberal-democratic politicians like FDR and Nixon in collusion with financial elites. The US dollar will inevitably lose its global reserve currency status through the weaknesses of those same politicians and elites, who cannot resist the lure of monetary inflation and debasement. The dollar will be replaced by bitcoin, a currency independent of any political sovereign, liberal-democratic or otherwise—a world historic innovation.

Cryptopartisans

Finally, to briefly consider a third network that may shape the future influence of the tech right, the cryptopartisans, we begin by asking how they come to take an interest in Bitcoin and other cryptographically secured technologies. They are not, as a rule, cyberlibertarians or technologists. Nor do they share any other ideology or political language save that prompted by their exclusion from mainstream platforms and services following their participation in activities they believe to be well within the bounds of liberal democracy. They turn into cryptopartisans out of necessity and illustrate how various political figures and groups, speaking their own languages of liberalism and democracy, come to interact with the hardening right in the technological sphere.[73]

As the political scientist Robert Pape has shown, most persons at the Capitol for Stop the Steal were not far right.[74] One suspects the same result will be found of the Canadian Freedom Convoy participants. But one notable figure at the Capitol can be characterized as such: Nicholas "Nick" J. Fuentes, a major Alt-right influencer and a strident Christian nationalist. Of Mexican-American descent, he identifies as Catholic, straight, and white. On January 6, he was 23 years old and one of the younger participants. But he had been prominent on the Alt-right since he was a teenager and founded America First, initially a YouTube livestream by which Fuentes garnered hundreds of thousands of followers before he was deplatformed. He filmed the stream in the basement of his childhood home in Chicago—a fact for which he was routinely lambasted, as this fit all-too-well a stereotype about the Alt-right as comprised of "extremely online" activists, typically young men who were unemployed, unmarried, and living with their parents. No doubt a key element in his deplatforming was his virulent antisemitism, which serves as a consistent theme in the livestream. Along with Christian nationalism, he advocates for immigration restrictionism in domestic policy. In foreign policy, he takes a pro-Putin and pro-Russian stance—including, after the 2022 Russian invasion of Ukraine, an anti-NATO position.[75] In 2022, he was also an advisor to "Ye," the hip-hop artist Kanye West, in his brief campaign for the US presidency.

Presumably for his *outré* views, Fuentes was deplatformed by YouTube and social media sites like Twitter (now known as X). He moved America First to other online streaming services, but never regained his earlier viewership. He claims to have been put on the No-Fly List of the US Department of Homeland Security and to have been blacklisted by major US-based banks, financial institutions, and payment processors. All this preceded January 6. Where, then, did his funding come from? How was he able to continue being a prominent activist, as at the Capitol that day?

After his deplatforming, Fuentes turned to Bitcoin as an alternative to mainstream financial services, a means of receiving continued contributions from his supporters. He had not previously been an advocate for Bitcoin or crypto. Nor would his turn to Bitcoin result in a newfound ideological commitment to such technologies. Yet one supporter would make headlines on this score. In October 2020, a French man sent Fuentes several bitcoin. At the time, these bitcoin were worth roughly a quarter million US dollars. By early 2021, however, those same bitcoin had gained in value and were worth approximately one million US dollars in aggregate (assuming Fuentes had not exchanged them for some other currency). Did this windfall help fund his participation in events like Stop the Steal?

More broadly, several far-right figures and groups have turned to bitcoin and other cryptocurrencies. The 2017 Unite the Right rally was a watershed. Figures there included Richard Spencer and various Alt-right groups like Vanguard America (subsequently Patriot Front) and the Rise Above Movement (RAM). As a result of Charlottesville, many were deplatformed by financial intermediaries like banks and payment processors.[76] They view these corporate intermediaries as quasi-state entities wielding tyrannical, illiberal, and undemocratic powers over American citizens—effectively "un-personing" them from the economic and financial system, denying all recourse and appeal—a financial state of exception, a sort of corporate

Guantanamo Bay. Hence, many on the Alt-right have turned into cryptopartisans, as have other excluded and deplatformed figures like writers for the white nationalist publisher Counter-Currents. It is unclear whether these figures and groups have profited from their turn to crypto to the degree enjoyed by Fuentes, but his windfall has surely been noted.

It is a sign of our times that financial and technological capabilities are becoming crucial to insurgent movements, including those on the far right, and the establishment forces that resist them. The cryptopartisan turn to Bitcoin and other cryptographically secured technologies is primarily pragmatic, a response to what they view as coordinated exclusion and deplatforming from mainstream institutions and services in Western liberal democracies. In "The Age of Neutralizations and Depoliticizations," originally given in the ominous circumstances of October 1929—that is, at the midpoint of the Great Crash and the month of Black Thursday—Schmitt observed that today "an economic catastrophe, such as a sharp monetary devaluation or crash, occasions widespread and acute interest both practical and theoretical."[77]

In his 1929 essay, Schmitt lays out four intellectual stages the Europeans have traversed in the past four centuries. In early modernity, theology constitutes the intellectual-political "central domain," whereas in subsequent centuries metaphysics, humanitarian-moral sentiments, and finally economics, in the nineteenth century, predominate. Only matters in each central domain truly activate the intellectual energies of the "active elite" and "respective vanguards" of each century.[78] Extending the Schmittian logic, we can conclude the central domain of the twentieth century is finance, while that of the twenty-first must surely involve aspects of cyberspace—including Bitcoin and other cryptographically secured technologies. No surprise, then, that crises for contemporary liberal democracy—like those which arose at Charlottesville, at the US Capitol, and in Ottawa—should play out in the realms of finance, money, and cyberspace.

Bitcoin arose in reaction to financial states of exception in which the true sovereigns in Western liberal democracy were supposedly revealed: an entrenched financial elite who can suspend economic and monetary laws at will and without accountability, purportedly to "save the system," the capitalist liberal-democratic order. From a purely analytical perspective, in witnessing who emerges to wield the power to decide upon and act in a state of exception one sees who is truly sovereign. From a practical political perspective, however, such power can appear deeply illegitimate. It can appear "dictatorial," despotic, tyrannical. Fierce populist movements arose in reaction to the global financial crisis and policymaker responses: On the populist right, the American Tea Party emerged in 2009, for instance, portraying policymakers like Barack Obama as tyrants akin to King George III. Such revolutionary, even insurrectionary, energies later fed into Trumpism and movements further to the right.

In Western liberal democracies the financial elite will no doubt continue to wield the powers of sovereignty—of deciding on and in the state of exception—for the foreseeable future. But these powers may increasingly come at higher prices than those who resist such powers have been able to exact until now. Bitcoin bros are developing an alternative economic and monetary system built on cutting-edge cryptography and technology. While they are comparatively nonpartisan, visionaries of a Bitcoin standard above and beyond the whims of nation-states, in their wake come true partisans. Keen to defend their vision of the liberal-democratic nation-state against governmental and quasi-state elites, perhaps Bitcoin and other cryptographically secured technologies will give such cryptopartisans a new edge against their foes.

Conclusion

It remains to be seen if the hardened statesmen envisaged by Thiel will need anything like the hardened money promoted by Buterin, the Thiel Fellow, and utilized by cryptopartisans like Fuentes, the riotous supporter of a Thiel-backed president. A state of exception is a moment of crisis in which the limits of law, including constitutional law, are reached. It is a moment in which an order, including a constitutional order, is called into question. Only a power beyond the law can save the law. As we have seen, Schmitt is unparalleled as a theorist of such matters. Pocock, in his account of the Machiavellian moment, has revealed their import in republicanism, including that of the American republic. The Anglo-American, bourgeois liberal tradition also contains awareness of such moments. Note the conceptualization of Lord Macaulay, the eighteenth-century Whig, who likens constitutional states of exception precisely to financial emergencies:

> Constitutions are in politics what paper money is in commerce. They afford great facilities and conveniences. But . . . they are not power, but symbols of power, and will, in an emergency, prove altogether useless unless the power for which they stand be forthcoming.[79]

In different ways, the networks of Thiel and the Bitcoin bros each prepare for Machiavellian moments in the life of liberal-democratic states. Thiel appears closer to the cryptopartisans, however, in his intention to save liberal democracies like the American republic. Bitcoin bros believe in the imminent downfall of state fiat currencies undergirding major liberal democracies—and often appear untroubled by the downfall of those liberal democracies *in toto*, for bourgeois freedoms and rights can now be secured outside the state through code. Again, Bitcoin bros earn their moniker precisely because of their unbounded masculine brio and futural optimism. They are the youngest sons of the Californian Ideology, itself born in a land of blond-haired, bronze-skinned, sun-kissed surfers, carefree scions of American economic and political dominance over a shattered postwar world.[80] In the Californian Ideology, technology is all. Since technology is always improving, what is there to worry about? "Let's hit the beach." That many Bitcoin bros—like many technology entrepreneurs and venture capitalists, to say nothing of Nick Fuentes—have indeed grown wealthy from this wager and long since absconded to beaches all over the world as "digital nomads" and global citizens is for some further confirmation of the validity of the Californian Ideology.[81] Yet, however, hardened their financial and technological capabilities, from a Thielian perspective Bitcoin bros appear escapist, evasive of the central problematics of our era: concerned with hardened money, yes, but not hardened states and hardened statesmen.

The Thielian moment contains its own tensions. In his 2007 essay, Thiel nowhere links his Schmittian reflections on states of exception and statesmanship to the central sources of his own wealth. Perhaps for obvious reasons: PayPal consummately intermediates commerce and consumerism, Facebook mimetic entertainment. Such corporations cater to the Last Man whiling away the end of history—anathema to a Schmittian commitment to the political sphere. In the essay, Thiel highlights ECHELON, a recently uncovered NSA program, as an instrument for global surveillance enabling an intelligence state of exception worldwide.[82] But Palantir, which may have been inspired by ECHELON, has been far less profitable than PayPal and Facebook. Furthermore, from the perspective of civil libertarians and cyberlibertarians, such corporations are among the most oppressive of quasi-state organizations, powerful instruments of surveillance and censorship—thus, they are anathema to Bitcoin bros. Palantir, critics allege, likely invades the privacy of American citizens. And it profits from defense spending paid in fiat currency.

Overall, while the right is certainly hardening in terms of its capabilities, it is not yet clear to what ends such capabilities will be wielded. In the coming decades, liberal democracies will doubtlessly encounter new and maybe greater crises, perhaps in major interstate conflict, civil war, or another financial emergency. We will then see whether the tech right has developed the capacities about which they speak. Figures like Thiel and the Bitcoin bros have been effective in pointing out the hypocrisies and inconsistencies in how liberal-democratic concepts are defined and employed by mainline liberal democrats. So far, they have been less effective at avoiding these same shortcomings themselves.

Notes

1 On this shift in right-wing language more broadly, see A. James McAdams and Alejandro Castrillon, eds., *Contemporary Far-Right Thinkers and the Future of*

Liberal Democracy (London: Routledge, 2021); and Chapters 2 and 12 by A. James McAdams and Samuel Piccolo, in this volume.
2 See Zúquete, Chapter 10, and Pittz, Chapter 9 of this volume.
3 J. G. A. Pocock, *The Machiavellian Moment: Florentine Political Thought and the Atlantic Republican Tradition* (Princeton: Princeton University Press, 1975); cf. Caroline Robbins, *The Eighteenth-Century Commonwealthman: Studies in the Transmission, Development, and Circumstance of English Liberal Thought From the Restoration of Charles II Until the War With the Thirteen Colonies* (Cambridge, MA: Harvard University Press, 1959); J. W. Burrow, *Whigs and Liberals: Continuity and Change in English Political Thought* (Oxford: Oxford University Press, 1988). As shown by Pocock and the burgeoning scholarship he has inspired, European and American liberal democracy develops *upon* or *out of* republicanism, suggesting republican concepts and discourses remain embedded within the contemporary languages of liberal democracy, ready for reactivation and revivification. The "Machiavellian moment" is one such concept. On the submerged history of republicanism see, for instance, Gordon Wood, *The Creation of the American Republic, 1776–1787* (Chapel Hill: University of North Carolina Press, 1969); Quentin Skinner and Martin van Gelderen, eds., *Republicanism: A Shared European Heritage*, 2 vols. (Cambridge: Cambridge University Press, 2002).
4 Pocock, *Machiavellian Moment*, viii.
5 As a Stanford undergraduate, Thiel founded a conservative student newspaper, *The Stanford Review*, in 1987. In terms of electoral politics, Thiel was a significant backer of Donald J. Trump in the 2016 presidential campaign. On these episodes and Thiel's life more broadly, see Max Chafkin, *The Contrarian: Peter Thiel and Silicon Valley's Pursuit of Power* (London: Bloomsbury, 2021). In the 2022 US midterm elections, Thiel backed two candidates for the Senate: in Arizona, Blake Masters—former chief operating officer of Thiel Capital, president of the Thiel Foundation, and the coauthor of Thiel's book *Zero to One*—and, in Ohio, J. D. Vance. The latter won.
6 Thiel has spoken at the national conservatism conferences hosted from 2019 by the Edmund Burke Foundation headed by the Israeli political theorist Yoram Hazony; Chafkin, *The Contrarian*, 287–89. For an example of his interest in the Nietzschean masculinist right, see Peter Thiel, "The Diversity Myth," *The New Criterion* 41, no. 10 (2023). On the masculinist right, including its relation to the "manosphere"—online male-dominated spaces in which the concerns, interests, and needs of men and boys are prioritized in reaction to allegedly androphobic and feminized societies—see Josh Vandiver, "Alt-Virilities: Masculinism, Rhizomatics, and the Contradictions of the American Alt-Right," *Politics, Religion & Ideology* 21, no. 2 (2020); ibid., "Metapolitics, Masculinity, and Technology in the Rise of 'Bronze Age Pervert,'" in *Far Right Thinkers and the Future of Liberal Democracy in the Twenty-First Century*, edited by A. James McAdams and Alejandro Castrillon (London: Routledge, 2021); ibid., "Masculinist Identitarians, Strategic Culture, and Eurocene Geopolitics," in *Global Identitarianism*, edited by José Pedro Zúquete and Riccardo Marchi (London: Routledge, 2023).
7 Peter Thiel, "The Straussian Moment," in *Politics and Apocalypse* (East Lansing: Michigan State University Press, 2007), 214–15, 207–08. The title (and substance) of Thiel's essay clearly alludes to Pocock's *Machiavellian Moment*, but it overtly references the thinking and followers of the German Jewish émigré Leo Strauss, a political theorist who long taught at the University of Chicago. Some of Strauss'

students (and students of students) became prominent foreign policy neoconservatives and strident advocates for the later Iraq war. Schmitt—a German jurist and theorist of politics, constitutionalism, and international law—is best known in the Anglo-Saxon world for Carl Schmitt, *The Concept of the Political*, 2nd ed. (1932; Chicago: University of Chicago Press, 2008), in which he posits the essence of "the political" as a concrete distinction between friends and enemies, and for his theory of the state of exception as developed across a number of works in the 1920s, including id., *Dictatorship* (1921; Cambridge: Polity Press, 2015); id., *Political Theology: Four Chapters on the Concept of Sovereignty* (1922; Chicago: University of Chicago Press, 2005). Both Strauss and Schmitt play prominent roles in Thiel's 2007 essay and broader political thought. On the "Christian statesman," see later.

8   The "Bitcoin bros" moniker is used both by critics and neutral observers—like Camila Russo, *The Infinite Machine: How an Army of Crypto-Hackers Is Building the Next Internet With Ethereum* (New York: HarperCollins, 2020)—to denote figures, from coders to influencers, deeply enmeshed within the male-dominated "crypto" ecosystem. According to a 2013 community survey, over 95% of Bitcoin users are male. Nigel Dodd, *The Social Life of Money* (Princeton: Princeton University Press, 2014), 369n. Among Bitcoin bros, certain forms of masculinity predominate, including "nerd" masculinities, on which see Lori Kendall, "'White and Nerdy': Computers, Race, and the Nerd Stereotype," *The Journal of Popular Culture* 44, no. 3 (2011).

9   On claims regarding "blockchain democracy," see William Magnuson, *Blockchain Democracy: Technology, Law and the Rule of the Crowd* (Cambridge: Cambridge University Press, 2020). On the "sovereign individual" supposedly enabled by contemporary technologies, see James Dale Davidson and William Rees-Mogg, *The Sovereign Individual: Mastering the Transition to the Information Age* (New York: Touchstone, 1997), a popular text among Bitcoin bros, as in Saifedean Ammous, *The Bitcoin Standard: The Decentralized Alternative to Central Banking* (Hoboken: John Wiley & Sons, 2018), 200: "In *The Sovereign Individual*, James Davidson and [Lord] William Rees-Mogg argue that the modern nation-state, with its restrictive laws, high taxes, and totalitarian impulses, has grown to a level of burdensome repression of its citizens' freedom comparable to that of the Church in the European Middle Ages, and as ripe for disruption." On the notion of "code is law," understood "as a statement that code is the *only* applicable normative constraint, defeating government regulation," see Michèle Finck, *Blockchain Regulation and Governance in Europe* (Cambridge: Cambridge University Press, 2018), 35, original emphasis.

10 On financial exclusions impacting the far right, see Austin Eggers and Jeffrey Hobbs, "Combatting the Financing of Hate Groups," *Journal of Money Laundering Control* 26, no. 1 (2023).

11 In a sense, they are akin to the "telluric" partisans—defenders of a determinate territory and constitutional order against hostile, even "foreign," governmental or extraterritorial forces—conceptualized by Carl Schmitt, *Theory of the Partisan: Intermediate Commentary on the Concept of the Political*, 2nd ed. (1975; New York: Telos Press, 2007).

12 Carl Schmitt, *Constitutional Theory*, trans. Jeffrey Seitzer (1928; Durham: Duke University Press, 2008), 169.

13 On such cases see A. James McAdams' introduction to this volume.

14 See Laura Field's analysis in Chapter 8 of this volume.
15 Peter Thiel, "The Education of a Libertarian," *Cato Unbound*, 13 April 2009, accessed June 22, 2023, www.cato-unbound.org/2009/04/13/peter-thiel/education-libertarian/. Other right-wing critiques of democracy include those of the short-lived neo-reaction (NRx) movement, on which see George Hawley, *Making Sense of the Alt-Right* (New York: Columbia University Press, 2017). More enduring has been the masculinist right, mentioned earlier, which evinces an aristocratic Nietzschean ethic often skeptical of mass democracy—paired, intriguingly, with an interest in crypto: "Nietzsche meets Bitcoin," as one wag aptly puts it. Kit Wilson, "The Rise of the Neoclassical Reactionaries," *The Spectator*, 24 November 2021, accessed June 11, 2023, www.spectator.co.uk/article/the-rise-of-the-neoclassical-reactionaries/.
16 As Schmitt, *Constitutional Theory*, 170, argues, the "principles of the modern, bourgeois Rechtsstaat constitution correspond to the constitutional ideal of bourgeois individualism," and thereby this constitutional form "contains a decision in the sense of bourgeois freedom: personal freedom, private property, contractual liberty, and freedom of commerce and profession." Such constitutional and other ideals, including of bourgeois freedoms, correspond to what is often called classical liberalism in American political language.
17 Richard Barbrook and Andy Cameron, "The Californian Ideology," *Science as Culture* 6, no. 1 (1996), 44; notably, as a sign of the apocalyptic implications of this convergence, the first section of this groundbreaking article is titled "As the dam bursts . . ." On PayPal and the Californian Ideology, see Jack Parkin, *Money, Code, Space: Hidden Power in Bitcoin, Blockchain, and Decentralisation* (Oxford: Oxford University Press, 2020), 184–87.
18 Finn Brunton, *Digital Cash: The Unknown History of the Anarchists, Utopians, and Technologists Who Created Cryptocurrency* (Princeton: Princeton University Press, 2019).
19 Quoted in id., *Digital Cash*, 198.
20 Parkin, *Money, Code, Space*, 185.
21 Magnuson, *Blockchain Democracy*, 11.
22 Pocock, *Machiavellian Moment*, chs. VI–VII; I return to this theme later and in the next section.
23 Barbrook and Cameron, "The Californian Ideology," 45, internal citation omitted.
24 On the distinction between the Bitcoin network and the bitcoin cryptocurrency (denoted by lowercase), which is hosted upon the Bitcoin network (denoted by uppercase), as the ether cryptocurrency is hosted upon the Ethereum network—but one of thousands of cryptocurrencies and other digital assets, now including non-fungible tokens (NFTs), on Ethereum—see Magnuson, *Blockchain Democracy*.
25 Pocock, *Machiavellian Moment*, viii–ix.
26 Myles A. McDonnell, *Roman Manliness: Virtus and the Roman Republic* (Cambridge: Cambridge University Press, 2006); Hanna Fenichel Pitkin, *Fortune Is a Woman: Gender and Politics in the Thought of Niccolò Machiavelli* (Berkeley: University of California Press, 1984).
27 Pocock, *Machiavellian Moment*, viii.
28 Charles W. Mahoney, "United States Defence Contractors and the Future of Military Operations," *Defense & Security Analysis* 36, no. 2 (2020), 12.

29 Andrew Iliadis and Amelia Acker, "The Seer and the Seen: Surveying Palantir's Surveillance Platform," *The Information Society* 38, no. 5 (2022).
30 On Tolkien and the European right, see Roger Griffin, "Revolts Against the Modern World: The Blend of Literary and Historical Fantasy in the Italian New Right," *Literature and History* 11, no. 1 (1985).
31 Lucy Suchman, "Algorithmic Warfare and the Reinvention of Accuracy," *Critical Studies on Security* 8, no. 2 (2020).
32 Mary Anne Franks, "The Desert of the Unreal: Inequality in Virtual and Augmented Reality," *University of California at Davis Law Review* 51, no. 2 (2017), 537. Andrew Anglin, "A Normie's Guide to the Alt-Right," *Daily* Stormer, 31 August 2016, accessed August 1, 2018, https://web.archive.org/web/20200102131759/https://dailystormer.name/a-normies-guide-to-the-Alt-Right/. On GamerGate in relation to the Alt-Right, see Hawley, *Making Sense of the Alt-Right*, 45–49.
33 Quoted in Suchman, "Algorithmic Warfare and the Reinvention of Accuracy," 182.
34 Thiel, "The Diversity Myth." For more on BAP, see Vandiver, "Metapolitics, Masculinity, and Technology."
35 These include "Peter Thiel's NeoEugenix research station in Baja" and a "Peter Thiel-funded underground network of gyms in Miami, Ft Lauderdale areas" where "Trump is training Russian gangs to destabilize Florida," presumably as part of President Trump's 2024 Republican primary contest with Governor Ron DeSantis.
36 E.g., Michael Anton, "Are the Kids Al(t)right?," *Claremont Review of Books* 19, no. 3 (2019).
37 Robert Hamerton-Kelly, "An Introductory Essay," in *Politics and Apocalypse*, edited by Robert Hamerton-Kelly (East Lansing: Michigan State University Press, 2007), 20; Wolfgang Palaver, "Carl Schmitt's 'Apocalyptic' Resistance Against Global Civil War," in *Politics and Apocalypse*, edited by Robert Hamerton-Kelly (East Lansing: Michigan State University Press, 2007), 69.
38 Robert Hamerton-Kelly, ed., *Politics and Apocalypse* (East Lansing: Michigan State University Press, 2007).
39 Thiel, "The Straussian Moment."
40 Id., "The Straussian Moment," 202. Alexandre Kojève's Hegelian account of the liberal end of history had been trumpeted in the previous decade by Francis Fukuyama, *The End of History and the Last Man* (New York: Free Press, 1992), a student of Straussians and a significant influence on neoconservative policymakers.
41 I allude here to the "hidden dialogue" between Schmitt and Strauss elaborated by Heinrich Meier, *Carl Schmitt and Leo Strauss: The Hidden Dialogue* (Chicago: University of Chicago Press, 1995), a work cited by Thiel, "The Straussian Moment," 203.
42 Leo Strauss, *Persecution and the Art of Writing* (1952; Chicago: University of Chicago Press, 1988), 36, quoted by Thiel, "The Straussian Moment," 204.
43 Id., "The Straussian Moment," 189.
44 Carl Schmitt, *The Nomos of the Earth in the International Law of the Jus Publicum Europaeum* (1950; New York: Telos Press, 2003); Palaver, "Carl Schmitt's 'Apocalyptic' Resistance," 75–76, 85.
45 Schmitt, *The Nomos of the Earth*, 140–47, and part IV, *passim*; on Schmittian *nomos* as "ordering order," see Jens Meierhenrich and Oliver Simons, "'A Fanatic

of Order in an Epoch of Confusing Turmoil': The Political, Legal, and Cultural Thought of Carl Schmitt," in *The Oxford Handbook of Carl Schmitt*, edited by Jens Meierhenrich and Oliver Simons (Oxford: Oxford University Press, 2016).
46 Thiel, "The Straussian Moment," 190–91; cp. Frantz Fanon, *The Wretched of the Earth* (New York: Grove Press, 1965).
47 Thiel, "The Straussian Moment," 190.
48 Ibid., 201.
49 Quoted by Ibid., 199.
50 Schmitt, *Political Theology*.
51 Thiel, "The Straussian Moment," 214–15.
52 Schmitt, *Dictatorship*.
53 Cultural and monetary theorists who study Bitcoin rightfully draw our attention to the "gendering of different forms of money and payment systems." Brunton, *Digital Cash*, 15n21. The most visible proponents of Bitcoin in Europe, North America, and Australia—and most users, as noted earlier—are men, typically relatively young men. Hence my insistence upon characterizing them in gendered terms as Bitcoin bros.
54 Schmitt, *Constitutional Theory*, 170.
55 Id., *Constitutional Theory*, 170, original emphases: "From the fundamental idea of bourgeois freedom follow two consequences, which constitute both principles of the Rechtsstaat component of every modern constitution. First, there is a *principle of distribution*. The individual's sphere of freedom is presupposed as something prior to the state, in particular the freedom of the individual is *in principle unlimited*, while the authority of the state for intrusions into this sphere is *in principle limited*."
56 G. Boyd Tarin, "The Bank for International Settlements: Keeping a Low Profile," *The Transnational Lawyer* 5 (1992); Carl Felsenfeld and Genci Bilali, "The Role of the Bank for International Settlements in Shaping the World Financial System," *University of Pennsylvania Journal of International Economic Law* 25 (2004).
57 Karl Marx, *A Contribution to the Critique of Political Economy* (1897; Chicago: Charles H. Kerr, 1904), 139, original emphasis, quoted in part by Dodd, *The Social Life of Money*, 211.
58 Id., *The Social Life of Money*, 212, 211.
59 Ibid., 55.
60 Ammous, *The Bitcoin Standard*; Thomas J. Anderson, *Money Without Boundaries: How Blockchain Will Facilitate the Denationalization of Money* (Hoboken: John Wiley & Sons, 2019). Was the nationalization of money—however brief and imperfect—in fact crucial to late modern democracy? Intriguingly, while not of course backed by gold (or any other commodity), the euro today is "akin to the gold standard: an external currency, beyond the reach of national governments." Dodd, *The Social Life of Money*, 46, summarizing Michel Aglietta, "The European Vortex," *New Left Review*, no. 75 (2012). However, in an undemocratic turn, as a "monetary standard to which member states must adhere . . . [as in] gold standard regimes in the past" the Eurozone monetary regime has reduced the elected governments of member nation-states to mere "municipal authorities." Dodd, *The Social Life of Money*, 79. Bitcoin bros rarely address the democratic deficits potentially arising from a Bitcoin standard, nor how state monetary

regimes are to be brought into adherence. Cf. Kenneth W. Dam, "From the *Gold Clause Cases* to the Gold Commission: A Half Century of American Monetary Law," *The University of Chicago Law Review* 50, no. 2 (1983), 506: "The gold standard can . . . be thought of as a purely domestic set of legal rules. . . . [O]ne has an international gold standard only when nations accounting for the great bulk of international trade and investment have such a domestic standard. Indeed, the international gold standard was never much more than the international result and interaction of domestic gold standard rules."

61 William E. Scheuerman, "The Economic State of Emergency," *Cardozo Law Review* 21, no. 5–6 (2000).
62 Bronze Age Pervert, *Bronze Age Mindset: An Exhortation* (San Bernadino: n.p., 2018), 119.
63 Dodd, *The Social Life of Money*, 222–26, 260–61.
64 Scheuerman, "The Economic State of Emergency," 1870, original emphasis.
65 Ammous, *The Bitcoin Standard*; Anderson, *Money Without Boundaries*.
66 Gerard N. Magliocca, "The *Gold Clause Cases* and Constitutional Necessity," *Florida Law Review* 64, no. 5 (2012). After FDR threatened not to comply with rulings that his actions were unconstitutional, the Supreme Court produced a muddled decision in *Perry v. United States* that forestalled direct confrontation with the president.
67 Scheuerman, "The Economic State of Emergency," 1869.
68 Dodd, *The Social Life of Money*, 224. On the experience of hyperinflation in Weimar Germany—and in Zimbabwe under the despotic Robert Mugabe—as context for understanding the emergence of Bitcoin, see Magnuson, *Blockchain Democracy*, 32–33.
69 E.g., Ammous, *The Bitcoin Standard*, 60–61: "Countries started trying to repatriate their gold reserves from the United States as they started to realize the diminishing purchasing power of their paper money. French president Charles de Gaulle even sent a French military carrier to New York to get his nation's gold back, but when the Germans attempted to repatriate their gold, the United States had decided it had had enough. Gold reserves were running low, and on August 15, 1971, President Richard Nixon announced the end of dollar convertibility to gold. . . . In effect, the United States had defaulted on its commitment to redeem its dollars in gold."
70 Several years ago, the possibility of pandemic-induced economic states of emergency was suggested by Bernadette Meyler, "Economic Emergency and the Rule of Law," *DePaul Law Review* 56, no. 2 (2007), 539, adducing a "potential bird flu pandemic."
71 Ammous, *The Bitcoin Standard*, 36–37, quoting Ludwig von Mises, *Human Action: A Treatise on Economics* (Auburn: Ludwig von Mises Institute, 1998), 472–73.
72 For a thoughtful consideration of the global disruptions potentially enabled by Bitcoin and crypto, see Ian Bremmer, "The Technopolar Moment: How Digital Powers Will Reshape the Global Order," *Foreign Affairs* 100 (November/December 2021), whose title references the geopolitical concept of the "unipolar moment," one the Straussian neoconservatives championed in the 1990s and acted upon after 9/11, as analyzed by Thiel in his 2007 essay.

73 In their opposition to elites they see as hostile to the common people, many cryptopartisans could be identified as populist so long as we acknowledge one crucial qualification. Their "populism" typically *followed* their exclusion or deplatforming: in their view, a betrayal of liberal democracy by the elites who target them for exclusion and deplatforming. Cryptopartisans are *defined by their exclusion* rather than by their sense of inclusion—in contrast, for instance, to populists who see themselves as representative of the "true" people opposed to other groups, including elites, as theorized by Jan-Werner Müller, *What Is Populism?* (Philadelphia: University of Pennsylvania Press, 2017).
74 Robert A. Pape, "American Face of Insurrection: Analysis of Individuals Charged for Storming the US Capitol on January 6, 2021," *Chicago Project on Security and Threats*, January 5, 2022, accessed June 13, 2023, https://d3qi0qp55mx5f5.cloudfront.net/cpost/i/docs/Pape_-_American_Face_of_Insurrection_(2022-01-05).pdf.
75 In these foreign policy views, Fuentes has charted a different course from Alt-right leaders like Richard B. Spencer, "For Ukraine, for Europe," *Alexandria*, February 23, 2023, https://radixjournal.substack.com/p/for-ukraine-for-europe (accessed May 15, 2023), who has vocally supported NATO.
76 Eggers and Hobbs, "Combatting the Financing of Hate Groups."
77 Carl Schmitt, "The Age of Neutralizations and Depoliticizations," in *The Concept of the Political* (1929; Chicago: University of Chicago Press, 2008), 86.
78 Ibid., 82.
79 Quoted in Burrow, *Whigs and Liberals*, 103.
80 Kirse Granat May, *Golden State, Golden Youth: The California Image in Popular Culture, 1955–1966* (Chapel Hill: University of North Carolina Press, 2002).
81 Fabiola Mancinelli, "Digital Nomads: Freedom, Responsibility and the Neoliberal Order," *Information Technology and Tourism* 22, no. 3 (2020).
82 Thiel, "The Straussian Moment," 208; regarding civil liberties-motivated efforts to uncover the existence of ECHELONfrom the 1970s onwards, see Steve Wright, "The ECHELON Trail: An Illegal Vision," *Surveillance & Society* 3, no. 2/3 (2005).

PART VI
Conclusion

12
LIBERALISM'S VULNERABILITIES AND TWO PATHS FOR THE FUTURE

Samuel Piccolo

Predicting the future is a fool's fancy. I will not end this book with a claim to predict how things will develop.[1] Throughout the volume, contributors have drawn up cases in which liberal democracy is endangered by Far-Right Newspeak. But by 2023 liberal democrats could find some reasons for relief, even if they may not wish to express such comfort publicly for fear of tempting fate in favor of the right-populists they consider dangerous to their way of life. In the United States, Donald Trump was ejected from office—not without event, but certainly without a doubt. In Brazil, Jair Bolsonaro departed with less disturbance than anticipated and went from worrying liberal democrats to wandering supermarkets in Florida. In the United Kingdom, the Conservative Party's flirtation with right populism diminished with the ascension of milquetoast banker Rishi Sunak to Number 10 Downing Street, and Labour leader Keir Starmer, far more Blairite than Corbynite, appears poised to win a majority government. Brexit may not be fully reversed, but the forces that propelled it have been—at least for now—tamed.

On the continent, France's Emmanuel Macron handily won a second term over Marine Le Pen and Eric Zemmour. Germany's Red/Green/Yellow leadership, though increasingly unpopular, is not seriously at risk of falling to the far-right Alternative for Germany (AfD), however increasingly well the AfD is polling. The AfD's popularity may well be tempered by other non-mainstream political movements such as Sara Wagenknecht's new leftist party. Poland's Law and Justice (PiS), which along with Hungary's Fidesz is a bête noir of traditional liberals, saw its support diminish in recent elections.

Nonetheless, parties like the AfD in Germany and the Netherlands' Party for Freedom have shown impressive staying power. Far-right parties remain influential and imposing in a way that simply was not the case

DOI: 10.4324/9781003436737-18

for many decades after the Second World War, as this volume's chapters show. A. James McAdams and Alejandro Castrillon's 2021 volume, *Far-Right Thinkers and the Future of Liberal Democracy*, surveyed and analyzed some of the most significant figures in the "new right." This volume, by contrast, has considered a single curious aspect of these figures' thought and rhetoric: their use of traditionally liberal language. As the essays in the preceding pages have argued, these figures have used the language of liberalism, such as the rights of minorities, appeals to equality, and democratic rule, while remaining—sometimes openly, sometimes esoterically—opposed to liberal democracy as it is understood by its defenders.[2] We have called this phenomenon "Far-Right Newspeak." The "new" refers to the fact that this development appears to be recent, or at least has recently intensified. Far-Right Newspeak, the volume's contributors have also argued, has been instrumental in making seemingly illiberal, or anti-liberal, ideas more appealing to broader audiences.

In this concluding chapter, I will not simply summarize the other contributors' arguments. I will rather comment upon what we have learned from the examples in this volume, and what the far right's challenge might teach us about what the defenders of liberal democracy must recognize and do. I intend to offer a more thorough approach to the topic that synthesizes contributors' suggestions to illuminate the present state of liberal democracy. I proceed in two main parts. First, speaking more empirically, I argue that mainstream understandings of the concepts employed as Far-Right Newspeak are—and remain—vulnerable to losing control over how these ideas are understood at large. By focusing on four key areas, including power centralization, information dissemination, gender, and the rule of law, I argue that shortcomings of traditional liberal forces in Western polities have helped to deplete public trust in them, making their opposition to the far right less persuasive than it might otherwise be. In a way this section serves to complement the foci of this volume's chapters. In addition to trying to understand purveyors of Far-Right Newspeak, liberal democrats should also look inward towards their own failings. Encouraging self-reflection and admission of shortcomings is one of liberal democracy's inherent strengths. Contrary to absolutist regimes wherein leaders admit no fault, liberal democracy's capacity for self-criticism is what allows it to improve and continue to exist.

In this chapter's second section, I focus on the theoretical question of what liberalism is. I argue that opponents of Far-Right Newspeak have two main options for successful resistance. Their first option is to defend an account of liberal ideas that does not reduce them to merely discursive—that is, socially constructed—status. Since without some definite idea of what liberal democracy is they cannot condemn any uses of liberal concepts as abuses, committed liberals must insist that liberal ideas are to some degree "thick," that is, hold some correspondence to a transhistorical understanding of justice and how humans should live with each other. This might be called a conservative liberalism. Their second option is to abandon any devotion to traditional liberal definitions altogether. This alternate route, I argue, means opponents of Far-Right Newspeak should openly endorse the redefinition of traditional liberal ideas and embrace a new mantle: leftist postliberals. While progressive postliberalism, as I describe it, will reject the way in which rightist figures redefine liberal concepts, they will—and already are—radically redefining traditional liberal language while retaining the familiar words. I conclude by suggesting that, to understand politics today, we must also study how leftist thinkers and political figures have transformed liberal ideas.

As A. James McAdams outlined in Chapter 1, it is not easy to say precisely what liberal democracy is. Contributors to his volume have used a general account of it as a system of institutions including the rule of law, free press, fair elections, separation of powers, and mixed representation. This has involved key concepts such as equality, democratic representation, and freedom. Liberal democracy has been instantiated in the constitutions and political traditions of North American and western European states. But contributors have also noted how liberal democracy is represented by more than just governments. Indeed, large and powerful media organizations see themselves as defenders of democracy.[3] When I describe liberal democrats in this chapter, then, I refer to mainline institutional powers in these states against whom far-right figures contrast themselves.

Vulnerabilities of Liberalism's Language

The contributors to this volume do not intend to generally endorse the ideas or actions of the individuals profiled in its pages. But, as scholars, they have been clear that there are numerous cases in which exponents of Far-Right Newspeak often have legitimate critiques of how the language of liberal democracy has been recently employed by established liberal political powers. Here, I argue that these critiques are connected to shortcomings in how liberal political concepts have been instantiated. I do not mean to suggest that all these conditions are directly attributable to failures of liberalism, merely that they have arisen under the watch of established political leadership that opposed the far-right figures profiled in this volume.

Centralization of Economic and Political Power

Scholars do not agree about liberal democracy's history, including whether liberalism is more properly Anglo-American or Franco-Germanic.[4] Yet in broad strokes we can recognize that it emerged primarily in monarchical societies that were gradually (and sometimes abruptly!) hemming in the power of the monarch. The emergence of liberal democracy was roughly contemporary to the mass centralization of power at the level of large states, first for the monarchy and its court, and then for a government more generally comprised of the people.[5] Thus liberal democracy has always had a contradictory relationship with the centralization of power. On the one hand, it seems to have historically required a significant centralization of political power to emerge, and then once it did emerge it acquired far more governing power than most monarchs ever had. On the other, critical to liberalism is some sense that government should be both limited and somewhat diffused—that is to say, authority ought to be split between different parts of society. Different liberal regimes reflect these principles in different ways. Bicameralism, for instance, typically involves one house with elite or aristocratic elements of society and another house representing the commons. Likewise, the intellectual elite is generally represented in the judiciary. Power is supposed to be separated between the judicial and legislative branches, and republican regimes have the added feature of dividing the executive from the legislative. Liberal democracy almost always involves regional representation and administration. And finally, liberalism is generally understood to involve some serious distinction between economic and political power, meaning that the government does not plan the economy and intervenes only when doing so would be both pragmatic and beneficial to the people whom the government is supposed to represent.

Yet in recent decades, Western liberal democracies have seen an unprecedented centralization of political and economic power. It is because of this centralization, I would like to suggest, that figures such as Marine Le Pen are so easily able to frame their vision as more democratic than the new "dominant ideology" liberalism has become, akin to the "divine monarchy" to which it initially arose in opposition.[6] Some of this increased power is both justifiable and inevitable, especially the economic interventions developed in the first half of the twentieth century in response to the privations of industrial capitalism, laid bare most grotesquely during the Great Depression. None but a few arch-libertarians could countenance returning the state to its pre-1900 size.

In many ways the centralization of political and economic power in Western liberal democracies has left many people—if not most—with the distinct sensation that the established political authorities favor government less for, of, and by the people than *over* them, an *over* that occurs in concert with big business. In the words of Joseph II of Austria: "Everything for the people, but nothing by the people." As economist Matt Stoller and others have convincingly shown, far too many sectors of our economy are run by monopolies or firms with strong monopolistic tendencies.[7] This trend, which began in the 1970s, reversed the anti-monopolistic efforts of democratic politics in the first two-thirds of the twentieth century. Now, in areas as distinct as advertising, news media, supermarkets, and general retail, citizens of liberal democracies must buy from an ever-diminishing number of firms—firms that exert ever-increasing power on markets and public policy.

The trend is even present in the realm of residential real estate, long the most reliable route to the middle class in North America and, to a lesser degree, in Europe. After the 2008 economic disaster, largely caused by egregiously irresponsible risk-taking in the finance industry, the collapse in house prices left millions of people underwater on their homes, and in many cases foreclosed upon. Yet, as has been well documented, the financial relief packages offered by the United States government overwhelmingly supported the very industry that had caused the crisis in the first place. Professional investors quickly created enormous real estate investment funds, buying up affordable housing and then renting it back to the individuals they had outbid.[8]

This gambit is reflective of many of the largest and most powerful firms in the world, which extract rents from local economies to be centralized in a few key population centers—in the United States, usually some combination of New York, San Francisco, Los Angeles, and Seattle, and in Europe, London, Paris, and Berlin. Take Uber as an example. When it first launched, users flocked to the application for its convenience and cost, which was typically significantly less than established taxicab services. Yet this lower cost was entirely a mirage. For many years, Uber aggressively subsidized rides with its vast reserves of venture capital funds. Uber only had a net quarterly profit in the second quarter of 2023, 13 years after its founding. Later, having effectively extinguished the local taxi industry in most places, Uber could cease subsidizing fares, leaving locals with prices no lower than before. Uber naturally long argued that they were actually *disrupters* of monopolies, since in most cities taxis functioned as local cartels with the number of medallions restricted by the municipal government. The key difference, though, is that these were *local* cartels, and there were hundreds—if not thousands—of them across the world. The decisions about the medallions were made by local authorities and fare money remained local. But now, the Uber monopoly (possibly a duopoly with Lyft) means that every cab fare in the world sends a significant percentage as rent directly to San Francisco.

The taxi industry is but one example. We could tell a similar story about the media or any number of other industries where ownership has concentrated ever more centrally to certain population centers around the globe.[9] This concentration, as José Pedro Zúquete shows in Chapter 10, is one important trend that anti-globalist agitators latch upon in their crusades against the "elite."[10] The central foe of these anti-globalist activists, who believe that a global elite is conspiring to enslave them and feed them a diet of insects, is the World Economic Forum (WEF). The WEF is the organization that holds the annual meeting in Davos, Switzerland, that has become a "Who's Who" of global power brokers. In 2016, the WEF published an essay that predicted that by 2030 "You'll own nothing, and you'll be happy."

Anti-globalists insist that this is a goal of the WEF, and, as Zúquete shows, argue that responses to the Covid-19 pandemic were intended to usher us closer to such a world—with some even arguing that the entire pandemic was a ruse for the Davos class to extend control.

Many of Zúquete's subjects see a planned plot of domination for which there is little evidence, and they lace their musings with antisemitism. Yet the degree to which private ownership of major parts of the economy has centralized in recent decades means that contemporary liberalism is deeply vulnerable to conspiracies like the ones Zúquete outlines. After all, even if the WEF was not endorsing a vision in which "you'll own nothing," many of the businesses represented at Davos surely are working towards a world in which they indeed do the owning and the rest of us the renting—at least for the assets that are likely to go up in value.

Likewise, had governments been more attuned to the perils of corporate power in today's liberal democracies, they might have been in a better position to understand some of the wariness of Covid vaccines I discuss later. Liberal democrats occupying institutional positions of power failed to reckon with citizens' legitimate worries that discussions around Covid-19 were being manipulated by corporations. Though I do not defend any particular position taken by those skeptical of official positions regarding Covid-19, I want to emphasize why many citizens might not have felt that their health authorities were genuinely oriented towards the interest of the general public. Widespread vaccine hesitancy emerged in a specific context, especially in the United States. This is a context in which large pharmaceutical companies have deliberately oversaturated Americans with prescription opioids, often in concert with medical doctors. Covid-19 and its accompanying vaccines—produced by Pfizer, Johnson & Johnson, and Moderna, among others—came immediately on the heels of this crisis. Most famous among opioid producers and pushers was Purdue Pharma, which was not involved in Covid vaccines. But Johnson & Johnson was. In Oklahoma, for instance, a state court ruled that J&J must pay $572 million in damages for its role in pushing opioids. The presiding judge wrote that J&J promoted the idea "that chronic pain was under-treated (creating a problem) and increased opioid prescribing was the solution." Among other things, the judge continued, J&J "sent sales representatives into Oklahoma doctors' offices to deliver misleading messages, they disseminated misleading pamphlets, coupons, and other printed materials for patients and doctors, and they misleadingly advertised their drugs over the internet."[11] Indeed, when Donald Trump was president, major media outlets paid some attention to this problem. Throughout 2020, the *New York Times* published a series of articles that outlined concerns about the connections between pharmaceutical companies and government operations.[12] But, seemingly when Trump left office, such matters were no longer considered sufficiently serious.

Covid vaccines are not opioids. But the point is that Americans learned that pharmaceutical companies lied to get them addicted to their products, addictions that have killed hundreds of thousands of citizens, especially the young. Two years later, amid another intense marketing push, this time for Covid vaccines (including Johnson & Johnson's), it is understandable that Americans might not have fully trusted the companies who produced them. It should not be surprising that many were skeptical when they were told that they needed an ever-long series of injections—extremely profitable ones for the producers—simply to eat at a restaurant or board an airplane. Liberal democracy's entanglements with the interests of corporations that too often seem unconcerned with the truth—not to mention the health and well-being of regular people—make many believe that medical and public health authorities are not really working for them. Liberal democrats' continual unwillingness to understand these conditions of broken trust makes them lastingly vulnerable to far-right figures who insist that they alone offer true democratic openness.

Though I have focused here on economic power, I need not detail just how much this centralization of economic power has centralized political power, too. Vast swaths of Western liberal democracies, often areas blighted by deindustrialization, grow increasingly distant from the centers of mainstream economic, cultural, and political power. Such areas include the United States' Midwest and the north of England and France—all areas that increasingly favor far-right politics. If liberal democrats do not work to redistribute institutional power and prosperity across political classes and geographic areas, liberal democracy will remain deeply vulnerable to charges that it is not democratic at all.

Government Legitimacy and Openness

As liberal-democratic ideas of limited government emerged in response to political absolutism of pre-Enlightenment Europe, liberal-democratic ideas of open information arose in response to the epistemological absolutism of that same time. Against the absolute power of churches and monarchs to declare what was true and false, liberal democracy heralded a new era in which legitimate knowledge came not from above but from the reasoned debate in which all parts of society could participate. The emergence of a free and critical press was critical to the spread of open information and skepticism of government claims. Liberal democracy, in its emphasis on dialogue and self-correction, is supposed to encourage governments to admit their own errors and to avoid them in the future.

In Chapter 9, Steven Pittz argues that conspiracy theorizing can be dangerously anti-liberal, with participants engaged in solipsistic storytelling without regard to verifiable evidence or the realities of the shared world. But Pittz argues that pragmatic conspiracism can also be constituted by liberal virtues. After all, as I have suggested, liberalism has always been distinct from absolute monarchies or totalitarian regimes where the power to set political realities resides in a single place. The liberal virtues of pragmatic conspiracism encourage citizens to be active participants in political life. They make it possible to question the claims of authority, and of those who seek to exempt themselves from such questioning. In recent years, governments in liberal democracies have been struggling to control the potential for chaos posed by the unlimited flow of information (of varying veracity) on the Internet while remaining committed to the freedoms necessary for pragmatic conspiracism.

We need not align ourselves with Raw Egg Nationalist and others that Zúquete profiles to say that, in recent years, liberal democracies have not always achieved an appropriate balance. As Pittz's and Zúquete's chapters indicate, liberal democracies are threatened by far-right figures who accuse mainstream figures of hiding important truths and manufacturing consensus. We need not agree with these far-right figures on substantive issues to see that liberal democracies' recent heavy-handed efforts to dominate information narratives from above have left many citizens no longer convinced that liberal democrats are oriented towards truth. Such citizens will be vulnerable to the messages of far-right conspiracists that Zúquete describes.

This much was evident in the lead-up to the 2003 invasion in Iraq, when parts of the United States government misled the public about Saddam Hussein's possession of weapons of mass destruction. This misleading was enabled by credulous media organizations, including the *New York Times*, which consistently ran coverage that was insufficiently skeptical of the administration's claims.[13] The US government, as well as other states such as the United Kingdom, used the tense circumstances following the 9/11 attacks to discourage the virtues of pragmatic conspiracism, which if properly practiced would have given citizens grave doubts about the Bush and Blair (in the UK) administrations' decision to invade Iraq. Though there were dissenting voices in government in the US and UK, the war initially received broad mainstream support. Tony Blair's Labour Party supported it in the UK, and many Democrats did in the United States. These governments did not practice censorship, per se, but they created an environment in which any sustained criticism of their policies was supposedly unpatriotic and potentially treasonous. When their accounts were shown to have been inaccurate, enormous trust was lost in government. By the 2016 Republican primary, Donald Trump could accuse the Bush Administration of lying about WMDs and win the nomination of Bush's own party. The primary campaign of Bush's brother Jeb, initially the preferred establishment candidate of the Republicans, wilted to pitiful finishes in the first two primaries before he withdrew.

Ultimately the virtues of pragmatic conspiracism triumphed in the case of Iraq, as it is now almost universally seen as an immense failure. But we could look to government responses to Covid-19 as a more recent example of more subtle failure when liberal-democratic governments did not always maintain an appropriate balance between openness to criticism and combatting forces of instability. Covid-19 is in part the subject of both Zúquete's and Pittz's chapters, and it is the most controversial recent political event. It also provides an instance where the failures of liberal democrats are less obvious and less universally acknowledged than in the case of Iraq, yet nevertheless resulted in considerably less trust in governments than before. The pandemic was a flashpoint for unhinged conspiracy, akin to Pittz's systemic classification. I pay these conspiracies little attention here, since as Pittz outlines such practices are not characteristic of liberal democracy. While liberal democrats have focused their Covid post-mortems on such systemic conspiracism and its detrimental effects, I consider it a mistake to place blame solely on this conspiracism for the damage done to trust in liberal democracies.

The rapid spread of Covid-19 posed a generational challenge to governments. This was not least because some extreme politicians and citizens refused to acknowledge that Covid-19 was a dangerous virus or that governments should enact policy responses to mitigate the number of casualties from it. Conspiracy theorists claimed many things, as outlandish as that Covid vaccines contained microchips or that they were intended to sterilize those who receive them. As Zúquete details, these conspiracy theorists came up with intricate accounts of a shadowy global cabal using Covid as a pretext to enslave populations with a series of technological interventions. Rightfully, governments saw it as their duty to combat false narratives in the public sphere. Yet there were times when the efforts of liberal-democratic governments to control the narrative around Covid-19 were too heavy-handed and failed to permit genuine discussion about the reality of the situation and the appropriate policy responses. These failures have left liberal democracy even more vulnerable to the spread of Far-Right Newspeak.

As knowledge of the virus increased, authorities too often presented the changing information as infallible, an infallibility undermined by how quickly the information changed.

Many originally criticized fears of the virus or suggestion of travel restrictions from China as anti-Asian racism. Former director of the National Institute of Allergy and Infectious Diseases Anthony Fauci initially said that masks were not effective in preventing transmission of the virus, and that "there was no reason to be walking around with a mask."[14] Then, within months, mask wearing became compulsory in all social settings. Citizens were commanded by public health officials to remain sequestered in their homes, at times indefinitely. Until, that is, amid widespread racial justice protests in the summer of 2020, the very same public health officials said that these gatherings were permissible because of the ongoing effects of racism in society. As even the *New York Times* put it, "Are Protests Dangerous? What Experts Say May Depend on Who's Protesting What: Public health experts decried the anti-lockdown protests as dangerous gatherings in a pandemic. Health experts seem less comfortable doing so now that the marches are against racism."[15] Understandably, this change in messaging—from insisting that the science should govern policy to focusing on politics—undermined the credibility of "trusting the science."

Even more troubling was the discourse around Covid's origins. At the very beginning, mainline politicians, media figures, and certain scientists claimed there was no doubt that the virus emerged naturally, probably in a wet market in Wuhan. They insisted that speculation of a leak from the Wuhan coronavirus laboratory was dangerous conspiracy. Pressured by certain American politicians, social media companies labeled discussion of the possibility of a lab leak "misinformation." But within a year, it emerged that there was considerable evidence that a lab leak was possible, and two US federal agencies eventually concluded as much. (Other agencies were less certain, yet recent reporting indicates that some of the very first people infected with Covid-like symptoms were employees of the Wuhan lab, among other irregularities.[16]) Fauci himself conceded that it was possible, and investigations continue. Many questions remain about to what degree the United States funded the lab's research via the NIH's grant to Ecohealth, and whether officials attempted to obscure this fact afterwards. As Stanford microbiologist David Relman told *Vanity Fair*, "It's just another chapter in a sad tale of inadequate oversight, disregard for risk, and insensitivity to the importance of transparency."[17]

Then came the battles over vaccines. At the same time as conspiracy theorists were musing about microchips, Fauci and President Joe Biden insisted that the vaccines were so effective that, having receive a full dosage, one could not transmit the virus to others. In Fauci's words, the vaccine made you a "dead end" to Covid-19. As it turned out, Covid vaccines did not create "dead ends" for the virus or prevent the vaccinated from spreading the virus to others. Nor did many research scientists say so at the time. In late 2021, *The Lancet*, the world's "highest-impact academic journal," published research suggesting, "the impact of vaccination on community transmission of circulating variants of SARS-CoV-2 appeared to be not significantly different from the impact among unvaccinated people." Wrote one contributor, "The scientific rationale for mandatory vaccination in the USA relies on the premise that vaccination prevents transmission to others." Yet since research indicated that vaccination did not prevent community transfer, the author called for "a reassessment of compulsory vaccination policies leading to the job dismissal [of the unvaccinated]."[18] Those who were even slightly hesitant in any way of vaccination were branded as dumb or malevolent. To defend these stances and the policies that followed from them, established authorities in liberal democracies appealed to "scientific consensus," even though such a thing did not exist precisely the way that authorities said it did.

With time we can see how murky this concept always was.[19] There was and is scientific consensus that Covid-19 was real and causing the deaths of a great many people. There was and is a consensus that the vaccines are generally safe and effective in mitigating the worst symptoms of the virus. But it was never clear that vaccines were entirely without risk for *all* people, or that they were a net benefit for every single individual. Side effects remain extremely low and nowhere remotely near what opponents claimed, but studies have indeed suggested that for some—especially young men—there may be some risks in receiving the vaccine. These risks mean that for certain people for whom Covid-19 is not a serious threat, it is not clear that receiving the vaccine is the correct medical decision.[20] The CDC itself now says that "evidence from multiple monitoring systems in the United States and around the globe support a causal association between mRNA COVID-19 vaccines (i.e., Moderna or Pfizer-BioNTech) and myocarditis and pericarditis."[21] Even back in 2020, scientists were publishing about the need for restraint on claims about what we knew about what vaccines could do, as there simply had not been sufficient research.[22] This does not mean that Covid vaccines should not have been encouraged or even required in certain environments. But it does mean that some of the official narrative around them was inaccurate and should have been subject to greater debate at the time, and if mandatory vaccination was going to be a policy aim it should have been debated with all relevant information.

Similarly, there was no scientific consensus on what sort of far-reaching damages certain lockdown policies could have. Very early on in the pandemic, it was clear that those at risk from Covid were the elderly and individuals with comorbidities. Considering this, some called for a policy response that focused protective efforts at those actually at risk, rather than at the entire population, protective efforts that could have oriented government resources towards preventing those actually at risk of dying from Covid from contracting the virus. While many factors were at play, it is unclear whether the low risk to children from Covid-19 justified the many pernicious effects of having no education and social interaction for up to two years—effects even more pronounced on the poorest and most disadvantaged children in society.[23] Indeed, laboratory research could only offer general guidance on such issues, and health officials who encouraged media organizations to discredit and dismiss medical professionals who offered conflicting evidence and analysis—for instance decrying professors from Harvard, Oxford, and Stanford as "fringe"—undermined considerable trust in their offices.[24]

Covid-19 presented a profoundly complicated situation for leaders, and at any given moment it was unclear what was true and which policy should have been pursued. Politicians and bureaucratic officials in liberal democracies had to make decisions with limited information as millions were falling sick. But, at times, the unwillingness of authorities to engage open debate about eminently complicated questions, or to admit that "the science" did not prescribe any one policy response, has understandably left millions of citizens of liberal democracies doubtful that current institutional powers truly wish to protect traditionally open liberal dialogue. When liberal democrats turn out to have been wrong—in addition to heavy-handed—they lose even more credibility. Their failings, especially when they are unwilling to admit error, provide ammunition for purveyors of Far-Right Newspeak, who use this as evidence that liberal democracies today have perverted the principles of openness and free debate.

Rule of Law

Perhaps no liberal principle is more important than the rule of law, which traces its roots in the Anglo-American tradition back to Magna Carta's restrictions on King John's powers in 1215. Far-right thinkers now challenge mainline understandings of that concept. As Tímea Drinóczi and Agnieszka Bień-Kacała show in Chapter 5, in Hungary and Poland leaders in recent years have redefined the rule of law to minimize the institutional limits on majorities, instead equating the rule of law with majoritarianism. Petra Mlejnková indicates in Chapter 4 that Tomio Okamura would do the same thing in the Czech Republic if given the opportunity.[25] Frank Wolff, likewise, demonstrates in Chapter 6 that certain figures have attempted to reframe the rule of law in Germany's constitutional tradition by arguing that the rule of law should have prevented Angela Merkel from admitting one million refugees in 2015. In the words of these far-right constitutional scholars, Merkel's acts made Germany an "unlawful" state.[26] And unsurprisingly, Donald Trump's attempts at self-pardoning and general belief that Richard Nixon was correct that "when the President does it, that means it's not illegal" evinced little respect for the rule of law. Trump's media and party supporters seem to generally agree that—at least when their man is in power—there ought to be no legal limits on the executive. They have even recently propounded the theory, in response to federal charges against Trump for mishandling classified documents, that he could legitimately take documents with him from the White House merely by thinking that they were not prohibited.

Why are liberal democracies vulnerable on this front? The issue is related to a general sense among citizens in liberal democracies that there is a class of people in society for whom law does not apply, while the state's policing power against everyone else only increases. Increasingly, I suspect people do not believe liberal institutional claims about equality under the law. Traditionally this was a position of the left. The experience of anti-Communist witch-hunts of the 1950s, FBI harassment of the Civil Rights movement and the Black Panthers in the 1960s and 1970s, and the emergence of mass incarceration of Black Americans leave many left-leaning Americans with the distinct impression that there exists no legal equality in the United States.

Likewise, in Canada, the policing and incarceration of Indigenous peoples elicits similar consternation. In France and the United Kingdom, scholars and more general observers have long noted that after 9/11 and other terrorist attacks by Islamic extremists, police scrutiny expanded.[27] Equality under the law, in the view of many critics from the left, was for non-Muslims only. Indeed, research has made it clear law enforcement agencies in the West were not only scrutinizing Muslim communities. They often employed undercover agents who essentially entrapped disaffected young Muslim men. Far from preventing radicalization, police forces helped to create radicals who mused over or actively plotted attacks, and then arrested these individuals for plans they would likely have never made without encouragement. The events occurred roughly contemporarily to conduct that produced the financial crisis of 2008. As has been well established, this catastrophe was largely produced by investment bankers engaging in profoundly reckless behavior. This was true especially around the creation of mortgage-backed securities based on subprime mortgages, securities that had been falsely represented as reliable investments.

The lives of millions of people were irrevocably damaged. People lost their homes, went bankrupt, and died prematurely. Yet virtually no one responsible was punished, and this reinforced the idea that equality under the law was nothing more than a liberal sham since there were either insufficient laws to govern financial criminals or the law was simply not enforced. The lack of consequences for those responsible for the cataclysm only solidified the impressions of many that financial crimes committed by the wealthy are prosecuted at subterranean levels.[28] Indeed, Josh Vandiver's contribution to this volume in Chapter 11 reveals that for "Bitcoin bros" and other right-wing figures seeking alternatives to state-backed currencies, the aftermath of the 2008 financial crisis was critical. As Vandiver details, in 2008 "existing financial laws and norms would have allowed large banks to fail like other businesses do when they make poor decisions. Yet policymakers across the West prevented these bank failures and claimed they saved the financial system . . . [deploying] extraordinary powers during an economic state of emergency."[29] These extraordinary powers, of course, a prorogation of the rule of law, were used most immediately to benefit the rich.

Such positions, as I said, are the traditional purview of the left, and I return to the left in the next section of this conclusion. Right-wing movements and thinkers, meanwhile, tend to support law enforcement, exemplified most by the "Thin Blue Line" pennants that fly as responses to Black Lives Matter flags. But far-right redefinitions of legal equality, and allegations of "deep state" conspiracy against major law enforcement agencies, are surely informed by a bipartisan sense that law enforcement acts less as a contributor to the common good than an independent center of unaccountable power. Who could forget, in the end, that as the FBI stormed the camp of the Branch Davidians in Waco, Texas, in 1993, these right-wing extremists hung a banner from their fortress that read: "Rodney King We Understand." This was a reference to the Black Angelino who was beaten by police the previous year, sparking mass anti-police protests and riots. We do not have to agree with this equivalency. King was an unarmed Black man assaulted without legitimate cause by law enforcement. The Branch Davidians were a cult with an amassed armory. Law enforcement intervention at Waco may have been justified, but as Jeff Guinn's recent work shows, there was no reason why the group's leader could not have been arrested when he was outside of the compound or why the FBI could not have attempted to de-escalate the situation before it got out of hand.[30] But, instead, the FBI deliberately deployed military force against Americans living in their homes, and the result was that over 70 people (including 24 children) were killed. The FBI's behavior at Waco was a radicalizing moment for right-wing extremist and Oklahoma City bomber Timothy McVeigh.

The far right tends to justify intense policing of ethnic minorities. Mainstream liberals and more leftist figures call for more policing of far-right movements. But both sides—to varying degrees—have the same intuition: Too often the liberal state and its policing powers are more interested in controlling populations far from the levers of power than in making sure established political and economic power is well-policed, too. Both sides also recognize that the police forces of liberal democracies (especially the United States, but also France and other European states) increasingly resemble militaries, from their equipment and weaponry to the way in which they speak. Some of these policed populations—be they Islamic extremists, gangs comprised of ethnic minorities, or white militias—indeed pose threats to the liberal order. Yet the way in which financial and political interests and others with established power have often flouted laws to augment their wealth and authority over others makes equality under the law less and less believable. Far-right figures who seek to redefine "equality under the law" to suit their political ends will continue to be aided by liberal democrats who accept over-policing in marginal communities while under-policing the rich and powerful.

Gender

Sarah Shurts shows in Chapter 3 how, in France, Marine Le Pen has articulated a theory of equality for women that diverges from most contemporary understandings of feminism. Le Pen, Shurts argues, abandons the feminist principle of absolute equality with men for an account that draws on some elements of complementarity among the sexes. For many of Le Pen's critics, this redefinition is a regressive reaction to the gains of feminist movements in recent decades. They also suggest that Le Pen is cynically articulating a form of feminism that aims to exclude and marginalize France's Muslim communities.[31] In a more radical realm, George Hawley describes the changes in discourse in the so-called manosphere. The story begins with activists making liberal arguments about the ways in which men's legal rights were being sidelined in favor of women, especially in divorce and child custody settlements. Hawley traces how these movements have largely lost this element of liberal language, in an opposite trajectory to many of the other phenomena in this volume. Instead, they have become increasingly more virulent in their hostility to women, often using outright misogynistic and even violent rhetoric. As Hawley writes, "energy within the manosphere shifted away from those calling for improvements in the cultural and legal treatment of men in contemporary Western democracies, and became increasingly dominated by the most hateful and bitter critics of both feminism as a movement and women overall."[32]

Hawley draws attention to the most worrying aspects of these uses and abuses of liberal language regarding contemporary gender relations. A. James McAdams details how Jordan Peterson has achieved enormous popularity among disaffected young men, as he peddles an evolutionary theory-infused Nietzscheanism as a paean to their sufferings.[33] But Hawley and Shurts also outline that the failure of liberal democracies to foster good relations between men and women has left societies open to these abuses of language. At least since the days of Mary Wollstonecraft and the French Revolution, in the late eighteenth century, liberalism and women's social and political recognition have been tied together. The twentieth century, and especially the availability of reliable birth control in the 1960s, saw women leave the household and enter the workforce in stupendous numbers. Abortion became widely accessible and largely unopposed in any significant sense in most liberal democracies, apart from the United States. On average people married later, if at all, and divorces became so common and accessible that the rate of divorce becomes a joke at every wedding. Falling birthrates in liberal democracies are kept afloat only by the families had by immigrants to these societies.

Most of these developments are championed by liberal democrats as the manifestation of genuine equality among men and women, a legal and cultural equality necessary for the emergence of social relations among peers. Yet even the most committed liberals must acknowledge that relations between men and women remain unsettled, and not all of this can be blamed on those who refuse to relinquish reactionary attitudes. As the MeToo movement showed, women who entered the workforce were often welcomed by men who claimed to be feminists and champions of working women but who proceeded to sexually harass them. Free of the patriarchal protections of the family, liberated from the *in loco parentis* of sex-segregated college dormitories or boarding-house landladies, women were not free of the men from whom the old system claimed to protect them.

Though the sexual revolution may have sundered sex from marriage culturally, more than one liberal has recognized that recent years have seen a general decline in satisfying sexual lives. Hawley shows that the manosphere is populated by men incensed by their inability to have romantic relationships with women. The vicious language these "incels" use rightfully makes us recoil. But their resentment may be merely a more virulent manifestation of the common experience of sexual relations today, even if we need not—following Hawley—accept incels' diagnosis for why this is so. We need only look to the female equivalent of the incel ("femcel") phenomenon to see the same dynamic at play among less unsavory subjects. Though nowhere near as prevalent as male incels, femcels describe a similar experience in their romantic lives. Femcels argue the modern dating market is structured in favor of "Stacys," their demeaning term for conventionally attractive women who have unlimited romantic options, just like male incels' description of "Chads." They find "the modern dating landscape—the image-based apps, the commodified dating 'market,' the illusory 'freedom' to be found in hookup culture—to be unnavigable."[34]

In the realm of employment, women rightly feel they remain underrepresented at the highest levels of power and earnings—from the media, to Hollywood, to boardrooms and governments. The continued dominance of men at the ceilings of various industries masks the way in which the floor has fallen out beneath an increasing number of men, meaning that while women remain frustrated that glass ceilings remain intact, men despair that their solid floors have melted away. The transformation of the economy and education system, which has generally helped women, has in some ways been zero-sum. It is not just denizens of the manosphere concerned about the state of men.[35] Men's educational achievements are cratering. For those who do not attend university, wages and employment prospects are dismal. Rates of addiction, suicide, and incarceration have continually risen. Men are increasingly absent from the economy and from familial life, and these are often the very men vulnerable to political radicalization. At the same time, the "female future" portended by women's educational success appears not to have buoyed their spirits in any meaningful way. Recent studies report that women's rates of depression and dissatisfaction with their lives are growing continuously. Especially upon young women, the effects of social media on well-being—and especially the competition that occurs on it—appear extremely detrimental.[36] For those men and women who do beat the odds, find satisfying partnerships, and plan to have families, the costs involved make doing so increasingly difficult. In short, in many ways the gender relations that have emerged under the management of traditional liberal cultural mores over the past century have replaced previous pathologies with new ones. Many people, not just those on the far-right, sense that liberal democracies have an empty and insufficient account of equality—or relations more generally—between men and women. This insufficiency will continue to leave liberals' language on gender equality vulnerable to those who seek to redefine gender equality in ways liberal democrats find unsavory.

In this section I aimed to outline four key areas of conflict covered in this volume's chapters. These areas reflect ongoing points of vulnerability for liberal democracy. I describe them not to justify right-wing responses to these vulnerabilities, but rather to re-emphasize that it is not enough for liberal democrats to reject right-wing ideologies—they must directly address the very real problems for which right-wing figures claim to have solutions. In the second section of the chapter, I turn to outlining two general theoretical approaches those hostile to right-wing uses of liberal ideas may take to prevent even greater success of these uses and abuses in the future.

Theoretical Responses to Uses and Abuses of Liberal Language

In the first part of this final chapter, I focused almost entirely on vulnerabilities in liberalism based on empirical conditions, conditions that leave citizens willing to entertain far-right accounts of liberal concepts to which this volume is devoted. The implication of this was that these empirical issues need to be better addressed by liberal politics. In this second section, I want to briefly step away from the empirical and supplement that overview with a consideration of how those hostile to right-wing uses of liberal language might approach the question theoretically. The problem, as I see it, is that unless liberal-democratic concepts are understood to have some fixed meaning, it is difficult to condemn any one instance of Far-Right Newspeak as a perversion of liberal-democratic ideas. Yet fixing the meaning of liberal-democratic ideas also runs contrary to certain strong progressive urges among liberal democrats today. Given this dilemma, I argue that liberal democrats have two main options: They can either recommit themselves to a form of conservative liberalism that insists that liberal concepts are both good and have an essential meaning which far-right figures are perverting, or alternatively they can concede that liberal concepts have neither essential meanings nor are necessarily worth preserving. I will call these two options conservative liberalism and progressive postliberalism respectively.

Conservative Liberalism

As contributors to this volume have shown, contemporary right-wing figures have redefined and redeployed liberal terms in ways that are different from how mainstream liberal democrats understand and use those same terms. From the perspective of conservative liberalism, these right-wing uses are generally *abuses* because they fundamentally transform the meaning of the terms. For conservative liberals, liberalism is a system of substantive ideas and institutions. It is comprised of moral and philosophic commitments to human dignity, natural equality among citizens, freedoms to expression and association, government by consent and contract, and freedoms from discrimination based on arbitrary attributes such as race and gender.

I cannot here offer a comprehensive philosophical history of these ideas, but many readers will recognize in them the principles of a foundational liberal tradition rooted in the thought of Immanuel Kant and John Locke. Lockean liberal democracy (though of course Locke's own relationship to "liberal democracy" is a complicated question) is based around the natural rights of life, liberty, and property. These natural rights predate government and the social contract, and government aims to preserve these natural rights that could not be long maintained without it. But government is also limited by these pre-political natural rights. Likewise, for Kant, ethics and politics are fundamentally grounded by the principles of reason, especially the categorical imperative. Theoretically speaking, we can contrast the conservative liberal tradition to the liberalism of thinkers like Richard Rorty and Isaiah Berlin as well as the later work of John Rawls, who whole-heartedly reject foundations and embrace value neutrality.[37]

Conservative liberalism in the twentieth century is also connected to the tradition of Christian democracy and philosophers such as Jacques Maritain, who aimed for a synthesis of Christian understandings of natural rights and natural law with liberal democracy. Conservative liberalism thus holds that liberalism is a historical discourse and praxis, but one intrinsically constrained by its correspondence with universal principles of truth and reason, as well as the pursuit of peaceful and secure domestic politics as so famously articulated by Thomas Hobbes, arguably the greatest illiberal forerunner to liberalism. By constrained by universal principles, I mean that conservative liberals understand reality to involve truths about humans and goodness—especially around natural equality, dignity, and so forth—that are transhistorical in nature. This is to say, these principles hold to a theory of truth that are not the aims of politics merely because of a contingent agreement among a certain people at a certain time.

This substantive account of liberalism offers a rebuke to the postliberalism that Laura K. Field describes in Chapter 8. The postliberals that Field profiles charge liberal democracy with having only negative understandings of freedom and equality—suggesting that liberal democracy only exists to remove external limits on individual autonomy. They argue that to avoid the emptiness of individualism, at home and in the market, we must reinstantiate older accounts of liberty and equality that are found in classical religious and philosophic traditions—ones that predate the emergence of liberal democracy. Yet the tradition of liberalism articulated by Locke, Kant, and others offers far more positive substance than Field's postliberals are willing to allow. Whereas Field's postliberals seem to equate liberal democracy with a society of individual wills, Lockeans and Kantians disagree.

Conservative liberals, then, can make a very clear case about the ways in which Far-Right Newspeak is indeed an abuse or perversion of liberal language. If liberalism is metaphysical, this means that its concepts have essences, essences that cannot be transformed by the discourses of right-wing figures. If the uses of liberal concepts by right-wing figures run contrary to the essence of liberalism, not only as a historical tradition but also as a collection of universal and rationally necessary principles, then these uses are illegitimate abuses. Conservative liberalism can make a clear stand on what liberalism is and is not: liberalism requires the rule of law, the separation of powers, free and regular elections, civilian control of the military, broad rights and protections for minorities, and many other entrenched constitutional principles. Conservative liberalism involves the idea that all individuals were born with some intrinsic equal worth. Any efforts to eliminate these attributes from a political system make it less and less liberal. In combatting right-wing uses of liberal language, conservative liberalism has a clear advantage in firm foundations from which to condemn the right. It also has a clear advantage in its efforts to maintain the accomplishments of liberalism more broadly. After all, liberalism has more than a set of constitutional commitments. Liberal states, at least internally, have enjoyed in recent centuries the most prolonged peace and prosperity in human history.

Yet conservative liberalism will not appeal to all who oppose Far-Right Newspeak. As it is grounded in some form of universalism, especially one mainly developed in Western history and philosophy, conservative liberals will be somewhat limited in their ability to accommodate certain types of political diversity. As James Tully has argued about constitutional liberalism, its instantiation in former colonies has involved the dismantling and suppression of Indigenous peoples' governance and lives.[38] Though conservative liberals can welcome Muslims into liberal democracies, they can only accept a certain type of Islam that has accommodated itself to some liberal principles. (The same is true, I should say, of certain forms of Christianity, especially integralist Catholicism.) Conservative liberals will also be deeply skeptical of contemporary developments that question or dismantle tradition liberal categories. For instance, conservative liberalism probably cannot accept non-human animals as rights-bearers—and even political actors—as has been recently proposed.[39] Likewise, nascent efforts to eliminate the liberal distinction between citizen and non-citizen cannot comport with a conservative liberalism. Nor will conservative liberalism be easily able to accept the emergence of technological hybrids that challenge the traditional understanding of the subject. Perhaps because of its Christian inheritance, and thus also Platonic heritage, traditional liberalism has had some sense of ensouled individuals as the base unit of political society.

Whether conservative liberalism takes a Lockean form, in which the state exists to protect a substantive idea of natural rights and individual self-ownership, or a more Hegelian form in which the state is the rational emergence of collective self-recognition of freedom required for individuals to realize their own freedom, my point is that conservative liberalism has boundaries. The concepts of freedom and equality cannot be limitlessly developed, for conservative liberals, even if plenty of people in a liberal society believe at any given point that they should be. Conservative liberalism permits some development and enlargement of democracy, freedoms, and equality to more people. But these must be amendments that correct accidental errors of liberal democracy—such as denying women the franchise—rather than essential elements, such as the distinction between citizen and non-citizen.

To summarize, recommitting to a conservative liberalism that combines both historical and metaphysical understandings of liberal concepts combats Far-Right Newspeak in several key ways. It means committing to the idea that there is something both essential and good in liberal democracy, and that it is possible to lose this essence if citizens are not attentive and do not actively nurture it. At the same time as conservative liberalism can steadfastly resist Far-Right Newspeak uses of liberal terms, it may not be able to accommodate what many progressives understand to be appropriate developments of liberal terms. For this reason, I will next outline another possible theoretical response that those hostile to Far-Right Newspeak may consider.

Progressive Postliberalism

The conservative liberalism I outlined in the last section sees the liberal-democratic constitutional state as the apotheosis of political development. Postliberal progressivism, meanwhile, argues that the development of freedom and equality do not stop in the liberal constitutional state. Freedom and equality must move beyond these liberal understandings. This postliberal progressivism is the other option to conservative liberalism for those who reject right-wing accounts of liberal concepts today, though of course it may take many different forms.

Conservative liberalism rejects the far right's articulations of liberal concepts, insisting that these articulations pervert the true meaning of liberal democracy. Progressive postliberalism, on the other hand, denies that there is a fundamental content to liberal democracy. This approach follows the philosophic critiques of thinkers such as Friedrich Nietzsche and Michel Foucault, who argue that discourses such as rights and equality are at root manifestations of power. Progressive postliberals may also follow more recent deconstructive theory, who generally suggest that we cannot say definitively what a particular tradition—such as liberalism—is, and therefore cannot say that any use of liberal language constitutes an abuse. (Because, for instance, liberal concepts have been used in many ways at many different times.) Where conservative liberals see the liberal discourses of rights and equality as political manifestations of genuinely good metaphysical principles, progressive postliberals see them as reflecting the particular power claims of those peoples and classes that instantiated liberal-democratic political orders. In this section I outline postliberal progressivism, an admittedly more difficult task than conservative liberalism because it is both newer and less clearly structured in thought and practice.

Postliberal progressivism cannot object to Far-Right Newspeak as a perversion of liberalism, since the approach does not entail a vision of liberal democracy that has some sort of true or good essence. Indeed, many postliberal progressives will be pleased that Far-Right Newspeak reveals the fundamental particularity and lack of universality to liberal-democratic claims. Yale law professor Samuel Moyn, for instance, one such postliberal progressive, has argued extensively that human rights in the twentieth and twenty-first centuries have functionally defended conservative understandings of liberty, family, and economic justice.[40] This volume has outlined a number of far-right thinkers and politicians who argue that true democracy means redefining how foundational liberal constitutional principles—such as the separation of powers or the independence of the judiciary—are understood. The reaction of a postliberal progressive like Moyn would be to agree that these constitutional principles should be superseded, only not in the way that the right suggests. In an op-ed in the *New York Times* last year, Moyn and co-author Ryan Doerfler argue that American progressives should abandon the Constitution. They write:

> By leaving democracy hostage to constraints that are harder to change than the rest of the legal order, constitutionalism of any sort demands extraordinary consensus for meaningful progress. It conditions democracy in which majority rule always must matter most on surviving vetoes from powerful minorities that invoke the constitutional past to obstruct a new future.[41]

Moyn and Doerfler's calls are not the same as Donald Trump's to abolish the Constitution. But they share with Trump an interest in eliminating higher-order legal principles from the past that constrain political possibilities in the present.

James Tully, meanwhile, proffers a deep critique of the universalism of liberal constitutionalism and the way in which it "yokes" irreducibly diverse cultural groups under a single political order that reflects one political tradition. To make Western societies more truly democratic, he seeks to replace liberal constitutional orders with constantly negotiated multicultural "strange multiplicities."[42] Others have a far more radical vision of how liberal concepts such as freedom and equality should be transformed. A whole branch of transhumanist philosophy predicts and welcomes the merging of humans and machines, and the concomitant dissolution of liberal subjectivity such a merging would bring.[43] Similarly, some radical feminists today argue that technology and other transformations—such as the abolition of the family and the socialization of all domestic work—are needed for women to achieve true equality.[44] Nowhere is postliberal progressivism more prominent than in discussions surrounding policing and the justice system. Postliberal progressives argue, as I hinted in the first section, that equality under the law—or the rule of law more broadly—is a sham that does not reflect the reality of legal systems in Western liberal democracies. They argue that racialized minorities, especially Black people, bear the brunt of legal systems that do not in any sense treat them as equal.

For such postliberal progressives, legal equality must be superseded by an anti-racist legal equity. The key difference is that anti-racist equity sees any distinctions among legal (as well as socioeconomic) outcomes among racial groups as reflective of racist systemic structures.[45] Such figures see these racist structures developed most fully in the United States, which they sometimes suggest was founded to defend slavery,[46] but also in the United Kingdom, Canada, France, Germany, and elsewhere.[47] These ideas have been extremely influential upon a new generation of legal academics, prosecutors, and politicians. The ideas generally involve a substantial transformation of the traditional liberal justice system—which focuses on individual guilt and innocence—into one which requires almost exclusive focus on social structures for the process to reflect genuine equality. It also seriously questions whether political equality among people of different races is possible, or at least suggests that this possibility requires radical changes to current politics. This skepticism of traditional liberal democracy, and accompanying redefinition of equality, is in many ways different from the Far-Right Newspeak's redefinition of equality and the critique of liberal democracy it implies. Yet they are both committed to the idea that liberal concepts such as democracy, equality, and freedom as defended by the liberal tradition are not truly just.

As I mentioned earlier, conservative liberalism may not satisfy critics of right-wing Newspeak, since a hardened understanding of liberal democracy can prevent progressive developments as well as right-wing alterations. Postliberal progressivism does not have this problem. Its critique of traditional liberal politics means that it remains open to new understandings of old liberal ideas—or left-wing Newspeak. Left-wing Newspeak, arguably, is what allows for the expansion of freedoms and equalities to people (and beings) where they were not previously found, since progressive postliberals do not recognize any distinction between "accidental" and "essential" elements of liberal democracy as does conservative liberalism. For postliberal progressives, contrary to the negative connotation that George Orwell gave Newspeak, there is nothing wrong with redefining old liberal terms and abandoning the traditional meanings—they just should be redefined much differently from the far right.

But there is also risk in progressive postliberalism, and we can see it illuminated in Moyn and Doerfler's concluding sentence in their essay calling for the abolition of the American Constitution. They write, "A politics of the American future [without the constitution] would make clear our ability to engage in the constant reinvention of our society under our own power, without the illusion that the past stands in the way." Since the French Revolution's "Year Zero," progressive forces in society have dreamed of throwing off the yokes of the past. Yet one of the strengths of liberal democracy is its ability to put limits on power—some principles agreed upon in the past *standing in the way*. Constitutions restrain leaders as much as empower them, and they especially constrain leaders of popular majorities. One would not be crazy to look back and wish that Robespierre and Napoleon—not to mention Hitler and Stalin—had something in the past standing in their way, or be thankful that Lyndon Johnson, Richard Nixon, Donald Trump, and other power-loving American presidents did face that same obstacle. Postliberal progressivism, in its rejection of basic liberal principles, contempt for moderation, and radical openness to the future, risks abandoning the institutions and practices of limited government that have made liberal democracy so remarkably successful.

This volume's focus is Far-Right Newspeak. But, to understand the current state of liberal-democratic ideas, and what they will look like in the future, we need to study left-wing transformations of liberal language, too. We hope this volume invites readers to consider this matter, though of course many of the substantial questions around left-wing Newspeak will be different, including around the question of structural justice and policing I discussed a moment ago. To consider another example, though, we might ask how left-wing thinkers and politicians have transformed liberalism's approach to gender relations. For centuries, liberal feminists sought to achieve political and social rights for women, with women construed as a natural category of human. Yet contemporary feminist theory and politics, deeply influenced by post-structural and postmodern investigations into gender, increasingly suggest that gender is primarily a matter of self-identification. This has led to highly contentious battles between traditional liberal feminists who generally do not believe that individuals born male can truly become women, and those who insist that "trans women are women."[48]

On the issue of gender, postliberal progressive Newspeak is very different from Far-Right Newspeak. But close study of progressive Newspeak on economic issues may reveal convergence with Far-Right Newspeak. Those committed to liberal democracy must look closely at its vulnerabilities, and especially at where left and right appear to be similarly disenchanted with the status quo, for these places offer opportunities to strengthen liberal democracy while appealing to both left and right. Liberal democracy has traditionally understood freedom to mean relative openness to the movement of capital across borders, minimal—or at least restrained—state involvement in the economy, and a general trend towards free trade. This understanding of freedom is increasingly less popular among the left and the right.

Instead, I suspect both left and right critics of conservative liberal democracy today believe that for citizens to have true (or genuine) economic freedom, the state must intervene aggressively in the economy to prevent the moneyed class from impoverishing the masses. The right and left postliberals agree that the corporate world has far too much power. They generally agree that there are too many industries in the Western capitalist world that have been subject to regulatory capture, with the foxes setting the rules about fences around the henhouse. Likewise, left and right both maintain that liberal democracies are awash with political figures who continually use their power and connections to enrich themselves.

Traditional liberal democrats inclined to resent any criticism of the established institutional order should not lament the existence of such implied critiques in left and right Newspeak. Instead, they should take these instances of Newspeak as clear smoke signals from bits of sparking dry brush in terrain where their accounts of the world are no longer accepted by many, sparks that could turn to wildfires if ignored. If they are committed to their principles, and unless they wish to abandon the idea that citizens should consent to their ruling regime, liberal democrats should view instances of Newspeak as places where they need to reconsider their own Oldspeak and why they are no longer persuading citizens. The alternative, as we may only see when it is too late to change course, is that when people no longer believe they live in a liberal democracy, they no longer act as if they do—or care whether its principles live or die.

Notes

1 My thanks to Jim McAdams and Connor Grubaugh for their comments and suggestions on this chapter.
2 I use liberal democracy and liberalism interchangeably in this chapter, though I acknowledge that this blending is historically—and contemporarily—troublesome.
3 The *Washington Post*, for instance, has as its tagline: "Democracy dies in darkness." In this conclusion, I assume that major mainline media organizations in western Europe and America (including the *New York Times*, the *Guardian*, *CNN*, *The Atlantic*, *The New Yorker*, *The Wall Street Journal*, *Der Spiegel*, and others) are representatives of liberal democracy. I understand that this is a complex question, especially since media organizations are not monolithic and because these

organizations scrutinize traditional liberal-democratic politicians in addition to right-wing figures.

4 For an account favoring the continent, see Helena Rosenblatt, *The Lost History of Liberalism* (Princeton, NJ: Princeton University Press, 2018). For one partial to Anglo-America, see Michael Zuckert, *Launching Liberalism: On Lockean Political Philosophy* (Lawrence, KS: University Press of Kansas, 2002).

5 For a classic account of the state's emergence, see James C. Scott, *Seeing Like a State: How Certain Schemes to Improve the Human Condition Have Failed* (New Haven, CT: Yale University Press, 1998).

6 Marine Le Pen, *Pour Que Vive La France* (Paris: Éditions Grancher, 2012), 90. See also McAdams, this volume.

7 Matt Stoller, *Goliath: The 100-Year War Between Monopoly Power and Democracy* (New York: Simon and Schuster, 2019).

8 Ryan Dezember, *Underwater: How Our American Dream of Homeownership Became a Nightmare* (New York: Thomas Dunne Books, 2019).

9 Eli Noam, *Media Ownership and Concentration in America* (Oxford: Oxford University Press, 2009).

10 Zúquete, Chapter 10 of this volume.

11 Chris McGreal, "Johnson & Johnson to Pay $572m for Fueling Oklahoma Opioid Crisis, Judge Rules," *The Guardian*, August 26, 2019, www.theguardian.com/us-news/2019/aug/26/johnson-and-johnson-opioid-crisis-ruling-responsibility-oklahoma-latest.

12 Sheila Kaplan, Matthew Goldstein, and Alexandra Stevenson, "Trump's Vaccine Chief Has Vast Ties to Drug Industry, Posing Possible Conflicts," May 20, 2020, www.nytimes.com/2020/05/20/health/coronavirus-vaccine-czar.html; David E. Sanger, "Trump Administration Selects Five Coronavirus Vaccine Candidates as Finalists," *The New York Times*, June 6, 2020, www.nytimes.com/2020/06/03/us/politics/coronavirus-vaccine-trump-moderna.html?searchResultPosition=30.

13 "The New York Times WMD Coverage," *PBS News Hour*, May 26, 2004, www.pbs.org/newshour/show/the-new-york-times-wmd-coverage.

14 "March 2020: Dr. Anthony Fauci Talks With Dr. Jon LaPook About Covid-19," *60 Minutes* (CBS, n.d.), www.youtube.com/watch?v=PRa6t_e7dgI.

15 Michael Powell, "Are Protests Dangerous? What Experts Say May Depend on Who's Protesting What," *The New York Times*, July 6, 2020, www.nytimes.com/2020/07/06/us/Epidemiologists-coronavirus-protests-quarantine.html; Dan Diamond, "Suddenly, Public Health Officials Say Social Justice Matters More Than Social Distance," *Politico*, June 4, 2020, www.politico.com/news/magazine/2020/06/04/public-health-protests-301534.

16 Jonathan Calvert and George Arbuthnott, "What Really Went on Inside the Wuhan Lab," *The Times*, October 6, 2023, www.thetimes.co.uk/article/inside-wuhan-lab-covid-pandemic-china-america-qhjwwwvm0; Michael R. Gordon and Warren P. Strobel, "U.S.-Funded Scientist Among Three Chinese Researchers Who Fell Ill Amid Early Covid-19 Outbreak," *The Wall Street Journal*, June 20, 2023, www.wsj.com/articles/u-s-funded-scientist-among-three-chinese-researchers-who-fell-ill-amid-early-covid-19-outbreak-3f919567.

17 Katherine Eban, "In Major Shift, NIH Admits Funding Risky Virus Research in Wuhan," *Vanity Fair*, October 22, 2021, www.vanityfair.com/news/2021/10/nih-admits-funding-risky-virus-research-in-wuhan.

18 Carlos Franco-Paredes, "Transmissibility of SARS-CoV-2 Among Fully Vaccinated Individuals," *The Lancet* 22 (2022): 16–17; Anika Singanayagam, Seran Hakki, and Jake Dunning, "Community Transmission and Viral Load Kinetics of the SARS-CoV-2 Delta (B.1.617.2) Variant in Vaccinated and Unvaccinated Individuals in the UK: A Prospective, Longitudinal, Cohort Study," *The Lancet* 22 (2021): 183–95.

19 Jason Blakely, "Doctor's Orders: Covid-19 and the New Science Wars," *Harper's Magazine*, July 2023, https://harpers.org/archive/2023/08/doctors-orders-jason-blakely/.

20 Joseph Fraiman et al., "Serious Adverse Events of Special Interest Following MRNA COVID-19 Vaccination in Randomized Trials in Adults," *Vaccine* 40 (2022).

21 "Clinical Considerations: Myocarditis and Pericarditis After Receipt of COVID-19 Vaccines Among Adolescents and Young Adults" (Centers for Disease Control and Prevention, March 23, 2023), www.cdc.gov/vaccines/covid-19/clinical-considerations/myocarditis.html.

22 Peter Doshi, "Will Covid-19 Vaccines Save Lives? Current Trials Aren't Designed to Tell Us," *British Medical Journal*, October 21, 2020, 1–4, https://doi.org/10.1136/bmj.m4037.

23 Colin Binkley, "Math and Reading Scores for American 13-Year-Olds Plunge to Lowest Levels in Decades," *Associated Press*, June 20, 2023, https://apnews.com/article/math-reading-test-scores-pandemic-school-032eafd7d087227f42808052fe447d76.

24 Vinay Prasad, "At a Time When the U.S. Needed Covid-19 Dialogue Between Scientists, Francis Collins Moved to Shut It Down," *Stat*, December 23, 2021, www.statnews.com/2021/12/23/at-a-time-when-the-u-s-needed-covid-19-dialogue-between-scientists-francis-collins-moved-to-shut-it-down/.

25 See Drinóczi and Bień-Kacała in Chapter 5 and Mlejnková in Chapter 4 of this volume.

26 See Wolff, Chapter 6 of this volume.

27 See, for instance, the films and journalism of Rokhaya Diallo.

28 Sheelah Kolhatkar, *Black Edge: Inside Information, Dirty Money, and the Quest to Bring Down the Most Wanted Man on Wall Street* (New York: Random House, 2017); James B. Stewart, *Den of Thieves* (New York: Simon and Schuster, 1992).

29 See Vandiver, Chapter 11 of this volume.

30 Jeff Guinn, *Waco: David Koresh, the Branch Davidians, and a Legacy of Rage* (New York: Simon and Schuster, 2023).

31 See Shurts, Chapter 3 of this volume.

32 See Hawley, Chapter 7 of this volume.

33 See McAdams, Chapter 2 of this volume.

34 Kaitlyn Tiffany, "What Do Female Incels Really Want?," *The Atlantic*, May 12, 2022, www.theatlantic.com/technology/archive/2022/05/femcel-meaning-female-incel-reddit/629836/.

35 Idrees Kahloon, "What's the Matter With Men?," *The New Yorker*, January 23, 2023, www.newyorker.com/magazine/2023/01/30/whats-the-matter-with-men.

36 "Youth Risk Behavior Survey" (Centers for Disease Control and Prevention, 2011–2021), www.cdc.gov/healthyyouth/data/yrbs/pdf/YRBS_Data-Summary-Trends_Report2023_508.pdf; Jonathan Haidt, "Social Media Is a Major Cause of the Mental Illness Epidemic in Teen Girls. Here's the Evidence," *After Babel*

(blog), February 22, 2023, https://jonathanhaidt.substack.com/p/social-media-mental-illness-epidemic.

37 John Rawls, *Political Liberalism* (New York, NY: Columbia University Press, 1993), 4. Rawls is obviously a complicated case. From *Political Liberalism* onwards, his work was avowedly non-metaphysical. Yet, for many reasons, I maintain that the political aims of *PL* are not self-evident without the metaphysical convictions that characterized his earlier work in *Theory of Justice*.

38 James Tully, *Public Philosophy in a New Key*, 2 vols. (Cambridge: Cambridge University Press, 2008).

39 Sue Donaldson and Will Kymlicka, *Zoopolis* (Oxford: Oxford University Press, 2013).

40 Samuel Moyn, *Christian Human Rights* (Philadelphia: University of Pennsylvania Press, 2015); Samuel Moyn, *Not Enough: Human Rights in an Unequal World* (Cambridge, MA: Harvard University Press, 2019).

41 Samuel Moyn and Ryan D. Doerfler, "The Constitution Is Broken and Should Not Be Reclaimed," *The New York Times*, August 19, 2022, www.nytimes.com/2022/08/19/opinion/liberals-constitution.html.

42 James Tully, *Strange Multiplicity* (Cambridge: Cambridge University Press, 1995); James Tully, "On Gaia Democracies," in *Democratic Multiplicity*, edited by James Tully et al. (Cambridge: Cambridge University Press, 2022), 349–73.

43 Nick Bostrom, "Letter From Utopia," *Studies in Ethics, Law, and Technology* 2, no. 1 (2008); Nick Bostrom, *Superintelligence* (Oxford: Oxford University Press, 2017); Nick Bostrom and Julian Savulescu, eds., *Human Enhancement* (Oxford: Oxford University Press, 2009).

44 Sophie Lewis, *Full Surrogacy Now: Feminism Against Family* (New York: Verso Books, 2019); Sophie Lewis, *Abolish the Family: A Manifesto for Care and Liberation* (New York: Verso Books, 2022).

45 Ibram X. Kendi, *How to Be an Antiracist* (New York: One World, 2019); Ibram X. Kendi, *Stamped From the Beginning: The Definitive History of Racist Ideas in America* (New York: Nation Books, 2016).

46 Nikole Hannah-Jones, *The 1619 Project: A New Origin Story* (New York: Random House, 2021).

47 See, for instance, Rokhaya Diallo's work on France, especially her documentary film *From Paris to Ferguson: Guilty of Being Black*.

48 This issue has become particularly inflammatory in the United Kingdom, with liberal feminists such as J. K. Rowling, Germaine Greer, and Kathleen Stock generating immense backlash over their stance on transgenderism.

BIBLIOGRAPHY

Chapter 1—Far-Right Newspeak and the Fragility of Liberal Democracy

Anheier, Helmut K. and Edward L. Knudsen. "The 21st Century Trust and Leadership Problem: Quoi Faire?" *Global Policy* 4, no. 1 (February 2023): 139–48.
Applebaum, Anne. *Twilight of Democracy*. New York: Doubleday, 2020.
Ashe, Stephen, Joel Busher, Graham Macklin, and Aaron Winter. *Researching the Far Right: Theory, Method and Practice*. Abingdon, Oxon: Routledge, 2020.
Beiner, Ronald. *Dangerous Minds: Nietzsche, Heidegger, and the Return of the Far Right*. Philadelphia: University of Pennsylvania, 2019.
Bermeo, Nancy. "On Democratic Backsliding." *Journal of Democracy* 27, no. 1 (January 2016): 5–19.
Berntzen, Lars Erik. *Liberal Roots of Far Right Activism: The Anti-Islamic Movement in the 21st Century*. London: Routledge, 2020.
Buchanan, Patrick J. "1992 Republican Convention Speech." August 17, 1992. https://buchanan.org/blog/1992-republican-national-convention-speech-148.
———. "The Cultural War for the Soul of America." September 14, 1992. https://buchanan.org/blog/the-cultural-war-for-the-soul-of-america-149.
———. "The Voice in the Desert." June 11, 1990. https://buchanan.org/blog/pjb-the-voice-in-the-desert-146?doing_wp_cron=1685470211.4164419174194335937500.
Camus, Jean-Yves and Nicolas Lebourg. *Far-Right Politics in Europe*. Cambridge, MA: Harvard University Press, 2017.
Corasaniti, Nick, Michael C. Bender, Ruth Igielnik, and Kristen Bayrakdarian. "Voters See Democracy in Peril, But Saving It Isn't a Priority." *New York Times*, October 18, 2022.
Crick, Nathan. *The Rhetoric of Fascism*. Tuscaloosa: The University of Alabama Press, 2022.
de Benoist, Alain. *Vu de Droite. Anthologie critique des idées contemporaines*. Paris: Éditions du Labyrinthe, 1977.

Drinóczi, Tímea and Agnieszka Bień-Kacała. *Rule of Law, Common Values, and Illiberal Constitutionalism: Poland and Hungary within the European Union.* London: Routledge, 2022.

Foa, R. S., A. Klassen, D. Wenger, A. Rand, and M. Slade. "*Youth and Satisfaction with Democracy: Reversing the Democratic Disconnect?*" Cambridge: Centre for the Future of Democracy, 2020. www.cam.ac.uk/system/files/youth_and_satisfaction_with_democracy.pdf.

Fox, Lauren. "The Hate Monger Next Door." *Salon*, September 13, 2013. www.salon.com/2013/09/29/the_hatemonger_next_door/.

Haggard, Stephan and Robert Kaufman. *Backsliding: Democratic Regress in the Contemporary World.* Cambridge: Cambridge University Press, 2021.

Hawley, George. *Making Sense of the Alt-Right.* New York: Columbia University Press, 2019.

Jackson, Paul, Matthew Feldman, Anton Shekhovtsov, Roger Griffin, Janet Wilson, Ruth Wodak, and Graham Macklin, eds. *Doublespeak: The Rhetoric of the Far Right Since 1945.* Stuttgart: Ibidem, 2014.

Kenes, Bulent. "Richard B. Spencer: The Founder of Alt-Right Presents Racism in a Chic New Outfit." *European Center for Populism Studies*, June 28, 2021. www.populismstudies.org/richard-b-spencer-the-founder-of-alt-right-presents-racism-in-a-chic-new-outfit/.

Kinkartz, Sabine. "Far-right AfD Emerges as Germany's Second Strongest Party." *Deutsche Welle*, July 7, 2023. www.dw.com/en/far-right-afd-emerges-as-germanys-second-strongest-party/a-66154675.

Kolakowski, Leszek. *Modernity on Endless Trial.* Chicago and London: The University of Chicago Press, 1990.

Kubitschek, Götz. "Drohen Finstere Tage?" November 25, 2021. https://sezession.de/65101/drohen-finstere-tageghttps://sezession.de/65101/drohen-finstere-tage.

Landa, Ishay. *The Apprentice's Sorcerer: Liberal Tradition and Fascism.* Chicago: Haymarket Books, 2012.

Laruelle, Marlene. "Aleksandr Dugin and Eurasianism." In *Key Thinkers of the Radical Right: Behind the New Threat to Liberal Democracy*, edited by Mark Sedgwick, 155–69. Oxford: Oxford University Press, 2019.

——, ed. *Eurasianism and the European Far Right: Reshaping the Europe-Russia Relationship.* Lanham, MA: Lexington Books, 2015.

——. "Illiberalism: A Conceptual Introduction." *East European Politics* 38, no. 2 (2022): 303–27.

Lewandowsky, M. and M. Jankowski. "Sympathy for the Devil? Voter Support for Illiberal Politicians." *European Political Science Review* 15, no. 1 (2023): 39–56.

Marx, Karl and Friedrich Engels. *The Communist Manifesto.* New York: Norton, 1988.

McAdams, A. James. *Vanguard of the Revolution: The Global Idea of the Communist Party.* Princeton: Princeton University Press, 2017.

Miller-Idriss, Cynthia. *The Extreme Gone Mainstream.* Princeton: Princeton University Press, 2017.

Mondon, Aurelian and Aaron Winter. *Reactionary Democracy: How Racism and the Populist Far Right Became Mainstream.* London: Verso, 2020.

Mudde, Cas. "Three Decades of Populist Radical Right Parties in Europe: So What?" *European Journal of Political Research* 52 (2013): 1–19.

Mudde, Cas and Cristóbal Rovira Kaltwasser. *Populism: A Very Short Introduction.* Oxford and New York: Oxford University Press, 2017.
Müller, Jan-Werner. *What Is Populism?* Philadelphia, PA: University of Pennsylvania Press, 2016.
Orwell, George. *1984.* New York: Signet Classic, 1961.
———. *Animal Farm.* New York: Signet Classic, 2004.
Plattner, Mark F. "Liberalism and Democracy: Can't Have One Without the Other." *Foreign Affairs* 77, no. 2 (1998): 171–80.
Rueda, Daniel. "A Certain Idea of France's Past: Marine Le Pen's History Wars." *European Politics and Society* (2022): 1–15. www.tandfonline.com/doi/full/10.1080/23745118.2022.2058751
Runciman, David. *How Democracy Ends.* New York: Basic Books, 2018.
Saull, Richard, Alexander Anievas, Neil Davidson, and Adam Fabry, eds. *The Long Durée of the Far Right.* London: Routledge, 2015.
Sedgwick, Mark, ed. *Key Thinkers of the Radical Right.* Oxford: Oxford University Press, 2019.
Tiles, Tiles. "'We Will Destroy These People,' Says Polish Leader Kaczyński in Response to Protests." *Notes from Poland*, December 8, 2022. https://notesfrompoland.com/2022/12/08/we-will-destroy-these-people-says-polish-leader-kaczynski-in-response-to-protests/.
Tucker, Aviezer. *Democracy Against Liberalism.* Cambridge: Polity, 2022.
V-Dem Institute. "Defiance in the Face of Autocratization." *Democracy Report*, 2023 www.v-dem.net/documents/29/V-dem_democracyreport2023_lowres.pdf.
Wagner, Thomas. *Die Angstmacher: 1968 und die neuen Rechten.* Berlin: Aufbau, 2017.
Weißmann, Karlheinz. "Gemeinwohl hat Vorrang." *Junge Freiheit*, November 28, 2021. https://jungefreiheit.de/debatte/kommentar/2021/fuer-impfpflicht/.
Wodak, Ruth. *The Politics of Fear.* London: Sage, 2021.
Wodak, Ruth and John E. Richardson, eds. *Analyzing Fascist Discourse: European Fascism in Talk and Text.* London: Routledge, 2013.

Chapter 2—Masters of Contemporary Newspeak: Tucker Carlson, Marine Le Pen, and Jordan Peterson

Burgis, Ben and Matt McManus. *Jacobin.* April 20, 2020. https://jacobin.com/2020/04/jordan-peterson-capitalism-postmodernism-ideology.
Camus, Renaud. *Le grand remplacement.* Paris: Reinharc, 2011.
Carlson, Tucker. *Fox News.* September 21, 2021. www.foxnews.com/opinion/tucker-carlson-joe-biden-revealed-why-supports-illegal-immigration-2015-change-the-country.
———. "The Great Replacement Is an Electoral Strategy." *Fox News*, July 19, 2022. www.foxnews.com/opinion/tucker-carlson-great-replacement-electoral-strategy.
———. "Joe Biden Revealed Why He Supports Illegal Immigration in 2015, He Wants to Change the Country." *Fox News*, April 28, 2022. www.youtube.com/watch?v=hextRF-7am0.
———. "The Key Difference Between 'Equality' and 'Equity'." *Fox News*, March 3, 2021. www.foxnews.com/transcript/tucker-the-key-difference-between-equality-and-equity.

———. *Ship of Fools*. New York: Free Press, 2018.
Confessore, Nicholas. "How Tucker Carlson Stoked White Fear to Conquer Cable." *New York Times*, April 30, 2022.
Eltchaninoff, Michel. *Inside the Mind of Marine Le Pen*. London: Hurst Publishers, 2018.
Fieschi, Catherine. "Muslims and the Secular City: How Right-Wing Populists Shape the French Debate Over Islam." *Brookings*, February 28, 2020. www.brookings.edu/articles/muslims-and-the-secular-city-how-right-wing-populists-shape-the-french-debate-over-islam/.
Flanagan, Caitlin. "Why the Left Is So Afraid of Jordan Peterson." *The Atlantic*, August 9, 2018. www.theatlantic.com/ideas/archive/2018/08/why-the-left-is-so-afraid-of-jordan-peterson/567110/.
Fournier, Théo. "A Constitutional Program Threatening the French Constitution." *Verfassungsblog*, March 2, 2017. https://verfassungsblog.de/marine-le-pen-a-constitutional-program-threatening-the-french-constitutional-regime/.
Haydon, Michael Edison. "It's OK to Be White: How Fox News Is Helping to Spread Neo-Nazi Propaganda." *Newsweek*, November 19, 2017. www.newsweek.com/neo-nazi-david-duke-backed-meme-was-reported-tucker-carlson-without-context-714655.
Hazareesingh, Sudhir. *How the French Think: An Affectionate Portrait of an Intellectual People*. New York: Basic Books, 2015.
Khan-Ruf, Safaya. "Is Marine Le Pen Far Right? It Depends on Who You Talk To." *The Independent*, April 23, 2022. www.independent.co.uk/voices/marine-le-pen-far-right-french-elections-b2060754.html.
Kranish, Michael. "How Tucker Carlson Became the Voice of White Grievance." *The Washington Post*, July 14, 2021. www.washingtonpost.com/politics/tucker-carlson/2021/07/13/398fa720-dd9f-11eb-a501-0e69b5d012e5_story.html.
Lam, Vivian. "Psychologist Jordan Peterson Says Lobsters Help to Explain Why Human Hierarchies Exist—Do They?" *The Conversation*, January 24, 2018. https://theconversation.com/psychologist-jordan-peterson-says-lobsters-help-to-explain-why-human-hierarchies-exist-do-they-90489.
Le Pen, Marine. CNBC Interview, December 21, 2016. www.cnbc.com/2016/11/21/cnbc-transcript-french-presidential-candidate-national-front-party-leader-marine-le-pen-speaks-with-cnbcs-michelle-caruso-cabrera-today.html.
———. "Je veux nationaliser les autoroutes et privatiser l'audiovisuel public." *Le Figaro*, September 8, 2021. www.lefigaro.fr/elections/presidentielles/marine-le-pen-je-veux-nationaliser-les-autoroutes-et-privatiser-l-audiovisuel-public-20210908.
———. "Le voile n'est pas un bout de tissu anodin, c'est un marqueur de radicalité." October 17, 2019. www.europe1.fr/politique/marine-le-pen-le-voile-nest-pas-un-bout-de-tissu-anodin-cest-un-marqueur-de-radicalite-3925985.
———. *Pour que vive la France*. Escalons, FR: Grancher, 2012.
"Le programme de Marine Le Pen à la présidentielle 2022." *Le Mond*, February 14, 2022. www.lemonde.fr/politique/article/2022/02/14/le-programme-de-marine-le-pen-a-la-presidentielle-2022_6113605_823448.html.
Newman, Cathy. Interview with Jordan Peterson. *Channel 4 News*, January 16, 2018. www.youtube.com/watch?v=E2iZvN5saNQ
Nussbaum, Ania. "Le Pen Goes Back to Basics With Immigration Referendum." *Bloomberg*, September 28, 2021. www.bloomberg.com/news/articles/2021-09-28/le-pen-joins-french-conservatives-seeking-immigration-referendum#xj4y7vzkg.

Peterson, Jordan. *12 Rules for Life: An Antidote for Chaos*. Toronto: Random House Canada, 2018.
———. "Equity: When the Left Goes Too Far." March 23, 2019. www.jordanbpeterson.com/political-correctness/equity-when-the-left-goes-too-far/.
———. *Maps of Meaning: The Architecture of Belief*. London: Routledge, 1999.
Plott, Elaina. "What Does Tucker Carlson Believe?" *The Atlantic*, December 15, 2019. www.theatlantic.com/politics/archive/2019/12/tucker-carlson-fox-news/603595/.
Robinson, Peter. Interview with Jordan Peterson. *Hoover Institution*, April 29, 2022. www.hoover.org/research/importance-being-ethical-jordan-peterson-1.
Rozsa, Matthew. "Tucker Carlson Bashes Capitalism, Says He Might Vote for Elizabeth Warren." *Salon*, January 26, 2019. https://docs.google.com/document/d/1HTztk4xDbjhralNlqgd5_Sdj9wd1dQDF7jGHhukybfc/edit.
Rueda, Daniel. "Is Populism a Political Strategy? A Critique of an Enduring Approach." *Political Studies* 69, no. 2 (2021): 167–84.
Trippenbach, Ivanne and Franck Johannès. "Marine Le Pen: A Fundamentally Far-Right Program Behind Her Softened Image." *Le Monde*, April 7, 2022.

Chapter 3—"We Are Looking for a New Feminism": Marine Le Pen's Reappropriation of the Liberal Language of Women's Rights and Gender Equality

Bacchetta, Paola and Margaret Power, eds. *Right-Wing Women: From Conservatives to Extremists Around the World*. New York: Routledge, 2002.
Bard, Christine, ed. *Un siècle d'antiféminisme*. Paris: Fayard, 1999.
Cudd, Anne E. *Capitalism, For and Against: A Feminist Debate*. Cambridge: Cambridge University Press, 2011.
Dietze, Gabriele and Julia Roth, eds. *Right-Wing Populism and Gender: European Perspectives and Beyond*. Bielefeld: Transcript Publishing, 2020.
Durham, Martin. *Women and Fascism*. London: Routledge, 1998.
Eltchaninoff, Michael. *Inside the Mind of Marine Le Pen*. London: Hurst & Company, 2018.
Everton, Elizabeth. "Christian Feminist and Nationalist: Marie Maugeret, Le Féminisme chrétien and the Ligue des Patriotes." *Paper presented for the Western Society for French History*, 2009. www.academia.edu/18162217/Christian_Feminist_and_Nationalist_Marie_Maugeret_Le_F%C3%A9minisme_chr%C3%A9tien_and_the_Ligue_des_Patriotes?email_work_card=view-paper.
Farris, Sara R. *In the Name of Women's Rights: The Rise of Femonationalism*. Durham: Duke University Press, 2017.
Gutsche, Elisa, ed. *Triumph of the Women? The Female Face of the Far and Populist Right in Europe*. Berlin: Friedrich Ebert Stiftung, 2018.
Hawley, George. *Conservatism in a Divided America: The Right and Identity Politics*. Notre Dame: University of Notre Dame Press, 2022.
Leidig, Eviane. *The Women of the Far Right: Social Media Influencers and Online Radicalization*. New York: Columbia University Press, 2023.
Schreiber, Ronnee. *Righting Feminism: Conservative Women and American Politics*. New York: Oxford University Press, 2008.

Scrinzi, Francesca. "A 'New' National Front? Gender, Religion, Secularism and the French Populist Radical Right." In *Gender and Far Right Politics in Europe*, edited by M. Köttig et al., 127–40. Cham: Palgrave Macmillan, 2017.
Shepard, Todd. *Sex, France, and Arab Men: 1962–1979*. Chicago: The University of Chicago Press, 2017.
Sibley, Alice. "Behind the British New Far-Right's Veil: Do Individuals Adopt Strategic Liberalism to Appear More Moderate or Are They Semi-Liberal?" *The British Journal of Politics and International Relations* (2023): 1–17.

Chapter 4—Far-Right Politics in the Czech Republic: Tomio Okamura's Liberal Language and Populist Playbook

Atlas vlivu. "Tomio Okamura a jeho systematické šíření dezinformací." Accessed May 24, 2013. www.atlasvlivu.cz/kauza/tomio-okamura-a-jeho-sireni-proruskych-narativu.
BBC1. "Dragon's Den." www.bbc.co.uk/programmes/b006vq92.
Cemper, Jan. "Jak je to s tím 'opičím morem' Tomia Okamury?" *Manipulátoři*, October 9, 2018. https://manipulatori.cz/jak-je-to-s-tim-opicim-morem-tomia-okamury/.
Český rozhlas. "Česká společnost 2019 — Rozdělená společnost." Online Data Set, ver. 1.0. (Praha: Czech social science data archive, 2020). Accessed November 30, 2022. https://doi.org/10.14473/CSDA00252.
Charter of Fundamental Rights and Freedoms. 1992. www.psp.cz/en/docs/laws/listina.html.
Charvat, Jakub, Denisa Charvatova, and Eva Niklesova. "Populism as a Communication Strategy: A Case Study of the Freedom and Direct Democracy Party and Tomio Okamura." *Communication Today*, no. 2 (2022): 106–20. www.proquest.com/scholarly-journals/populism-as-communication-strategy-case-study/docview/2778657547/se-2.
ČTK. "Choďte venčit prasata kolem mešit, vyzývá Okamura." *Aktuálně.cz*, January 3, 2015. https://zpravy.aktualne.cz/domaci/okamura-chodte-vencit-prasata-kolem-mesit-nekupujte-kebaby/r~4cd0f8a4935811e4a7d8002590604f2e/.
CVVM. "Politická orientace českých občanů—září 2019." https://cvvm.soc.cas.cz/media/com_form2content/documents/c2/a5021/f9/po191024.pdf.
Dolejší, Milan. "Halík, Höschl a Kysela: Přímá demokracie by byla diktaturou většiny. Menšinám na úkor." *ČT24*, February 18, 2018. https://ct24.ceskatelevize.cz/domaci/2394715-halik-hoschl-a-kysela-prima-demokracie-byla-diktaturou-vetsiny-mensinam-na-ukor.
Dugin, Alexander. "Liberalism 2.0." *The Fourth Political Theory*. Accessed May 24, 2023. www.4pt.su/en/content/liberalism-20.
———. "Proud to Be Illiberal." *The Fourth Political Theory*. Accessed May 24, 2023. www.4pt.su/en/content/proud-be-illiberal.
European Commission, Directorate-General for Communication. "Standard Eurobarometer 88: Standard Eurobarometer 88." (v1.00), Data Set, 2018. http://data.europa.eu/88u/dataset/S2143_88_3_STD88_ENG.
———. "Standard Eurobarometer 92: Standard Eurobarometer 92." (v1.00), data set, 2020. http://data.europa.eu/88u/dataset/S2255_92_3_STD92_ENG.

———. "Standard Eurobarometer 95: Standard Eurobarometer 95 — Spring 2021." (v1.00), data set, 2021. http://data.europa.eu/88u/dataset/S2532_95_3_95_ENG.

———. "Standard Eurobarometer STD97: Standard Eurobarometer 97 — Summer 2022." (v1.00), data set, 2022. http://data.europa.eu/88u/dataset/S2693_97_5_STD97_ENG.

Freedom House. "Czech Republic." 2023. Accessed May 23, 2023. https://freedomhouse.org/country/czech-republic/freedom-world/2023.

Gordon, Sarah. "Bear Necessities: Czech Travel Agency Promises to Show Stuffed Toys the Sights of Prague." *Daily Mail*, February 26, 2010. www.dailymail.co.uk/travel/article-1253386/Czech-travel-agency-takes-teddy-bears-Prague-sightseeing-tour.html.

Hanley, Sean. "Dynamika utváření nových stran v České republice v letech 1996–2010: hledání možných příčin politického zemětřesení." *Czech Sociological Review*, no. 1 (2011): 115–36. https://sreview.soc.cas.cz/artkey/csr-201101-0006_dynamics-of-new-party-formation-in-the-czech-republic-1996-2010-looking-for-the-origins-of-a-political-earthqu.php.

Janáková, Barbora Mašát. "Okamura varuje, že migranti šíří opičí mor. Nemoc neexistuje, je to dětská hra." *Deník N*, October 4, 2018. https://denikn.cz/2335/okamura-varuje-ze-migranti-siri-opici-mor-nemoc-neexistuje-je-to-detska-hra/.

Koulová, Zuzana. "Tomio Okamura povstává proti hnutí Black Lives Matter. Vyjmenoval největší dárce a má jasno, o co tu jde ve skutečnosti." *Parlamentní listy*, July 19, 2020. www.parlamentnilisty.cz/arena/rozhovory/Tomio-Okamura-povstava-proti-hnuti-Black-Lives-Matter-Vyjmenoval-nejvetsi-darce-a-ma-jasno-o-co-tu-jde-ve-skutecnosti-630986.

Machová, Martina. "Zbraně Ukrajině ano, nebo ne? SPD se snaží vysvětlit změny názoru." *Seznam Zprávy*, March 12, 2022. www.seznamzpravy.cz/clanek/domaci-politika-zbrane-ukrajine-ano-nebo-ne-spd-se-snazi-vysvetlit-zmeny-nazoru-193104.

Mareš, Miroslav. "Konstituování krajní pravice v českém stranicko-politickém systému." *Politologický časopis*, no. 2 (2000): 157–68. www.politologickycasopis.cz/userfiles/file/2000/2/2000-2-4-Mare%C3%81-Konstituov%E2%80%A0n%C2%B0%20krajn%C2%B0%20pravice%20v%20%C3%BCesk%C4%81m%20stranicko-politick%C4%81m%20syst%C4%81mu.pdf.

———. *Pravicový extremismus a radikalismus v ČR*. Brno: Barrister & Principal, 2003.

Ministerstvo vnitra ČR. "Výroční zprávy o extremismu a koncepce boje proti extremismu." Accessed May 24, 2023. www.mvcr.cz/clanek/extremismus-vyrocni-zpravy-o-extremismu-a-strategie-boje-proti-extremismu.aspx.

McGoldrick, Stella. "Vypnutí dezinformačních webů bude přechodné, to je jasné, míní Fiala." *iDnes.cz*, June 6, 2022. www.idnes.cz/zpravy/domaci/vlada-dezinformacni-web-opatreni-fiala.A220606_124231_domaci_iste.

Monteiro, Emanuel. "Vídeo visto 1,6 milhões de vezes mostra migrantes a agredir uma mulher numa estação de comboios da linha de Sintra?" *Poligrafo*, June 21, 2020. https://poligrafo.sapo.pt/fact-check/video-visto-16-milhoes-de-vezes-mostra-migrantes-a-agredir-uma-mulher-numa-estacao-de-comboios-da-linha-de-sintra.

Muller, Robert and Jan Lopatka. "Far-Right Scores Surprise Success in Czech Election." *Reuters*, October 21, 2017. www.reuters.com/article/us-czech-election-farright-idUSKBN1CQ0T3.

Okamura, Tomio. "About Me." Official webpage. Accessed May 23, 2023. https://tomio.cz/o-mne/.

———. "Hnutí SPD odmítá snahy eurokomisařky Jourové a Evropské komise cenzurovat sociální sítě." *SPD*, June 2, 2021. www.spd.cz/hnuti-spd-odmita-snahy-eurokomisarky-jourove-a-evropske-komise-cenzurovat-socialni-site/.

———. "Je nepřípustné, aby sociální sítě a EU svévolně cenzurovaly svobodu projevu a porušovaly základní lidská práva daná ústavou." 2021. Accessed May 24, 2023. www.spd.cz/je-nepripustne-aby-socialni-site-a-eu-svevolne-cenzurovaly-svobodu-projevu-a-porusovaly-zakladni-lidska-prava-dana-ustavou-3/.

———. "Můj dnešní rozhovor pro Parlamentní listy o aktuálním ohrožení svobody slova." *SPD*, June 30, 2021. www.spd.cz/tomio-okamura-v-rozhovoru-pro-parlamentni-listy-40/.

———. "Okamura (SPD): Evropská unie svobodu slova a pluralitu potlačuje." *Parlamentní listy*, November 29, 2020. www.parlamentnilisty.cz/politika/politici-volicum/Okamura-SPD-Evropska-unie-svobodu-slova-a-pluralitu-potlacuje-645618.

Okamura, Tomio and Jaroslav Novák Večerníček. "nám dal BAN." *Facebook*. www.facebook.com/groups/1215511288852239.

———. "SPD." *Facebook*. www.facebook.com/tomio.cz.

———. *Umění přímé demokracie*. Praha: Fragment, 2013.

O'Shaughnessy, Nicolas. *Politics and Propaganda. Weapons of Mass Seduction*. Manchester: Manchester University Press, 2004.

Pappas, Takis S. "Populists in Power." *Journal of Democracy*, no. 2 (2019): 70–84. https://doi.org/10.1353/jod.2019.0026.

Rindisbacher, Hans J. "Direct Democracy, Populism, and the Rule of the Right People." *The European Legacy*, no. 6 (2022): 622–27. https://doi.org/10.1080/10848770.2021.1991655.

Seongcheol, Kim. "Between Illiberalism and Hyper-Neoliberalism: Competing Populist Discourses in the Czech Republic." *European Politics and Society*, no. 5 (2020): 618–33. https://doi.org/10.1080/23745118.2020.1709368.

Seznam Zprávy. "'Nejúspěšnější' dezinformátoři v Česku: vyniká SPD i Ledecký." March 3, 2021. www.seznamzpravy.cz/clanek/zebricek-nejuspesnejsich-dezinformatoru-vede-spd-i-csakova-148558.

Sládek, Miroslav. "Hlavní referát přednesený předsedou strany PhDr. Miroslavem Sládkem." In *Sdružení pro Republiku—republikánská strana Československa: Materiály z ustavujícího sjezdu konaného dne 24. února 1990 v Praze*, n.d.

Smolík, Josef. "Krajněpravicové politické strany v zemích V4: historie a současnost." *Sociológia*, no. 4 (2013): 385–410. www.sav.sk/journals/uploads/09030849Smolik%20-%20OK.pdf.

STEM. "Česko společně." *Aktuálně.cz*, 2022. https://zpravy.aktualne.cz/domaci/cesko-spolecne-vsechna-dotazovana-temata/r~be30a9764aee11edbc030cc47ab5f122/.

———. "V Česku i na Slovensku převládá pocit nedostatečné spravedlnosti 2021." 2021. www.stem.cz/v-cesku-i-na-slovensku-prevlada-pocit-nedostatecne-spravedlnosti/.

Suchánek, Jonáš and Jiří Hasman. "Nativist With(out) a Cause: A Geographical Analysis of the Populist Radical Right in the 2017 and 2021 Czech Parliamentary Elections." *Territory, Politics, Governance* (2022). https://doi.org/10.1080/21622671.2022.2150287.

Universal Declaration of Human Rights. "Article 10: Freedom of Expression." www.equalityhumanrights.com/human-rights/human-rights-act/article-10-freedom-expression.

Voda, Petr and Vlastimil Havlík. "The Rise of Populists and Decline of Others: Explanation of Changes in Party Support in the Czech Republic." *Problems of Post-Communism*, no. 4 (2021): 279–91. https://doi.org/10.1080/10758216.2020.1869906.

Willoughby, Ian. "Okamura Registers New Anti-Immigrant Party Freedom and Direct Democracy." *Radio Prague International*, June 16, 2015. https://english.radio.cz/okamura-registers-new-anti-immigrant-party-freedom-and-direct-democracy-8256951.

Wirnitzer, Jan. "Okamura: Na většině Ukrajiny není válka. Mapa: Leda pokud za válku nepočítáme rakety a okupaci." *Deník N*, June 15, 2022. https://denikn.cz/900038/okamura-na-vetsine-ukrajiny-neni-valka-mapa-leda-pokud-za-valku-nepocitame-rakety-a-okupaci/.

Zpráva Komise Evropského parlamentu a Radě o provedení rámcového rozhodnutí Rady 2008/913/SVV. 2018. https://eur-lex.europa.eu/legal-content/CS/TXT/HTML/?uri=CELEX:52014DC0027&from=CS.

Chapter 5—The Transition From Liberal to Illiberal Constitutionalism in Poland and Hungary: The Language of Rights and Equality

Balogh, L. "'Reproductive Rights in Danger'?: Reflections From the Semi-Periphery." *Culture Wars Papers*, No. 23, 2022. www.illiberalism.org/reproductive-rights-in-danger-reflections-from-the-semi-periphery/.

Balogh, L. and T. Drinóczi. "The Missing Arc of Backlash? Thirty Years of Constitutional Debates On 'women's equality' in Hungary." *Intersection* 8, no. 4. (2022): 112–31. https://doi.org/10.17356/ieejsp.v8i4.969.

Baraggia, A. and M. Bonelli. "Linking Money to Values: The New Rule of Law Conditionality Regulation and Its Constitutional Challenges." *German Law Journal* 23, no. 2 (2022): 131–56. https://doi.org/10.1017/glj.2022.17.

Bárd, P. and V. Z. Kazai. "Enforcement of a Formal Conception of the Rule of Law as a Potential Way Forward to Address Backsliding: Hungary as a Case Study." *Hague Journal on the Rule of Law* 14 (2022): 165–93.

BBC. "Black Monday: Polish Women Strike Against Abortion Ban." 2016. www.bbc.com/news/world-europe-37540139.

Bień-Kacała, Agnieszka. "Informal Constitutional Change: The Case of Poland." *Przegląd Prawa Konstytucyjnego* 6, no. 40 (2017).

———. "Gloss to the Judgement of Constitutional Tribunal of 16 March 2017 (Kp 1/17)." *Przegląd Prawa Konstytucyjnego* 4 (2017): 255–62.

Bień-Kacała, Agnieszka and T. Drinóczi. *Abortion and Illiberal Constitutional Courts*, edited by M. Ziegler. Cheltenham: Edward Elgar, 2023.

Bień-Kacała, Agnieszka and J. Kapelańska-Pręgowska. "Niższy wiek emerytalny kobiet: przywilej czy dyskryminacja? Perspektywa prawnomiędzynarodowa I konstytucyjna [A Lower Retirement Age for Women: A Privilege or Discrimination? Constitutional Law and International Law Perspective]." *Praca i Zabezpieczenie Społeczne/Labour and Social Security Journal* (January 2022): 12–22. https://doi.org/10.33226/0032-6186.2022.1.2.

Bień-Kacała, Agnieszka, J. Kapelańska-Pręgowska, and A. Tarnowska. "Rise and Fall of Gender Equality in Poland." In *The Rights of Women in Comparative Constitutional Law. . .*, edited by V. Scotti et al. London: Routledge, 2023.

Dixon, R. and D. Landau. "1989–2019: From Democratic to Abusive Constitutional Borrowing." *International Journal of Constitutional Law* 17, no. 489 (2019).

———. *Abusive Constitutional Borrowing: Legal Globalization and the Subversion of Liberal Democracy*. Oxford: Oxford University Press, 2023.

Drinóczi, T. "Sham and Smokescreen: Hungary and the Rule of Law Conditionality Mechanism." *VerfBlog*. October 5, 2022. https://verfassungsblog.de/sham-and-smokescreen/.

———. "The Unfolding Illiberalism in Hungary." *Review of Central and East European Law* 3–4 (December 2022): 352–80. Brill. https://doi.org/10.1163/15730352-bja10071.

Drinóczi, T. and A. Bień-Kacała. *Illiberal Constitutionalism in Poland and Hungary: The Deterioration of Democracy, Misuse of Human Rights and Abuse of the Rule of Law*. London: Routledge, 2022.

———, eds. *Rule of Law, Common Values and Illiberal Constitutionalism. Poland and Hungary within the European Union*. London: Routledge, 2021.

Duffy, Nick. "Hungarian Prime Minister Viktor Orbán Demands Gay People 'Leave Our Children Alone' in Sinister Attack on Lesbian Cinderella Book." 2020. www.pinknews.co.uk/2020/10/06/hungary-prime-minister-viktor-orban-gay-children-lesbian-cinderella-book.

Explanatory Memorandum 2015. Explanatory Memorandum, 26. www.sejm.gov.pl/sejm8.nsf/druk.xsp?nr=62.

Explanatory Memorandum 2016. www.parlament.hu/irom41/00332/00332.pdf.

Explanatory Memorandum 2020. "Explanatory Memorandum to the Ninth Amendment to the FL." www.parlament.hu/irom41/13647/13647.pdf.

Florczak-Wątor, M. "Comments on the PCT Decision." 2017. https://konstytucyjny.pl/glosa-do-wyroku-tk-z-dnia-16-marca-2017-r-sygn-akt-kp-117-monika-florczak-wator/.

Freedom House, 2022. https://freedomhouse.org/explore-the-map?type=fotn&year=2022.

Frick, Marie-Luisa. "Illiberalism and Human rights." In *Routledge Handbook of Illiberalism*, edited by A. Sajó, R. Uitz, and S. Holmes, 861–75. London: Routledge, 2022.

Haász, János. "Hungarian Judicial Council, a Stakeholder in Judicial Reform Package, Disagrees with Several Points of Draft." 2023. https://telex.hu/english/2023/02/01/hungarian-judicial-council-a-stakeholder-in-judicial-reform-package-disagrees-with-several-points-of-draft.

Heper, Altan. "The Idea of Equality." In *Encyclopedia of the Philosophy of Law and Social Philosophy*, edited by M. Sellers and S. Kirste. Springer. https://doi.org/10.1007/978-94-007-6730-0_812-1.

Ipsos. "Global Views on Abortion in 2021: Favorability Toward Legalization of Abortion in 27 Countries." 2021. www.ipsos.com/sites/default/files/ct/news/documents/2021-09/Global-views-on-abortion-report-2021.pdf.

Katarzyna, Eliasz and Wojciech Załuski. "Freedom." In *Encyclopedia of the Philosophy of Law and Social Philosophy*, edited by M. Sellers and S. Kirste. Springer. https://doi.org/10.1007/978-94-007-6730-0_234-2

Koncewicz, Tomasz Tadeusz. "When Legal Fundamentalism Meets Political Justice: The Case of Poland." *Israel Law Review* 55, no. 3 (2022): 302–59.

Laruelle, Marlene. "Illiberalism: A Conceptual Introduction." *East European Politics* 38, no. 2 (2022): 303–27. https://doi.org/10.1080/21599165.2022.2037079.

Marcisz, Pawel. "A Chamber of Certain Liability: A Story of Latest Reforms in the Polish Supreme Court." *VerfBlog*, October 31, 2022. https://verfassungsblog.de/a-chamber-of-certain-liability/. https://doi.org/10.17176/20221031-215613-0.

May, C. and A. Winchester, eds. *Handbook of the Rule of Law*. Cheltenham: Edward Elgar, 2018.

Młynarska-Sobaczewska, A. "Unconstitutionality of Access to Abortion for Embryo-Pathological Reasons." *International Human Rights Law Review* 10 (2021): 168–79.

MTI 2021. "2021-ben is folytatodik a nok 40." https://kormany.hu/hirek/2021-ben-is-folytatodik-a-nok-40.

Pech, Laurent. "Covering Up and Rewarding the Destruction of the Rule of Law One Milestone at a Time." *VerfBlog*, June 21, 2022. https://verfassungsblog.de/covering-up-and-rewarding-the-destruction-of-the-rule-of-law-one-milestone-at-a-time/. https://doi.org/10.17176/20220621-153415-0.

Pech, Laurent, P. Wachowiec, and D. Mazur. "Poland's Rule of Law Breakdown: A Five-Year Assessment of EU's (In)Action." *Hague Journal on the Rule of Law* 13 (2021): 1–43.

Press Information. "Wybory Parlamentarne. PiS: obniżymy wiek emerytalny." 2015. https://polskieradio24.pl/42/273/artykul/1532526,wybory-parlamentarne-2015-pis-obnizymy-wiek-emerytalny.

Rosta, G. and A. Hámori. "Declining Religiosity Among Hungarian Youth After the Turn of Millennium—Main Trends and Possible Explanations." In *Confessionality and University in the Modern World*, edited by E. Sepsi, P. Balla and M. Csanády. L'Harmattan, Budapest: Károli University, 2014.

Scheppele, Kim Lane and John Morijn. "Are Hungary's EU Funds Being Cut (or Not)?: Funding Confusions, Separate Tracks and What May Lie Ahead." *VerfBlog*, November 14, 2022. https://verfassungsblog.de/are-hungarys-eu-funds-being-cut-or-not/.

Tomka, M. *Expanding Religion: Religious Revival in Post-Communist Central and Eastern Europe*. Berlin: De Gruyter, 2011.

Tushnet, M. "The Possibility of Illiberal Constitutionalism." *Florida Law Review* 69 (2017).

V-Dem Institute. "Democracy Report 2022. Autocratization Changing Nature?" https://v-dem.net/media/publications/dr_2022.pdf 25

Waller, Julian G. "Distinction with a Difference: Illiberalism and Authoritarianism in Scholarly Study." *Political Studies Review* (2023): 1–22.

Chapter 6—When Legal Language Meets Apocalypse Anxiety: Democracy, Constitutional Scholars, and the Rise of the German Far Right After 2015

AfD-Fraktion im Bundestag and Ulrich Vosgerau. "Herrschaft Des Unrechts: AfD Fraktion klagt vor Verfassungsgericht!" May 18, 2018. https://youtu.be/J7hvBe9tzb4.

Anderson, Benedict. *Imagined Communities. Reflections on the Origin and Spread of Nationalism*. London: Verso, 1983.

Bibliography

Baberowski, Jörg. "Ungesteuerte Einwanderung: Europa ist gar keine Wertegemeinschaft." *FAZ*, September 14, 2015. www.faz.net/aktuell/feuilleton/debatten/joerg-baberowski-ueber-ungesteuerte-einwanderung-13800909.html.

Bendersky, Joseph. "The Expendable Kronjurist: Carl Schmitt and National Socialism, 1933–36." *Journal of Contemporary History* 14, no. 2 (1979): 309–28.

Berlinghoff, Marcel. "Über die 'Grenzen der Aufnahmefähigkeit' hinaus." *Netzwerk Flüchtlingsforschung*, September 28, 2015. http://fluechtlingsforschung.net/uber-die-grenzen-der-aufnahmefahigkeit-hinaus/.

"CSU-Landesgruppenchef: Dobrindt Will 'konservative Revolution' unterstützen." *Der Tagesspiegel*, January 4, 2018. www.tagesspiegel.de/politik/dobrindt-will-konservative-revolution-unterstutzen-5511829.html.

Depenheuer, Otto. "Flüchtlingskrise als Ernstfall des menschenrechtlichen Universalismus." In *Der Staat in der Flüchtlingskrise: Zwischen gutem Willen und geltendem Recht*, edited by Otto Depenheuer and Christoph Grabenwarter, 18–39. Bd. 5. Paderborn: Ferdinand Schöningh, 2016.

Depenheuer, Otto and Christoph Grabenwarter, eds. *Der Staat in der Flüchtlingskrise: Zwischen gutem Willen und geltendem Recht*. Bd. 5. Paderborn: Ferdinand Schöningh, 2016.

———. "Vorwort." In *Der Staat in der Flüchtlingskrise: Zwischen gutem Willen und geltendem Recht*, edited by Otto Depenheuer and Christoph Grabenwarter, 7–8. Paderborn: Ferdinand Schöningh, 2016.

Detjen, Stephan and Maximilian Steinbeis. *Die Zauberlehrlinge: Der Streit um die Flüchtlingspolitik und der Mythos vom Rechtsbruch*. Stuttgart: Klett-Cotta, 2019.

Die Welt. "Ex-Verfassungsrichter: Papier rechnet mit deutscher Flüchtlingspolitik ab." January 12, 2016. www.welt.de/politik/deutschland/article150894661/Papier-rechnet-mit-deutscher-Fluechtlingspolitik-ab.html.

Dresdner. *Gespräche mit Björn Höcke*. Dresden: Compact TV, 2017. https://youtu.be/WDUWh1LfDeA.

Feldkamp, Michael F. *Der Parlamentarische Rat 1948–1949: Die Entstehung des Grundgesetzes*. Göttingen: Vandenhoeck & Ruprecht, 2019.

Genova, Nicholas de. "Migrant 'Illegality' and Deportability in Everyday Life." *Annual Review of Anthropology* 31 (2002): 419–47.

Hailbronner, Kay, Hans-Georg Maaßen, Jan Hecker, and Marcel Kau, eds. *Staatsangehörigkeitsrecht 6. Neu Bearbeitete Auflage*. München: C. H. Beck, 2017.

Hartwig, Roland. "Auszüge aus dem Gutachten von Prof. Dr. Dieter Murswiek." *netzpolitik.org*, October 22, 2018. https://netzpolitik.org/2018/wir-veroeffentlichen-wie-sich-die-afd-ihre-eigene-verfassungsfeindlichkeit-bescheinigen-laesst/.

Holtmann, Everhard. "Die DDR—ein Unrechtsstaat?" *bpb.de*, May 11, 2020. www.bpb.de/themen/deutsche-einheit/lange-wege-der-deutschen-einheit/47560/die-ddr-ein-unrechtsstaat/.

Hunger, Anna. "Gut vernetzt—Der Kopp-Verlag und die schillernde rechte Publizistenszene." In *Strategien der extremen Rechten: Hintergründe—Analysen—Antworten*, edited by Stephan Braun, Alexander Geisler, and Martin Gerster, 425–37. Wiesbaden: Springer Fachmedien, 2016.

Kewenig, Wilhelm A. "Die Deutsche Staatsbürgerschaft—Klammer der Nation?" *Europa-Archiv* 42, no. 18 (1987): 517–22.

Kingreen, Thorsten. "Mit gutem Willen und etwas Recht: Staatsrechtslehrer in der Flüchtlingskrise." *JuristenZeitung* 71, no. 18 (2016): 887–90.

Klefke, Heike and Matthias Meisner, eds. *Extreme Sicherheit: Rechtsradikale in Polizei, Verfassungsschutz, Bundeswehr und Justiz*. Freiburg: Herder, 2019.

Maaßen, Hans-Georg, and Alexander Wallasch. "Nach grün-roter Rassenlehre sind Weiße eine minderwertige Rasse." *Alexander-wallasch.de*, January 16, 2023.

McAdams, A. James. "Making the Case for 'Difference': From the Nouvelle Droite to the Identitarians and the New Vanguardists." In *Contemporary Far-Right Thinkers and the Future of Liberal Democracy*, edited by A. James McAdams and Alejandro Castrillon, 85–102. London and New York: Routledge, 2022.

Meier-Braun, Karl-Heinz and Reinhold Weber, eds. *Deutschland Einwanderungsland: Begriffe—Fakten—Kontroversen*. Bonn: Bundeszentrale für politische Bildung, 2017.

Murswiek, Dietrich. "Nationalstaatlichkeit, Staatsvolk und Einwanderung." In *Der Staat in der Flüchtlingskrise: Zwischen gutem Willen und geltendem Recht*, edited by Otto Depenheuer and Christoph Grabenwarter, 123–39. Paderborn: Ferdinand Schöningh, 2016.

Niethammer, Lutz. *Kollektive Identität: heimliche Quellen einer unheimlichen Konjunktur*. Reinbek bei Hamburg: Rowohlt, 2000.

Oltmer, Jochen. "'Weltvergessen' und 'geschichtsblind': Kritik am deutschen Blick auf Migration." *Deutschlandfunk*, March 5, 2017.

Panagiotidis, Jannis. "Heute und damals: Es waren einmal drei Millionen." *FAZ*, September 3, 2015. www.faz.net/aktuell/wissen/leben-gene/fluechtlinge-wie-integration-gelingen-kann-13775770.html.

Pichl, Maximilian and Eric von Dömming. "Autoritäre Inszenierung und Umdeutung—Die Rechtspolitik der 'Alternative für Deutschland'." *Kritische Justiz* 53, no. 3 (2020): 299–310.

Rath, Martin. "Staatsrechtslehrer unter Migrationsstress." *Legal Tribune Online*, March 27, 2016. www.lto.de/recht/feuilleton/f/depenheuer-grabenwarter-der-staat-in-der-fluechtlingskrise-rezension/.

Reimann, Anna and Christina Hebel. "Die wirre Welt der Wohlstandsbürger." *Der Spiegel*, December 16, 2014.

Rich, Anna-Katharina. "Asylerstantragsteller in Deutschland im Jahr 2015: Sozialstruktur, Qualifikationsniveau und Berufstätigkeit." *BAMF-Kurzanalyse* 3 (2016): 1–11.

Rothberg, Michael. *The Implicated Subject: Beyond Victims and Perpetrators*. Stanford, CA: Stanford University Press, 2019.

Sarrazin, Thilo. *Deutschland schafft sich ab: Wie wir unser Land aufs Spiel setzen*. München: Deutsche Verlags-Anstalt, 2010.

Schachtschneider, Karl A. "Das Unrecht der Masseneinwanderung. Auszug aus der Verfassungsbeschwerde." November 4, 2017. www.kaschachtschneider.de/das-unrecht-der-masseneinwanderung/.

Schlink, Bernhard. "Die Entthronung der Staatsrechtswissenschaft durch die Verfassungsgerichtsbarkeit." *Der Staat* 28, no. 2 (1989): 161–72.

Schorkopf, Frank. "Das Romantische und die Notwendigkeit eines normativen Realismus." In *Der Staat in der Flüchtlingskrise: Zwischen gutem Willen und geltendem Recht*, edited by Otto Depenheuer and Christoph Grabenwarter, 11–17. Paderborn: Ferdinand Schöningh, 2016.

SD. "Der Staat in der Flüchtlingskrise." *Truppendienst*, May 23, 2017. www.truppendienst.com/themen/beitraege/artikel/der-staat-in-der-fluechtlingskrise.

"Seehofer unterstellt Merkel 'Herrschaft des Unrechts'." *Merkur*, February 9, 2016. www.merkur.de/politik/seehofer-unterstellt-merkel-herrschaft-unrechts-zr-6109526.html.

Skordas, Achilles. "A Very German Cultural War: Migrants and the Law." *ZaöRV* 79 (2019): 923–34.

Steinbeis, Maximilian. "Die AfD und ihr Rechtsbruch-Mythos: Im Felde unbesiegt." *Verfassungsblog*, December 18, 2018. https://verfassungsblog.de/die-afd-und-ihr-rechtsbruch-mythos-im-felde-unbesiegt/.

Stolleis, Michael. *Geschichte des öffentlichen Rechts in Deutschland, Vol. 3, Weimarer Republik und Nationalsozialismus 1914–1945*. München: C. H. Beck, 2002.

———. *Geschichte des öffentlichen Rechts in Deutschland, Vol. 4: Staats- und Verwaltungsrechtswissenschaft in West und Ost 1945–1990*. München: C. H. Beck, 2012.

Thränhardt, Dietrich and Karin Weiss. "Die Einbeziehung des Islam in Deutschland zwischen Integrations- und Religionspolitik." In *Staat und Islam: Interdisziplinäre Perspektiven*, edited by Uwe Hunger and Nils Johann Schröder, 23–41. Islam und Politik. Wiesbaden: Springer Fachmedien, 2016.

Thym, Daniel. "Der Rechtsbruch-Mythos und wie man ihn widerlegt." *Verfassungsblog*, May 2, 2018. https://verfassungsblog.de/der-rechtsbruch-mythos-und-wie-man-ihn-widerlegt/.

Ty, Michelle. "The Myth of What We Can Take In: Global Migration and the 'Receptive Capacity' of the Nation-State." *Theory & Event* 22, no. 4 (2019): 869–90.

"Viele Bewertungen beruhen auf einer falschen rechtlichen Grundlage." *AfD TV*, January 19, 2020. www.presseportal.de/pm/110332/4496751.

Vosgerau, Ulrich. "Demokratie ohne Demos?—Die ethnisch-kulturelle Identität des deutschen Volkes wahren zu wollen, ist nicht verfassungsfeindlich." *Tumult* 2 (2022): 78–82.

———. *Die Herrschaft des Unrechts: die Asylkrise, die Krise des Verfassungsstaates und die Rolle der Massenmedien*. Rottenburg: Kopp Verlag, 2018.

———. "Für Recht und Freiheit." *Die Zeit*, May 5, 1995. www.zeit.de/1995/19/Fuer_Recht_und_Freiheit.

———. "Herrschaft des Unrechts." *Cicero* 12 (2015): 92–98.

———. *Organstreitverfahren der AfD-Fraktion im Bundestag*. Berlin, 2018. https://www.bundesverfassungsgericht.de/SharedDocs/Pressemitteilungen/DE/2022/bvg22-026.html.

———. "Veröffentlichungen." 2022. www.ulrich-vosgerau.de/veroeffentlichungen/.

Wagner, Joachim. *Rechte Richter: AfD-Richter, -Staatsanwälte und -Schöffen: Eine Gefahr für den Rechtsstaat?* Berlin: Berliner Wissenschafts-Verlag, 2021.

Weiß, Volker. "Die 'Konservative Revolution'." In *Erinnerungsorte der extremen Rechten*, edited by Martin Langebach and Michael Sturm, 101–20. Wiesbaden: Springer Fachmedien, 2015.

Wengeler, Martin. *Topos und Diskurs: Begründung einer argumentationsanalytischen Methode und ihre Anwendung auf den Migrationsdiskurs (1960–1985)*. Tübingen: Niemeyer, 2003.

Wildt, Michael. *Die Ambivalenz des Volkes: Der Nationalsozialismus als Gesellschaftsgeschichte*. Berlin: Suhrkamp, 2019.

———. *Volk, Volksgemeinschaft, AfD*. Hamburg: Hamburger Edition HIS, 2017.

Wolff, Frank. "Rechtsgeschichte als Gesellschaftsgeschichte? Die Staatsbürgerschaft der DDR als Kampfmittel im Kalten Krieg." *Kritische Justiz* 51, no. 4 (2018): 413–30.

Chapter 7—From Practical Critics to Hateful Malcontents: The Rise and Fall of the Online "Manosphere"

Alter, Karen J. and Michael Zürn. "Theorising Backlash Politics." *The British Journal of Politics and International Relations* 22 (2020): 739–52.
Costello, William, Vania Rolon, Andrew G. Thomas, and David Schmitt. "Levels of Well-Being Among Men Who Are Incel (Involuntarily Celibate)." *Evolutionary Psychological Science* 8 (2022): 375–90.
Diani, Mario. "The Concept of a Social Movement." *The Sociological Review* 40 (1992): 1–25.
Fasteau, Marc Fiegen. *The Male Machine*. New York: McGraw-Hill, 1974.
Ferrell, Warren. *The Liberated Man*. New York: Random House, 1974.
Goldberg, Herb. *The Hazards of Being Male: Surviving the Myth of Masculine Privilege*. New York: Signet, 1976.
Hawley, George. *Making Sense of the Alt-Right*. New York: Columbia University Press, 2017.
Lewis, Andrew R. *The Rights Turn in Conservative Christian Politics*. New York: Cambridge University Press, 2017.
Lin, Jie Liang. "Anti-Feminism Online. MGTOW (Men Going Their Own Way)." In *Digital Environments: Ethnographic Perspectives Across Global Online and Offline Spaces*, edited by Urte Undine Frömming, Steffen Köhn, Samantha Fox, and Mike Terry, 77–96. Bielefeld: Transcript Verlag, 2017.
Messner, Michael A. "The Limits of 'The Male Sex Role': An Analysis of the Men's Liberation Movement and the Men's Rights Movements' Discourse." *Gender and Society* 12 (1998): 255–76.
Mystery, Lovedrop and Chris Odom. *The Mystery Method: How to Get Beautiful Women Into Bed*. New York: St. Martin's Press, 2007.
Nichols, Jack. *Men's Liberation: A New Definition of Masculinity*. New York: Penguin, 1975.
Ribeiro, Manoel Horta, Jeremy Blackburn, Barry Bradlyn, Emiliano De Cristofaro, Gianluca Stringhini, Summer Long, Stephanie Greenberg, and Savvas Zannettou. "The Evolution of the Manosphere Across the Web." *Proceedings of the International AAAI Conference on Web and Social Media* 15 (2021): 196–207.
Smith, Helen. *Men on Strike: Why Men Are Boycotting Marriage, Fatherhood, and the American Dream—And Why It Matters*. New York: Encounter Books, 2013.
Strauss, Neil. *The Game: Penetrating the Secret Society of Pickup Artists*. New York: Harper Collins, 2005.
Vallerga, Michael and Eileen L. Zurbriggen. "Hegemonic Masculinities in the 'Manosphere': A Thematic Analysis of Beliefs About Men and Women on The Red Pill and Incel." *Analyses of Social Issues and Public Policies* 22 (2022): 602–25.

Chapter 8—Forced to Be Free? America's "Postliberals" on Freedom and Liberty

Barr, William P. "Attorney General William P. Barr Delivers Remarks to the Law School and the de Nicola Center for Ethics and Culture at the University of Notre

Dame." South Bend, IN, Friday, October 11, 2019. www.justice.gov/opa/speech/attorney-general-william-p-barr-delivers-remarks-law-school-and-de-nicola-center-ethics.
———. "Barr Says He Believes Trump 'Knew Well He Lost the Election'." *CNN*, August 3, 2021. www.youtube.com/watch?v=X6m72ZQRBh8.
———. Letter, Barr to President Donald J. Trump, December 14, 2020. www.documentcloud.org/documents/20424018-attorney-general-william-barr-resignation-letter.
Beauchamp, Zach. "It Happened There: How Democracy Died in Hungary." *Vox*, September 13, 2018. www.vox.com/policy-and-politics/2018/9/13/17823488/hungary-democracy-authoritarianism-trump.
Berlin, Isaiah. "Two Concepts of Liberty." In *Four Essays on Liberty*. Oxford: Oxford University Press, 1969.
Cho, Emmy and Isabella Cho. "Harvard Law School Organizations Petition to Denounce Professor Adrian Vermeule's 'Highly Offensive' Online Rhetoric." *The Crimson*, January 13, 2021. www.thecrimson.com/article/2021/1/13/harvard-law-school-petition-vermeule/.
Churchwell, Sarah. "American Fascism: It Has Happened Here." *NYRB*, June 22, 2020. www.nybooks.com/online/2020/06/22/american-fascism-it-has-happened-here/.
Constant, Benjamin. "The Liberty of the Ancients Compared With That of the Moderns," 1819. https://oll.libertyfund.org/title/constant-the-liberty-of-ancients-compared-with-that-of-moderns-1819.
Deneen, Patrick. "After Obergefell: A First Things Symposium," *First Things*, 2015. www.firstthings.com/web-exclusives/2015/06/after-obergefell-a-first-things-symposium.
———. *Regime Change*. New York: Sentinel Press, 2023
———. *Why Liberalism Failed*. New Haven: Yale University Press, 2018.
Deneen, Patrick and Gladden Pappin. "Dispatch From Budapest: Notes on a Conversation With Hungary's Viktor Orbán." *Postliberal Order Substack*, August 5, 2022. https://postliberalorder.substack.com/p/dispatch-from-budapest.
Drinóczi, Tímea and Agnieszka Bień-Kacała. "Illiberal Constitutionalism: The Case of Hungary and Poland." *German Law Journal*, no. 20 (2019): 1140–66. https://doi.org/10.1017/glj.2019.83.
Field, Laura K. "On the Highbrow Conspiracism of the New Intellectual Right: A Sampling From the Trump Years." *Niskanen Center*, April 2019. www.niskanen-center.org/the-highbrow-conspiracism-of-the-new-intellectual-right-a-sampling-from-the-trump-years/.
———. "Revisiting Why Liberalism Failed." *Niskanen Center*, December 21, 2020. www.niskanencenter.org/revisiting-why-liberalism-failed-a-five-part-series/.
Pappin, Gladden. "Within the West, Hungary Has Set the Standard for a Reasonable Approach." *Postliberal Order Substack*, April 14 2023. https://postliberalorder.substack.com/p/within-the-west-hungary-has-set-the.
Sata, Robert and Pawel Karolewsk. "Caesarean Politics in Hungary and Poland." *East European Politics* 36, no. 2 (2020): 206–25. https://doi.org/10.1080/21599165.2019.1703694.
Scheppele, Kim Lane. "How Viktor Orbán Wins." *Journal of Democracy* (July 2022): 45–61. www.journalofdemocracy.org/articles/how-viktor-orban-wins/.
Schwartzman, Micah and Richard Schwagger. "What Common Good?" *The American Prospect*, July 2022.
Vermeule, Adrian. *Common Good Constitutionalism*. Cambridge: Polity Press, 2022.

———. "Common Good Constitutionalism." *The Atlantic*, March 31, 2021. www.theatlantic.com/ideas/archive/2020/03/common-good-constitutionalism/609037/.

———. "Integralism From Within." *American Affairs*, Spring 2018. https://americanaffairsjournal.org/2018/02/integration-from-within/.

Waldstein, Edmund. "Contrasting Concepts of Freedom." *The Josias*, November 11, 2016. https://thejosias.com/2016/11/11/contrasting-concepts-of-freedom/.

———. "Integralism in Three Sentences." *The Josias*, October 17, 2016. https://thejosias.com/2016/10/17/integralism-in-three-sentences/.

Weiseltier, Leon. "Christianism." In *Liberties*. Spring 2022. https://libertiesjournal.com/articles/christianism/.

Chapter 9—Shine a Light or Burn It Down? Conspiracism and Liberal Ideas

Hoppe, Hans-Herman. "Libertarianism and the Alt-Right: In Search of a Libertarian Strategy for Social Change" (speech from Property and Freedom Society meeting in Bodrum, Turkey, September 17, 2017). *Free Life*. https://libertarianism.uk/2017/10/20/libertarianism-and-the-alt-right-hoppe-speech-2017/.

Koppelman, Andrew. *Burning Down the House: How Libertarian Philosophy Was Corrupted by Delusion and Greed*. New York: Saint Martin's Press, 2022.

Muirhead, Russell and Nancy Rosenblum. *A Lot of People Are Saying: The New Conspiracism and the Assault on Democracy*. Princeton: Princeton University Press, 2019.

Rothbard, Murray. "Right-Wing Populism: A Strategy for the Paleo Movement." *Rothbard-Rockwell Report*, January 1992. https://www.rothbard.it/articles/right-wing-populism.pdf.

Urbinati, Nadia. "For a Tripartite Model of Conspiracy." *Contemporary Political Theory* 19 (2020): 142–74.

Chapter 10—Against the Global Prison-Society: The Far Right's Language of the Opposition to the Great Reset

Alice, Margaret Anna. "Dissident Dialogues: C. J. Hopkins." August 8, 2022. https://margaretannaalice.substack.com/p/dissident-dialogues-cj-hopkins.

Anonymous. *Manifeste Conspirationniste*. Paris: Seuil, 2022.

Baudet, Thierry. "Het COVID-Plan." January 14, 2022. https://twitter.com/thierrybaudet/status/1482072174118719489?lang=en.

———. "The Speech That Shook Parliament." September 26, 2022. https://fvdinternational.com/article/the-speech-that-shook-parliament.

———. "Thierry Baudet's Speech in Dutch Parliament About the Agenda Behind Covid-19." October 21, 2021. CTV News, "Truth Tracker: Analyzing the World Economic Forum 'Great Reset' Conspiracy Theory," May 28, 2022. www.ctvnews.ca/canada/truth-tracker-analyzing-the-world-economic-forum-great-reset-conspiracy-theory-1.5922314.

BlazeTV Staff. "ESG Scores EXPLAINED: This Is Why Companies Are Going Woke." January 25, 2022. www.glennbeck.com/esg-the-great-reset.

Breizh-info. "Lucien Cerise: 'Les Blancs n'ont pas le droit d'avoir une conscience raciale'." October 5, 2021. www.breizh-info.com/2021/10/05/171735/lucien-cerise-blancs-conscience-raciale/.

Canlorbe, Grégoire. "A Conversation With French Writer Renaud Camus." July 5, 2018. www.gatestoneinstitute.org/12604/renaud-camus-interview.

CTV News. "Truth Tracker: Analyzing the World Economic Forum 'Great Reset' Conspiracy Theory." May 28, 2022. www.ctvnews.ca/canada/truth-tracker-analyzing-the-world-economic-forum-great-reset-conspiracy-theory-1.5922314.

Cudenec, Paul. E-mail communication with author, September 16, 2022.

———. "Our Insurrection Will Be Impure!" February 17, 2022. https://network23.org/paulcudenec/2022/02/17/our-insurrection-will-be-impure/.

Engels, David. E-mail communication with author, August 13, 2022.

The Epoch Times. "Why Freedom Depends More Than Ever on Our Health and Fitness—Raw Egg Nationalist." November 8, 2022. www.theepochtimes.com/why-freedom-depends-more-than-ever-on-our-health-and-fitness_4832419.html.

Geopolitics & Empire Podcast. "C. J. Hopkins: The Virus of Mass Destruction & Brave New Totalitarian Normal." July 25, 2020. https://american-podcasts.com/podcast/podcast-geopolitics-empire/c-j-hopkins-the-virus-of-mass-destruction-brave-ne.

Ghilionn, John Mac and Raw Egg Nationalist. "No Antidote to Globalist Chaos." *The American Mind*, February 14, 2023. https://americanmind.org/salvo/no-antidote-to-globalist-chaos/.

Granza, Mark. "Thierry Baudet: Europe's Hopeful Pessimist." June 15, 2021. https://im1776.com/2021/06/22/interview-thierry-baudet/.

Griffin, Nick. November 20, 2021. https://twitter.com/NickGriffinBU/status/1462081473087946772.

———. February 25, 2022. https://vk.com/wall292118168_1648.

———. "Le Grand Reset . . . ou Le grand ménage?" # *5 Great Reset et Moeurs*, May 14, 2022. https://podcasts.apple.com/us/podcast/le-grand-reset-ou-le-grand-m%C3%A9nage/id1624596805.

Johnson, Greg. E-mail communication with author, September 1, 2022.

Klein, Naomi. "The Great Reset Conspiracy Smoothie." December 8, 2020. https://theintercept.com/2020/12/08/great-reset-conspiracy/.

Kulchur Lodge Radio. "'Only a God Can Save Us'—Morgoth on the Plan for a Metaverse Tech-Dystopia." *Kulchur Lodge Radio* #35, February 10, 2022. https://podcastaddict.com/episode/135310411.

Lichtmesz, Martin. "Dugins 'Das Große Erwachen gegen den Great Reset' (4/5)." March 21, 2022. https://sezession.de/65577/dugins-das-grosse-erwachen-gegen-den-great-reset-4-5.

———. E-mail communication with author, August 3, 2022.

Live Stream. "Nick Griffin Live—The Great Reset." May 6, 2021. www.purged.tv/l/3206212459/8pm-Live-Stream-Nick-Griffin-Live-The-Great-Reset-6-5-21.

Manifesto. "Man's World Magazine." 2021. https://mansworldmag.online/manifesto/.

Markovics, Alexander. E-mail communication with author, October 16, 2022.

Noor Bin Ladin Calls . . . Raw Egg Nationalist #2, September 19, 2022. https://noorbinladincalls.podbean.com/e/noor-bin-ladin-calls-raw-egg-nationalist-2/.

Raw Egg Nationalist. "The Great Reset Agenda to Be Weak and Effeminate EXPOSED [Raw Egg Nationalist]." October 17, 2022. https://theinfowar.tv/watch?id=634cb96866c27b0d30d5439e.

Rebellion. "Entretien Avec Lucien Cerise." May 6, 2020. https://rebellion-sre.fr/entretien-avec-lucien-cerise-face-au-biopouvoir-nous-navons-pas-le-capital-economique-mais-nous-avons-le-capital-humain/.

Rubin Report. "Why the Great Reset Is No Longer a Conspiracy Theory | Glenn Beck | POLITICS." February 6, 2022. www.youtube.com/watch?v=pwVjlPJTxV8.

Schwab, Klaus and Thierry Malleret. *The Great Narrative for a Better Future*. Geneva, Switzerland: Forum Publishing, 2022.

Sellner, Martin. E-mail communication with author, August 2, 2022.

Strategika. "La plus grave menace de tous les temps—entretien avec Lucien Cerise." March 9, 2022. https://strategika.fr/2022/03/09/la-plus-grave-menace-de-tous-les-temps-culture-populaire-sentretient-avec-lucien-cerise/.

Templar Report, July 16, 2022. www.purged.tv/l/3453444824/Templar-Report-July-26-2022.

WEF-World Economic Forum. "8 Predictions for the World in 2030." www.weforum.org/agenda/2016/11/8-predictions-for-the-world-in-2030/.

———. "The Great Reset." www.weforum.org/focus/the-great-reset.

Woods, Keith. E-mail communication with author, November 1, 2022.

———. "The Truth About the World Economic Forum." April 4, 2021. www.youtube.com/watch?v=LXIwnlAcUqQ.

Zúquete, José Pedro. "Beyond America: The Rise of the European Alt-Right." In *Contemporary Far-Right Thinkers and the Future of Liberal Democracy*, edited by A. James McAdams and Alejandro Castrillon, 207–22. London: Routledge, 2021.

Chapter 11—Hard Men, Hard Money, Hardening Right: Bitcoin, Peter Thiel, and Schmittian States of Exception

Aglietta, Michel. "The European Vortex." *New Left Review*, no. 75 (2012): 15–36.

Ammous, Saifedean. *The Bitcoin Standard: The Decentralized Alternative to Central Banking*. Hoboken: John Wiley & Sons, 2018.

Anderson, Thomas J. *Money Without Boundaries: How Blockchain Will Facilitate the Denationalization of Money*. Hoboken: John Wiley & Sons, 2019.

Anglin, Andrew. "A Normie's Guide to the Alt-Right." *Daily Stormer*, 2016. Published electronically August 31. https://dailystormer.name/a-normies-guide-to-the-alt-right.

Anton, Michael. "Are the Kids Al(t)right?" *Claremont Review of Books* 19, no. 3 (Summer 2019): 50–56.

Barbrook, Richard and Andy Cameron. "The Californian Ideology." *Science as Culture* 6, no. 1 (1996): 44–72.

Bremmer, Ian. "The Technopolar Moment: How Digital Powers Will Reshape the Global Order." *Foreign Affairs* 100 (November/December 2021).

Bronze Age Pervert. *Bronze Age Mindset: An Exhortation*. San Bernadino: n.p., 2018.

Brunton, Finn. *Digital Cash: The Unknown History of the Anarchists, Utopians, and Technologists Who Created Cryptocurrency*. Princeton: Princeton University Press, 2019.

Burrow, J. W. *Whigs and Liberals: Continuity and Change in English Political Thought*. Oxford: Oxford University Press, 1988.

Chafkin, Max. *The Contrarian: Peter Thiel and Silicon Valley's Pursuit of Power*. London: Bloomsbury, 2021.

Dam, Kenneth W. "From the *Gold Clause Cases* to the Gold Commission: A Half Century of American Monetary Law." *The University of Chicago Law Review* 50, no. 2 (1983): 504–32.
Davidson, James Dale and William Rees-Mogg. *The Sovereign Individual: Mastering the Transition to the Information Age*. New York: Touchstone, 1997.
Dodd, Nigel. *The Social Life of Money*. Princeton: Princeton University Press, 2014.
Eggers, Austin and Jeffrey Hobbs. "Combatting the Financing of Hate Groups." *Journal of Money Laundering Control* 26, no. 1 (2023): 14–23.
Fanon, Frantz. *The Wretched of the Earth*. New York: Grove Press, 1965.
Felsenfeld, Carl and Genci Bilali. "The Role of the Bank for International Settlements in Shaping the World Financial System." *University of Pennsylvania Journal of International Economic Law* 25 (2004): 945–1045.
Finck, Michèle. *Blockchain Regulation and Governance in Europe*. Cambridge: Cambridge University Press, 2018.
Franks, Mary Anne. "The Desert of the Unreal: Inequality in Virtual and Augmented Reality." *University of California at Davis Law Review* 51, no. 2 (2017): 499–538.
Fukuyama, Francis. *The End of History and the Last Man*. New York: Free Press, 1992.
Griffin, Roger. "Revolts Against the Modern World: The Blend of Literary and Historical Fantasy in the Italian New Right." *Literature and History* 11, no. 1 (1985): 101–23.
Hamerton-Kelly, Robert. "An Introductory Essay." In *Politics and Apocalypse*, edited by Robert Hamerton-Kelly, 1–28. East Lansing: Michigan State University Press, 2007.
———, ed. *Politics and Apocalypse*. East Lansing: Michigan State University Press, 2007.
Hawley, George. *Making Sense of the Alt-Right*. New York: Columbia University Press, 2017.
Iliadis, Andrew and Amelia Acker. "The Seer and the Seen: Surveying Palantir's Surveillance Platform." *The Information Society* 38, no. 5 (2022): 334–63.
Kendall, Lori. "'White and Nerdy': Computers, Race, and the Nerd Stereotype." *The Journal of Popular Culture* 44, no. 3 (2011): 505–24.
Magliocca, Gerard N. "The *Gold Clause Cases* and Constitutional Necessity." *Florida Law Review* 64, no. 5 (2012): 1243–78.
Magnuson, William J. *Blockchain Democracy: Technology, Law and the Rule of the Crowd*. Cambridge: Cambridge University Press, 2020.
Mahoney, Charles W. "United States Defence Contractors and the Future of Military Operations." *Defense & Security Analysis* 36, no. 2 (2020): 180–200.
Mancinelli, Fabiola. "Digital Nomads: Freedom, Responsibility and the Neoliberal Order." *Information Technology and Tourism* 22, no. 3 (2020): 417–37.
Marx, Karl. *A Contribution to the Critique of Political Economy*. Chicago: Charles H. Kerr, 1904. First published 1897.
May, Kirse Granat. *Golden State, Golden Youth: The California Image in Popular Culture, 1955–1966*. Chapel Hill: University of North Carolina Press, 2002.
McAdams, A. James and Alejandro Castrillon. *Contemporary Far-Right Thinkers and the Future of Liberal Democracy*. London: Routledge, 2021.
McDonnell, Myles A. *Roman Manliness: Virtus and the Roman Republic*. Cambridge: Cambridge University Press, 2006.
Meier, Heinrich. *Carl Schmitt and Leo Strauss: The Hidden Dialogue*. Chicago: University of Chicago Press, 1995.

Meierhenrich, Jens and Oliver Simons. "'A Fanatic of Order in an Epoch of Confusing Turmoil': The Political, Legal, and Cultural Thought of Carl Schmitt." In *The Oxford Handbook of Carl Schmitt*, edited by Jens Meierhenrich and Oliver Simons, 3–70. Oxford: Oxford University Press, 2016.

Meyler, Bernadette. "Economic Emergency and the Rule of Law." *DePaul Law Review* 56, no. 2 (2007): 539–68.

Mises, Ludwig von. *Human Action: A Treatise on Economics*. Auburn: Ludwig von Mises Institute, 1998.

Müller, Jan-Werner. *What Is Populism?* Philadelphia: University of Pennsylvania Press, 2017.

Palaver, Wolfgang. "Carl Schmitt's 'Apocalyptic' Resistance against Global Civil War." In *Politics and Apocalypse*, edited by Robert Hamerton-Kelly, 69–94. East Lansing: Michigan State University Press, 2007.

Pape, Robert A. "American Face of Insurrection: Analysis of Individuals Charged for Storming the US Capitol on January 6, 2021." 2022. Published electronically 5 January. https://d3qi0qp55mx5f5.cloudfront.net/cpost/i/docs/Pape_-_American_Face_of_Insurrection_(2022-01-05).pdf.

Parkin, Jack. *Money, Code, Space: Hidden Power in Bitcoin, Blockchain, and Decentralisation*. Oxford: Oxford University Press, 2020.

Pitkin, Hanna Fenichel. *Fortune Is a Woman: Gender and Politics in the Thought of Niccolò Machiavelli*. Berkeley: University of California Press, 1984.

Pocock, J. G. A. *The Machiavellian Moment: Florentine Political Thought and the Atlantic Republican Tradition*. Princeton: Princeton University Press, 1975.

Robbins, Caroline. *The Eighteenth-Century Commonwealthman: Studies in the Transmission, Development, and Circumstance of English Liberal Thought from the Restoration of Charles II Until the War With the Thirteen Colonies*. Cambridge, MA: Harvard University Press, 1959.

Russo, Camila. *The Infinite Machine: How an Army of Crypto-Hackers Is Building the Next Internet With Ethereum*. New York: HarperCollins, 2020.

Scheuerman, William E. "The Economic State of Emergency." *Cardozo Law Review* 21, no. 5–6 (2000): 1869–94.

Schmitt, Carl. "The Age of Neutralizations and Depoliticizations." In *The Concept of the Political*, 80–96. Chicago: University of Chicago Press, 2008. First published 1929.

———. *The Concept of the Political*, 2nd ed. Chicago: University of Chicago Press, 2008. First published 1932.

———. *Constitutional Theory*. Translated by Jeffrey Seitzer. Durham: Duke University Press, 2008. First published 1928.

———. *Dictatorship*. Cambridge: Polity Press, 2015. First published 1921.

———. *The Nomos of the Earth in the International Law of the Jus Publicum Europaeum*. New York: Telos Press, 2003. First published 1950.

———. *Political Theology: Four Chapters on the Concept of Sovereignty*. Chicago: University of Chicago Press, 2005. First published 1922.

———. *Theory of the Partisan: Intermediate Commentary on the Concept of the Political*, 2nd ed. New York: Telos Press, 2007. First published 1975.

Skinner, Quentin and Martin van Gelderen, eds. *Republicanism: A Shared European Heritage*. 2 vols. Cambridge: Cambridge University Press, 2002.

Spencer, Richard B. "For Ukraine, for Europe." *Alexandria*, 2023. Published electronically February 23. https://radixjournal.substack.com/p/for-ukraine-for-europe.

Strauss, Leo. *Persecution and the Art of Writing.* Chicago: University of Chicago Press, 1988. First published 1952.

Suchman, Lucy. "Algorithmic Warfare and the Reinvention of Accuracy." *Critical Studies on Security* 8, no. 2 (2020): 175–87.

Tarin, G. Boyd. "The Bank for International Settlements: Keeping a Low Profile." *The Transnational Lawyer* 5 (1992): 839–71.

Thiel, Peter. "The Diversity Myth." *The New Criterion* 41, no. 10 (2023).

———. "The Education of a Libertarian." *Cato Unbound*, 2009. Published electronically April 13. www.cato-unbound.org/2009/04/13/peter-thiel/education-libertarian/.

———. "The Straussian Moment." In *Politics and Apocalypse*, 189–215. East Lansing: Michigan State University Press, 2007.

Vandiver, Josh. "Alt-Virilities: Masculinism, Rhizomatics, and the Contradictions of the American Alt-Right." *Politics, Religion & Ideology* 21, no. 2 (2020): 153–76.

———. "'Apollo Has Saved Us!' Global Ambition and Metapolitical Warfare in Alt-Right Religion." *Journal for the Study of Radicalism* 16, no. 1 (2022): 135–82.

———. "Masculinist Identitarians, Strategic Culture, and Eurocene Geopolitics." In *Global Identitarianism*, edited by José Pedro Zúquete and Riccardo Marchi, 175–96. London: Routledge, 2023.

———. "Metapolitics, Masculinity, and Technology in the Rise of 'Bronze Age Pervert'." In *Far-Right Thinkers and the Future of Liberal Democracy in the Twenty-First Century*, edited by A. James McAdams and Alejandro Castrillon, 242–63. London: Routledge, 2021.

Wilson, Kit. "The Rise of the Neoclassical Reactionaries." *The Spectator*, 2021. Published electronically November 24. www.spectator.co.uk/article/the-rise-of-the-neoclassical-reactionaries/.

Wood, Gordon. *The Creation of the American Republic, 1776–1787.* Chapel Hill: University of North Carolina Press, 1969.

Wright, Steve. "The ECHELON Trail: An Illegal Vision." *Surveillance & Society* 3, no. 2/3 (2005): 198–215.

Chapter 12—Liberalism's Vulnerabilities and Two Paths for the Future

Binkley, Colin. "Math and Reading Scores for American 13-Year-Olds Plunge to Lowest Levels in Decades." *ABC News*, June 21, 2023. https://abcnews.go.com/US/wireStory/math-scores-plunge-13-year-olds-pandemic-setbacks-100263778?

Blakely, Jason. "Doctor's Orders: Covid-19 and the New Science Wars." *Harper's Magazine*, July 2023. https://harpers.org/archive/2023/08/doctors-orders-jason-blakely/.

Bostrom, Nick. "Letter from Utopia." *Studies in Ethics, Law, and Technology* 2, no. 1 (2008).

———. *Superintelligence.* Oxford: Oxford University Press, 2017.

Bostrom, Nick, and Julian Savulescu, eds. *Human Enhancement.* Oxford: Oxford University Press, 2009.

Calvert, Jonathan and George Arbuthnott. "What Really Went on Inside the Wuhan Lab." *The Times of London*, June 10, 2023. www.thetimes.co.uk/article/inside-wuhan-lab-covid-pandemic-china-america-qhjwwwvm0.

"Clinical Considerations: Myocarditis and Pericarditis After Receipt of COVID-19 Vaccines Among Adolescents and Young Adults." *Centers for Disease Control and Prevention*, March 23, 2023. www.cdc.gov/vaccines/covid-19/clinical-considerations/myocarditis.html.

Dan Diamond. "Suddenly, Public Health Officials Say Social Justice Matters More Than Social Distance." *Politico*, June 4, 2020. www.politico.com/news/magazine/2020/06/04/public-health-protests-301534.

Dezember, Ryan. *Underwater: How Our American Dream of Homeownership Became a Nightmare*. New York: Thomas Dunne Books, 2019.

Donaldson, Sue and Will Kymlicka. *Zoopolis*. Oxford: Oxford University Press, 2013.

Doshi, Peter. "Will Covid-19 Vaccines Save Lives? Current Trials Aren't Designed to Tell Us." *British Medical Journal* (October 21, 2020): 1–4. https://doi.org/10.1136/bmj.m4037.

Eban, Katherine. "In Major Shift, NIH Admits Funding Risky Virus Research in Wuhan." *Vanity Fair*, October 22, 2021. www.vanityfair.com/news/2021/10/nih-admits-funding-risky-virus-research-in-wuhan.

Fraiman, Joseph, Juan Erviti, Sander Greenland, Patrick Whelan, Robert M. Kaplan, and Peter Doshi. "Serious Adverse Events of Special Interest Following MRNA COVID-19 Vaccination in Randomized Trials in Adults." *Vaccine* 40 (2022).

Franco-Paredes, Carlos. "Transmissibility of SARS-CoV-2 Among Fully Vaccinated Individuals." *The Lancet* 22 (2022): 16–17.

Gordon, Michael R. and Warren P. Strobel. "U.S.-Funded Scientist Among Three Chinese Researchers Who Fell Ill Amid Early Covid-19 Outbreak." *The Wall Street Journal*, June 20, 2023. www.wsj.com/articles/u-s-funded-scientist-among-three-chinese-researchers-who-fell-ill-amid-early-covid-19-outbreak-3f919567?mod=hp_lead_pos11.

Guinn, Jeff. *Waco: David Koresh, the Branch Davidians, and a Legacy of Rage*. New York: Simon and Schuster, 2023.

Haidt, Jonathan. "Social Media Is a Major Cause of the Mental Illness Epidemic in Teen Girls. Here's the Evidence." *After Babel* (blog), February 22, 2023. https://jonathanhaidt.substack.com/p/social-media-mental-illness-epidemic.

Hannah-Jones, Nikole. *The 1619 Project: A New Origin Story*. New York: Random House, 2021.

Kahloon, Idrees. "What's the Matter with Men?" *The New Yorker*, January 23, 2023. www.newyorker.com/magazine/2023/01/30/whats-the-matter-with-men.

Kaplan, Sheila, Matthew Goldstein, and Alexandra Stevenson. "Trump's Vaccine Chief Has Vast Ties to Drug Industry, Posing Possible Conflicts." May 20, 2020. www.nytimes.com/2020/05/20/health/coronavirus-vaccine-czar.html.

Kendi, Ibram X. *How to Be an Antiracist*. New York: One World, 2019.

———. *Stamped from the Beginning: The Definitive History of Racist Ideas in America*. New York: Nation Books, 2016.

Kolhatkar, Sheelah. *Black Edge: Inside Information, Dirty Money, and the Quest to Bring Down the Most Wanted Man on Wall Street*. New York: Random House, 2017.

Le Pen, Marine. *Pour Que Vivre La France*. Paris: Éditions Grancher, 2012.

Lewis, Sophie. *Abolish the Family: A Manifesto for Care and Liberation*. New York: Verso Books, 2022.

———. *Full Surrogacy Now: Feminism Against Family*. New York: Verso Books, 2019.

"March 2020: Dr. Anthony Fauci Talks With Dr. Jon Lapook About Covid-19." *60 Minutes*. CBS, n.d. www.youtube.com/watch?v=PRa6t_e7dgI.

McGreal, Chris. "Johnson & Johnson to Pay $572m for Fueling Oklahoma Opioid Crisis, Judge Rules." *The Guardian*, August 26, 2019. www.theguardian.com/us-news/2019/aug/26/johnson-and-johnson-opioid-crisis-ruling-responsibility-oklahoma-latest.

Moyn, Samuel. *Christian Human Rights*. Philadelphia: University of Pennsylvania Press, 2015.

———. *Not Enough: Human Rights in an Unequal World*. Cambridge, MA: Harvard University Press, 2019.

Moyn, Samuel and Ryan D. Doerfler. "The Constitution Is Broken and Should Not Be Reclaimed." *The New York Times*, August 19, 2022. www.nytimes.com/2022/08/19/opinion/liberals-constitution.html.

"The New York Times WMD Coverage." *PBS News Hour*, May 26, 2004. www.pbs.org/newshour/show/the-new-york-times-wmd-coverage.

Noam, Eli. *Media Ownership and Concentration in America*. Oxford: Oxford University Press, 2009.

Powell, Michael. "Are Protests Dangerous? What Experts Say May Depend on Who's Protesting What." *The New York Times*, July 6, 2020. www.nytimes.com/2020/07/06/us/Epidemiologists-coronavirus-protests-quarantine.html.

Prasad, Vinay. "At a Time When the U.S. Needed Covid-19 Dialogue between Scientists, Francis Collins Moved to Shut It Down." *Stat*, December 23, 2021. www.statnews.com/2021/12/23/at-a-time-when-the-u-s-needed-covid-19-dialogue-between-scientists-francis-collins-moved-to-shut-it-down/.

Rawls, John. *Political Liberalism*. New York: Columbia University Press, 1993.

Rosenblatt, Helena. *The Lost History of Liberalism*. Princeton, NJ: Princeton University Press, 2018.

Sanger, David E. "Trump Administration Selects Five Coronavirus Vaccine Candidates as Finalists." *The New York Times*, June 3, 2020. www.nytimes.com/2020/06/03/us/politics/coronavirus-vaccine-trump-moderna.html?searchResultPosition=30.

Scott, James C. *Seeing Like a State: How Certain Schemes to Improve the Human Condition Have Failed*. New Haven, CT: Yale University Press, 1998.

Singanayagam, Anika, Seran Hakki, and Jake Dunning. "Community Transmission and Viral Load Kinetics of the SARS-CoV-2 Delta (B.1.617.2) Variant in Vaccinated and Unvaccinated Individuals in the UK: A Prospective, Longitudinal, Cohort Study." *The Lancet* 22 (2021): 183–95.

Stewart, James B. *Den of Thieves*. New York: Simon and Schuster, 1992.

Stoller, Matt. *Goliath: The 100-Year War Between Monopoly Power and Democracy*. New York: Simon and Schuster, 2019.

Tiffany, Kaitlyn. "What Do Female Incels Really Want?" *The Atlantic*, May 12, 2022. www.theatlantic.com/technology/archive/2022/05/femcel-meaning-female-incel-reddit/629836/.

Tully, James. "On Gaia Democracies." In *Democratic Multiplicity*, edited by James Tully, Keith Cherry, Fonna Forman, and Jeanne Morefield, 349–73. Cambridge: Cambridge University Press, 2022.

———. *Public Philosophy in a New Key.* Vol. 1. 2 vols. Cambridge: Cambridge University Press, 2008.
———. *Strange Multiplicity.* Cambridge: Cambridge University Press, 1995.
"Youth Risk Behavior Survey." *Centers for Disease Control and Prevention*, 2021, 2011. www.cdc.gov/healthyyouth/data/yrbs/pdf/YRBS_Data-Summary-Trends_Report2023_508.pdf.
Zuckert, Michael. *Launching Liberalism: On Lockean Political Philosophy.* Lawrence, KS: University Press of Kansas, 2002.

INDEX

Note: Page numbers followed by "n" with numbers refer to notes.

abortion: in Hungary 96–98; Le Pen's view of ('of convenience') 52, 57, 61; in Poland 94–98
Africa 37, 39, 119, 197
Alternative for Germany (AfD) 5, 16, 107, 117, 119–122, 233
Alt-right: blogosphere 112; cryptopartisans and 219–221; and GamerGate 211; Fuentes, Nick as, influencer 219–220; and Libertarian Party (LP) 177–179
America First 175–176, 220
American Civil Liberties Union (ACLU) 214
anti-feminist: movements 19, 126–127, 130–131; subculture 124; *see also* manosphere
anti-immigration: 51–52, 58, 60, 61, 178–179
Aristotle 161, 164n29
artificial intelligence (AI) 211
Asperl, Walter 5
Association for the Republic—Republican Party of Czechoslovakia (SPR—RSČ) 66–67
Atlas Shrugged (Rand) 133, 141n16
authority: public 156, 158; skepticism of 167–169
autonomy: bodily 89, 94–98, 102; liberal 148, 151, 178

Baberowski, Jörg 109
Babiš, Andrej 68, 74
Bank of International Settlements (BIS) 215
Bannon, Steve 11
Barbrook, Richard 209, 226n17, 226n23
Barr, William 146, 158, 161; constitutionalism 147–150
Baudet, Thierry 190, 192–193, 195–196, 202n9, 203n17, 203n25, 203n31
Beck, Glenn 193, 199
Beierle, Scott Paul 136
Biden, Joe 157, 242
Bień-Kacała, Agnieszka 18–19, 78, 146, 244
Bitcoin 20, 206, 209–210, 222–223; cryptopartisans 219–222; moment 215–219
"Bitcoin bros" 207–209, 210, 215–223; 225n8, 228n53; *see also* Thiel, Peter
Black people 153, 254
Brand, Russell 167, 170–171, 181–182; conspiracism of 173–175; *Stay Free With Russell Brand* (podcast) 169, 171
Braun, Jürgen 120
British National Party 4, 190

Bronze Age Pervert (BAP) 211–212, 217, 229n62
Buchanan, Pat 6, 10–11
bureaucracy 154
Burnham, James 192
Buterin, Vitalik 209–210

Cameron, Andy 209, 226n17, 226n23
Camus, Renaud 37, 46n26; Davocracy 191
Canada 6, 136, 245, 254; The Freedom Convoy (truckers' protest) 199, 205;
Canadian Human Rights Act 33
capitalism 23n34, 196, 210, 218–219; "disaster" 192–195; industrial 236; Woke 5
Carlson, Tucker 14, 27–29: newspeak and audience 29–38; possible consequences of views 42–45; "replacement theory" 11–12; *Ship of Fools* 31, 37, 43
Catholic Church 12, 91, 94
Cato Institute 177, 180
CDU *see* Christian Democratic Union
Center for Libertarian Studies (CLS) 180
Central Intelligence Agency (CIA) 211
Christian Democratic Union (CDU) (Germany) 108, 111
Christianity 21n8, 137, 159, 251
Christian Social Union (CSU) (Germany) 108
citizenship 192; French 38–39; German 109, 114–116, 118, 121
climate change 193–194
common good 11, 13–14, 18, 246
Common Good Constitutionalism (Vermeule) 146, 153–156, 162
communitarianism 44
Conservative Party (United Kingdom) 233
conservative: American, women's movements 53, 158; conceptions, in Germany 111–114; liberalism 235, 249–252; mainstream 15, 35, 211–212; manosphere 139–140; moderate 30; national 7; podcasts 169–171; "revolution by the people" 108–109; social 177; traditional 42; views in Hungary 158–159
conspiracism 20, 166–169, 180–182, 240–241; Joe Rogan and Russell Brand as conspiracists 171–175

conspiracy theories 37, 167–168, 177, 180, 245; Covid-19 241–242
constitutionalism: Bitcoin bros, defenders of liberal-democratic 215; constitutional scholars and legal argumentation as Newspeak in Germany 109–118, 121–122; critique of liberal-democratic (Thiel, P.) 206–207, 213–214; critique of universalism of 253–254; from liberal to illiberal, in Hungary and Poland 87–92; *see also Common Good Constitutionalism*; Barr, William
corporations 194–195, 199–200, 202, 223
Court of Justice of the European Union 100, 102
courts 17; Czech Constitutional 78; German Constitutional 113–115, 119–120; Poland and Hungary's constitutional 87–88, 91–93, 96, 98–102
Covid-19 pandemic 166, 238, 241–243
COVID-19: The Great Reset 191
Craig, Andy 176
cryptocurrency 20, 206, 210, 220
cryptopartisans 20, 207–208, 219–222, 230n73; *see also* Bitcoin; Bitcoin bros
Cudenec, Paul 200, 204nn46–47
culture 161: American 43, 137, 177; cancel 4, 77, 171; Catholic 101; constitutional 89; European 69; French 18, 27, 55 49; traditional 151, 161; transmitters of 55; *see also* manosphere
Czech Republic 16, 65–70, 75–79, 95, 244; *see also* Okamura, Tomio
Czechoslovakia 65–66, 75

Davos 191, 237–238
de Beauvoir, Simone 60
de Benoist, Alain 10–11
Declaration of Independence 9, 149–150, 156
de Gaulle, Charles 44
Democratic Party (United States) 36–38
Deneen, Patrick 19–21, 145–146, 150, 160–162; and postliberal reduction of liberty 150–153; postliberalism in practice 157–160; and Vermeule 153–157; *see also* Vermeule, Adrian
Department of Defense (DoD) 211

Depenheuer, Otto 114–116, 120
dictatorship 7: communist, in Czechoslovakia 66, 75–76; eco- 197; global corporate 200; "European Union dictatorship" (Okamura) 77; health 197–198; left-wing 109; Nazi 108
Dobrindt, Alexander 108–109
Dodd, Nigel 216, 218
Doerfler, Ryan 253, 255, 259n41
Drinóczi, Tímea 18–19, 78, 146, 244
Dugin, Aleksandr 6, 8–9, 76–77, 83n46; *The Great Awakening vs. The Great Reset* 200–201

ECtHR *see* European Court of Human Rights
egalitarianism 44
égalité 5, 55–56, 58
Eisenhower, Dwight D. 180
Elam, Paul 131, 138
electoral system 16, 161
Engels, David 191, 200, 202n7, 204n49
environmentalism 199
equality 91; equal rights of LGBTQIA+ people 98–103; and freedom 252–254; and freedom as antagonistic (Carlson, Le Pen, Peterson) 35–36, 38–39, 41, 42; gender 246–249; legal, in USA 244–245; Le Pen's view of women's rights and gender 48–50, 52, 54; Le Pen's reconceptualization of 55–62; natural 250–252; Okamura on gender 72–73
equality of opportunity: guarantee of, compromised (Carlson) 31; Le Pen's view 56; Peterson's view of 33–35;
equal rights 6, 9–11, 14, 36, 56, 89, 93; of LGBTQAI+ People 98–102; *see also* feminism
equity 33–34, 128, 254
ESG scores 193
ethnicity 6, 31, 36–37, 40, 42–43, 60, 112; anxiety about diminishing German 113–118
European Court of Human Rights (ECHR) 99, 102
European Union (EU), the 12, 30, 68, 71–73, 80, 160; dictatorship 77

family: abolition of 254; institution of 100; liberal 138; sanctity of 11; traditional 99
Farmer-Citizen Movement 5
far right, the: in Czech Republic 67; female leaders of, appropriating women's right 50; figures on the, using liberal principles 166; in Germany 108–109, 111–114, 122; opposition learning from challenges of 234–235; and progressive postliberalism 252–256; women's equal rights vs. the far right 51–53, 61–62
Farris, Sara 59, 64n53, 64n59
fascist, fascism 5–6, 8, 75–76, 99, 179, 201
Fauci, Anthony 241–242
Federal Office for the Protection of the Constitution (BfV) 120–121
Federal Reserve 207, 215
feminism: Le Pen's (neo-feminism) 53–62; right-wing vs. left-wing 48–53, 247
Fidesz (Hungary) 88, 90–91, 96–97, 100–101, 233
Field, Laura K. 19–20, 250–251
FN *see* Front National
FN Women's council (CNFE) 55
Forum for Democracy 16
Foucault, Michel 252
France 4, 10, 39–40; *see also* Le Pen, Marine
freedom: of assembly 99; of association 178; bourgeois 219; of choice 97; of conscience 176; core of 149; deepest form of 158; defender of 171; genuine 158, 162, 256; guarantee of 90; individual *see* individual freedom; language of 38, 49, 69–75, 147; liberal *see* liberal freedom; liberal religious 148–149; of movement 179; of opinion 201; political 157; postliberal 159; rights and 35; of speech 12, 17, 31, 70–73, 75–76, 178; threat to 78–80; of thought 70, 76; true 152, 159, 256; women's 58–61; *see also* Okamura, Tomio
Freedom and Direct Democracy, SPD (Czech Republic) 68–74, 76, 79
free speech: Carlson Tucker and 30–31; Jordan Peterson and 33; Libertarian

Party and 177–179, 181; Okamura and 70–73, 75, 79; *see also* podcasts
Front National (FN) (France) 28, 50–52
Fuentes, Nick 219–223
Fundamental Law, 2012 92, 96, 100–102

Gates, Bill 196
gender 246–249; Fundamental Law and 100–101; MGTOW movement view on gender roles 133; Le Pen and 51–52, 55–56, 58, 61–62; Peterson on 33, 39; roles changing 129; Okamura on 72; Tate, Andrew, and 139
genocide 70, 74, 117
geopolitics 195
Germany 11, 16; AfD in 16, 119, 233–234; "rule of injustice" 106, 112, 119; constitutional scholars and legal argumentation as Newspeak in 109–118, 121–122; ethnicity in 'danger' 113–118; parliamentary junctions 118–121; rule of law in 110; Syrian refugees in 2015 and political ambience 106–109
Girard, René 212, 214
global financial crisis 207, 216–218, 221
globalism 169, 191–192
globalization 192, 195–197, 199; economic 169, 218
God 11, 41, 44
Grabenwarter, Christoph 114–115, 120
Great Replacement Theory 37, 197–198
Great Reset, the 189–190; and Great Replacement 197–198; deep roots 190–192; disaster capitalism 192–195; freedom, democracy and dystopia 200–202; Great Revolt 198–200; technological reset 195–197;
Great Resist, the 189–190, 193
Great Revolt, the 198–200
Griffin, Nick 190, 193–196, 203n26, 203n33
Guatemala 37
Guinn, Jeff 246, 258n30

Habermas, Jürgen 116
Hawley, George: manosphere 19, 63n22, 142n30, 182n4, 247–248; real antiracists and feminists 53
Hobbes, Thomas 209, 250

homosexuality 100–101
Hopkins, C. J. 193
Hoppe, Hans-Hermann 177, 179, 184n42
Hudak, John 176
human rights: In Hungary and Poland 89–93, 96; of LGBTQIA+ People 99, 192; Okamura 'defending' 69–71, 74; Peterson condemning Canadian Human Rights Act amendment 33–34; universalism 115–16
Hungary: abortion and the Fundamental law 96–98; liberal to illiberal constitutionalism in, 87–92; LGBTQIA+ rights 98–102; Viktor Orbán's regime 87–89, 102–103

identitarians 11, 17, 114; Austrian identitarian movement 190, 196–197, 199
identity: Czech 66, 69; Hungary, constitutional 92; within anti-Great Reset and anti-Great Replacement framework 197; Hungary, individual 100–101; digital 193; French national 18, 39, 44, 49, 52, 57; gender 101; in Germany 111–113, 114–118, 121; group 16; national 66, 117, 121, 195; white 8–9
identity politics 200
Igounet, Valérie 52
illiberal democracy 7, 16, 77, 89, 157, 208
illiberal politics 65
immigration: Carlson on 38; Front National on 52; in Germany 108, 111, 117, 121; Le Pen on 39–49, 51–52, 60–62; Libertarian Party on 178–179; Okamura on 68, 71–72
Immigration and Customs Enforcement (ICE) 211
Immigration and Nationality Act, 1965 38
incels 127–128, 134–139, 248
Independent Women's Forum (IWF) 53
Indigenous people 153, 245, 251
individual freedom 6, 8–9, 15, 20, 89; exercise of 28, 42; guarantee of 35; and national sovereignty 92; rhetoric of 80
individualism 92–93, 191–192, 201, 250; bourgeois 208, 226n16; excessive 16, 151, 152; heroic 10

individual rights: and equality 18–19, 87–88; and fairness 137; language of 18; and liberties 147, 152; protections 150–151; recognition of 80; *see also* equality
inequality 29; between men and women 58; human 93; income 171; social and economic 30
International Monetary Fund (IMF) 213
Internet 127, 240; democratization 139; MGOTW 134; men's rights activists on 128–130; pickup artists 132; rise of extreme right movements on 138–139; Rumble 171; *see also* Bitcoin bros; manosphere; Raw Egg Nationalist (REN)
Internet of Bodies (IoB) 196
In-Q-Tel (IQT) 211
Islam/Islamism 251; Islamo-Leftists 32; Le Pen's views on 39–40, 49, 51, 58–61; Okamura's views on 69, 71, 72–73; Thiel on 214
Islamophobia 61, 72

Joe Rogan Experience, The (United States) 166, 169, 170, 172
John Birch Society (JBS) 180
Johnson, Gary 176, 197–198, 204n36
Jones, Alex 170–171

Kaczyński, Jarosław 6, 12, 14, 16–18, 78, 87–89, 94–95, 99, 101, 103n2; *see also* Poland
Kant, Immanuel 152, 250–251
Khmer Rouge, the 34, 45
Koch, Charles 180
Koch, Fred 180
Kolakowski, Leszek 21n11, 23n31; "perpetual antinomy" 6, 13, 16, 35
Koppelman, Andrew 176, 183n29
Kövér, László 101
Kubitschek, Götz 6, 11–12, 14

laïcité 39–40, 59
language of liberalism/liberal language (appropriated/manipulated) 4, 10, 18, 31–32, 48, 65, 87–88, 119, 137, 18–139, 161
Law and Justice party (PiS) (Poland) 12, 88
laws: absence of, to govern financial criminals 245; Bitcoin bros arguing financial 216, 221; Deneen on 158; in Hungary 96–97, 101; Okamura and 77; in Poland 91, 94, 102; Thiel and constitutional 214; Vermeule, tradition and laws 156
left, the 4, 7–8, 15, 34–37, 245, 256
leftist: activists 43; extremism 9; politicians 14, 32; postliberals 235; progressivism 35
left-wing 135; Democrats 10; dictatorship 109; elites 108; feminism 5, 56–58, 61; Newspeak 254–255
Legal Tribune Online (LTO) 118
legitimacy: constitutional 97; electoral 158; legislative 116
Lenin, V. I. 14, 184n32
Le Pen, Marine 4–5, 6, 18, 236; on abortion ('of convenience') 52, 57, 61; feminism (neo-feminism) of 53–62, 247; on gender 51–52, 55–56, 58, 61–62; newspeak and audience 27–30, 31–32, 35, 38–40; possible consequences of views 42, 44–45
LGBTQAI+ persons/people 98–99, 101–102
liberal conservative party 67
liberal democracy xiv–xv: according to Deneen 151, 153, 156–157; Bitcoin bros and 218–219; crisis of 221; fragility of 3–4, 6–7, 15–18; modern bourgeoisie of 208; Okamura and 76–80; preserving, ways of 234–236, 239, 241, 249–256; Rogan and 174–175; Vermeule on 154, 156
liberal democrats: of genuine skepticism 173; mainline 190, 223; traditional 174–175, 256
liberal freedom: Deneen on 150–151; and rights 215; Waldstein opinion on 154
liberalism: classical 3, 10, 34, 40, 45, 176, 179, 208; conservative 249–252; contemporary 238; democratic 78; dominant ideology 236; legitimacy of 208; liberalism 2.0 76; minoritarian 201; modern 147, 151–152, 156; progressive 252–256; totalitarian 76; vocabulary of 74
libertarianism 206, 209, 211–212; American 180, 215; paleo- 175, 177; right-wing 29
Libertarian Party (LP) 175–181
liberté 58

liberty: American 149; Christian 159; moral 153; negative 146, 150–151; political 148–149; positive 151; republican promise of 60; right to 70, 202; self-determination and free will 90; sexual 56; *see also* religious liberty/freedom
Lichtmesz, Martin 198, 201, 204n38, 204n43, 204n51
Limbaugh, Rush 169
Locke, John 33, 35, 178–179, 209, 213, 250–251
LP *see* Libertarian Party
Luckey, Palmer 211

Machiavelli, Niccolo 157, 209
Macron, Emmanuel 28, 32, 39–40, 50, 57, 233
majoritarianism 10, 89, 93, 103, 244
Malone, Robert 166, 170
manosphere 126–127, 130–131; demise 137–139; incel movement 134–136; men's rights before the Internet 128–130; MGTOW movement 133–134; pickup artists 128, 132–133, 138; succeeding despite itself 139–140
Maoism 45
Maříková, Karla 72–73, 76
Maritain, Jacques 250
Marx, Karl 14, 23n34, 216, 228n57
Marxism 45
McAdams, A. James 65, 89, 114, 124n39, 177, 234, 247
McArdle, Angela 177, 181
media: alternative media and conspiracies 169; Covid-19 and vaccines and 238, 242–243; decline of traditional 138; Fox News 28; in Germany, Vosgerau 112–113, 122 (alt-right blogosphere); Hungary LGBTQIA+ and 101; manipulation of (Hungary and Poland) 161; mainstream 113, 127, 131, 167, 171–172, 181; man's rights movement and mainstream 131; Okamura and 71, 74; Orbán and 159; powerful, organizations 235, 243; *see also* manosphere; podcasts; social media
Meloni, Giorgia 4–5, 49
"men going their own way" (MGTOW) 128, 133–134, 137, 139

men's rights: activists 127–128, 130–131, 135, 137–138; movement 127, 129–131, 133–135, 137–138
Merkel, Angela 108–109, 111, 117, 120; rule of law 244
metapolitical facts 112
metapolitics 140
Mexico 37, 216
Middle East 37, 119
migration: crisis, 2015 106; dangers of 69; illegal 72; law 120; mass 108–109, 120; social reality of 111; of users 137
Mill, John Stuart 33, 35
Minassian, Alek 136
Ministry of the Interior (Czech Republic) 69, 75
minorities: ethnic 29, 36, 38, 246; demands of 14; racial 6, 29, 36, 38, 254; religious 38, 71; rights and freedoms of 155, 234
Mises Caucus 175, 177–181
Mlejnková, Petra 18, 178, 184n39, 244; *see also* Okamura, Tomio
monetary policy 215, 217
monopolies 5, 15, 45, 236; disrupters of 237; Uber 237
Moyn, Samuel 253, 255, 259nn40–41
multiculturalism 32, 112, 161, 197; society 117
Murswiek, Dietrich 116–117, 120–121, 125n49, 125n51
Musk, Elon 170, 208
Muslim 251; in Canada 245; Okamura's views on 71, 73; Le Pen on Muslim immigrants 39–40, 58–61, 247

National Conservatism 159, 206
nationalism 57, 61, 77
National Rally (RN) (France) 49–50
National Security Agency (NSA) 211
National Socialism 5, 108, 120
nativism 65, 69, 92
Nazis 36, 76
neo-Marxists 76
Netherlands, the 6, 16, 233
New Right 10, 118, 145, 150, 158, 234
New World Order 76, 189–190, 199
New York Times 238, 240, 242, 253
Nietzsche, Friedrich 35, 217, 247, 252
9/11 attacks 167, 240

Nixon, Richard 218–219, 229n69, 244, 255
Nouvelle Droite (France) 10, 112

Occupy Wall Street 199, 216
Okamura, Tomio 18, 65–66: free speech, defense 72, 75–78; direct democracy 77–80; historical background of Czech Republic's political scene 66–67; language of freedom 69–75; political career 67–69; as threat to freedom and democracy 78–80; "Tomio Okamura Banned Us" Facebook group 75
old-right 10
Oldspeak 3, 7, 256
openness 239; democratic 239; liberal 172; radical 255
open society 113, 201
Orbán, Viktor 87–89, 101, 109, 146–147, 159–160; *see also* Hungary; Fidesz
Orwell, George 3–4, 15, 20, 21n1, 23n34, 65, 126, 255
Overton window 4, 21n6, 27, 39, 138, 177

Palaver, Wolfgang 212–213
paleoconservative/paleoconservatism 175
Pape, Robert 219, 230n74
Pappas, Takis 78, 83n55
Pappin, Gladden 147, 159–160; *see also* Orbán, Viktor
Parkin, Jack 209, 226n20
parliament: on abortion, Hungarian 96–97; on abortion, Polish 94–95, 99; on LGBTQIA+, Hungarian 101: Czech (SPR—RSČ) in 66–68, 72–73, 76–77; Hungary, Fidesz in 91–92; Polish, PiS in 12, 87–88, 92
parliamentary junctions 118–121
PayPal 208–209, 223
Pegida 111–112
perpetual antinomy 6, 13, 16, 80
Peterson, Jordan 27–30; manosphere and 139, 247; newspeak and audience 32–35, 40–42; possible consequences of views 42, 44–45; *12 Rules for Life: An Antidote to Chaos* 28, 34, 45
Piccolo, Samuel 20, 173, 190
pickup artists (PUAs) 128, 132–136, 138

Pittz, Steven 20, 29, 149, 190, 205, 239–241
Plato 151–152, 164n29, 192
Pocock, J. D. A. 206, 209–211
podcasts: and free speech 169–171; Griffin, Nick 193; Soral, Alain 193; *see also* conspiracy theories; Brand, Russell; Rogan, Joe
Poland: abortion in 94–96, 97–98; Jarosław Kaczyński's regime 87–89, 102–103; liberal to illiberal constitutionalism in, 87–92; LGBTQIA+ rights 98–102
Polish Constitutional Tribunal 91, 94–95, 97, 102
populism 175–177, 179, 182, 192, 201, 209, 230n73
postliberal: American thought 20–21, 147–148, 160–162, 250–251; extremism 153–157; Deneen and, reduction of liberty 150–153; practice 157–160; progressivism 252–256; *see also* Barr, William; Deneen, Patrick; Vermeule, Adrian
postliberalism 145, 147, 160–162; in practice 157–160; progressive 235, 252–256
Postliberal Order 153, 159
power: centralization of 235–239; emergency 218; governmental 156; institutional 174–17, 239, 244; political 9, 12, 16, 43, 79; public 90; of sovereignty 222; state 211; superior 202; symbolic 198; tyrannical 207, 215

race 6, 8, 10, 31, 42–43, 116, 250; war 12
Rand, Ayn 23n36, 133, 141n16
rationalism 8
"Raw Egg Nationalist" (REN): anti-Great Reset 199; on diet, influence of 192, 194–195; on masculinity and diet 139–140
Rawls, John 250, 259n37
Rechtsstaat 208, 228n55
refugee crisis 107, 109, 121
religion 6, 44, 70, 90–91, 97, 161; Christian 175; traditional 148–149
religious liberty/freedom 147–148, 150
republicanism 59, 206, 210, 222, 224n3
Republican Party (United States) 10

rhetoric 4, 52, 234; anti-democratic 6; anti-establishment 113; avenue 45; device 167; hateful 126; inflammatory 69; liberal constitutional 19; neofascist 6; populist 68, 77; power 168–169; question 111; racist 67; violent 247
right, the 8, 167, 221, 256; of individuals 101
rights: active 90; -bearers 251; civil 99; constitutional 3, 95; fundamental 17, 91, 150; gay 32; minority 78–79; natural 250, 252; negative 90; positive 91; property 178; sovereign 45; unalienable 43
right-wing: backlash movements 126, 139; "equality of the sexes" 55–57; extremists 88, 157, 246; libertarianism 29; natalism 57; nationalist 49; politicians 5, 52; populism 157, 178–179; projects 62; social media masculine influencers 139; thinking 16, 19, 147; values 57–58; women 53
right-wing uses of liberal ideas 249–256
Rise Above Movement (RAM) 220
Rockwell, Lew 175–176
Rodger, Elliot 127, 136
Rogan, Joe 166–167, 169–171, 181–182; conspiracism of 171–173, 174–175; *The Joe Rogan Experience* (podcast) 166, 169, 170, 172
Roma population 67
Roosevelt, Eleanor 76
Roosevelt, Franklin Delano 218
Rothbard, Murray N. 175–177, 179–180, 183n27, 184n30
rule of law 244–246; breaching 109; democratic state of the 89; foundational element of 113
Russia 17, 69, 192, 195, 208

Scheuerman, William 217, 229n61, 229n64, 229n67
Schmitt, Carl: "The Concept of the Political" 114, 225; *Dictatorship* 214, 228n52; modern constitutionalism 215; *Nomos of the Earth* 213, 227nn44–45; *Political Theology* 214; "state of exception" 207, 214, 217–218, 223; Thielian moment and 211–214, 217–218, 221, 223
Schorkopf, Frank 115, 124n44
Schreiber, Ronnee 53, 63n20
Schwab, Klaus 190, 196, 202n4
secularism 8, 39, 44, 59, 161
Seehofer, Horst 108–111, 119–120
Sellner, Martin 190, 195, 197–198, 203n27, 204n35, 204n39
sexism 33
sexuality 99
Shurts, Sarah 18, 28, 147, 246–247
Sládek, Miroslav 67, 80n4
Slovakia 65–66
Slovenian National Party 16
Smith, Dave 181, 185nn54–55
Social Democratic Party (Germany) 5-
social hierarchies 42, 93
Social Life of Money, The (Dodd) 217, 225n8, 228n57, 228n60, 229n63, 229n68
social media 5, 9, 18, 71, 220; influencers/personalities 139–140, 190, 192; effect of, on well-being (of young women) 248; *see also* manosphere; Raw Egg Nationalist (REN)
Southern Poverty Law Center, 2022 42
Soviet Union 8, 66
Special Operations Command (SOCOM) 211
Spencer, Richard 6, 8–9, 220
Stay Free With Russell Brand (United Kingdom) 169, 171
Stoller, Matt 236, 257n7
Strauss, Leo 212–213, 227n42
Supreme Administrative Court (SAC) 98–99
surveillance 193, 195–196, 206–207, 211; global 223; mass 200; totalitarian 202

technology 195–196; military 211
terrorism 12, 70, 74, 136; Islamic 193
Thiel, Peter 20, 206, 208, 222–224, 224n5, 224n6; Thielian moment 212–215; Thielian network 208–212; *see also* Bitcoin bros
de Tocqueville, Alexis 79, 192
tolerance 3, 7, 28, 73, 76, 178
Troy, Dave 180, 185n52

Trump, Donald 3–4, 11, 149–150, 238–240, 244, 253
truths, esoteric 132
Tully, James 251, 253–254, 259n38, 259n42

Ukraine 73–74, 181, 195, 220
United Kingdom 6, 233, 240, 245, 254
United Nations High Commissioner for Refugees (UNHCR) 108
United States 10–11, 17, 158–159, 205–206, 218, 237–247
Universal Declaration of Human Rights 70–71

Valizadeh, Daryush 137, 141n17, 142n26
Vandiver, Josh 20, 174, 183n23, 193, 245
Vanguard America 220
Venezuela 37
Venner, Fiammetta 51, 62n5, 62n7
Vermeule, Adrian: 20–21, 147–148, 150, 160–162; postliberal extremism 153–157; postliberalism in practice 157–160
Vietnam War 218
violence 70–71, 121, 135–136; brutal 136; masculine 51
vocabulary 3–4, 36, 116, 120; liberal 9, 18, 27, 33, 74
von Mises, Ludwig 180, 218
Voice for Men, A (Elam) 131
Vosgerau, Ulrich 110; in *Cicero* 112; rule of injustice 111

Waldstein, Edmund 154, 163n24
war 192; against Islamism/Islamic practice 40; and Bitcoin bros 217–218; "bracketed" war in Europe 213; Cold War 114, 191; crimes 71; race 12; with Russia 195; on terror 206, 212; in Ukraine 74, 173
WEF *see* World Economic Forum
Weißmann, Karlheinz 11
Wieseltier, Leon 154, 161
Western civilization 8–9, 37, 55, 59, 112; values 78
white nationalism/nationalists 12, 37, 197–198, 221
white supremacists 4, 8; feminism 53
Wildt, Michael 113, 124n27
wokeism 32, 185n53
women's rights: in Hungary 98; Le Pen and 18, 48–50, 52–53, 57–62, 97; in Poland 97–98
Woods, Keith 196, 200–201, 203n32, 204n50
words 3, 30; "freedom" and "democracy", Okamura's 66; giving old new meaning 48; key 15; polarizing 92; postliberalism as most Orwellian word 162
World Bank 213
World Economic Forum (WEF) 20, 189, 202n3, 237–238
World War I 66, 217
World War II 3–4, 9, 38, 66, 213, 234

Zuckerberg, Mark 170, 216

Printed in the United States
by Baker & Taylor Publisher Services